Ethnic Recordings in America
A Neglected Heritage

Ethnic Recordings in America

A Neglected Heritage

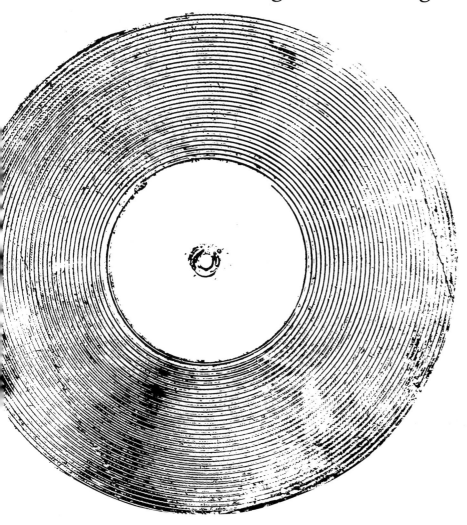

American Folklife Center

Library of Congress
Washington 1982

Studies in American Folklife, No. 1

Library of Congress Cataloging in Publication Data

Main entry under title:

Ethnic recordings in America.

    (Studies in American Folklife; no. 1)

    Includes bibliographical references and index.
    CONTENTS: Gronow, P. Ethnic recordings : an introduction.—Spottswood, R. K. Commercial ethnic recordings in the United States.—Hickerson, J.C. The Archive of Folk song : early interest in ethnic music.—[etc.]
    SUPT. of Docs. no.: LC39.2:R24
    1. Folk music—United States—Congresses. 2. Sound recordings—Congresses. I. American Folklife Center.
II. Series.
ML3551.E75   789.9'121773   80-607133
ISBN 0-8444-0339-3   AACR2

For sale by the Superintendent of Documents,
U.S. Government Printing Office, Washington, D.C. 20402

Contents

Foreword

On January 24–26, 1977, the American Folklife Center convened a meeting at the Library of Congress on the subject "Ethnic Recordings in America: A Neglected Heritage." The conference brought together scholars, producers, performers, collectors, and community leaders who had participated in and were concerned about the subject of ethnic recordings—in particular, those ethnic recordings that had been produced on commercial labels in the United States since the turn of the century. These recordings, drawn directly from various ethnic groups in the United States and sold directly back to them, have documented and reinforced the identities of ethnic cultures in this country. Although they form a vast and important body of artistic expression, they have received virtually no attention from cultural institutions, researchers, and the general public.

An aura of excitement and anticipation hovered about the opening of the conference. The subject had never been dealt with in a public forum—much less under the auspices of a national institution like the Library of Congress. The conferees were drawn from many walks of life, and many had never met each other before. In addition, it was the first major public event of the newly inaugurated American Folklife Center, which had been created by an Act of Congress, the American Folklife Preservation Act (P.L. 94–201), in 1976. Surrounded by the warm ambience of the Library's Whittall Pavilion, the assembled group heard Daniel J. Boorstin, the Librarian of Congress, open the conference.

This book is not a transcription of the proceedings of the conference, nor does it begin to represent the papers, talks, roundtable discussions, and audience contributions that made up the meeting. Rather, it carries the initiative of the conference a step further—exploring more deeply some themes and exemplary figures contemplated at the conference, and beginning the task of assembling the research tools requisite to serious future investigation of the subject.

Yet in certain ways the spirit of the conference lives on in this volume. Scholars, collectors, record producers and dealers, shop-owners, and recording artists all attended the conference—a rare and magical mix of all the concerned parties in one assembly. For me the emblematic moment of the conference occurred when Pekka Gronow, moderating a roundtable discussion with ethnic record producers and distributors, introduced Chicago Polish record producer Alvin Sajewski. Fellow pioneer producer Myron Surmach, whose record and book store served New York's Ukrainian community, had just shared his thoughts and recollections with the conference. As Sajewski was being introduced, he rose, saying, "Excuse me, I want to shake hands with Mr. Surmach." They had never met, though they had known of each other for decades, and a warm and lively discussion of shared experiences ensued. Sajewski's experiences are more amply explored in this volume in Richard K. Spottswood's "The Sajewski Story: Eighty Years of Polish Music in Chicago," and Surmach reappears in Spottswood's "Commercial Ethnic Recordings in the United States."

The conference included an evening concert in the Library's Coolidge Auditorium. The first half of the concert presented the Polish Highlanders from Chicago. The second half featured Lydia Mendoza, whose artistry has made her a living legend along the Southwest border. Lydia Mendoza not only performed for but participated in the conference: With James S. Griffith serving as her interlocutor, she spoke at a roundtable discussion with recording artists on the second day. This volume relives and expands that moment in the conference, for Griffith subsequently visited her in Houston in order to help her assemble a fuller autobiography for publication.

During the conference an exhibit on ethnic recordings in America was mounted in the Library of Congress. The exhibit not only stood as a testimony to the value of primary documents for exploring the subject, but through those documents made a statement about the history and importance of ethnic recordings. Richard K. Spottswood, who was responsible for preparing the exhibit in cooperation with the Library's Exhibit Office, lent from his own collection and secured from other private sources a number of items to supplement the materials drawn from the holdings of the Library. The exhibit dramatized one unanimous conclusion of the conferees: The preservation of primary documents relating to ethnic recordings—the original recordings themselves, related publications and commercial catalogs, and materials pertaining to the business of record production and distribution—is an urgent prerequisite to an adequate understanding of their significance to American civilization. I hope that the illustrations included in this book help to convey the value of these documents and the urgency of that concern.

This book, then, is another step toward the goals articulated by the conference on "Ethnic Recordings in America." Three of the contributors have devoted essays to limning the subject in its broad outlines and exploring some fundamental issues the subject raises: Pekka Gronow's "Ethnic Recordings: An Introduction," Richard K. Spottswood's "Commerical Ethnic Recordings in the United States," and Joseph C. Hickerson's "Early Field Recordings of Ethnic Music." Three more contributions examine particular examples in greater depth: Mick Moloney's "Irish Ethnic Recordings and the Irish-American Imagination," which looks at a single ethnic group's recording activities as a reflection of the changing tastes and preferences of its American experience; "La Alondra de la Frontera," an essay in autobiography prefaced by James S. Griffith's remarks about Lydia Mendoza as a Mexican-American artist; and "The Sajewski Story," in which Richard K. Spottswood reflects on the crucial role of a producer and distributor of recordings and music publications in an American ethnic community. And finally, Norm Cohen and Paul Wells of the John Edwards Memorial Foundation have provided a much-needed resource guide to help launch what we all hope will be an era of concerted preservation of ethnic recordings and increased research into their significance as documents and artifacts of our civilization.

The American Folklife Center is grateful to all the contributors whose essays comprise this book. We are likewise grateful to others whose participation made the conference such a success. I should like to acknowledge in particular the efforts of Elena Bradunas and Carl Fleischhauer of the center staff, who worked on both the conference and the book; Richard K. Spottswood, who helped organize the conference and accompanying exhibit and contributed in many ways beyond the essays included here; Howard W. Marshall and Brett Topping, who assisted in the development of the manuscript; Judith McCulloh, whose fine editorial hand helped steer us from an idea to a book; and the staff of the Library's Publishing Office, who assisted in the latter stages of production.

For ethnic recordings in America this volume is definitive only in that it defines the task before us. It is published in the hope that, as we move into the second century of recordings as a communicative and cultural medium, collecting and research will continue until ethnic recordings assume their proper place in our national consciousness of our national heritage.

Alan Jabbour
Director, American Folklife Center

Welcoming Remarks to the Conference on Ethnic Recordings in America

This is a historic as well as a historical occasion, because it is the first conference to be held by the new American Folklife Center in the Library of Congress. The Library has of course been a pioneer in enlarging our concept of American civilization and in bringing together all the materials that are related to it. Our collection of folksongs goes back to 1928, and in some respects earlier. We hope that the Folklife Center will make it possible for us to be even more active, more wide-ranging, more imaginative in the exploration of the folk cultural aspects of American civilization.

I should like briefly to put this meeting in the perspective of American civilization. The title of the conference is "Ethnic Recordings in America: A Neglected Heritage." In that title and in the purpose of our meeting there are three distinctive features of American civilization: music, technology, and ethnicity.

Music in this country has had a quite distinct character. The American achievement has not been expressed in chamber music, or in symphony, or in grand opera, but in popular music. The line between popular music and folk music is a difficult one, and I shall leave its definition to more competent hands, but there is certainly some connection between the special character of folk music and the spectacular success of popular music in the United States. Wherever you go in the world, whatever you may hear said about American civilization, you will find juxtaposed to those comments performances of American popular music, usually from phonograph recordings.

But we ourselves have found it hard to come to terms with popular music. We have found it hard to give musical comedy the dignity which seems to come with grand opera or the music of high culture. Our most articulate wits and pundits have had trouble finding the proper place for music in our civilization. This puzzlement was perhaps best expressed by Mark Twain when he observed that Wagner's music is better than it sounds. The assumption that somehow there is a cultural measure or standard for music which is different from the way it sounds has, of course, plagued all of us.

Popular music has been a special feature of American life, and it has had a special relationship to technology. The phonograph is as good a symbol as any of the peculiar intrusion of technology in America into the traditional categories of culture. I think perhaps someone should compile an anthology of the comments about the phonograph when it was first invented. It was treated primarily as a threat; in *The Americans: The Democratic Experience* I have explored some of the consequences of John Philip Sousa's attack on what he called "the menace of mechanical music." We forget now that, just as when movable type was introduced people preferred hand-made Bibles to the machine-made Bibles, so when the phonograph came in people tended to prefer hand-made music to machine-made music. There were many quips by more witty people than John Philip Sousa. Ambrose Bierce, for example, defined the phonograph as "an irritating toy that restores life to dead noises."

The phonograph asserted itself in American life largely because it was a democratic instrument. It was a machine which not only repeated experience but democratized it. While Ambrose Bierce and Sousa could indicate their fears of the phonograph around 1906, within a decade or two it was one of the primary resources for reaching everybody with music—including the high-brow music that so aroused the suspicion of Mark Twain and others.

Finally, let me mention the third element which is brought together in this conference—ethnicity. We have heard again and again—in fact, so often that perhaps our ears have become immune to the message—that this is a nation of nations, that we were comprised of many peoples. That multiplicity is expressed in our language, in the fact that the real American language is broken English, familiar to many of us as it was spoken by our parents or grandparents. One of the reasons, perhaps, why foreign language study has not been popular in the United States, is that so many Americans already speak another language. We are interested in this pluralism of American life. It is interesting to note that the cover of our conference program reproduces a Victor record label for a Ukrainian-American recording which uses the Cyrillic alphabet. We are here celebrating the multiplicity of American life, the manyness of it, the subtlety of it.

This label appeared on the program for the conference "Ethnic Recordings in America: A Neglected Heritage." The recording was made in 1927 by a group of Ukrainian actors, singers, and musicians led by E. I. Tziorogh and presents a skit celebrating Jordan's Eve, a holiday marking the climax of the Christmas season.

This conference is significant because it serves the large purpose of the Library of Congress, which is not only to celebrate but to understand and reach deep into American civilization—to discover how it has been limited, how it has been fulfilled and how we can make it more fulfilling. We here bring together these three elements which have been characteristic of American civilization: the popularity and the democratic character of our music, the speed and effectiveness and vitality of our technology, and the vividness and richness of our ethnicity. We have high hopes for this, our debut for the Folklife Center. We trust it is a signal and a symbol of much more to come.

Daniel J. Boorstin
The Librarian of Congress

Ethnic Recordings: An Introduction

Pekka Gronow

Erik Kivi's recording.
Courtesy of Pekka Gronow.

In August 1926, the Victor Talking Machine Company was busy recording Gene Austin, Waring's Pennsylvanians, the Savoy Bearcats, and Paul Whiteman and His Orchestra. On August 17, after twelve rejected takes, Gladys Rice and Billy Murray produced a successful recording of "The Girl Is You and the Boy Is Me," a classic statement of the basic theme of twentieth-century American popular music.[1] Other artists featured in the Victor catalog included Enrico Caruso, John McCormack, Fritz Kreisler, Frank Crumit, Vernon Dalhart, Homer Rodeheaver, and the Benson Orchestra of Chicago.[2] In 1926, $70 million worth of phonograph records were sold in the United States,[3] and Victor, the leading company in the field, accounted for a considerable portion of those sales.

On August 9, a man named Erik Kivi entered the Victor studios in New York to record four Finnish folksongs to his own fiddle accompaniment. The first two, "Merimiehen valssi" and "Porin poika," were issued in November on Victor 78882, and the other two titles, "Laula kukko" and "Masuska," were released the following month on Victor 78907. The records sold a total of 1,069 and 652 copies, respectively, hardly anything to compete with Paul Whiteman, or with Vernon Dalhart, whose Victor recording of "The Prisoner's Song"/"Wreck of the Old 97" sold 957,635 copies in 1925-26.[4] Yet Victor was sufficiently satisfied with Erik Kivi to call him back to the studios three times to record a total of eighteen numbers.

Erik Kivi was the earliest Finnish folk musician to record commercially; in Finland, no commercial recordings of traditional fiddling were made until the 1950s. Nothing is known about his career except that he lived on the East Coast and was rumored to have a violin made of toothpicks.[5] His recordings were part of the little-known field of "foreign-language records" that flourished in the United States from the turn of the century to the 1950s along with the better-known popular, classical, "race," and "country" recordings. During this period Victor alone issued more than 15,000 so-called foreign records, recordings made by immigrant artists ranging from Finnish fiddlers to Sicilian bagpipe players.

None of Erik Kivi's recordings seem to have sold many more than a thousand copies. A survey of the sales of Victor's Finnish-American records

From the Finnish newspaper
New Yorkin Uutiset,
March 5, 1927. Courtesy of
Pekka Gronow.

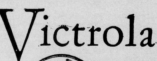

suggests that many sold fewer than that.[6] Why did the company that was selling Paul Whiteman and Vernon Dalhart by the hundreds of thousands go to the trouble of recording Erik Kivi and other Finnish-American artists, processing the recordings, publishing special Finnish catalog supplements, and advertising regularly in the Finnish-American press?

There may be several explanations. For one thing, selling 1,069 copies of a recording was perhaps not such bad business after all. If the company did not insist on covering a large part of its fixed costs with the sales of the foreign-language department, a thousand copies may well have been enough to make a profit, or at least to keep the pressing plant running while it had nothing else to do. Very little is known about the economics of the record industry, but in the 1950s, when recording techniques were not much different from those of the 1920s, record producers in Finland estimated that a 78 rpm record had to sell 1,200 copies to make a profit.

Of course, the Finns were among the smaller immigrant groups, and recordings by Italian-American or German-American artists might be expected to sell considerably more. There are unconfirmed reports of foreign-language recordings selling 100,000 copies or more.[7] In addition, we must remember that Victor and the other large record companies of the period were not in business only to sell records. They also sold phonographs, or "talking machines," and the sale of one phonograph could equal the sale of a few hundred records. About a million phonographs were sold in the United States in 1927.[8] It was certainly easier to sell a talking machine to a Finnish-American if a recording of a popular Finnish comedian, a Finnish folksong, or the national anthem of Finland went with it. No wonder that Victor's main competitor, the Columbia Phonograph Company, urged its dealers in the company's house organ in 1909 to

> remember that in all large cities and in most towns there are sections where people of one nationality or another congregate in "colonies." Most of these people keep up the habits and prefer to speak the language of the old country. Speak to them in their own tongue, if you can, and see their faces light up with a smile that linger and hear the streak of language they will give you in reply. To these people RECORDS IN THEIR OWN LANGUAGE have an irresistible attraction, and they will buy them readily.[9]

And again, two years later:

> Don't wait until you have sold every American-born individual in your locality a Columbia before giving the one-time foreigner attention. You will probably find a good deal of much easier business among the people of foreign nationality.[10]

The industrial revolution caused tremendous changes in our communication systems, many of which we are only now beginning to understand. Today we obtain both our news and our dreams through the mass media, industrially produced to suit the needs of the largest possible audience. Although students of the mass media have often forgotten the phonograph record, it is certainly as much a mass medium as, say, the film. Records seem to consume more of our time and our money than do films, and most of the music that the average person in the industrialized world hears today comes from records, either directly or by radio.[11]

By definition, the mass media strive to reach a large audience. Their expensive technology and production methods demand that the product— whether a film, a broadcast, or a record—be acceptable to a considerable number of people. Although students of mass communication have shown little interest in music, musicologists have often pointed out the dangers inherent in the mass production of music, the "cultural gray-out" that will result.[12]

There is no doubt that the development of the record industry and radio broadcasting has contributed to the leveling of musical tastes. Yet in some cases, the record industry has contributed to the continued existence and development of the musical traditions of relatively small groups, such as many ethnic groups in the United States. I believe it is time to put the questions in a different way. The importance of the mass media, especially the record industry, to music today is undeniable. But what effect will this have on the development of musical traditions? Under what conditions will the mass media promote change or stagnation? When will they accelerate the culturral gray-out, and when will they add to the variety and diversity of traditions? What other effects will they have?

The record industry has been studied so little that it is still too early to answer these questions definitively. But the history of ethnic, or foreign-language, recordings in the United States offers us a rare chance to study these problems under almost laboratory conditions. This was probably the first country in the world where record players and records were widely distributed among large parts of the population. At the same time, there were—and still are—many different ethnic groups in the country. Each of these groups has had its own musical traditions, and each has used the new media in its own way.

In order to understand the situation fully, we must first look at the development of the record industry from a global perspective. At the beginning of this century, the industrialized part of the world was ready for large-scale production and consumption of household technology. This was the era of the bicycle, the sewing machine, and the phonograph. Growing international trade encouraged new industries to expand to less developed countries. Patent legislation helped establish monopolies or near-monopolies.[13]

After a series of legal and economic battles at the turn of the century, three firms had a virtual monopoly in the production of recordings and record players in the United States: the Victor Talking Machine Company, the Columbia Phonograph Company, and Edison.[14] All three operated on a global scale. By 1907, Edison's National Phonograph Company had offices in New York, London, Paris, Berlin, Brussels, Mexico City, Sydney, and Buenos Aires.[15] In 1898, Victor established a sister company in England, the Gramophone Company, financed in part by English capital. In 1907 the two companies agreed to division of territory, so that Victor operated in the Americas, Japan, and China, and the Gramophone Company in the rest of the world.[16] The French Pathé Frères and the German Carl Lindström and Beka companies (which soon merged) also set out to conquer the world.

Recent research has unearthed interesting details of the Gramophone Company's activities in Europe and Asia.[17] By 1905 the company had already made recordings in most European and Asian countries, including such remote localities as Helsinki, Tiflis, and Rangoon. At the same time, Victor's engineers toured South America and the Caribbean. The two companies obviously tried to penetrate every possible market from Tibet to Bolivia. To give just one example: Iceland had 78,000 inhabitants in 1900;[18] yet beginning in 1910, the Gramophone Company took pains to record Icelandic artists fairly regularly, first in Copenhagen and later in Reykjavik.[19]

These examples illustrate the record industry's unique capacity to adapt its product to the needs of different groups. The same phonographs could be sold anywhere. The same patented processes were used to manufacture records. Yet the industry could offer each group its own music, and it did. Between 1898 and 1921, the Gramophone Company alone made about 200,000 recordings in its part of the world. Of course, the largest number of recordings were made in the countries where the record companies had their headquarters: England, France, Germany, and the United States.

The record industry did not set out to change musical traditions. It recorded whatever it thought could be sold, seeking its artists from the opera houses as well as the music halls. In the United States this meant both the Metropolitan Opera, and the beer gardens where young Irving Berlin was starting his career as a singing waiter. But the artists had to be professionals in their own field, performing in the urban centers where the industry operated.

At the beginning of the century, immigration was a highly visible phenomenon in the New York area, where the recording industry was concentrated. In 1900, 13.5 percent of the population of the United States was foreign born, and the figure was much higher in metropolitan areas such as New York.[20] The foreign-language press was an important part of the American press. In 1910, for instance, there were 700 foreign-language dailies or weeklies in the United States with a total circulation exceeding 5 million.[21] There were also foreign-language theaters in large cities.

In this situation it was natural for the record companies to use the same methods at home and abroad. The "foreign-speaking population," as the companies called it, was a market that had to be taken into consideration. Very soon American companies were recording immigrant artists, and in fact, their activities at home and abroad complemented each other. Recordings made in Europe and Asia could also be sold to members of the same groups in the United States, just as recordings made by immigrant artists in New York could be exported to their home countries.

Of course, some recordings crossed ethnic barriers, especially in the field of classical music. The recordings of Caruso were best-sellers in the American "domestic" market, outselling recordings by American singers. A considerable number of the artists listed in the Victor Red Seal catalog were foreign and sang in languages other than English.[22] But even in this field, minor artists were usually relegated to their own ethnic markets. Aino Ackté, a Finnish soprano who appeared at the Metropolitan Opera in the early years of this century, made the Red Seal catalog, while Väinö Sola, the leading tenor of the Helsinki Opera, was consigned to Victor's foreign catalog.[23]

From 1900 to 1920, the record industry enjoyed a period of almost uninterrupted growth.[24] Victor, Columbia, and Edison issued increasing numbers of foreign records in addition to their domestic releases. To give just one example: Between 1908 and 1923, Columbia issued about 5,000 domestic (mainly popular) records in the "A" catalog series and about 6,000 foreign records in the "E" series.

By the late 1910s, many new companies had entered the lucrative record

business. In the early 1920s there were already about 150 record companies,
and overproduction was causing the industry difficulties. Many of the new
firms were trying to survive by cutting prices and concentrating on the latest
popular hits. Obviously they had little interest in minority audiences. But the
larger and better-financed new companies found it necessary to start producing foreign records. These companies include at least Brunswick, Emerson,
Gennett, Pathé, Plaza (Banner), and Vocalion. And the General Phonograph
Corporation, "makers of the famous OKeh records," which had close connections with the German Lindström company, was soon competing seriously
with Victor and Columbia in the ethnic field.

Examples of ethnic records produced by smaller companies in the 1920s: a Parsekian Armenian record, a Macksoud Arabic record, and a Srpske Gusle Serbian record. Courtesy of Pekka Gronow.

The establishment of independent pressing plants made it possible for almost anyone to enter the record business with little capital. This period saw the beginning of specialization in the industry. Many music store owners and other small entrepreneurs in ethnic communities became involved on a small scale. In New York, Harry Pace's Black Swan company specialized in producing race records for the black market. In Chicago, Wallin's Music Store issued about twenty-five Swedish records between 1922 and 1927, using the technical resources of Paramount and Autograph (Marsh Laboratories). Other ethnic labels of the 1920s include Gaelic, Jugoslavia, Italianstyle, Panhellenion (Greek), Parsekian (Armenian), Srpske Gusle (Serbian), La Patrie (French-Canadian), and Macksoud (Arabic). It is possible that in some cases these small companies were closer to the tastes of the ethnic communities than were the large companies, which sometimes used assembly-line methods to produce foreign records, assigning their regular studio orchestra to accompany ethnic performers.

On the other hand, the major companies were expanding their recording activities outside New York. Around 1920 they had discovered the existence of a black audience and had embarked on the production of race records. By the mid-1920s, they had also found out that rural record buyers, especially in the South, had a taste for "old-time tunes" that differed markedly from the popular music consumed by northern urban audiences. Soon the production of old-time tunes, or "hillbilly music," was an important part of the industry. Record companies were able to apply many of the methods that they had developed in the production and marketing of foreign-language records to these new fields. Race records and old-time tunes were assigned their special numerical series, new releases were announced in special supplements, and (in the case of race records) they were advertised in the ethnic press. Just as the major companies automatically advertised their new Finnish releases in *New Yorkin Uutiset,* advertisements for new race releases appeared in the *Chicago Defender.*

To obtain material for their race and old-time catalogs, the record companies had to go outside New York. Soon they were making regular recording expeditions as far as New Orleans and San Antonio. Permanent recording facilities were established in Chicago, which soon became an important recording center on its own. (Columbia had made recordings for its foreign catalog in Chicago as early as 1915.)

The companies seem to have been willing to try almost any artist the local record retailer suggested. In this way, during the 1920s they discovered the French-speaking Acadians, or "Cajuns," of Louisiana, the Czech communities in Texas, the Spanish-speaking population of the Southwest, the Scandinavians of the Midwest, and possibly others. The following story of Joseph Falcon, the first Cajun accordionist to make records, illustrates this process:

George Burrow, a jewelry store owner in Rayne, persuaded Falcon to go to New Orleans with him to make some records to be sold in Burrow's Rayne store.

"We went over there," Falcon recalled. "They looked at us— we was but two, just myself and my wife Clemo Breaux, she played the guitar—but they were used to recording with orchestras. 'That's not enough music to make a record,' they said. So George had 250 records paid for before I even went to make them. So George started talking; 'We got to run it through because that man there,' he said, pointing to me, 'is popular in Rayne; the people are crazy about his music and they want the records.' But they said, 'We don't know if it's going to sell.' They then turned around and asked him, 'How much would you buy?' He told them he wanted 500 copies as the first order. 'Ah,' they said, '500! When are you gonna get through selling that?' 'That's my worry,' he said, 'I want 500.' And he made out a check for 500 records. They started looking at each other. 'Well,' they said, 'you go ahead and play us a tune just for us to hear.' "[25]

Thus was the first Cajun record, "Alons à Lafayette," made in 1928. The passage just quoted supports the hypothesis that ethnic recordings did not have to sell by the thousands to satisfy the companies. In the same interview, Joseph Falcon also observed that the fact that one of their own people had cut a record made a great impression on the Cajuns: "Even some of the poorest country fellows, they buy as high as two records. They ain't got no Victrola, but they buy and go to their neighbor's and play it!"

After the 1929 crash, record sales deteriorated rapidly. Only $6 million worth of records were sold in 1933, a tremendous decrease from $75 million in 1929. By the mid-1930s there were only three compaines in the business: RCA Victor (the old Victor Talking Machine Company had been acquired by the Radio Corporation of America), the Brunswick-Columbia-American Record Corporation group (the result of numerous mergers), and the recently established Decca Records.

But even though record sales were low, these companies continued a steady, if small, output of ethnic recordings throughout the lean years. They relied mostly on imported masters from their European affiliates for their foreign output, but they also did some recording in the United States. To a certain extent radio seems to have replaced records as a source of music in ethnic communities as well as in the nation as a whole. There were now foreign-language broadcasts in many cities, and music played an important role in these programs.[26]

By 1938, record sales were increasing again, thanks in part to the popularity of juke boxes. The bars and saloons in ethnic communities also had juke boxes, and Columbia was quick to publish a list of suitable foreign records.[27] Will Glahé's "Beer Barrel Polka" was a big juke-box hit in many ethnic communities. The number of foreign releases picked up, but soon the wartime shellac shortage and union disputes (the "Petrillo ban") were giving the industry so much trouble that it was happy just to be able to meet the demand for popular records.

To the major companies, ethnic recordings had by then become an unimportant sideline. However, to the record dealers in an ethnic community, such as the Scandinavian Music House in Brooklyn's Scandinavian section, foreign records were their bread and butter. Many of them started looking for other suppliers. Some imported records from overseas, while others encouraged the growth of small specialist labels or started record production on their own. Many small companies began making unauthorized "pirate" pressings of recordings produced abroad, which was easy because United States copyright law did not cover sound recordings.

"Cajan" Folk Song Recorded by General Phono Corp.

Folk Song of the Acadians, Who Live in the Louisiana Bayous, Recorded by Dr. James F. Roach, New Orleans, for Okeh Records

Although the first Cajun record was produced by Columbia in 1928, this notice in *Talking Machine World* (July 15, 1925, p. 12) indicates an earlier attempt by OKeh in 1925. OKeh did not use the recording, which appeared instead on the singer's own Roach label with a piano solo by his wife, Agnes Farrell Roach, on the reverse side. Motion Picture, Broadcasting, and Recorded Sound Division, Library of Congress.

NEW ORLEANS, LA., July 6.—The first recording of a "Cajan" folk song for Okeh records has been made by the Hart Piano House, Southern jobbers for the Okeh line.

The "Cajans," or Acadians, have a type of music all their own. They are the descendants of the French colonists banished from Grand Pré by the British after the cession to England of some of the French holdings off the Canadian shore, near Newfoundland. These people have lived along the Louisiana bayous, weaving and spinning and raising the peculiarly tinted cotton made famous in the cloths they weave, and the dialect they speak and the songs they sing in the fields and over the cradles are heard only in the bayou country. As portraits of bayou life they are real poetry, connoisseurs say, telling stories of the strange water creatures that inhabit the bayous, and the uneventful life of fisherfolk.

The initial record is "Gue Gue Solingail," or "Song of the Crocodile." It is sung for the Okeh by Dr. James F. Roach, a new Orleans non-professional, who is gaining a widespread reputation for amateur and radio appearances. The success of the first recording will mean, it is believed, further experiment along the same line and the introduction of typical Cajan music and dialect lyrics to many music lovers, via the talking machine.

After the war the major companies attempted briefly to re-enter the ethnic market. Old records were reissued, new recordings cut. But total record sales were now rapidly growing—$224 million in 1947—and the introduction of LP and 45 rpm records gave them other things to worry about. And they were no longer in touch with the tastes of the ethnic communities. Columbia (now part of the CBS concern) conducted a market survey of American musical interests and did not even mention the music of the non-English-speaking ethnic groups. The following quotation from Lloyd Dunn, a Capitol Records executive, illustrates the attitude of major American labels in the 1950s:

During my travels, I soon became aware that in Europe, and most of the world, American popular records were in great demand. . . . But our foreign associates insisted that we reciprocate by selling more of *their* records. They pointed out that there are more Italians in New York than in Rome. And more Germans in Milwaukee than—etc., etc. True, perhaps. But second-generation Europeans are *Americans*, particularly in their musical tastes.[28]

At the same time, nevertheless, dozens of small companies were able to make a living by supplying ethnic communities with their music. Some produced records in a wide variety of languages and idioms, such as Tetos Demetriades' Standard Records, which could draw from Demetriades' experience and contacts as former head of Victor's foreign department. Other labels identified closely with one area or language were Balkan, Scandinavia Sings, Fennia, and so forth. A parallel development was occurring in the fields of country-and-western and black music (now called rhythm-and-blues), where independent labels took over the market from the major companies.[29]

By the 1960s, the transition to LP and the decreasing size of many ethnic groups was radically changing the field of ethnic recordings. The sixties, however, are beyond the scope of this article. I shall note only that while Spanish-speaking communities now became the leading consumers of non-English-language recordings, many other groups also continued their own production; but in many cases the line between recordings produced for ethnic communities and folk music recordings produced for the general public became vague.

At this point it may prove instructive to look more closely at recording activities among a variety of ethnic groups: Finns, Irish, Jews, Hawaiians, Native Americans, and Hispanic Americans.

Since the 1890s, the Cape Ann area in Massachusetts has been one of the centers of Finnish immigration in the United States. By the 1910s, Rockport and Lanesville each had a Finnish Lutheran church, a Temperance Hall, and a Socialist Hall, which were the social and cultural centers of the Finnish community. The halls were active in putting on plays, having dances, and supporting brass bands.

Two members of the Väinölä Temperance Society brass band of Lanesville were to leave their mark in the history of recorded music. The first, Antti Syrjäniemi, was born in Haapajärvi, Finland, in 1892. He came to America in his teens and, like many other Finns, found his first employment in the granite quarries of Cape Ann. Later he opened a shoe-repair shop, which he ran until his retirement in 1957. Syrjäniemi was one of the moving forces in the cultural life of the Finnish community. Besides playing E-flat alto and baritone horns in the brass band, he organized athletic groups, appeared in plays, and was a popular singer who was well known in Finnish halls all over Massachusetts. He was famous for his topical songs, which he composed while working on his customers' shoes, and in 1929 he was asked to go to New York to record five titles for Victor's Finnish catalog. One of the songs was a satirical commentary on the famous Scopes trial; another described the happenings at a Finnish dance on Cape Ann, celebrating another Finnish-American recording artist, the accordionist Viola Turpeinen. By the time the records were released, the Depression had cut records sales to

Sylvester Ahola. Courtesy of Pekka Gronow.

a fraction of the peak years of the 1920s. Antti Syrjäniemi was not asked to record again, but he remained active in the Finnish community until his death in 1962. In 1956 the fortieth wedding anniversary of Mr. and Mrs. Andrew Niemi—as Syrjäniemi and his wife were known by then— was a major social event.[30]

The Väinölä band's cornettist, Sylvester Ahola, was born in Lanesville in 1902. His parents had emigrated from the same region of Finland as Antti Syrjäniemi. For a while Ahola worked on his parents' farm, but then he decided to become a professional musician. He studied in Boston and was soon playing with dance bands there and in nearby cities. He made his first recordings in Boston with Frank Ward's Orchestra. In 1925 he went to New York to join the Paul Specht Orchestra at the Moulin Rouge at Forty-seventh and Broadway, and recorded with a number of different groups. In 1927 he sailed to London to join the Savoy Orpheans. The next year he joined Bert Ambrose's famous orchestra at the May Fair Hotel, and, with dozens of different studio groups, he started a prolific recording career that lasted until his return to New York in 1931. During the 1930s he was an active studio musician in New York, appearing frequently on the Bing Crosby radio show.[31] In 1940 he decided to leave New York and the "big time." He went back to Gloucester, Massachusetts, performed frequently at local functions, and became a sexton of the local church. He often played with Antti Syrjäniemi's daughters Miriam and Mary, who played accordion and piano, respectively.

Antti Syrjäniemi and Sylvester Ahola represent two different relationships between Finnish-Americans and the record industry. Although he never lost his Finnish-American identity, Ahola joined the mainstream of the industry and recorded for the general American and international public.

Mäki Orkesteri soittaa

Tanssit

BIWABIK'IN PAVILJONGISSA,
Tiistai-iltana, t. k. 6 p.

ANGORA, ALANGON HAALILLA,
Keskiviikko-iltana, t. k. 7 p.

ZIM, FARMERS CLUB'IN HAALILLA
Torstai-iltana, t. k. 8 p.

MARKHAM, WORKERS HAALILLA,
Perjantai-iltana, t. k. 9 p.

KEEWATIN, SUOMAL. HAALILLA,
Lauantai-iltana, t. k. 10 p.

CALUMET, KELJULAN HAALILLA,
Sunnuntai-iltana, t. k. 11 p.

MÄKI TRIO SOITTAA TEIDÄN
MIELIKSENNE!

Advertisement for Mäki Orchestra appearances at dances in Finnish-American community halls; from the Finnish newspaper *Työmies*, Superior, Wisconsin, May 3, 1930. Courtesy of Pekka Gronow.

Syrjäniemi's records were specifically aimed at the Finnish-American community. In his case, their circulation was quite limited, but one should not underestimate the importance of the ethnic record market. Between 1900 and the 1950s, American companies issued at least 30,000 78 rpm records aimed at the non-English-speaking communities in the United States. And although many ethnic records had only a limited sale, a great many popular records sold poorly, too. Many of Sylvester Ahola's recordings are now very rare, for example, and are eagerly sought by jazz collectors.

The 800 Finnish recordings issued by American companies clearly do not form a unified group. They include the archaic fiddling and singing of Erik Kivi; the topical songs of Antti Syrjäniemi, Arthur Kylander, and Hiski Salomaa; songs of the Finnish section of the Industrial Workers of the World; religious hymns; Massenet's "Elegy" and other classical selections; and a large number of accordion solos. Some of them were not even performed by Finns. Columbia 3174–F, issued as by Manhattanin Suomalainen Orkesteri (Manhattan Finnish Orchestra), was in fact a reissue of record 20231–F from the Russian series, where it appeared as by the Russian orchestra Moskwa. The record companies frequently promoted such crossovers to get more mileage from their repertory.

Many Finnish-American records were obviously aimed at subgroups within the community. A supporter of the IWW could hardly be expected to buy religious records, and vice versa. Yet the Finnish community would certainly have identified all these recordings as Finnish, just as the record companies did. They were distributed through record shops with a Finnish-American clientele, advertised in Finnish-American newspapers, and released in specific Finnish catalog series such as the Columbia 3000–F series.

The term "ethnic" has become a convenient label for groups that have maintained a language and/or culture that sets them apart from the dominant English-speaking culture of the United States. There are several theoretical problems inherent in the concept; these have been outlined elsewhere.[32] Still, for a discussion of the American record industry, the term serves a purpose. We can readily call all Finnish-American recordings "ethnic recordings," keeping in mind the fact that they range from traditional folk fiddling to classical selections. The same applies for the recordings of many other groups. However, in other cases the term "ethnic recordings" may cause difficulties; for instance, recordings made by or for Irish-Americans, Spanish-Americans, Jews, Hawaiians, and Native Americans do not always fall into the general pattern.

We often equate "immigrant" with "non-English-speaking," but of course an important number of immigrants to the United States came from the British Isles. There were a few Celtic-speaking people among them, but the majority were English-speaking. Immigrants from England were quick to merge with the dominant American population, and no record company issued "English-American" records. But although most Irish-Americans were English-speaking, they remained culturally apart.

Irish and pseudo-Irish music appeared in record catalogs from the very first years of the industry. Studio orchestras played jigs and reels; Irish accordionists and fiddlers made recordings; tenors sang "When Irish Eyes Are Smiling." But when record companies started to assign separate numerical series for their domestic and foreign recordings (Columbia in 1908, Victor ca. 1912), Irish records were systematically placed in the domestic series.

In the early 1920s there appeared small labels such as Gaelic and New Republic that specialized in Irish music. When Columbia revised its numerical system in 1923, assigning separate numerical series with an "F" suffix to each foreign nationality, Irish was at first not included. However, in 1925 the Irish were given (out of alphabetical sequence, as an afterthought) their own 33000-F series. Victor, OKeh, and Brunswick did likewise, but it is interesting to note that Columbia continued to list Irish releases in both domestic and foreign catalogs.[33]

At the beginning of the century, Irish music and American popular music were still sufficiently close that the average mainstream record buyer might well purchase an Irish jig. By the 1920s, Irish-American music and American popular music had grown apart, and record companies began to view the Irish as a foreign group, just like the Italians or the Finns.

In the 1920s, Victor and Columbia often recorded popular American hits of the day in other languages for the ethnic market, but only 1 to 2 percent of Irish-American recordings were sung in Gaelic. Those Irish-Americans who wished to enjoy the current popular hits could readily use the original versions; and there was no need to record a Gaelic version of "I Kiss Your Hand, Madame." Instead, the Irish series contained a much higher proportion of folk music than did the recordings of many other immigrant groups. The violin solos of Michael Coleman, James Morrison, and the other great violinists in the Columbia 33000-F series are among the finest examples of traditional music ever issued on commercial recordings.

Most of the major record companies also issued what they variously designated as "Jewish," "Hebrew-Jewish," or "Hebrew-Yiddish" records. The confusion of the record companies reflects the complexity of Jewish music.

Liturgical music in Hebrew is certainly the most widely known form of Jewish music. Josef Rosenblatt, David Roitman, Mordechay Hershman, and other famous cantors are indeed prominently featured in record catalogs. But until fairly recently, nobody spoke Hebrew as his mother tongue.[34] Jews came to America from many countries and spoke several different languages. However, the largest immigration came from Eastern Europe, where Yiddish was the language of Jewish communities. There soon developed a large-circulation Yiddish press in the United States, and a flourishing Yiddish theater in New York. Most "Jewish" records issued in the United States were Yiddish pieces—folksongs, popular songs, theatrical songs, and so on. A third important category was instrumental dance music from the Jewish communities in Eastern Europe and the Balkans. One of the most popular Jewish recording artists of the 1910s and 1920s was the bandleader Abe Schwartz. Advertisements for his Columbia records stressed the attraction of tradition: "To bring joy in life is a worthy art and when you hear Abe Schwartz's Orchestra playing on a Columbia record you will not be able to help yourself you must become lively and happy and begin dancing. . . . When you hear a 'Schwartz' record you become young and you think that you are standing with your loved one under the wedding canopy."[35] To make matters more complicated, there also appeared a small number of "Spanish-Hebrew" (actually Judezmo) recordings, and in the 1940s a new category emerged, secular or Zionist songs in Hebrew.

In spite of the great variety of Jewish recordings, their total number remained small compared with the output of other immigrant groups of

Recordings by Abe
Schwartz's Orchestra.
Courtesy of Pekka Gronow.

equal size. One cannot help thinking of the great number of Jewish entertainers who have, since the days of Al Jolson, made themselves a name in the
larger field of American popular music.

Earlier I noted how Irish-American music seems to have moved from the
popular mainstream to an ethnic category. The case of Hawaiian music is the
opposite. When Hawaii was annexed to the United States in 1898, the Islands
already had a hybrid popular music that combined native and Euro-Ameri-
can elements. The population of the Islands at that time was about 150,000.[36]
Around 1905, Victor issued some fifty Hawaiian records in a special 15000
catalog series. They may have been recorded on the Islands and were probably intended mainly for sale there, as they were listed in the company's
foreign catalog. [37]

Then as now, Hawaii, its music, and its dances held a romantic attraction for mainlanders. Hawaiian performers appeared in vaudeville, and the
1915 Panama-Pacific Exhibition in San Francisco made the Islands even better known. Record companies started recording Hawaiian guitarists for their
popular series. The 1915 Victor catalog commented on this transition:

> The Victor recently announced a fine list of favorite Hawaiian
> numbers, rendered by the now famous Hawaiian Quintette, who
> have made such a success in the "Bird of Paradise" Company; the
> gifted Toots Paka Troupe, and the Irene West Royal Hawaiians,
> who have been appearing in vaudeville.
>
> Although these fine records were intended mainly for
> customers in the Hawaiian Islands, they have been largely acquired
> by those Victor customers who like quaint and fascinating music
> such as this.[38]

Hawaiian music became part of the popular music of the day, and Tin Pan
Alley composers began writing songs about Honolulu and hula girls.[39]

In the late 1910s Columbia had an obscure Hawaiian "Y" series which
seems to have been intended for sale on the Islands. But most of Columbia's
Hawaiian records were issued in the popular "A," later "D," series.

The Toots Paka Hawaiian Troupe in the Victor 1916 Hawaiian catalog. Courtesy of Pekka Gronow.

Throughout the 1920's and 1930s, most recordings of Hawaiian music were made primarily for sale to non-Hawaiians, often by non-Hawaiian artists. Regular recording activity in Hawaii began first in the 1940s with the establishment of Bell Records.

The first commercial recordings by a Native American were made for Berliner records in the 1890s. In 1904 Ho-Nu-Ses recorded Iroquois Songs for the Victor Talking Machine Company. In the years following, additional recordings of Indian music were made occasionally, sometimes by Indians appearing on the stage, sometimes for ethnographic purposes, such as the Gennett Hopi recordings of 1926. They were obviously intended for sale to people who were not Indians.[41]

Commercial recordings of their own music first became important in Indian communities in the 1950s, when Raymond Boley's Canyon Records in Phoenix and a few other small companies in the Southwest started producing recordings of Indian music. Native Americans were obviously the last ethnic group (or groups) in the United States to adopt sound recordings as a medium for musical communication. There were many reasons for this: the small population of many Indian tribes, low incomes, and the fact that most Indians lived away from the old recording centers. But the growing popularity of records among Indians today shows that the medium can be adapted to musical traditions quite different from most other recorded music.[42]

Cape Verdean music recorded in America on Columbia's Portugese series, 1934. Courtesy of Pekka Gronow.

When United States record companies set out to conquer the world at the beginning of the century, Latin America was a natural target for their operations. In 1904, Columbia announced the establishment of "a complete record making laboratory in the City of Mexico."[43] Victor followed suit in 1905, and by 1915 the company had made recordings in Buenos Aires, Santiago, Montevideo, Lima, Rio, Trinidad, and other South American locations, and had established local agencies. The recordings were at first usually pressed in the United States and then exported back to the countries of origin, but by the 1920s factories were established in Mexico, Argentina, and possibly other Latin American countries.

Record company executives considered these recordings a third category apart from domestic and foreign records. In the 1920s Columbia used the letter "D" to denote domestic popular records, "M" for classical, and "F" for foreign records. Spanish and Portuguese records were grouped under "X" together with Chinese and Filipino records, indicating that they were mainly intended for the export trade.[44] Since the United States had a considerable Hispanic population, many of these export records were also sold at home. But the main market was outside the country, where in fact most of the recordings had been made.

In the 1920s, record companies began to make field recordings in the South. In San Antonio they found Mexican-American performers along with blues singers and hillbilly musicians, and there has been continuous recording activity in that area ever since. Many of these recordings are in the local *norteño* idiom, which is not particularly popular south of the border.

There are other Hispanic groups in the United States that have no connections with Latin America, such as the Cape Verdean Portuguese community in New England. Some Cape Verdean recordings appeared in the Columbia "X" series; it is not known whether they were sold outside the United States.

The role of the United States record industry in Latin America is a puzzling mosaic that has been little studied. In some cases it merely acted as the manufacturer of discs that were both recorded and sold abroad. In rare cases it produced records for Latin groups in the United States—such as the Texas-Mexicans or the Cape Verdeans—that can really be considered ethnic recordings in the same sense as Finish-American records. But usually the situation is much more complex. Cuban music was recorded in both Cuba and New York; it was sold in Cuba and other Latin-American countries and to Cubans and other Latins in the United States; at times it even entered the popular mainstream, when Latin-American dances enjoyed a period of popularity. Here the term "ethnic" soon loses all meaning. But from one point of view, of course, all records are ethnic.

How representative are ethnic recordings? In the late 1930s, the Library of Congress Archive of American Folk Song made a considerable number of field recordings in midwestern Finnish communities. Hardly any of these titles duplicate the songs issued on Finnish-American commercial recordings.[45] Most Finnish communities had choirs and brass bands, which played an important role in the activities of Finnish-American civic groups.[46] Yet they made extremely few commercial recordings and the Library of Congress was not interested in them, either.

Commercial recordings obviously do not represent all forms of music that existed in Finnish-American communities. Recording artists were usually professional entertainers in their own communities. We find their names regularly in advertisements in the Finnish-American press; they played at dances, gave concerts, and appeared in leading roles in the operettas presented by amateur theatrical groups. Finnish-Americans were willing to pay to hear them, both in person and on records. The industry used them because they had professional experience and their names were already known. There was no need to record the music that anyone could sing for himself at home.

At the time the record industry was born, folk music was already yielding to new forms of popular entertainment in most European countries. During the nineteenth century, urbanization, the growth of sheet-music publishing, and the development of vaudeville and other forms of commercial entertainment had given rise to music that was usually produced by professionals for a mass audience. The songs from music publishers in Berlin, London, and Paris were easily learned, and they soon replaced—at least in part—traditional forms of music, even in many rural areas.[47]

Advertisement for Viola Turpeinen's performance at a local hall in Duluth, Minnesota. From the Finnish newspaper *Työmies*, Superior, Wisconsin, May 3, 1930. Courtesy of Pekka Gronow.

By the turn of the century, the less industrialized, more remote parts of Europe had not yet fully adopted modern forms of entertainment, and folk music still played a prominent part in their culture. In the Balkan countries, folk traditions were influenced by Turkish-Arabic music, and it seems that modern popular music spread to these areas more slowly than to other parts of Europe. On the other hand, by 1900 all European countries had had some contact with the European art music tradition, and most countries had opera houses, conservatories, and symphony orchestras. In that nationalistic era, classically trained composers wrote popular patriotic songs. New mass movements, such as socialism, Zionism, and revivalistic religions, also developed their own special songs. Thus in most cases immigrants had several musical traditions to bring from their homelands, traditions that had to compete for survival in the new country.

Art music had a long tradition of professionalism, and also great prestige. The early foreign catalogs contain many recordings by classically trained singers, performing arias or lieder by composers of the home country, or translations of famous classics. But art music had appealed to a minority audience in the old countries, and in American ethnic communities the number of potential buyers was even smaller. The proportion of art music remained low, and the same singers also recorded patriotic songs (starting, of course, with the national anthem) and folksong arrangements in the fashion of the Romantic era, with piano or orchestra.

Popular music was something record company executives could readily identify. Many of its features were international, although repertories and styles varied from country to country. In many cases record companies could use their staff arrangers and musicians to accompany ethnic performers without difficulty. The Victor recording ledgers carry an interesting comment for January 30, 1928, when the Finnish comedians Matti Jurva and Tatu Pekkarinen were scheduled for a recording session in New York. A pianist named Cortese and a flute player named Barone (both musicians much used by the company) had been called in to accompany the singers. Evidently Pekkarinen felt uncomfortable with the pianist, as the files state "Cortese called but not used, as Pekkarinen wanted Jurva to play piano for him." On the recordings we can hear Jurva playing piano and Clement Barone, who obviously did not understand what the songs were about, supplying a competent flute obligato.

Since folk music is typically used for private amusement or communal music-making, performing it out of such contexts, for profit, would often be unthinkable. On the other hand, in many folk music traditions there was room for professional or semiprofessional performers, such as fiddlers who played for dances.[48] And at the beginning of the century, many European countries were already consciously trying to revive folk music and were promoting publications and competitions.

Traditional music must have had an important place in the life of most immigrant groups in the United States. However, many aspects of folk music were not easily adapted to the purposes of the record industry. Instrumental dance music was the type of folk music most frequently recorded. But even here, the archaic fiddling of Erik Kivi was unique in Finnish-American recordings; nothing comparable ever appeared on Swedish-American records. Both groups produced a large number of accordion recordings that stylistically and historically range from authentic folk music to popular music of the 1930s.

It must also be noted that ethnic groups varied greatly in the type of recorded music they preferred. Irish-Americans, Ukrainian-Americans, and Greek-Americans, for example, were especially interested in folk music. Religious songs dominated Norwegian-American records. Dutch- and Danish-Americans produced hardly any recordings at all and probably preferred standard popular or classical records. And in the case of Oriental groups, these distinctions were not always meaningful.

Swedish accordian players John Lager and Eric Olson in the Columbia 1920 Scandinavian catalog. Music Division, Library of Congress.

Record companies must have had great difficulties in judging ethnic folk performers, although record retailers in ethnic communities no doubt helped in the selection of artists. When Gunleik Smedal won the Norwegian-American Hardanger violin championship in Albert Lea, Minnesota, in 1928, he was a safe bet for Victor, and the company engaged him to record four sides for their Norwegian catalog.[49] But working in the studio with folk performers sometimes presented difficulties. One of Erik Kivi's folksongs had bawdy words, so it had to be sold under the counter in Finnish communities, which probably resulted in some negative feedback to the company.[50] Perhaps such experiences alarmed the industry. When Columbia engineers recorded the Cajun accordionist Dewey Segura in New Orleans in 1929, for instance, they told him, "We don't know what you're singing, we ask you just one thing: don't sing anything dirty." [51]

During the era of 78 rpm discs, which lasted for half a century, major United States companies issued ethnic recordings in at least thirty different languages. Among European nationalities or ethnic groups, it is easier to count those that did not record. As far as I have been able to determine, there were no Estonian, Latvian, Byelorussian, or Basque 78 rpm recordings made in the United States. Of course, smaller minority groups, such as Frisians, Faroese, or Lapps, did not record either, but otherwise every European language from Albanian to Welsh can be heard on recordings made in this country. Asia is not evenly represented. Only Turkish, Arabic, Armenian, Persian, Indian, Chinese, Japanese, and Filipino recordings were made in the United States. No African or Oceanic groups (except the Hawaiians) recorded, no doubt due to their small number in America. (Of course, this does not include the large English-speaking Afro-American population, which is beyond the scope of this paper.)

The output of these groups varied from several thousand to just a few recordings. The Icelanders are among the smaller immigrant groups in the United States; the 1930 census reported 2,764 persons born in Iceland. To obtain an exact picture of the potential market for Icelandic-American records we should also know whether their distribution extended to Canada, where there is an Icelandic community, or to Iceland. In any case, the market was small. The total number of Icelandic-speaking people in the world in the 1910s was not much over 100,000. In 1916, in New York, Columbia recorded four titles by Icelandic singer Einar Hjaltestad, and slightly later an instrumental version of the Icelandic national anthem. In the 1920s, Victor released two Icelandic records made in Europe, and in the 1940s an Icelandic singer had RCA custom press a record. The total known output of Icelandic 78 rpm recordings in the United States is six records, twelve titles. It seems reasonable to conclude that recordings did not play an important role in the development of Icelandic-American music. The remarkable thing is that record companies gave it a try. [52]

The 1920 census reported 149,824 persons born in Finland. The 1940 census, the first to give the mother tongue of native-born Americans, reported 230,420 Finnish speakers, which made the Finns the sixteenth largest non-English-speaking group in the United States. A group this size was able to support fairly regular record production for five decades. Victor and Columbia alone issued about 700 Finnish records. Almost 500 were recorded in the United States; the others were pressed from masters recorded in Europe. To these can be added about 100 records issued by other companies, mainly original American recordings. In the most active year, 1929, ninety new Finnish records were issued in the United States.

Table 1 shows the annual variation in the number of Finnish-American releases, which seems to follow a curve fairly typical of most ethnic groups. After production got under way in the late 1910s, this pattern obviously reflects the variation in total United States record sales.[53] Many ethnic groups produced more records than did the Finns. But the size of the groups does not predict its record output very well; see table 2 for a comparison of the size of some ethnic groups with their record production. Unfortunately, it is not yet possible to estimate the total record output of all American companies in all languages at different periods. The two sets of figures used in table 2 are fairly representative: Columbia's foreign series for 1923–52 (the "F" series) and Victor's foreign series for 1929–42 (the "V" series). The inclusion of other record companies would not alter the picture radically, but the inclusion of the period before 1923 would result in many changes.

It is very difficult to obtain adequate statistics on ethnic groups. The country of origin of immigrants is well documented, but many European countries have an ethnically mixed population, and it does not help to estimate the number of American-born members of ethnic groups. Here I have chosen the 1940 census data on mother tongue for reasons explained by Joshua Fishman in his pioneering work *Language Loyalty in the United States.*[49] For groups for which language data are not available (usually relatively small groups), I have given the country-of-birth data, but it should be remembered that the two sets of data are not comparable. Spanish- and Portuguese-speaking groups are excluded because of the impossibility of obtaining comparable figures on record production.

Although the figures must be used with caution, some interesting facts emerge. It is obvious that the smallest groups were not able to support regular record production. These groups include the Albanians, Armenians, Bulgarians, Welsh, most Asiatics—and, somewhat surprisingly, the Danes, Norwegians, and Dutch. Releases were sporadic, and sound recordings can hardly have played any important role in their musical life. At the end of the scale, it is not surprising that the Italians lead in record production; but the biggest non-English-speaking group, the Germans, falls below expectations. The number of Yiddish recordings is also smaller than might be expected, perhaps because of the many ethnic subdivisions within the group. Groups extremely active for their size are the Greeks and Ukrainians. The census figures for the Ukrainians are probably misleading—many Ukrainians were classified as Russians or Poles—but still their record output is impressive.

To explain these differences fully, we ought to know a great deal more about the history of the various groups, their internal divisions, their musical traditions in the old country and in the United States. But some tentative explanations can be suggested.

The most active groups were usually those who had recently immigrated. The number of Ukrainian and Greek speakers increased from 1940 to 1960 (but so did the number of Dutch speakers). Their home countries were little industrialized and had strong folk music traditions. Passive groups such as the Danes and the Dutch came from highly industrialized countries and spoke languages closely related to English. There was still some Danish recording activity in the United States in the 1910s, but it vanished in the 1920s.

Pawlo Humeniuk. From the Columbia 1927–28 Ukrainian-Russian catalog. Courtesy of Richard K. Spottswood.

The Norwegian case is more difficult. At the time of the most extensive emigration, Norway was a predominantly agricultural country with rich folk music traditions. But Norwegians are culturally and linguistically related to Swedes, and record companies issued "Scandinavian instrumental" recordings, (here classified with Swedish), which would appeal to Norwegians as well as to Swedes. In addition, Norwegian-Americans lived far from the main recording centers, and religion had considerable influence in their lives; records were perhaps considered too-worldly amusement. In the late 1910s and early 1920s, when Norwegian-American recording activity was at its peak, religious songs formed a large part of the recorded repertory. There are several times more Norwegians than Ukrainians in the United States, and yet the Ukrainians were far more productive in the recording field. Were the Norwegians assimilated more rapidly? Was there something about the Norwegian tradition that made their fiddle music less suitable for recording purposes than Ukrainian fiddling? Or was it because Ukrainians lived on the East Coast, while Norwegians were in the Midwest, far from recording centers?

At the same time the study of ethnic recordings leads us to ask many interesting questions about the history of the groups that made them, we must not dismiss the influence of a few creative individuals. The history of Ukrainian-American music, for instance, would certainly have been different without Pawlo Humeniuk, the violinist whose successful recordings in the 1920s influenced ethnic recordings far beyond the field of Ukrainian-American music.

In this discussion of ethnic recordings in the United States, we should bear in mind that many of the recordings issued by American companies in their foreign series were simply recordings that had originally been made in Europe for local consumption. The companies obtained the masters from their European affiliates and pressed the discs for the American market with their own labels. Since the recording expenses had already been covered in the country of origin, the cost of issuing such recordings was small. On the other hand, American record companies did not have to rely entirely on domestic sales in the production of ethnic records. In many cases the records could also be sold in the old country; almost all Finnish-American records made by Columbia between 1925 and 1930, for example, were also pressed by Columbia's European affiliates for sale in Finland. Canada was a natural market for ethnic records, and at least in the 1930s RCA's subsidiary was marketing ethnic recordings made in the United States for the larger immigrant groups in Argentina.[55]

The ratio of original American recordings to imports varied from time to time and from group to group, even from company to company. Table 1 shows how Columbia and Victor first made a large number of Finnish recordings in the United States but later relied mainly on imports. During the 1910s and 1920s recording activity was great in all ethnic groups; during the 1930s imports dominated. Germany was one of the leading record-producing countries in the world, and German recordings were readily available to American companies. Yet they usually found it necessary to record German-American performers, too. On the other hand, very few Ukrainian recordings were made in Europe during the 1920s, so American companies had to depend on their own initiative. Some ethnic groups, such as the Cajuns, had no other source than their own performers to draw from.

Table 1
Victor and Columbia Finnish Releases, 1907–53

Note: US = American recordings; USr = reissue of American recording; Fin = Finnish recording; Fr = reissue of Finnish recording previously issued in the United States; Unkn = unknown (missing numbers).

ª Exact release date unknown, but between 1944 and 1947. The release dates of early (pre-1925) Columbia issues are estimated, but the error can hardly be more than one year.

Year	Victor						Columbia					Grand Total
	US	USr	Fin	Fr	Unkn	Total	US	USr	Fin	Unkn	Total	
1907	20					20						20
1908												
1909												
1910	9					9						9
1911							4				4	4
1912												
1913	3					3						3
1914												
1915							11				11	11
1916	7					7	13				13	20
1917	4					4	13				13	17
1918							6				6	6
1919	6					6	3				3	9
1920	7					7	6				6	13
1921	1					1	5				5	6
1922	2		2			4	2				2	6
1923	2		1			3	2				2	5
1924	6					6	8				8	14
1925	2		1			3	8				8	11
1926	5		4			9	19				19	28
1927	22		8			30	27				27	57
1928	37		9			46	32			1	33	79
1929	36		19			55	35				35	90
1930	$26\frac{1}{2}$		$15\frac{1}{2}$			42	29	5			34	76
1931	7		12	2		21	24		9		33	54
1932	$9\frac{1}{2}$		$7\frac{1}{2}$	1		18	7		1	2	10	28
1933	1		2	2		5	1		4		5	10
1934	8	1				9			7	2	9	18
1935												
1936									2		2	2
1937									2		2	2
1938		8	13	2		23			3	1	4	27
1939	1	1	14			16			3	1	4	20
1940	6					6			6	3	9	15
1941							2		3		5	5
1942												
1943												
1944												
1945												
1946		12		17		29ª						29
1947												
1948				6		6						6
1949									6		6	6
1950												
1951												
1952												
1953	3					3						3
Total	225	22	114	25	5	391	257	5	46	10	318	709

Table 2
Ethnic Groups and Record Production

Ethnic Group			Columbia		Victor	
Mother Tongue (1940 Census)	Rank	Population	Rank	Records Issued, 1923-52	Rank	Records Issued, 1929-42
German	1	4,949,780	4	649	3	614
Italian	2	3,766,820	1	1,312	1	625
Polish	3	2,416,320	2	799	2	617
(Spanish		1,861,400)		—ᵃ		—ᵃ
Yiddish	4	1,751,100	9	361	11	150
French	5	1,412,060	3	759ᵇ	7	169ᶜ
Swedish	6	830,900	6	463ᵈ	4	314ᵈ
Norwegian	7	658,220	19	12	14	83
Russian	8	585,080	8	389	9	165ᵉ
Czech (Bohemian)	9	520,440	11	338	10	164
Slovak	10	484,360	15	238	5	218
Hungarian	11	453,000	10	340	8	167
Dutch	12	289,580	18	22		0
Greek	13	273,520	5	649	13	143ᶠ
Lithuanian	14	272,680	12	335	15	82
Finnish	15	230,420	14	253	6	195
Danish	16	226,740	20	6		0
(Portuguese		215,660)		—ᵃ		—ᵃ
Slovenian	17	178,640	16	204	16	43
Serbo-Croatian	18	153,080	13	303	12	147
(Arabic		107,420)		—ᵃ		—ᵃ
Ukrainian	19	83,600ᵍ	7	430		—ʰ
Rumanian	20	65,520	17	126	17	29
Country of Birth and Year of Census						
Albania (1930)		8,814		49		17
Armenia (1930)		32,166		27		0
Bulgaria (1930)		9,399		40		40
Japan (1930)		70,993		29		—ᵃ
China (1930)		46,129		—ᵃ		—ᵃ
Turkey (European and Asian areas, 1930)		48,911		118		50
Ireland (1930)		744,810		563ⁱ		79

ᵃ Comparable figures not available.
ᵇ Includes "French," "French-Canadian," and "Acadian-French."
ᶜ Does not include "Acadian-French."
ᵈ Includes "Scandinavian instrumental."
ᵉ Includes Ukrainian.
ᶠ Does not include Greek records pressed on the Ortophonic label.
ᵍ Census figures on Ukrainian-speakers are unreliable, since many Ukrainians were classified as Russian.
ʰ Included with Russian.
ⁱ Does not include the postwar 33500-F series.

Of course, many of the original American recordings could just as well have been made in Europe. The first Finnish-American recordings, made by John M. Erikson for Victor in 1907, are well-known Finnish patriotic songs and folksongs that have also been recorded many times in Finland. No doubt Finnish-Americans purchased these recordings because they reminded them of the old country, not of the new. Many immigrant groups "imported" artists from their homelands to tour meeting halls, dances, or summer festivals, and often these artists also recorded while passing through New York. Thus the famous Swedish singer Jussi Björling made his first recordings in 1920 for Columbia's Swedish catalog while touring America with his brothers as the Juvenile Trio.

By the 1920s, however, ethnic recordings begin to show local color. Some popular Finnish-American performers of the time, such as accordionist Antti Kosola, had been born in the United States. Others were immigrants but started their performing careers in the meeting halls of Finnish-American communities. Hannes Saari, who recorded profusely for Columbia, directed Finnish choirs in the New York area. While the songs he recorded come mostly from Finland, his recordings sound quite different from popular recordings made in Finland in the 1920s. New songs were also being written in the United States. Accordionists wrote dance tunes in traditional style; William E. Stein, a pianist from New York, composed operettas for Finnish-American organizations; Finnish-American political groups had their songs recorded.

The most interesting Finnish-American songwriters were Hiski Salomaa and Arthur Kylander, whose topical songs often dealt with life in the ethnic community. They sang about the immigrant's first difficulties, the life of the miner and the lumberjack, Prohibition and the Depression. Hiski Salomaa even wrote a song about the current fad for making records.[56] Their songs revealed both humor and social pathos:

> Kun helluni jätti niin tämä poika läksi
> näille Amerikan kultamaille.
> Mut kun köyhästä torpasta kotoisin mä olen
> niin rikkautta jäin minä vaille.
>
> (When my sweetheart left me, I went
> to the golden land of America.
> But because I was born in a poor shanty
> I could not get rich there.)[57]

I have investigated fairly thoroughly the entire output of Finnish-American and Swedish-American recordings. Although there are fewer Finnish recordings, they contain more original American material than do the Swedish ones. There is no Swedish counterpart to Hiski Salomaa or Arthur Kylander. The famous Swedish-American comic Olle i Skratthult (Hjalmar Peterson) seems to have recorded little original material composed in the United States. The most productive Swedish-American songwriter was the Reverend J. A. Hultman of Worcester, Massachusetts (1861–1942), whose "sunshine songs" (solskenssånger) sold in large quantities in book and record form both in Sweden and among Swedish-Americans.[58]

Ethnic pieces created in America are relatively frequent in record catalogs of the late 1920s. "Maksa na burtu u Detroidu," "Învârtita dela Chicago," "Szport amerykanskyj," "L' Arrivo di de pinedo in America," and "Hurray for New York" are typical examples.[59] It is perhaps not coincidental that the new homeland appears most frequently in comic songs. However, the amount of original American material clearly varied from group to group. Extensive research will be needed before anything definite can be said on this question. To take just one example: Considering the large number of German-speaking people in America, it is surprising that so little original German-American music appeared, at least on records. On the other hand, the relatively small Cajun French community constantly produced new music.

Swedish dialect parody that sold over a million copies. Courtesy of Pekka Gronow.

Relatively few ethnic recordings were made in the 1930s. When recording activity increased rapidly in the 1940s, thanks to the many new independent companies, the music presented was often distinctly American. In Europe, popular music traditions had changed throughout the years, with the result that many immigrants, who had only occasional contact with the old country, found the new popular music there alien. But their own musical tastes had also changed. They had come under the influence of American popular music, including country music, which in the 1940s was still unknown in Europe. Now there appeared recording artists like the Barry Sisters, who sang Yiddish songs in a style borrowed from the Andrews Sisters. Slim Jim and the Vagabond Kid, a Norwegian-American duo from Minneapolis, sang Swedish comic songs, Norwegian hymns, and American country-and-western songs to guitar and accordion accompaniment. Hawaiian guitarists who were actually Ukrainian appeared on records. Bilingual records with one verse in English and another in the language of the ethnic group were also an innovation of this era. "I Yust Go Nuts at Christmas," a Swedish-American comic song, became a million-seller.[60]

The emergence of "polka music" also characterized this period. The polka and the waltz had been popular folk dances in Central and Eastern Europe in the nineteenth century, and they are also common in sheet-music publications of the day. The polka served as a common denominator among German-speaking and Western Slavic areas of Europe. By 1945, the younger generation of these ethnic groups in America usually spoke English better than they spoke the language of their parents. Many had been to war. Still, these groups were so large that immediate "Anglo-Americanization" was not possible.

In the 1930s record companies were already issuing instrumental polkas and waltzes for a "pan-ethnic" audience. Hans Wilfahrt and his Concertina Orchestra of New Ulm, Minnesota, made their first recordings for the OKeh German series in the 1920s. By the mid-1930s he had become "Whoopee John" Wilfahrt on the Vocalion 15000 series. Will Glahé's "Beer Barrel Polka" (a European recording) became a hit and was covered by the Andrews Sisters. In the 1940s such transitions were commonplace. Edmund Terlikowski and his orchestra became the Juke Box Serenaders, while the Orkiestra Polskiej Karuzeli became the Windy City Five on Columbia.

In New York, Dana Records had considerable success with the Polish bands of Gene Wisniewski, Frank Wojnarowski, and Walt Solek. Many other companies followed suit. Their style was, however, quite different from anything heard in Europe:

> For many years, while such groups provided Polish language radio programs with traditional *mazurkas*, *polkas* and *obereks*, they attracted only a Polish audience. Then they changed their style, added a batch of hot licks, put in a Gene Krupa beat (he too is a Pole), translated old lyrics into English and wrote a batch of new lively ones. Suddenly, low-power radio stations found themselves capturing network audiences as millions of high school live wires began arguing the relative merits of Frank Wojnarowski's pressing of *Broke But Happy Polka* versus Bernie Wilkowski's recording of *Wha, He Say Mambo*. In Chicago recently, one disc dockey casually asked his listeners to name their favorite polka band. Within three days he had received more than 22,000 post cards.[61]

This report by Albert Q. Maisel, first published in *Reader's Digest* in 1956, summarizes what was happening in Chicago, Milwaukee, or Detroit in the late 1940s and early 1950s. The polka bands used a rhythm section much like the popular dance bands of the era, often with accordion added. And although they did not feature improvised solos, the phrasing of the horns shows clear dance-bands influence—if not of Benny Goodman, at least of Lawrence Welk.

For a while polka music showed promise of entering the mainstream of American popular music, just like Hawaiian music in the 1910s and swing in the 1930s. Frankie Yankovich, who had started his career in the Columbia Slovenian series, enjoyed a million-selling hit in 1948 with "Blue Skirt Waltz," [62] a record that must have been purchased by many people who had no recent European roots. The rise of rock-and-roll in the mid-1950s, however, made any such development impossible. It was black music, not polka music, that proved dominant during the next decades. Polkas were relegated back to ethnic status. The *Milwaukee Journal* offered this survey in 1963:

The "Blue Skirt Waltz" by Frankie Yankovich was a million-seller hit in 1948. Courtesy of Pekka Gronow.

> The polka belt runs north to Buffalo, N.Y., east to Newark—it doesn't cross the Hudson river—south to the Pennsylvania line, and then west, roughly north of the Indiana turnpike, through Michigan, Wisconsin, Iowa, the Dakotas and Nebraska. It covers northern Indiana and northern Illinois. The polka is a many splintered thing. There are four main styles, and a multitude of variations on them, said Norman Marggraff, the WMIL disc dockey who is better known as Fritz the Plumber, spinner of polka platters.
>
> There is, for instance, the Cleveland, or Slovenian, style, practiced by Yankovich and Pecon. It is fast tempoed. No. 2 is the Bohemian, or brass, style à la Romy Gosz. There is the ump-pah-pah, or German, style along Six Fat Dutchmen lines, and the Polish style, as played by Little Wally of Chicago. [63]

Most of the record companies of the polka era have already disappeared. It is perhaps significant that the most successful of the remaining labels, Jay Jay Records of polka bandleader Li'l Wally (Walter Jagiello), now operates from Florida.

The era of ethnic recordings is by no means over in the United States. In the early 1970s, for example, the record industry trade paper *Billboard* found it necessary to publish regular lists of best-selling "Latin" discs in addition to the traditional "Hot 100," "Country," and "Soul" charts. Latin music is an important and growing branch of the record industry.

But while the production of Spanish-American recordings is flourishing, activity in many other ethnic communities is limited. For instance, it seems extremely unlikely that the production of Finnish-American recordings will ever reach the same proportions as in the 1950s, not to speak of the 1920s. Finnish-American recordings are now part of history, both American and Finnish. The songs of Hiski Salomaa or Arthur Kylander summarize in a unique way the Finnish experience in America:

Eikä nuo Atlannin laineetkaan kasvanu ruusuja punasia
Vaanhan ne tuuti New Yorkin rantaan poikia tuhansia.

(The waves of the Atlantic did not grow red roses
But they rocked us to New York's shores by the thousands.)[64]

Much of this history will be lost unless urgent steps are taken to collect and preserve these documents. There is apparently not a single public archive or library in the United States with a good collection of the recordings of any ethnic group. Fortunately, RCA and CBS, the successors of Victor and Columbia, have good if not complete archives, and one hopes that these materials can be made available for research. But most of the smaller labels have disappeared, and many recordings are probably lost forever.

The study of ethnic recordings need not serve only historical research. Immigration continues both in America and in other parts of the world. Today there are almost as many Finnish immigrants in Sweden as there were in the United States in the 1920s. Finnish recording activity is just beginning in Sweden, and perhaps something can be learned there from the history of Finnish-American recordings. And from a global perspective, in this time of rapidly increasing international contact we are all equally ethnic.

Promotional flyer. Courtesy of Pekka Gronow.

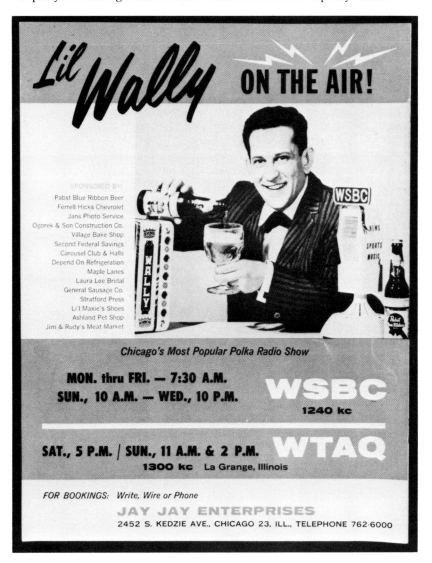

Notes

Very little has been written about ethnic recordings in America, and this study would not have been possible without the help of numerous individuals. I would especially like to thank Maury Bernstein, Walter Eriksson, the late Edwin Jarl, Rudolph Kemppa, Steve Maksymjuk, Chris Strachwitz, and Myron Surmach for their help. In addition, Tim Brooks, William Bryant, Björn Englund, Brian Rust, Richard K. Spottswood, and many other discographers have helped reconstruct the total operations of the record companies that produced ethnic records.

1. Brian Rust, *The Victor Master Book, Volume 2 (1925-1936)* (Hatch End, Middlesex, England: By the author, 1969), pp. 65–73. Further references in this article to Victor recordings are based on data in the Victor archives (now RCA Records, New York).

2. *1926 Catalog of Victor Records* (Camden, N.J.: Victor Talking Machine Co., 1926).

3. All references to U.S. record sales in this article are based on figures compiled by the Record Industry Association of America and published from time to time in *Billboard* (e.g., September 18, 1971, sect. 2, p.9).

4. Norm Cohen, "Commercial Music Documents: Number Six," *JEMF Quarterly* 6, no. 24 (Winter 1971):173. See also Charles Wolfe, "Columbia Records and Old-Time Music," ibid. 14, no. 51 (Autumn 1978):118–25, 144; Joseph Murrells, *The Book of Golden Discs*, enl. ed. (London: Barrie and Jenkins, 1978); and Norm Cohen, "Early Pionners," in *Stars of Country Music: Uncle Dave Macon to Johnny Rodriguez*, ed. Bill C. Malone and Judith McCulloh (Urbana: University of Illinois Press, 1975), pp. 3–10, for information on record sales.

5. Rudolph Kemppa, pionner Finnish disc jockey in Hancock, Mich., to Pekka Gronow, August 18, 1970. Kemppa's large collection of Finnish-American recordings is now in the Suomen Äänitearkisto (Finnish Institute of Recorded Sound), Helsinki.

6. Pekka Gronow, *Studies in Scandinavian-American Discography*, vol. 1 (Helsinki: Suomen Äänitearkisto [Finnish Institute of Recorded Sound], 1977), p. 6.

7. Pekka Gronow, "Recording for the 'Foreign' Series," *JEMF Quarterly* 12, no. 41 (Spring 1976):15–20.

8. U.S. Department of Commerce, Bureau of the Census, *Historical Statistics of the United States* (Washington, D.C., 1975), p. 696.

9. *Columbia Record* 7, no. 9 (September 1909).

10. Ibid. 9, no. 3 (March 1911).

11. For a discussion of these themes, see Pekka Gronow, "The Record Industry, Multi-National Corporations and National Musical Traditions," in *The Canada Music Book*, vols. 11–12 (Montreal: Canadian Music Council, 1975), pp. 175–81.

12. Alan Lomax, *Folk Song Style and Culture* (Washington, D.C.: American Association for the Advancement of Science, 1968), pp. 4–6.

13. For general background, see, e.g., A. G. Lockwood and A. L. Lougheed, *The Growth of the International Economy 1820–1960* (London: George Allen and Unwin, 1971), especially pp. 182–85.

14. For a general history of sound recording, see Oliver Read and Walter L. Welch, *From Tin Foil to Stereo*, 2d ed. (Indianapolis: H. W. Sams, 1976).

15. According to contemporary Edison catalogs, e.g., *French Edison Gold Moulded Records* (Orange, N.J., 1907).

16. John F. Perkins, Alan Kelly, and John Ward, "On Gramophone Company Matrix Numbers, 1898 to 1921," *Record Collector* 23, nos. 3–4 (May 1976):57.

17. Ibid.

18. *Yearbook of Nordic Statistics, 1975* (Stockholm: Nordic Council, 1976), p. 32.

19. Karleric Liliedahl, *The Gramophone Co.: Acoustic Recordings in Scandinavia and for the Scandinavian Market* (Helsinki: Suomen Äänitearkisto [Finnish Institute of Recorded Sound], 1977).

20. *Historical Statistics of the United States* (1975). All subsequent references to U.S. census figures are from this source.

21. Joshua A. Fishman, Robert G. Hayden, and Mary E. Warshauer, "The Non-English and the Ethnic Group Press, 1910–1960," in *Language Loyalty in the United States*, ed. Joshua A. Fishman. (The Hague: Mouton, 1966). See also Robert E. Park, *The Immigrant Press and Its Control* (New York: Harper and Brothers, 1922).

22. Red Seal records featured famous opera singers and other performers in the classical field, both European and American. Victor promoted the Red Seal line heavily in its catalogs and advertising.

23. Aino Ackté's "Ballade du roi du Thule" appeared on Victor Red Seal 91044; Väinö Sola was featured on the cover of the *Uusia Victor Suomalaisia Rekordeja* (New Victor Finnish records) (Camden, N.J.: Victor Talking Machine Co.) supplement for June, 1926, where he was referred to as "the Caruso of Finland."

24. This section is largely based on my own research; the sources include record company files and catalogs and, of course, the records themselves. For further references see the introductions to Pekka Gronow, *Studies in Scandinavian-American Discography*, vols. 1–2 (Helsinki: Suomen Äänitearkisto, 1977). These publications also contain bibliographies of record company catalogs containing listings of foreign records. For the parallel fields of hillbilly and race records, see Archie Green, "Hillbilly Music: Source and Symbol," *Journal of American Folkore* 78 (July–September 1965):204–28, and Robert M. W. Dixon and John Godrich, *Recording the Blues* (London: Studio Vista, 1970).

25. Chris A. Strachwitz, "Cajun Country," in *The American Folk Music Occasional*, [no. 2], ed. Chris Strachwitz and Pete Welding (New York: Oak Publications, 1970), p. 15. This volume also contains an interesting article on Texas Czech music.

26. Rudolf Arnheim and Martha Collins Bayne, "Foreign Language Broadcasts over Local American Stations," in *Radio Research, 1941*, ed. Paul F. Lazarsfeld and Frank N. Stanton (New York: Essential Books, 1941), pp. 3–64.

27. *Columbia Foreign Records Suitable for Automatic Machines* (New York: Columbia Phonograph Co., ca. 1937).

28. Lloyd Dunn, *On the Flip Side* (New York: Billboard Publications, 1975), p. 29. The Columbia market survey referred to is "Selected Data on Musical Preferences and the Market for Records" (New York: CBS Research Department, 1947). A copy of this mimeographic report is in the Library of Congress. Among the musical categories included in this study were "Hawaiian music," which was liked by 10 percent of the adults surveyed, "Latin-American music" (9 percent), and "cowboy and hillbilly songs" (7 percent). The most popular categories were "hit selections from movies and shows," "sweet music," and "symphonies."

29. Charlie Gillett, *The Sound of the City: The Rise of Rock and Roll* (New York: Outerbridge and Dienstfrey, 1970), pp. 1–29, 48–51.

30. I am grateful to Miriam Niemi Lane, daughter of Antti Syrjäniemi, for information about her father and the cultural activities of the Cape Ann Finns. Elis Sulkanen, *Amerikan suomalaisen työväenliikkeen historia* (Fitchburg, Mass.: Amerikan Suomalainen Kansanvallan Liitto ja Raivaaja, 1951), especially pp. 110–23, has additional information on Finnish-American cultural activities.

31. This section is based on my correspondence with Sylvester Ahola and on Brian Rust, "An American in London: A Portrait of a Great Musician," parts 1–5, *Vintage Jazz Mart*, June 1966, September 1966, November 1966, February 1967, and July 1967. Some of Ahola's 1927–30 recordings have been reissued on Quality Records QRS 1001: *Sylvester Ahola* (The Fabulous Finns, vol. 1).

32. See, e.g., Sallie TeSelle, ed., *The Rediscovery of Ethnicity* (New York: Harper and Row, 1974).

33. Pekka Gronow, *The Columbia 33000-F Irish Series*, JEMF Special Series no. 10 (Los Angeles: John Edwards Memorial Foundation, 1979).

Ethnic Recordings: An Introduction   29

34. Joshua A. Fishman, *Yiddish in America*, Publication of the Indiana University Research Center in Anthropology, Folklore, and Linguistics, no. 36 (Bloomington, 1965). For a case study see Joseph Greenberger, "Cantor Josef Rosenblatt," *Record Collector* 20, nos. 6–7 (May 1972): 125–45.

35. "Arayntsugebn fray in lebn iz a vikhtege kunst, un ven ir hert Abe Schwartz's orchestra shpilen oif a Columbia record, kent ir zikh nit helfn ir must vern lebendig un freilakh un onhoibn tansn . . . Ven ir hert a 'Schwartz' record vert ir vider yung un ir denkt az ir shteyt mit ayer gelibter oder gelibten unter der khupa." *Columbia Hebrew-Jewish Record Catalogue; Contains All Selections Up to and Including October, 1921* (New York: Columbia Graphophone Co., 1921), p. 29. I am grateful to Henry Sapoznik for the translation.

36. On early Hawaiian popular music see Wolfgang Laade, *Neue Musik in Afrika, Asien und Ozeanien* (Heidelberg: By the author, 1971), pp. 350–414; Tony Todaro, *The Golden Years of Hawaiian Entertainment, 1874–1974* (Honolulu: T. Todaro Publishing Co., 1974), pp. 15–17, 64–65; and annual volumes of *Ha ilono Mele* magazine (Honolulu, 1975–).

37. *Victor Records in Spanish, German, Italian, French, Hebrew, Russian, Polish* (Camden, N.J.: Victor Talking Machine Co., ca. 1907), pp. 47–48.

38. *Victor Records, November 1915* (Camden, N.J., 1915), "Hawaiian music" section.

39. Sigmund Spaeth, *A History of Popular Music in America* (New York: Random House, 1948), pp. 399–400.

40. See "Who's Who in Music, September, 1945–September, 1946: The Billboard 1946–47 Encyclopedia of Music," *Record Research*, nos. 146–147 (May–June 1977), p. 5.

41. "Starr Co. Sending Expedition to Make Records of Melodies of Hopi Indians," *Talking Machine World*, July 15, 1925, p. 15. The Ho-Nu-Ses recordings were listed in the 1907 Victor foreign catalog (cited in n. 37), which makes one wonder whether they were actually intended for sale to the Iroquois.

42. Interview with Raymond Boley, Washington, D.C., January 24, 1977.

43. "Spanish Records; Mexican Specialties; Record Making Plant Established in Mexico," *Columbia Record* 2, no. 1 (January 1904): 2.

44. See, e.g., *1930–1931 Numerical Catalogue of Columbia Ten- and Twelve-Inch Double Discs Domestic Series Records* (New York: Columbia Phonograph Co., 1930), p. 2, and *1930 Numerical Catalogue of Columbia Foreign Records* (New York: Columbia Phonograph Co., 1929), p. 2.

45. File cards in the Library of Congress, Music Division, Recorded Sound Section.

46. Reino Kero, "Finnish Immigrant Culture in America," in *Old Friends—Strong Ties*, ed. Vilho Niitemaa, Jussi Saukkonen, Tauri Aaltio, and Olavi Koivukangas (Turku: Institute for Migration, 1976), pp. 115–44. This volume, published in connection with the Bicentennial, is a good general introduction in English to Finnish immigration to America.

47. See, e.g., Peter Czerny and Heinz P. Hofmann, *Der Schlager*, vol. 1 (Berlin: VEB Lied der Zeit, 1968), pp. 12–128.

48. Anne and Norm Cohen, "Folk and Hillbilly Music: Further Thoughts on Their Relation," *JEMF Quarterly* 8, no. 46 (Summer 1977): 50–57, compare the repertories of early hillbilly recordings and folksong collections and introduce the concepts of "domestic" and "assembly" traditions, suggesting that folksong collectors were more interested in the former, while record companies (and record purchasers) preferred the latter. My experience suggests that the assembly tradition should be further divided into "communal" (such as choral singing, where participation is often more important than performance) and "performance" (such as instrumental dance music by professionals or semiprofessionals). The last category clearly dominates commercial recordings of ethnic music.

49. "Gunleik Smedal, Mester Hardanger Violinist af Amerika. Vandt denne aere i Albert Lea, Minn. 29de–30te juni, 1928." See *Victor Skivor på Skandinaviska, Svenska-Norska* (Camden, N.J.: Victor Talking Machine Co., 1929), p. 11.

50. I have heard this story independently from Rudolph Kemppa and from Kuuno Sevander, Finnish-American Columbia recording artist now living in Petrozavodsk, USSR. The record itself has not been found.

51. As told to Richard K. Spottswood.

52. Jón R. Kjartansson, *Skra yfir íslenzkar hljómplötur 1907–1955* (Reykjavik: by the author, n.d.); Gronow, *Studies in Scandinavian-American Discography,* vol. 2, Columbia "E" series listing; RCA files.

53. The figures are based on the numerical listings published in Gronow, *Studies in Scandinavian-American Discography,* vols. 1–2.

54. Census figures quoted in Joshua A. Fishman and John E. Hofman, "Mother Tongue and Nativity in the American Population," in Fishman, *Language Loyalty,* pp. 36, 44. The figures on record production are based on the highest catalog numbers known in the Columbia "F" and Victor "V" series. Further research may necessitate revising these figures, but any changes are likely to be small.

55. See, e.g., *Catálogo de Discos Victor No. 38* (Buenos Aires: RCA Victor Argentina, 1938).

56. Hiski Salomaa, "Laulu taiteilioista," Columbia 3073–F (matrix 108729–2), released in 1928.

57. Hiski Salomaa, "Talvella maa on valkoinen," Columbia 3169–F (matrix 112129–1), released in 1930.

58. "Hultman, Johannes Alfred," *Sohlmans Musiklexikon,* vol. 3 (Stockholm: Sohlmans Förlag, 1976), p. 494.

59. Maksim Prdić i Milka Trtić, "Maksa na burtu u Detroidu," Columbia 1138–F (Serbo-Croatian); Joan Haţegan, "Învârtita dela Chicago," Columbia 31049–F (Rumanian); Ewgen Zukowsky, "Szport Amerykanskyj," Columbia 27124–F (Ukrainian); Compagnia Mignonette, "L'Arrivo di de pinedo in America," Columbia 14284–F (Italian); Peisachke Burstein, "Hurray far New York," Columbia 8178–F (Yiddish).

60. Murrells, *Book of Golden Discs,* p. 73.

61. Albert Q. Maisel, *They All Chose America* (New York: T. Nelson, 1957), p. 217.

62. Murrells, *Book of Golden Discs,* p. 68.

63. Donald H. Dooley, "Royalty of Polka Bands Meet in Milwaukee to Make Album," *Milwaukee Journal,* February 8, 1963.

64. Salomaa, "Talvella maa on valkoinen."

A Checklist of 78 Rpm Foreign-Language Records

To facilitate stockkeeping and ordering, record companies usually give each record released a *catalog number*, beginning with 1, 100, 1001, or any other arbitrarily chosen starting point. Often (but not always) the catalog number indicates the order in which records were released by the company: Record number 14301 was released before 14305. When Victor and Columbia, the leading American companies, started issuing disc records at the turn of the century, the first record was simply numbered 1, and the subsequent ones 2, 3, 4, and so on. Soon, however, the companies were compelled to use several different catalog number series to indicate size, price, or the type of music recorded. Different numerical series were used for ten- and twelve-inch records, and classical and popular records, foreign and domestic records, and so on.

The study of catalog numbers is interesting for several reasons. Knowledge of the numerical system often helps us determine when a particular record was released. Different catalog series tell us how record companies conceptualized the music they recorded: What categories did they use? Thorough acquaintance with the numerical system helps us make a quantitative analysis of the output of a particular record company: How many records did it issue annually in each category?

The following checklist surveys all United States record manufacturers known to have issued "foreign-language," or ethnic, records during the era of 78 rpm discs, roughly from 1900 to the mid-1950s. The principal companies, Victor and Columbia, are listed first. They are followed by other labels, both major labels that issued standard popular and classical ("domestic") records as well as "foreign" records, and small specialist labels that issued only ethnic recordings. The listings are still far from complete. Many small ethnic labels are certainly missing, but the survey of major companies is fairly exhaustive.

Catalog numbers should not be confused with *matrix numbers*. The matrix (or "master") number was the number given by record companies to the stamper used to press records. The matrix number, which is often also found on record labels, is different on each side of the record.

The checklist will—within limitations—answer questions such as these:

Which American companies have issued 78 rpm Hungarian records?
How many foreign records did Columbia issue between 1908 and 1923?
Which ethnic groups preferred twelve-inch records (instead of the regular ten-inch size, with shorter playing time)?
When was Odeon record number 26045 issued?

Once a person who is interested in a specific ethnic musical tradition has found out which companies have issued recordings of that music, when the recordings were issued, and the extent of recording activity, he will probably want to hear the records, or at least learn more about them—artists' names, titles recorded, and so on. Unfortunately, since very few archives contain commercially published ethnic recordings, the researcher will have to rely mainly on his own initiative. The most likely sources, of course, are the elderly in ethnic communities, who may have saved old recordings. There may be record stores that have boxes of unsold 78s in the basement. It is advisable to try more general sources, also: antique shops, Salvation Army stores, collectors of other types of music. This procedure is slow; one may have to browse through ten thousand old records to find one interesting item. But German, Polish, Italian, and Yiddish records, especially, often turn up this way, as they were originally sold in considerable quantities.

Old catalogs issued by record companies are an excellent source of additional information on ethnic recordings. Unfortunately, the most common catalogs do not list ethnic recordings. The companies usually did not list them in their general catalogs, but instead published special catalogs and supplements for each ethnic group. These catalogs were often bilingual and had titles such as "Victor Finnish Records— Victor suomalaisia rekordeja." In addition, many record companies issued special *numerical* catalogs for their dealers for stockkeeping purposes, which listed both foreign and domestic releases. Since these catalogs were not made available to the general public, they are extremely rare today.

Like other ethnic record catalogs, this Columbia 1921 German catalog had a colorful cover with an idealized scene from the homeland. Music Division, Library of Congress.

Few libraries were farsighted enough to collect catalogs at the time they were published, and consequently they have become collectors' items that in some cases are even rarer than the records they list. As far as I know, only two libraries in the United States have good—but far from complete—collections of old record company catalogs listing ethnic recordings: the Library of Congress and the Rodgers and Hammerstein Archives of Recorded Sound at the New York Public Library. Other libraries and archives with recorded sound collections may also have a sampling of such materials.

Victor

The Victor Talking Machine Company was founded in 1901 as a successor to the Berliner Phonograph Company. In 1928 it became part of the Radio Corporation of America (RCA).

1900–1908

The earliest Victor catalog series, which started at 1 in 1900, included both domestic and foreign recordings. Soon other series were also used for twelve-inch recordings, and for recordings intended mainly for export.

1908–29

In 1908–9, with the introduction of double-sided discs, Victor started several new catalog series. The black-label 75¢ ten-inch 16000 series and $1.25 twelve-inch 35000 series at first included both domestic and foreign recordings, as did the more expensive blue-label 45000 (10″) and 55000 (12″) series.

Around 1912, however, it was decided to reserve a separate catalog series for foreign recordings. For reasons explained in my *Studies in Scandinavian-American Discography*, vol. 1, the series had to make several jumps in the numerical sequence, with the following results:

> 10″: 62000–63999, 65000–65999, 67000–67999, 69000–69999, 72000–73999, 77000–81100s
>
> 12″: 68000–68999, 59000–?

Talking Machine World, September 1928, page 9. Motion Picture, Broadcasting, and Recorded Sound Division, Library of Congress.

In addition, other catalog series were used for South American and Oriental recordings. During this period, Victor issued recordings for at least the following groups: Albanian, Arabian-Syrian, Armenian, Bohemian, Bulgarian, Cajun, Chinese, Croatian, Danish, Dutch, Filipino, Finnish, French, German, Greek, Hebrew and

Victor Foreign-Domestic Catalog Contains Wealth of Musical Gems

Many Dealers Are Unaware of the Sales Possibilities of the Records Made for the Foreign Born—D. Des Foldes Writes Foot-notes for Bulletins Listing Records

Despite the fact that one of the greatest classes of record buyers of the present day is that of foreign-born residents many dealers have neglected to solicit this business. It is a known fact that the peoples of many European countries are far in advance of citizens of this country in musical appreciation, and this love of music has been transmitted by them to their children. Record manufacturers have recognized the vast market which is represented by the foreign born and are regularly releasing records for their consumption. Nevertheless many dealers have been loath to study the possibilities of encouraging this trade, with the result that the business naturally gravitates to some competitor who is more alert and more willing to make himself acquainted with the wants of this type of record buyer.

A glance at a recent issue of a bulletin (No. 18) sent out on behalf of the foreign-domestic series of records, issued by the Victor Talking Machine Co., gives an idea of the wealth of material available in this class of record. A great number of dealers are no more aware of these releases than they are of the releases of some record company whose products they do not carry, yet music is said to be the universal language and is an art which boundaries of nations or languages do not limit.

The bulletin in question was sent out to Victor dealers last month and contained records to be placed on sale on August 17. Foot-notes with explanatory remarks regarding each record were supplied by D. Des Foldes, head of the foreign-domestic department. They included: In the International Series a coupling of two polkas, "Nava" and "Ha! Ha!" novelty selections, especially suited for outdoor or store-door playing and "Dreams of Schubert," a medley of popular Viennese waltz tunes, timely because of the interest in the Schubert Centennial now being celebrated all over the world; in the Croatian-Serbian series, a comic sketch, "The Divorce," with a native orchestra is featured. The foot-note to this release gives the Jugoslav population of fourteen of the larger cities in the United States, stating that Chicago has 20,000 of this race with New York housing 15,000 and Pittsburgh third with 12,000, giving an idea of the large market.

Other languages included in this bulletin are Finnish, German, Greek, Jewish, Italian, Lithuanian, Polish, Swedish and Spanish-Mexican. Naturally the records listed in each instance are intended primarily for the natives of the countries mentioned, yet the greater majority of these records could be played before an audience of native-born music lovers and find a ready market. Some years ago, well within the memory of every dealer, a waltz record, "Cielito Lindo" was issued as part of the Spanish-Mexican listing. After a time this record had become so popular that practically every record manufacturer released the selection played by a modern dance orchestra and as part of the regular popular releases. This is one instance of the sales that are possible of gems hidden in the foreign language series.

Aside from the sales possibilities among the entire record-buying population there are enough foreign born and their descendants in this country to insure a handsome profit by selling these records only to those for whom they were originally intended. There is scarcely a talking machine dealer to-day in whose territory there are not some foreign born. As the Victor bulletin points out, there are over 183,700 Lithuanians in eighteen of the principal cities of the United States—Chicago being the principal haven with over 87,000 of this race making their homes there. Lithuanians are good record customers, and for a dealer to neglect the sales possibilities of this nationality or of any nationality is to overlook a sure source of profit.

Another angle, and one that should not be overlooked, is that to these people who still speak the mother language of their countries the talking machine is still the principal and, in fact, only means of home entertainment, whereas English-speaking people divide their attention between the talking machine and radio receiver. There are, it is true, some programs being broadcast in foreign languages, but at best they are few and far between, and are concerned with but a few of the foreign languages. Look over this Victor bulletin on U. S. foreign records. Then study your market, decide what records should be carried and go after this extra record business with vigor.

9

Yiddish, Hungarian, Icelandic, Irish, Italian, Japanese, Korean, Lithuanian, Mexican-Spanish, Norwegian, Polish, Portuguese, Rumanian, Russian, Ukrainian, Scandinavian, Serbian, Slovak, Slovenian, Swedish, Swiss, Turkish, Welsh, West Indian. (The variation in the way ethnic groups are cited in this Appendix reflects record company usage.)

1929-42

In 1929 the numerical system was revised, and each ethnic group was allocated its own "V"-prefix series:

	10"		12"
International[a]	V-1	-216	V-50000-50048
International Novelties	V-500	-818	
Bohemian	V-1000	-1161	V-51000-51001
Bulgarian	V-2000	-2039	
Croatian	V-3000	-3146	
Finnish	V-4000	-4194	
French	V-5000	-5135	
French[b]	V-5500	-5532	
German	V-6000	-6526	V-56000-56086
Greek	V-8000	-8023	V-58000-58118
Hebrew-Jewish	V-9000	-9109	V-59000-59039
Hungarian	V-11000-11164		V-60000-60001
Italian	V-12000-12601		V-62000-62022
Lithuanian	V-14000-14081		
Norwegian	V-15000-15082		V-65000
Polish	V-16000-16607		V-66000-66008
Rumanian	V-19000-19028		
Scandinavian[c]	V-20000-20122		
Russian-Ukrainian	V-21000-21142		V-71000-71021
Slovak	V-22000-22190		V-72000-72026
Slovenian	V-23000-23039		V-73000-73002
Swedish	V-24000-24189		V-74000
Syrian	V-25000-25006		V-75000-75001
Turkish	V-26000-26045		V-76000-76003
Albanian	V-28000-28014		V-78000-78001
Irish	V-29000-29078		

[a] Later issues were called Continental Gems.
[b] The V-5500 block comprised imported masters.
[c] Instrumental recordings.

Bluebird records, 1934-39

In the 1930s, RCA Victor issued foreign recordings also on its cheaper Bluebird label:

Cajun	B 2171-2199, B 2000-2092
Bohemian, Italian, French-Canadian	B 2500-
Hungarian, Slovak, Polish	B 2600-
Scandinavian	B 2725-2739
Slovak	B 2776-2780
Irish, French-Canadian, hillbilly	B 4900-
Mexican	B 2200, 2300, 2400, 3000, 3100, 3200, 3300, 3400, 3500 (not a continuous series)

RCA label, 1942–1950s

In October, 1942, the old Victor label was replaced with an RCA label, and the numerical system was revised. The following RCA foreign series were used; in many cases the recordings were simply reissues of older "V" series recordings:

	10''	12''
Latin-American	23-0001, 23-5000	
Continental Gems	25-0001–	38-2001–
International Novelties	25-1001–	
Bohemian	25-2001–2054	
Croatian-Serbian-Slovenian	25-3001–3074	
German	25-4001–4136	38-0001–
Hebrew-Jewish	25-5001–5105	38-1001–1039
Hungarian	25-6001–6093	
Italian	25-7001–7148	
Norwegian	25-8001–8036	
Polish	25-9001–9227	
Scandinavian	26-0001–0059	
Portuguese	26-0500–	
Swedish	26-1001–1089	
Turkish	26-2000–2065	
Filipino	26-3000–	
Russian-Ukrainian	26-5001–5041	
Finnish	26-6001–6038	
Calypso	26-6500–	
French and French-Canadian	26-7001–	
Irish	26-7501–	
Greek	26-8001–8245	38-3001–3150
Latin-American	26-9001–	38-5000–
Albanian		38-4000–4002
Latin-American	60-0000	
Latin-American	70-7000	
Latin-American	90-0500	

Columbia

The Columbia label has undergone many changes of ownership since the 1880s, when it was first introduced, but its activities show a remarkable continuity throughout the years. While the first Columbia recordings were cylinders and included many foreign recordings, I shall start here with the introduction of the disc.

1902–8

The first series of single-sided discs included both domestic and foreign recordings: 1–1999, 3000–4000s. (The 2000 block was reserved for the Far East.)

1908–23

With the introduction of double-sided discs in 1908, it was decided to reserve the "A" series for domestic and "E" for foreign ("European") recordings. The "E" series included Albanian, Arabian-Syrian, Armenian, Bohemian, Bulgarian, Croatian-Serbian, Danish, Dutch, Finnish, Flemish, French, German, Greek, Hebrew and Jewish, Hungarian, Icelandic, Italian, Lithuanian, Norwegian, Polish, Portuguese, Rumanian, Russian, Scandinavian, Slavish-Slovak, Slovenian ("Krainer"), Swedish, Swiss, Turkish, Welsh, and Ukrainian ("Ruthenian") records.

"E" series

10": E 1–4999, 6000–6140, 7000–7999, 9000–9112
12": E 5000–5283, 8000–8001

Other ethnic series

The following series were probably mainly for export:

Portuguese-Brazilian	B 1–
Spanish-Mexican	C 1–
South American (classical)	H
Javanese, Malaysian, Japanese	J
Trinidadian	L
Filipino	M
Peruvian	P
South American	S
Argentinian	T
Hawaiian	Y 1–

1923–early 1950s

In 1923 the numerical system was revised. The "D" series was used for domestic, "F" for foreign, and "X" for export records.

The Oriental Trio in the Columbia 1920 Turkish catalog. The first musician with the *keman* is Kemany Minas, another musician with either the *oud* or *canoun* is Merdjan Garubet, the third musician is unidentified. Music Division, Library of Congress.

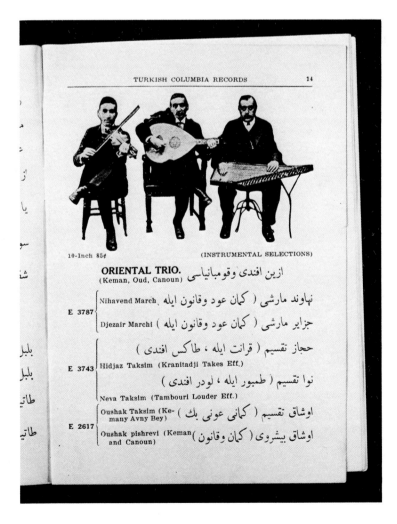

"F" series

The highest known issue is listed.

	10''	12''
Bohemian	1 F–324 F	50000 F–50013-F
Croatian (Serbo-Croatian)	1000 F–1267 F	
Danish (1923-25)	2000 F–2005 F	
Dutch (1949-51)	2000 F–2007 F	
Finnish	3000 F–3252 F	
French	4000 F–4131 F	
German	5000 F–5364 F	55000 F–55283 F
Greek	7000 F–7304 F	56000 F–56390 F
Hebrew-Jewish	8000 F–8277 F	57000 F–57082 F
Hungarian	10000 F–10324 F	58000 F–58014 F
Instrumental	12000 F–12566 F	59000 F–59063 F
Italian	14000 F–15245 F	60000 F–60050 F
Lithuanian	16000 F–16328 F	61000 F–61005 F
Norwegian (1923-27)	17000 F–17011 F	
Polish	18000 F–18784 F	63000 F–63013 F
Russian	20000 F–20380 F	64000 F–64007 F
Scandinavian	22000 F–22191 F	65000 F–65002 F
Serbian (1923-26)	23000 F–23034 F	
Slavish-Slovak (Slovak)	24000 F–24223 F	67000 F–67013 F
Slovenian	25000 F–25196 F	68000 F–68006 F
Swedish	26000 F–26266 F	69000 F
Ukrainian	27000 F–27401 F	70000 F–70017 F
Armenian (1928-)	28000 F–28020 F	71000 F–71005 F
Albanian (1940s)		72000 F–72048 F
Bulgarian (1928-)	29000 F–29039 F	
Holland-Dutch [sic] (1927)	30000 F–30011 F	73000 F–73001 F
Rumanian	31000 F–31125 F	
Turkish	32000 F–32044 F	75000 F–75021 F
Irish (1926-37)	33000 F–33562 F	
Irish (1947-51)	33500 F–33532 F	
French-Canadian	34000 F–34608 F	
Spanish-Hebrew		78000 F–78001 F
Scottish (1928-)	37000 F–37029 F	
		80000 F (one issue only)
Novelty (1928-)	38000 F–38011 F	
Turkish (higher priced)	40000 F–40050 F	
Arcadian-French (ca. 1930)	40500 F–40517 F	
Japanese (ca. 1930)	41000 F–41029 F	
Persian (ca. 1930)	42000 F–42012 F	82000 F–82001 F
Italian operatic	43000 F–43003 F	83000 F–83015 F

"X" series

	10''	12''
Syrian-Arabic	1 X	50000 X
Portuguese (Brazilian)	1000 X	51000 X
Spanish-Mexican-Filipino	2000 X	52000 X
Chinese-Amoy	15000 X	54000 X
Chinese-Cantonese	17000 X	55000 X
Chinese-Pekinese	19000 X	56000 X
Chinese-Swatow	21000 X	57000 X
Chinese	61000	

Attuned to the sensitive cultural and linguistic identities of ethnic groups, Columbia's 1927–28 catalog with its hyphenated title divided the listings into two separate sections: Ukrainian and Russian. Courtesy of Richard K. Spottswood.

In addition, Columbia issued Chinese records on the Beka label.

1950s

In the 1950s, shortly before discontinuing the production of 78 rpm records, Columbia issued some best-selling foreign records from the various "F" series, renumbered, in a 10000 series.

Other major prewar labels

For the most part, the companies listed in this section issued standard popular (and, to some extent, classical) recordings. However, they also found it necessary to compete in the foreign field with Columbia and Victor, the market leaders.

Actuelle

See Pathé.

Autograph

This Chicago company issued some Swedish records in the mid-1920s, possibly as a custom-pressing job.

Banner

The Plaza Music Company issued some Yiddish records on its Banner label in the mid-1920s (not to be confused with the postwar Banner label).

Beka

See Columbia.

Bluebird

See Victor.

Brunswick

The Brunswick-Balke-Collender company entered record production in 1920. In the mid-1920s about 150 foreign records were issued in special 40000 (10") and 45000 (12") series, which contained the music of many ethnic groups. Around 1927 the numerical system was revised, and separate series were assigned to records of various nationalities:

The Lion (Hubert Raphael Charles) was a well-known calypso man from the late 1920s onward. He is still occasionally active in Port of Spain in Trinidad but now goes under the name DeLeon. This recording was made on April 2, 1936, in New York. Motion Picture, Broadcasting, and Recorded Sound Division, Library of Congress.

	10"	12"
Spanish	40000	
French-Canadian	52000	
German	53000	77000
Italian	58000	78000
Russian-Ukrainian	59000	79000
Swedish	6100	
Polish	60000	
Finnish	62000	
Jewish	67000–67181	75000–75012
Irish	68000–68012	

After 1930 the Brunswick label underwent many changes of ownership, but several of the above series were continued for many years. For instance, the Spanish series reached 41,644 by July, 1934. *See also* Vocalion.

Connorized

This company had an Italian series in the early 1920s.

Decca

Decca Records, founded in 1934, started issuing foreign recordings in the late 1930s; many of the series continued until the early 1950s. Much of the material was drawn from the catalog of the European Carl Lindström company. All records are ten-inch unless otherwise specified.

Mexican	10000-10513[a]
Irish	12000-12287
Scotch	14000-14033
East Indian	16500-16515
Acadian-French	17000-17059
Calypso	17250-17484
Hispana	21000-21348
Armenian	30100-30103
Greek (10'')	31000-31220
Turkish	32000-32052
Bohemian	33000-33001
Greek (12'')	35000-35029
International	45000
Latin-American	50000
Italian	70000-70024

[a] The listing shows highest issue known. Some of the series may have gone beyond this point.

Edison

The Edison company at first issued only cylinder recordings, including foreign recordings in a number of different series. The thick, vertical-cut Edison Diamond Discs were issued from 1912 to 1929, and the following foreign series were used:

	10''	12''
German	57001-57034	73001-73013
French	58001-58028	74001-74015
Scandinavian	59001-59016	78001-78021
Finnish	59300-59307	
Hebrew and Yiddish	59500-59518	
Spanish and Cuban	60001-60078	76001-76021
Italian	64001-64002	
Bohemian	65001-65026	
Polish	65300-65323	
Russian	65500-65511	

Emerson

The Emerson company was founded in 1915. An international division, Emerson International, was founded in 1919, and the following series probably date from this period. Emerson's record production ended in the mid-1920s.

	9''	10''	12''
Polish	1100	11000	
Italian	1200	12000	1200-X
Hebrew and Yiddish	1300	13000	1300-X, 13000-X
Slovak	1400		
Russian and Ukrainian	1500		
Swedish		18000	
German and Swiss		19000	
International (semi-classical and operatic)	02000	20000	02000-X

Emerson also had a cheaper label, Regal, mainly for popular releases. Polish, German, "Hebrew-Jewish," and Italian records have been reported on this label.

Gennett

Gennett records were issued by the Starr Piano Company of Richmond, Indiana, in the late 1910s and throughout the 1920s. The company's main popular series, which started at 4500 in 1918 and went beyond 6300 in the late 1920s, included a considerable number of "Czecho Slovak," German, Hungarian, Italian, Jewish (Yiddish), Spanish, Polish, Swedish, and Welsh material. In addition, the company had a 11000 French-Canadian series.

ODEON-OKEH

Odeon was the trademark of the German Carl Lindström company. OKeh was the trademark of the Otto Heineman Phonograph Company (after 1920, General Phonograph Corporation; after 1926, OKeh Phonograph Company), which also represented Odeon records in the United States. Around 1921 the General Phonograph Corporation began issuing foreign records on a large scale, both imported European and original United States recordings. Usually the Odeon label was used for the former and the OKeh label for the latter, although there are numerous exceptions. In 1926, Columbia purchased OKeh, and the two companies merged in the early 1930s. The OKeh label was revived in 1939. *See also* Vocalion.

OKeh-Odeon 10″ foreign series (1921?–1930?)

The same series were used for both OKeh and Odeon releases. Usually, but not always, the OKeh label denotes American recordings, while Odeon denotes European (Lindström-derived) recordings.

		1923	1926	1928	Highest known number
9001	Italian	9085	9276	9379	9482
10001	German and polyglot [a]	10211	10401	10484	10559 [b]
11001	Polish	11104	11272	11364	11458
12001	Hungarian	12071	12127		
13001	Rumanian		13074		
13501	Finnish		13521		
14001	Hebrew-Jewish	14061	14083		
15001	Russian	15008	15072	15078	
15501	Ukrainian		15537	15563	15609
16001	Mexican	16046	16208	16256	16292
16400	Mexican	16441	16576	16583	16814
17001	Bohemian	17153	17302	17328	17359
18001	Slovak	18002	18055		
19001	Scandinavian [c]	19036	19188	19234	19326-Y [d]
20001	Danish				20009
21001	Irish [e]				21081
22001	French	22020			
23001	Serbo-Croatian [f]	23008	23065		
23501	Croatian		23533		
24001	Slovenian (Krainer)	24014	24052		
25001	Norwegian	25009	25078		
26001	Lithuanian	26010	26037	26059	26082
27001	Swiss	27004			
27501	Welsh		27510		
28001	Greek		28036	28068	
29001	Portuguese		29036		

—continued	1923	1926	1928	Highest known number
29000 Chinese			29040	
33001 Spanish ($1.00)			33023	
65001 West Indian[g]				
66001 Spanish				
69001 Bulgarian		69012		
77001 Armenian		77005		

[a] "Polyglot" = instrumental recordings.
[b] Shown in the February, 1930, Odeon German supplement.
[c] The 19001 series comprised Scandinavian instrumental and Swedish recordings.
[d] On the Columbia-Odeon label.
[e] Not listed in the foreign catalog.
[f] Called Serbian in the 1926 catalog.
[g] Not listed in the foreign catalog.
The listing above shows the highest number included in the foreign catalogs for March, 1923, July, 1926, and May, 1928, as well as the highest record number seen to date.

OKeh-Odeon 10¾" and 12" foreign series (1920s)

The listing shows the highest issue known.

10¾"		12"	
Armenian	78001–78004	Greek	82501–82513
Hebrew-Jewish	80001–80005	Rumanian	83501
Portuguese	80501–80513	German and polyglot	85001–85155
German and polyglot	81001–81012	Italian	86001–86024
Greek	82001–82023	Hungarian	86501–86502
Turkish	83001–83085	Polish ($1.25)	87001–87009
Italian	84001–84002	Polish ($1.50)	67001–67003
		Mexican	88001–88006
		Bohemian	89001–89019

New OKeh series (1939–)

Mexican [a]	8000, 9000–
International [a]	15000, 16000–
Irish [b]	84000–84189
Cajun [c]	90000–90018

[a] Earlier issues on the Vocalion label.
[b] From the Columbia 33000-F series.
[c] From the Columbia 40500-F series.

Paramount

Paramount records were issued during the 1920s by the New York Recording Laboratories of Port Washington, Wisconsin. Some German records have been reported on Paramount and associated labels such as Broadway, Claxtonola, Puritan, and Triangle. Some Polish material also appeared on Broadway.

Pathé

The Pathé Fréres Phonograph Company started operations in the United States in 1914. The earliest discs were vertical cut and seem to have been mainly drawn from the company's European catalog. The following foreign series were used around 1920:

	10"	12"
French	500	49500

—continued	10''	12''
German	1000	
Hungarian	1500	
German	1800	
Italian	2000	
Polish	2500	49000
Russian	3000	
Hebrew-Jewish	3500	49100
Slovak	4000	
Bohemian	4500	
Dutch	5500	
International instrumental	6000	
Spanish-Mexican	6500	
Scandinavian	7000	
Finnish	7500	
Miscellaneous		49200

In 1921 the company started issuing regular lateral-cut discs. In the 1920s, at least Italian, German, and Yiddish records appeared in the 01000, 02000, and 03000 series on the Pathé Actuelle and Actuelle labels. (The name of the company was later changed to Pathé Radio and Phonograph Company.)

Regal

See Emerson.

Vocalion

The Aeolian company started issuing Vocalion records in 1918. In the early 1920s, Yiddish, Mexican, Norwegian, and other foreign records appeared in the 14000 popular series. In 1925, when the Vocalion label was sold to Brunswick, the following foreign series were in use:

	10''	12''
German	9000	09000
German	10000	010000
Jewish	2000	
Jewish	13000	
Italian	17000	017000
Polish	18000	018000

Later there may have been some overlap with Brunswick. The 60000 Vocalion Polish series may have been a continuation of the Brunswick series. In the mid-1930s, an 8000 Mexican series was started, and the old 14000 (now 15000) series was used for "international" recordings. When Vocalion was acquired by CBS in 1938, these two series were used on the OKeh label.

Zonophone

The short-lived International Zonophone Company seems to have been the first record company to allocate different catalog series for different ethnic groups. The following series appeared about 1904:

Single-sided discs

Hebrew-Yiddish	9''	2000
Spanish	9''	2200
Spanish	7'', 9''	2400
Italian	9'', 11''	2500
French	7'', 9''	2900
Hebrew-Yiddish	10''	3000

Single-sided discs—continued

German	9''	3200
Bohemian	10''	3200
Hungarian	9''	3500
German	10'', 12''	3500
Italian (Neapolitan)	10''	3600
Hungarian	10'', 12''	3700
Hebrew-Rumanian	10''	8000
Italian	9'', 11''	10000
French	10''	11000
Italian	10''	12500
Spanish	10''	13000
Portuguese	10''	14000
French	10''	15000
Portuguese	10''	16000
Italian	12''	24000

Double-sided discs

Spanish-Italian	10''	40000
Spanish-Italian	12''	45000
German	10''	46000
German	12''	47000
Hebrew-Yiddish	10''	50000
Polish	10''	54000
Russian	10''	60000

Other labels

Several other early record companies apparently also issued occasional foreign records. Japanese records have been recorded on the Phono-Cut label of the 1910s. Some Cajun and French-Canadian records appeared on American Record Corporation's Melotone label in the 1930s. Foreign items have also been reported on Lyric and Rishell. Further research will no doubt reveal more.

Prewar ethnic labels

During the 1920s there appeared a number of small record companies that specialized in the music of a single ethnic group. The records were often issued by record or music stores in ethnic neighborhoods, and the pressing was usually done by a larger company. The following labels have so far been discovered; all are from the 1920s unless otherwise indicated.

Label	Language	Location	Manufacturer
Arion	German		Gennett
Excellent	Italian	New York	
Gaelic	Irish	New York	
Geniale	Italian	New York	
Greek Record Company	Greek		
Hermes	Greek		
Italianstyle	Italian	New York	
Jugoslavia	Serbo-Croatian	Detroit	Gennett
Joseph Jiran	Bohemian	Chicago	Victor
Macksoud	Arabic	New York	Scranton Button
Maloof	Arabic	New York	
Marrache	Arabic	New York	
Mermaid	Polish	Milwaukee	Paramount

Label	Language	Location	Manufacturer
New Republic	Irish		
Nofrio	Italian		
O'Byrne De Witt	Irish	New York and Roxbury, Mass.	
Panhellenion	Greek	New York	Emerson
Parsekian	Armenian, Turkish	New York	Perfect
La Patrie	French-Canadian	Lawrence, Mass.	
Pharos	Armenian	New York	
Phonotype	Italian	New York	
Sokhag	Armenian		
Splendor	Italian	New York	
Srpske Gusle	Serbian	Chicago	Autograph/ Paramount
Strong	German	New York	
United Hebrew Disc and Cylinder Company (early 1900s)	Hebrew		
Universal	Mexican	El Paso	Gennett
Wallin's Svenska Records	Swedish	Chicago	Autograph/ Paramount
Yorktown	Irish		Victor (1930s)

General postwar labels

The bigger new companies that were established in the 1940s no longer showed much interest in foreign records. Capitol had a short-lived 52000 International series with Polish, Yiddish, and Mexican records. Mercury Records of Chicago issued some Greek, Czech, Serbo-Croatian, and Russian records. But many of the smaller companies in the South and Southwest that specialized in country or blues records also issued some Cajun or Mexican material. These labels include Colonial, De Luxe, Goldband, Gold Star, Imperial, and Macy's. Among other smaller companies that issued foreign records as part of their general output, Stinson (Hebrew, Russian, and Ukrainian) and Keynote (Russian) should be mentioned.

Postwar ethnic labels

Several hundred small, local record companies issued 78 rpm ethnic recordings in the 1940s and 1950s. Most of them specialized in one language or ethnic group; a few may also have issued English-language material, but not enough information is presently available to confirm this. Some companies apparently issued only one record. Larger firms with an extensive output in a single language include Balkan, Continental, Scandinavia, and Standard. Some of the companies issued recordings made in Europe, while others made recordings in the United States.

The following list is probably not equally representative for all ethnic groups. The listings of Finnish, Scandinavian, Ukrainian, Cajun, and Greek labels are believed to be fairly comprehensive, thanks to the help of specialists in these fields. Other areas have not been covered so well. Some Canadian labels that are known to have been distributed in the United States are also included. Labels identified as Jewish may represent Hebrew and/or Yiddish.

Label	Language	Location
Acapulco	Mexican	Los Angeles
Aguila	Mexican	Los Angeles
Alamphon	Arabic	

The Balkan Phonograph Record Company, one of the larger postwar ethnic companies, issued recordings in Slovenian, Serbo-Croatian, Turkish, Albanian, and Greek. Courtesy of Pekka Gronow.

Bilingual recording in the postwar period. Courtesy of Pekka Gronow.

Label		Language	Location
Alkawakeb		Arabic	
Alpine		Swiss	San Mateo, Calif.
Amuke		Ukrainian	
Arabphon		Arabic	
Argee		Russian, Ukrainian, Byelorussian	
Arka		Ukrainian	
Aristophone		Greek	
Armenaphone		Armenian	
Arziv		Turkish	
Atticon		Greek	Chicago
Azteca		Mexican	Los Angeles
Balkan	001	Slovenian	There were two Balkan companies, one in New York, the other in Chicago.
	500	Serbo-Croatian	
	800	Greek	
	4000	Turkish	
Banner		Jewish	
Batt Masian		Armenian	
Bayan		Ukrainian	New York
Bazar		Ukrainian	Toronto
Beaver		Finnish	Canada
Bell Novelty		Jewish	New York
Big Mamou		Cajun	Ville Platte, La.
Cajun		Cajun	
Cajun Classics		Cajun	Paris, Tex.
Carnival		Jewish	New York
Chicago		Polish	
Chwyli Dnistra		Ukrainian	Cleveland
Cinemart		Finnish	New York
Cordion		Scandinavian	New York
Continental	1	Bohemian	New York
	200	Serbo-Croatian	
	400	Slovenian	
	500	Lithuanian	
	700, 800	Polish	
	900	Scandinavian	
	1000	International	
Copley		Irish, Scottish	
Corona		Mexican	Texas
Csardas		Hungarian	New York
Dana		Polish	New York
Del Valle		Mexican	Texas
DSF		Ukrainian	Canada
Dublin		Irish	
Echo		Ukrainian	Montreal
Edelweiss		Swiss	Union City, N.J.
Elite		German	New York
Etna		Italian	New York
Fais-Do-Do		Cajun	Crowley, La.
Falcon		Mexican	Texas
FDC		Czech	Rosenberg, Tex.
Feature		Cajun	Crowley, La.
Fennia		Finnish	Canada
Flint		Greek	San Francisco
FM		Norwegian	Hollywood
Folkstar		Cajun	Lake Charles, La.

Jay Jay Records are produced by Walter Jagiello or Li'l Wally, the well-known bandleader, composer, and songwriter. Courtesy of Pekka Gronow.

The Kismet Record Company, a postwar enterprise, featured Ukrainian and Russian music. Motion Picture, Broadcasting, and Recorded Sound Division, Library of Congress.

Label		Language	Location
Forssa		Finnish	
Fortuna		Ukrainian	New York
French Hits		Cajun	Crowley, La.
Frontier		Polka	Denver
Globe		Mexican	Texas
Grecian Artists		Greek	
G.S.		Chinese	San Francisco
Harmony Music		Scandinavian	Berkeley, Calif.
Harpha		Ukrainian	
Ideal		Mexican	Texas
Irish			
Israel			
Italdisc		Italian	New York
Jan		Polish	Hartford, Conn.
Jay Jay		Polish	Chicago
Kalos Diskos		Greek	
Kervorkian		Armenian	Fresno, Calif.
Khoury		Cajun	Lake Charles, La.
Kismet		Russian, Ukrainian	New York
Liberty		Greek	New York
Linden		Scandinavian	Seattle
Lyric		Cajun	Lake Charles, La.
Meladee		Cajun	New Orleans
Melotone (not the 1930s label)		Jewish	New York
Menorah		Hebrew	
Metropolitan	100	Greek	
	3000	Spanish-Hebrew	
	7000	Armenian	
Musicale		Polish	Toledo, Ohio
Musico		Polish	
Nina		Greek	
Nordic		Norwegian	
Odeum		German	
Onni Laine		Finnish	
Opera		Cajun	Lake Charles, La.
Ortophonic (produced by RCA Manufacturing Company for Standard Phono Company)		Greek, Turkish, Albanian	New York
OT		Cajun	Lake Charles, La.
Oudi Hrant		Turkish	Los Angeles
Pašvaisté		Lithuanian	
Peerless		Mexican	Los Angeles
Perfectaphone		Turkish	
Piknik		Polka	New York
Pilotone		Jewish	Long Island City, N.Y.
Podhalan Medleys		Polish	Chicago
Polart		Polish	New York
Polkaland		Polka	Sheboygan, Wis.
Polka King		Polka	Sheboygan, Wis.
Polkatunes		Polish	
Polo		Polish, Lithuanian	
Poprad		Lemko-Ukrainian	
Popular		Turkish, Armenian	
Printone		Slovenian	Cleveland
Quality		Swedish	Chicago

Liberty, a postwar label, issued Greek recordings. Motion Picture, Broadcasting, and Recorded Sound Division, Library of Congress.

A record from Standard's "Gems of Music" series. Motion Picture, Broadcasting, and Recorded Sound Division, Library of Congress.

Label	Language	Location
Radiant	Polka	Chicago
Radiodisque	German	New York
Rio	Mexican	Texas
Rocky Mountain	Polka	Greeley, Colo.
Rondo	Polish	
Rönkä Levyt	Finnish	North Hollywood, Calif.
Royal	Polka	Berwyn, Ill.
Rudder	Swedish	
Sajkas	Serbo-Croatian	
Sarkisian	Armenian	Hollywood
Scandinavia(n)	Swedish, Norwegian, Finnish	New York
Scandinavia.Sings	Swedish	Minneapolis
Schirmer	Hungarian	
Seva	Russian, Ukrainian	
Shamrock	Irish	
Simfonia [sic]	Ukrainian	New York
Slavtone	Serbo-Croatian	Hollywood
Solos	Finnish	Brooklyn
Sonart	Serbo-Croatian, Ukrainian	New York
Sonora	Scandinavian	New York
Southern	Cajun	Lake Charles, La.
Spiro's Records	Polish	New York
SRC	Scandinavian	Spokane, Wash.
Stanchel	Serbo-Croatian	Los Angeles
Standard		New York
T-100	International—Operators' Special	
T-2000	Gems of Music	
F-2000	Russian	
F-3000	Polish	
F-4000	Latin-American	
F-5000	Scandinavian	
F-6000	Italian	
F-7000	Czechoslovakian	
F-8000	Jewish	
F-9000	Greek	
F-11000	German-Austrian	
F-12000	Serbo-Croatian	
F-13000	French-Canadian	
F-14000	Irish	
F-15000	Hungarian	
F-16000	Slovak	
F-17000	Arabian-Syrian	
F-18000	Slovenian	
F-19000	Lithuanian	
Stella	Polish	
Sun (not the Memphis label)	Jewish	New York
Sunrise	Tagalog, Ilocano	Los Angeles
Surma	Ukrainian	New York
Taxco	Mexican	
Tempo	Swedish	Hollywood
Tikva	Jewish	
Tone-Art	Norwegian	
Trembita	Ukrainian	
Trident	Ukrainian	
UFM	Ukrainian	Canada
Ukrainian		
Ukrainian Bandurist's Chorus		

The White Eagle label illustrated with the Polish national emblem. Motion Picture, Broadcasting, and Recorded Sound Division, Library of Congress.

Label	Language	Location
Ukrainska Radioperedacha Vasilya Sharvana		Buffalo, N.Y.
Velvetone (not the Columbia label of the 1920s)	Ukrainian	
Victory	Greek	
Vienna	Austrian	Los Angeles
Viking	Finnish	
Vita-Tone	Polish	
White Eagle (issued by Continental records)	Polish	
Zimra	Jewish	
Zimrot Haaretz	Jewish	

Notes

A preliminary version of this checklist appeared in the *JEMF Quarterly* 9, no. 29 (Spring 1973):24–31. I am grateful to CBS Rcords, RCA Records, the Library of Congress, the Rodgers and Hammerstein Archives of Recorded Sound at the New York Public Library, and the John Edwards Memorial Foundation for their assistance. Individual collectors who have contributed to the listings include the late Walter C. Allen, Tim Brooks, William Bryant, Sam Chianis, Robert Crumb, Björn Englund, Mike Kaptanis, Rudolph Kemppa, Steve Maksymjuk, Louis Pyritz, Tony Russell, Brian Rust, Richard K. Spottswood, Chris Strachwitz, and Ray Wile. For further details and a bibliography, see my *Studies in Scandinavian-American Discography*, vols. 1 and 2 (Helsinki: Suomen Äänitearkisto [Finnish Institute of Recorded Sound], 1977). Readers with additions or corrections are urged to send them to Pekka Gronow, Lumikintie 3D 137 00820 Helsinki 82, Finland.

Commercial Ethnic Recordings in the United States

Richard K. Spottswood

Ethnic music—the music of cultural minorities—is an area that has fascinated me as long as I can remember. By the time I was ten, I had heard some of the music of Duke Ellington, Jelly Roll Morton, Charlie Parker, Bessie Smith, and other early and recent representatives of our jazz tradition. A few years later I had learned of the Carter Family, Blind Lemon Jefferson, and other folk musicians, black and white, who began during the 1920s to find their way from the rural South to recording studios in the North. I didn't know much about the music—any of it—at the time, but I did recognize that the best of it contained a special emotional and personal appeal missing not only from mass-marketed pop music, but also from what is often called "good music"—that is, the symphonic, chamber, and vocal music of European art tradition. By these standards the music I liked was not art at all, because it had never encountered the discipline of the academies or, in most cases, formal instruction or written notation. I learned that what I liked could be called folk music, but only in a special sense, because even as folk music it had nothing to do with the rarified versions of Negro spirituals or British ballads that at one time were staples of the concert hall. Nor did it have much to do with the polished, eclectic product popularized by groups like the Kingston Trio or Peter, Paul, and Mary. I adopted a proprietary attitude toward what I liked, and began to feel that too many Americans were short-changing themselves in accepting diluted and derivative forms of folk music and overlooking its more authentic, less compromising forms.

But only a few years ago did I begin to discover that there was another element in American folk music of which I'd been almost totally ignorant. When I was young, I had experienced ethnic music in folk-dancing classes, learning a few international dances accompanied by instructional records that employed simple, unornamented melody lines and an uncomplicated, overstressed beat. I had no way of knowing that the music I heard was unrepresentative, and I'm afraid I was guilty of dismissing all Old World folk music as lacking both vigor and complexity.

When I agreed to assemble and edit the Library of Congress LP series *Folk Music in America* in 1974, I knew that ethnic music was an area I would need to deal with. From reading Pekka Gronow's articles in the *JEMF*

Quarterly,[1] I had learned that there were surprisingly large quantities of foreign-language records made in the United States. I wrote to Gronow for help, and he replied generously with information, suggestions, and original recordings that helped immeasurably to put me on the right track; he showed me that there was music on American records from other cultures that was every bit as exciting as Charlie Parker or the Carter Family. Shortly thereafter, I had a chance encounter with the Ukrainian-American musicologist and discographer Stefan Maksymjuk, who invited me home to listen to an extensive variety of recordings from his personal collection. He in turn led me to Myron Surmach, who turned me loose in the basement of his New York City store and invited me to choose from many thousands of early and recent Ukrainian, Polish, and other records that he had accumulated through six decades; these discs provided an indispensable resource for the *Folk Music in America* series.[2]

My own level of involvement with this field is indicated by something that happened at the 1977 Ethnic Recordings in America conference. Several months before that, I had become especially interested in the music and related traditions of the Polish *górale,* or Highlanders, the people who emigrated from the mountain region of Podlhale in southern Poland. I helped negotiate the appearance at the conference of the singers, dancers, and musicians from Chicago who represent the Highlander tradition, and while they were rehearsing in the Coolidge Auditorium, my pleasure in watching them must have been obvious, because Alvin Sajewski came up to me and said, with a grin, "Are you sure you don't have some Polish blood in you?" I don't, but still I thought it was one of the finest compliments I'd ever been paid.

Chicago's Polish Highlanders perform in the Coolidge Auditorium at the Library of Congress, January 1977. Photograph by Carl Fleischhauer, American Folklife Center, Library of Congress.

And that raised an interesting question: Is it appropriate that a native-born WASP American like me should be involved with musical artifacts from other cultures whose languages and many of whose ambient traditions and folkways are unfamiliar to me? The answer has to be yes, and yes precisely because I *am* an American and have a unique opportunity to learn from other cultures that have been transplanted from the Old World to my own, cultures that have managed to thrive on American soil and, in the process, offer us all depth and diversity.

The history of ethnic recordings in the United States begins not so much with the recording industry as with those foreign-born peoples and their descendents whose music was available for record companies to exploit.

Most of us learned in school about the pre-Revolution emigrants who settled the colonies to escape religious and political persecution, or those who came to explore the new land and increase their wealth. By 1820 the industrial revolution had begun in Europe; it spread from England to Ireland, to Germany in the 1840s, then to the Scandinavian countries and the Balkans, and finally to Poland, Greece, and most of the rest of Europe, producing successive waves of emigrants made up of the small farmers and artisans whose lands and livelihoods were suddenly removed. Since land was plentiful in the United States, and labor scarce outside the southern slave states, the immigrants could find ready employment in the mines, mills, and factories, where they were welcomed by employers who were able to pay them much lower wages than native Americans would have accepted. Emigration was hastened by famines and pestilence in several Old World countries, beginning with the Irish famine of the 1840s. This pattern of escape to America was interrupted only by the outbreak of World War I. Restrictive admissions policies adopted after the war effectively sealed the gates, but not until the United states had become a new home for millions. These immigrants brought with them not just their skills and needs, but also shared memories of home, religion, tales, music, and other remnants of lifestyles they desperately needed to preserve in a new, alien, and sometimes hostile society. By the end of the century, a revolutionary invention had made it possible to preserve and perpetuate these memories in a new way.

Though Thomas Alva Edison's talking machine was widely heralded in 1877–78 as a major scientific breakthrough, nearly twenty years passed before his crude toy was sufficiently developed to make a major impact on society. By the mid-1890s it was evident that the future of the phonograph (as it was later called) lay primarily in providing home entertainment and secondarily in serving as a coin-operated device in places of public amusement. There was some attention to ethnic groups from the mid-1890s onward. An 1895 listing of "plates" from the fledgling Berliner Company included an announcement of several "Hebrew songs," and a relatively small number of Polish, Spanish, and French songs emerged with slowly increasing momentum from more companies as the turn of the century drew near. Advertisements and other documents of that era do not reveal that record companies had discerned that they might appeal to special and continuing audiences, and it is likely that the records were produced more as novelty items than as an attempt to reach a selected group of potential buyers. Such sophisticated marketing concepts were a long time developing. The industry was plagued also during its early years with a series of patent infringement suits that hindered the growth and development of the recording art.

Some of the dust began to settle in the 1900s. Patents were more widely shared, and as cylinders were slowly phased out of production, a standard ten- or twelve-inch two-sided disc that played at seventy eight revolutions per minute for 2½ to 4½ minutes per side, recorded and reproduced with a laterally undulating stylus, gradually came to be the norm. With technical standardization came an even greater public acceptance of the medium, so that by World War I the phonograph had become essential in many American homes.

To the person who spoke another language the phonograph assumed a more important role. In a country with strange customs and values, where other people spoke an unfamiliar language, a phonograph could and did provide a means of emotional retreat to one's homeland. Records of familiar songs reinforced traditional values and an immigrant's sense of self-worth. If a Mexican *corrido*, a Polish *sztajerek*, or a Cretan *pentozali* was worthy of attention from Columbia or Victor, that fact went far in making up for neighbors or shopkeepers who did not know the immigrant's language and made fun of his clothes. It meant that at least one American business was soliciting his patronage by recognizing, respectfully, who he was.

For their part, record companies were astute enough to recognize the need for foreign-language records during the early 1900s when they began to seriously build and diversify their catalogs and offerings. By 1908, Columbia, Victor, and smaller companies had begun issuing two-sided popular records for seventy-five cents—only ten cents over the cost of single-sided discs. Even before this, there were at least token offerings. A 1906 Columbia catalog for example, offered discs and cylinders in German, Italian, French, Czech, Swedish, Danish, Norwegian, Polish, Hungarian, Hebrew, and Russian. A note on the last page indicates that there was an entirely separate catalog for records in Spanish.

By World War I sales of records and phonographs to nonnative peoples had become big business. Columbia and Victor rapidly expanded their catalogs, offering a wide choice of material recorded domestically and supplementing it with popular recordings drawn from overseas affiliates in London, Kiev, Berlin, and other large Old World cities. New language series were introduced, and it became more and more worthwhile for everyone to own a phonograph as a continuing source of popular entertainment. Even less populous groups were catered to. If, say, the Albanian-American community was not significantly large, record sales would be low; but still, each person who wanted a record could also be persuaded to buy a phonograph, and eventually some other kinds of records to play on it. This particular example is not drawn out of a hat; both Victor and Columbia maintained Albanian series for a time, and pressing figures range from a high of 300 to a low of 25. Since these figures represent the total number of copies ever made, such records are of course extremely rare today.

How did the record companies themselves view these operations, and how systematically did they move into foreign-language recording? Unfortunately, we do not have corporate histories that would readily yield such information. The Edison company's output was small, hindered by its reliance on cylinders and "diamond discs," neither of which was compatible with the popular, inexpensive machines made by Victor and Columbia. Victor had issued nearly 6,000 ethnic records by 1920, offering records in Lithuanian, Ukrainian, Dutch, Serbian, Croatian, Yiddish, Rumanian, Slovak,

A Chinese Circular

Miss Helen Moore, manager of the record department of the Kieselhorst Piano Co., St. Louis, Mo., overlooks no opportunity to increase the clientele of the store and to render every possible service to customers. The store has a number of Chinese customers, and Miss Moore decided to send a circular letter to them and to other Chinese in the city in order to increase the sale of Chinese records. She had one of her Chinese customers lay off "Spotting-up" laundry tickets long enough to get up a special letter in Chinese characters to send the Kieselhorst message to the Orientals. The text of the letter, which is reproduced herewith, is translated by Miss Moore as follows: "Come here for your Chinese records and Victrolas. Time payments. Complete stock carried here. Kieselhorst Piano Co. Ask for Miss Moore."

Finnish, Hawaiian, Armenian, Syrian, Portuguese, Slovenian, Arabic, and Turkish, in addition to all those languages Columbia was offering in 1906. Victor and Columbia were also making records in various oriental tongues; they were manufactured and marketed on a separate basis.

Columbia introduced an "E" prefix to denote its foreign records when it began issuing double-sided discs in 1908. Its output over the following years rivaled Victor's, and its advertising and promotion in this area were far more aggressive. Witness this 1914 message to dealers:

Foreign Record Field

Energetic Dealers Find Alien Trade Profitable,
Active, and Easily Acquired

Getting the foreign trade is not a mysterious art or science as so many of the dealers seem to think. It doesn't require you to be an accomplished linguist. You don't have to "talk Spanish" to sell Spanish selections; juggle spaghetti when Antonio asks for some of Daddi's Neapolitan street songs; nor get the palms of your hands sunburned to convince Abe Rosinsky he wants Cantor Karniol's records. For these foreigners have been quick to learn "when in America, do as the Americans" meaning first of all, speak English. This 99% of them can do and while they speak it with varying degrees of proficiency, all can either ask for the music they want or point out the record number in the catalog.

With from five to eight thousand miles between them and the land of their birth, in a country with strange speech and customs, the 35,000,000 foreigners making their home here are keenly on the alert for anything and everything which will keep alive the memories of their fatherland—build them a mental bridge back to their native land. They are literally starving for amusements. With no theatres, except in one or two of the larger cities, few books in their native tongue, it is easy to realize why the talking machine appeals to them so potently, so irresistibly. Their own home music, played or sung by artists whose names are household words in their homeland— these they must have. They are patriotic, these foreigners, and their own intense interest in their own native music is strengthened by their desire that their children, brought or born in this *new* country shall share their love of the old.

The immense stirring of patriotic fervor due to the European war has given an impetus to the sale of Columbia records of foreign music which is truly phenomenal.

If you are not getting your share of it, you are overlooking a large and profitable business which, moreover, is right at your door. . . .[3]

Columbia catalog from 1906. Music Division, Library of Congress.

The message is convincing—and, judging by the large quantities of the old green-label "E" series still in existence, dealers took the message seriously.

When war broke out in 1914, one immediate effect upon record production in the United States was that European-made masters were no longer available. At the same time, Old World loyalties were rekindled among Americans descended from the various warring nations, and sales of patriotic and war-related songs rose dramatically. The companies redoubled their efforts to turn out records for the ethnic markets, often using special decorative labels, flags, and war scenes to further tempt purchasers.

Inevitably the companies were forced to rely more and more on domestic talent to provide new material. Some of the slack was taken up by studio musicians who churned out instrumentals and were given names like Columbia Polish Orchestra or Victor International Orchestra. Some releases began to appear in international or polyglot series, with titles given in as many as four languages on one record label. In still other cases ethnic musicians were used to record; but if the result was a waltz, polka, or another dance with multinational appeal, the record would be reissued for other nationalities with misleading artist credits to make the purchaser think he was buying something intended especially for him.

But what ultimately changed the course of ethnic recordings most was the attempt to recruit more immigrant talent. During the early years the only significant American recording activity took place in New York, primarily because the equipment was cumbersome and expensive to transport. But in 1915, as a direct result of the war, Columbia shipped recording equipment to Chicago to take advantage of the talent there, and recorded extensively. Victor had already undertaken earlier forays through Trinidad, Mexico, and Central America; we do not know when the company began recording regularly in Chicago, though they were clearly active there by the early 1920s.

Talking Machine World, September 1928, page 12. Motion Picture, Broadcasting, and Recorded Sound Division, Library of Congress.

Price Specializes in Language Records

Seattle Talking Machine Dealer Carries Records in Forty-two Languages

Where Fred Price Does a Large Foreign Record Business

FRED P. PRICE has the unique distinction of conducting the only foreign record booth in Seattle, and has been operating it for nearly seven years. He is located in the Seattle Pike Place Market and his booth is the haven for record seekers from every land. Besides Mr. Price himself, the sales personnel includes Mrs. William King, who efficiently carries on the business during his absence, and Earle Hatch.

Records, new or second-hand, classical or sacred, in every language are available. The counters are divided into partitions which are each devoted to records from a certain country. A card with the name of the country on it helps to identify the records in each partition, which taken in order, read something like this: German, Suomalaisia, Scandinavia, Swedish, Norske, Danish, Classical Imported Records, Italian, Croatian, Serbian, Armenian, Russian, Greek, Turkish, Polish, Ukrainian, Spanish, Hungarian, Bethanian, Holland-Dutch, Roumanian, French, Welsh, Arabian-Serbian, Belgium, Gaelic, etc., forty-two languages in all being represented.

All domestic records are carried in Columbia, Victor and Brunswick, and include everything from old-time music to the very latest hits. Complete catalogs are carried in all makes of records. The stocks consist of every record

that is made and every record that can possibly be obtained in any foreign language. Four average-sized hearing rooms are used.

"A big mail order business has been built up and is very successfully carried on. Records are shipped extensively throughout the territory west of the Rocky Mountains as well as throughout the entire country. An occasional shipment has been made to Australia, while it is not at all unusual to ship them frequently to the old country," stated Price.

With regard to business conditions Mr. Price declared: "Business is very good, and it is good the entire year around. While most dealers were not doing so well during July, for us it was one of the best months that we have ever had. We did nearly 30 per cent more business at that time this year than we did last year. There is nearly always a crowd buying records, and we have never seen a slack time yet."

Newspaper advertising is used in many of the foreign papers. In local American papers, ads are tied up with most of the Columbia, Victor and Brunswick activities.

Radio station KVL is furnished with all of the

record music used by that station from Mr. Price's booth. At all odd times these records are used to fill in during the various broadcasts and sometimes for two- and three-hour periods during the day nothing but such records are played.

Although Price specializes in records he does sell an occasional phonograph. He handles the Victor, Columbia and Brunswick lines.

Okay Shop Opens Branch

The Okay Radio Shop, Washington, D. C., recently opened a branch store in the Transportation Building, Seventeenth and H streets, N. W., where a complete line of radio products, including the Crosley and Freshman lines of radio receiving sets, will be carried.

Sells Radiolas to Hotel

BRISTOL, VA., September 4.—The Bristol Radio Co., Inc., of this city, recently installed several models of Radiola 17 in the Hotel Bristol. Every room in the hotel has radio service.

Such activity had its effect on other areas, too: It was in Chicago that many significant jazz and blues performers were recorded during their prime.

The wartime momentum in foreign record sales did not let up after the Armistice. The new prosperity was reflected in greater record and phonograph sales; many millions of records were sold each year, reaching a peak in 1921. There would have been no stopping the companies' corporate growth

Victor 1923 catalog of Chinese records in Cantonese dialect. Music Division, Library of Congress.

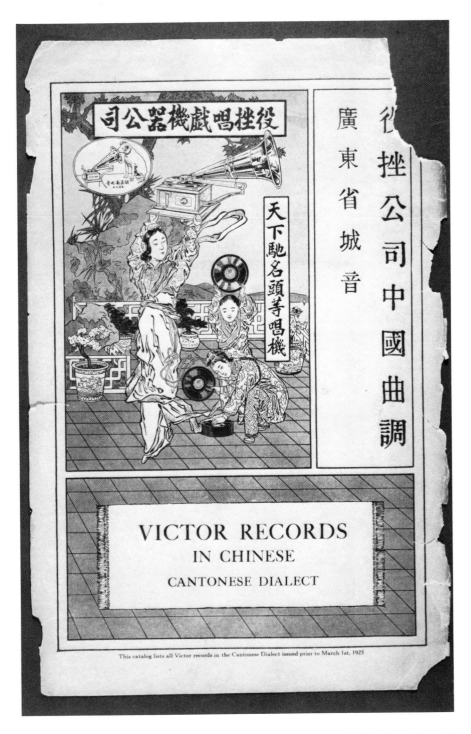

司公器機戲挫役

廣東省城音

役挫公司中國曲調

天下馳名頭等唱機

VICTOR RECORDS
IN CHINESE
CANTONESE DIALECT

This catalog lists all Victor records in the Cantonese Dialect issued prior to March 1st, 1923

and expansion had it not it been for the introduction and immediate popularity of radio, which by 1925 had become a serious competitor for amusement dollars.

Record and phonograph profits had been so handsome in the 1910s that the intense research and technological competition of earlier years had virtually come to a standstill. Radio had two significant advantages: It provided varied entertainment without further investment, and electronic amplification gave it a sound markedly superior to records, which were still being made by the acoustical horn method. By 1925, this second advantage was countered, when the same system was adapted to recording techniques. The increase in fidelity was astounding, and the new process proved the greatest recording advance until the introduction of magnetic tape. Unfortunately, it did not do the record companies much good. Radio's inroads were already permanent, and inexpenive phonographs capable of reproducing the new records electronically were not available for a number of years. Sales declined gradually, bottoming out during the worst years of the Depression. The period 1925–34 saw every major record company either change ownership or simply go out of business.

Still, the area we are considering was one of the least affected, as the music of American minorities continued to be produced and released in relatively stable and even increasing quantities until 1930. Radio, from the first, had been directed to a general audience, and its offerings reflected the tastes and inclinations of the undifferentiated mainstream. There were occasional exceptions: Myron Surmach produced a Ukrainain broadcast in New York City once a week for twenty-seven years; an item in *Talking Machine World* mentions a special Chicago Polish broadcast in 1927 featuring record artists.[4] But these efforts were occasional, barely sufficient to meet the entertainment needs of ethnic Americans. As a result, the music of these minorities, as well as that of blacks and rural whites, enjoyed a greater share of the companies' attention than ever before.

In 1918 several crucial patents owned almost exclusively by Victor and Columbia were declared invalid by the courts. As a result, a number of independent companies were formed, and several older firms began producing laterally recorded discs that were compatible with Victor and Columbia phonographs. Eventually most of them took an interest in ethnic music. Pathé and Vocalion issued Irish records in the early 1920s. Around 1920, Emerson (which later abandoned records for radio manufacture) was issuing records in Swedish, Yiddish, Italian, Polish, and other languages.

More important was the General Phonograph Corporation, which began as a parts manufacturer and began issuing its records in 1918. A year or two later, it acquired rights to release masters from the Lindström company in Germany. This gave General exclusive rights to the fabled Fonotipia opera series and to Lindström's Odeon label. General began issuing records in many languages on a combined OKeh-Odeon series, using the Odeon label for European-made material. OKeh-Odeon became an important competitor, and when General merged with Columbia in 1926, these series continued without interruption in addition to Columbia's own output.

Fourth behind Victor, Columbia, and OKeh-Odeon was the Brunswick-Balke-Collender Company, best known for its bowling equipment. Vocalion had begun production in 1917, and by 1923 had issued a few records in ten languages (including Irish). It merged with Brunswick in 1924, probably to combine efforts at getting electrically made recordings into production. Brunswick, which had had little previous experience in the ethnic field, then began extensive production, and material in several languages appeared on both Brunswick and Vocalion for some years. Gennett and Paramount, noted for their blues, jazz, country, and gospel activity, evidently produced ethnic records, too, but their releases have been only sketchily documented.

Actually, the parallels between the industry's response to black and southern white music and to ethnic music are striking. Certainly, the fortunes of race and hillbilly records (as they were then known) and ethnic releases rose and ebbed together, and there also seems to have been mutual influence. A brief sketch of early race and hillbilly records will help make these parallels clearer.

In 1920, at the repeated promptings of an insistent black songwriter and publisher, OKeh decided to release one of his songs and, at his request, to record it using a popular black cabaret singer named Mamie Smith. The disc sold reasonably well, and Smith was called back six months later. Her second release, "Crazy Blues," was a big hit, and OKeh, along with its competitors, quickly found itself in the profitable business of selling black music to black people.

Three years later, OKeh was pressured into another profitable and precedent-setting recording, this time by a fifty-five-year-old traditional mountain singer who provided his own accompaniment, Fiddlin' John Carson. Carson's first release, "The Old Hen Cackled and the Rooster's Going to Crow," did for hillbilly music what Mamie Smith had done for the blues, revealing an extensive market for the tradition-oriented music of southern whites.

Smith, Carson, and their successors filled an important void, comparable to one that Myron Surmach describes. When he became seriously interested in record retailing in the early twenties, his Ukrainian customers had to

Myron Surmach and the exhibit case highlighting his contributions to Ukrainian music and culture from the 1977 Ethnic Recordings in America Conference. Photograph by Carl Fleischhauer, American Folklife Center, Library of Congress.

Columbia's August 1926 supplement of Russian and Ukrainian records. Music Division, Library of Congress.

On this 1936 release Humeniuk's name is spelled in the Polish form. Motion Picture, Broadcasting, and Recorded Sound Division, Library of Congress.

choose from a limited offering. The trained singers, studio orchestras, military bands, comedians, and small choruses who were making Ukrainian records had a united appeal to the people who had migrated from the farms and small villages of the old country. It never occurred to anyone to seek out an Old World counterpart to Fiddlin' John until one day in 1925, when an OKeh representative dropped in at Surmach's shop to ask if there were any good musicians around who could make recordings. As it happened, a fiddler and instrument maker Pawlo Humeniuk was in the store, and Surmach introduced them. A bargain was struck, and Humeniuk was in the OKeh studios with an instrumental quartet in December, 1925. The two resulting records did well, but this time OKeh failed to follow up. A few weeks later Humeniuk was under contract to Columbia, who wanted more of his peasant song and dance tunes. OKeh apparently never realized what it had lost, and made no further attempts to record rural music from the Ukraine—strange, considering the company's ready exploitation of Mamie Smith and John Carson and others like them. It would be instructive to know whether the OKeh scout was only seeking new talent to record, or whether he had recognized that a large spectrum of music was missing from the company's offerings.

Humeniuk recorded extensively for the next ten years. Early in 1926, Columbia released his "Ukrainske Wesilie" (Ukrainian Wedding), which occupied both sides of a twelve-inch 78 rpm disc. It was a simply prepared skit combining dialog, songs, and dance music; but it was authentic, and it had the feel of life as many had experienced it in the Old World and were trying desperately to hang onto in the New. It was a runaway hit, not only among Ukrainians, but also among other minority groups with similar feelings, who, while they might not understand the words, knew well enough what it was all about. According to Surmach, the record sold at least 100,000 copies, and possibly a good many more. One immediate result was the establishment of Humeniuk as an enduring and versatile artist. Originally from Galicia, he was as well versed in the Polish language, music, and customs as in his own. He began recording prodigiously in Columbia's Polish series, altering his name slightly (to Pawel Humeniak), and proved as appealing there as he was for the Ukrainians. Alvin Sajewski reports that Humeniuk's 1927 "Polka 'Kanarek'" was one of the biggest Polish sellers of its time.

But Humeniuk's success had further ramifications. Within a few months after "Ukrainske Wesilie" was released, other county fiddlers and their groups could be heard, not only on Polish and Ukranian records, but on those intended for many other nationalities as well. While Humeniuk may not have done it singlehandedly, he seems to have been the catalyst for the hundreds, perhaps thousands, of records that followed his, presenting the folk music of his own and other countries in authentic and informal settings, and turning the ten years following 1925 into an incredibly rich era of ethnic folk recording activity. His creation of an awareness of and demand for "the real thing" is an accomplishment of no less stature than Mamie Smith's or John Carson's.

There is one more intriguing parallel: In 1927, Columbia issued "A Fiddler's Convention in Georgia" and "A Corn Licker Still in Georgia" by Gid Tanner, Riley Puckett, Clayton McMichen, Fate Norris, and other members of the Skillet Lickers band of north Georgia. Like "Ukrainske Wesilie," these records featured skits with songs and fiddle music. Like

"Ukrainske Wesilie," the discs were influential and inspired imitations. While Humeniuk's various skits were about weddings, engagements, and christenings, the Skillet Lickers' "Corn Licker Still," which eventually occupied fourteen sides, was joined by other topical skits about country stores, possum hunts, hog butchering, and census taking. The moonshining and Prohibition themes by the Skillet Lickers and others remained popular; even the ethnic series eventually featured a few.

Obviously, this is no more than an interesting series of coincidences, and many questions remain to be answered: Did the success of Fiddlin' John Carson alert OKeh to the need for rural-based music in its ethnic series? Are there earlier precedents for the recorded narrative skits with songs and fiddle music? Was "Ukrainske Wesilie" responsible, directly or indirectly, for "A Corn Licker Still in Georgia"? Did radio figure in these skits' origin and popularity?

What we *can* assert, on the basis of ample evidence, is that this was a "Golden Era" for ethnic folk recordings, much like that for precommercial styles of jazz, blues, gospel, and country music. Instrumentalists of all kinds were presented, and singing styles compare favorably with those of the best blues and hillbilly singers of the day. Current technology made it possible to record any type of music, including the high, delicate frequencies of stringed instruments, with accuracy, clarity, and vitality. At that time record companies were still in the process of discovering new markets and catering to them.

As the Columbia advertisement quoted earlier indicates, the notion of weaning people's tastes away from their own ethnic forms and fostering a reliance on mainstream popular music was there from the beginning. Nevertheless, those days were a long way from our own, in which we have a giant, superbly coordinated music industry capable of determining a schedule of mass-produced hits that is amazingly consistent throughout the country, narrowing our tastes into a litany of Top Tens, Top Twenties, and Top Forties. In the late 1920s that was not yet possible, and folk and regional music of every description was readily and widely available on records. By 1930, Victor and Columbia dealer's catalogs offered predominantly American-made releases in all the following series: Acadian French, Albanian, Annamite, Arabic (Syrian), Armenian, Bohemian (Czech), Bulgarian, Cambodian, Chinese (Cantonese), Chinese (Mandarin), Croatian, Cuban, Danish, Dutch, Finnish, Franco-Annamite, French, French-Canadian, German, Greek, Hawaiian, Hebrew-Yiddish, Hungarian, Indo-Chinese, International, Irish, Italian, Japanese, Korean, Lithuanian, Mexican, Norwegian, Novelty, Persian, Philippine (Tagalog), Polish, Puerto Rican, Portuguese, Rumanian, Russian, Scandinavian, Serbian, Slovak, Slovenian, Swedish, Swiss, Tonkinese, Turkish, Ukrainian, Welsh, and West Indian. Literally thousands of recordings captured a wealth of style and tradition from every significant national group in our country. And by 1930 a high proportion of these were performances of significant folk value. In the Ukrainian and Polish series, for instance, one finds examples of the mountain dance music of the western Carpathians, street beggar songs accompanied by fiddle or hurdy-gurdy, comic singers accompanying themselves with concertina or accordion, and beautiful religious music derived from the Catholic or Orthodox devotions. The Irish series contains fiddling, piping, accordion music, and traditional singing. The various Spanish-language series include Afro-Cuban marimba

The Talking Machine World, New York, October, 1928

Columbia

Of Vital Interest to
Foreign Language Record Dealers

¶ Columbia offers you the greatest library of foreign language records. They cease to be a "foreign language" when recorded by Columbia—they are "native" in the purest and best sense.

¶ The whole wide world is the arena of Columbia Recordings. Each nation has its own individual type of music, its own distinctive interpretations, which native artists can best portray.

¶ Therefore, Columbia records native artists in the following languages:

Armenian	Hebrew-Jewish	Russian
Bohemian	Hungarian	Scandinavian
Bulgarian	Irish	Swedish
Chinese	Italian	Scotch
Croatian-Serbian	Lithuanian	Slovak
Finnish	Mexican	Slovenian
French-Canadian	Polish	Syrian-Arabic
German	Portuguese	Turkish
Greek	Roumanian	Ukrainian

Columbia runs an extensive advertising campaign each month in native language papers. Stock up now on Columbia Foreign Language Records recorded in the "native" languages—you will find it highly profitable.

COLUMBIA PHONOGRAPH COMPANY
1819 Broadway, New York City
Canada Columbia Phonograph Co., Ltd., Toronto

"MAGIC NOTES"

music from central America, *jarocho* (harp) and *huasteca* (fiddle) bands from the Veracruz region, the *corridos* of the street musicians from Texas and northern Mexico (the long narrative ballads that celebrated the romantic outlaw heroes of the border region), and even the calypsoes and other West Indian songs and dances from Trinidad and Barbados.

As diverse, as cosmopolitan, as these offerings were, they still represent a uniquely American phenomenon. Many of these traditions, though maintained in the Old World, went virtually unrecorded except in the United States. That counterparts to our Golden Era heritage are almost nonexistent elsewhere is largely a result of economics: Folk music is not the product of affluent classes, and the people among whom it does flourish are precisely those who felt compelled to come to America seeking economic opportunities they did not have at home. The impoverished classes they left behind, in the country and small villages, could not afford to purchase luxuries like phonographs and records, and thus did not constitute an audience for their own traditional entertainment, so far as making and marketing records was concerned.

We have to be grateful for the early intense activity in this country, for the record companies' unwitting gift to us of the traditional, regional, and ephemeral music they captured and preserved. If we could return to 1930, we could still easily hear their music and obtain all the recordings in those thick dealer's catalogs. But that was a half-century ago, and many of the discs have been worn out or destroyed. This is all the more a pity because 1930 marked the beginning of the decline in ethnic production. Americans began to feel the effects of the Depression that year. As businesses folded and unemployment rose, records more and more became an expendable luxury. New releases in 1931 were a fraction of the 1929 totals, and sales figures were correspondingly lower. In 1930, Columbia began to pad its catalog by remastering and reissuing acoustical records, declaring that they were "electrically recorded." Both Columbia and Victor recycled instrumental polkas, waltzes, and occasional songs, assigning them new release numbers in different national series, disguising artist and title credits in the process. Smaller companies ceased ethnic production entirely; by 1932–33 only Victor's and Columbia's most active series enjoyed even a token number of newly produced recordings—and many of these were once again being reissued from foreign masters.

In 1929, the Victor Talking Machine Company was purchased by RCA. Columbia had already changed hands, and the Depression hastened the process for other firms—witness the sale, consolidation, or demise of OKeh, Gennett, Vocalion, Brunswick, and Paramount. The scene brightened somewhat in 1933 and 1934 when Victor introduced its thirty-five-cent Bluebird label and English Decca began its American operation, retailing records for the same low price. Both labels were active in releasing Mexican, Cajun, Irish, and West Indian music. What was left of other series remained available on Victor and Columbia, selling at from fifty to seventy-five cents per disc.

The operations that had once catered to European immigrants lay virtually dormant. Pawlo Humeniuk made a last handful of sides for both Victor and Columbia in 1936 and, except for four more sides in 1940, was not heard from again on records. He and his generation were being replaced by more homogeneous groups like those led by Ted Johnson (Swedish), "Whoopee John" Wilfahrt (German), Wasyl Gula (Bill Gale, Ukrainian),

Wasyl Gula, better known in the 1940s as Bill Gale. Release date ca. 1936. Motion Picture, Broadcasting, and Recorded Sound Division, Library of Congress.

Jolly Jack Robel (Polish), and others, who were consciously aiming their music at the widest possible audience, turning out a steady fare of polkas and waltzes, eschewing the more distinctively regional dances like the *kolomyika, hambo, czardas,* and *oberek.* When singers were featured, they often sang in English or alternated English with the mother tongue. As far as the record companies were concerned, the melting pot was the way of profits. By World War II, this homogenized music was nearly all that was left.

Fortunately, Victor and Columbia both recognized the continuing need for at least token diversity, and they responded by leaving many of the Golden Era records in their catalogs. Even after the war, it was still possible to buy new pressings of more than three dozen Humeniuk recordings, and records of traditional artists of other nationalities were still available, albeit in diminished quantity. But record making changed again during those years. Tape mastering was in wide use by 1948, the same year Columbia introduced its 33⅓ rpm long-playing discs. Victor countered the following year with its 45s. A "War of the Speeds" ensued and the standard 78s were rapidly phased out. By this time new releases were infrequent, and it was no longer worth the cost to remaster the old ethnic records and make them available again at the new speeds. In 1952 both Victor and Columbia quietly bowed out of the ethnic recording business.

This might be the end of our story, but fortunately, others were aware of the gap the major labels were leaving unfilled. If magnetic tape contributed to the end of major-label operations, the portability and low cost of tape recorders also made it possible for more modest operations to spring up all over the country. By the mid-fifties there were hundreds of full- and part-time recording firms throughout the country. Myron Surmach was producing new Ukrainian records and reissuing selected old ones on his Surma and Boyan labels. Dana and Jay Jay in Chicago were distributing Polish records to stores and juke boxes wherever they could locate a Polish audience. Violet Ruparcich founded Greyko Records in Pittsburgh, a thriving company specializing in Serbian and Croatian music, with a catalog that today includes everything from opera to rock. Ray Boley started Canyon Records in Phoenix to record, release, and distribute the music of American and Canadian Indians—peoples who were in a relatively impoverished position during the Golden Era and were correspondingly almost ignored by American record companies. Today Canyon produces a wide variety of popular and tribal music on everything from 45 rpm discs to eight-track tape cartridges. Standard-International, a thriving multifaceted company begun in the 1930s, has issued recordings of many ethnic groups, thanks in large part to the effort and enthusiasm contributed by Walter Erikkson during his thirty-five-year association with that firm.

Interest in historical ethnic recordings has been slight among folk music scholars, but not totally nonexistent. Folkways Records and its founder, Moses Asch, were involved from the inception of the company in 1950. A number of its ethnic sampler records have used material that had appeared on early 78s. The Folkways anthology *American Folk Music,* issued in 1952, included seven Cajun selections that found wide favor because of what that music has in common with southern breakdowns and blues. Further recordings were produced by Harry Oster and Chris Strachwitz, and Strachwitz's activities include an important reissue program as well. Recently, he has developed an interest in the fascinating music of the Mexico-Texas border, and through Arhoolie he has recorded and reissued a great deal of important music from this area. Love Records in Finland has reissued two LPs of Finnish-American folksongs derived from 78s that Pekka Gronow located in the United States.

And finally there is the *Folk Music in America* series I referred to at the beginning of this article. Much of the fifteen albums of dance music, religious music, and various topical songs rests, of course, on the familiar base of southern and southern-derived English-language folk music, in part because the South has always been a vital wellspring of our traditional music and in part because I had only limited access to the wealth of American-made foreign-language folk recordings. Nevertheless, approximately 20 percent of the music included is from Irish, Indian, Polish, Ukrainian, Armenian, Cajun, West Indian, Spanish, German, Hebrew, and other sources, and it will, I hope, serve to introduce this magnificent and rewarding music to new audiences.

Already the series has had some worthwhile spin-offs. New World Records, funded by a large grant from the Rockefeller Foundation to produce the *Recorded Anthology of American Music*, expressed interest in

Folk Music in America volume 4, record cover.

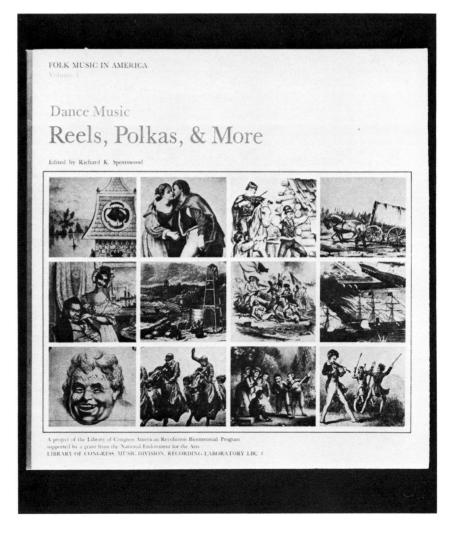

albums of American-recorded music from Europe and the Near East. A two-record set of Ukrainian-American dance music is available from Folklyric; two Polish companies in Chicago are beginning reissue programs; and Ted Johnson, the popular Swedish bandleader from Minneapolis, is reissuing some of his own vintage recordings.[15]

Many of us in the United States tend to think of ourselves as belonging to an English-speaking nation, directly descended from the country to whom this one belonged two centuries ago. Yet our lives are filled, both culturally and practically, with the products of artists and artisans who left a multitude of countries for this one. Recordings are a very special part of this phenomenon; they document for us more than eight decades of the musical, spoken, and other sounds that form a unique and essential part of our collective history, and for which there is no equivalent. The Ethnic Recordings in America conference came at an especially fitting time. We had just completed the year of America's bicentennial celebration, a year that commemorated among other things, our ethnic diversity. Nineteen seventy-seven was also the centennial of Thomas Edison's discovery that sound could be captured and reproduced at will, thus enabling the world to preserve its past in a new and revolutionary medium. This juxtaposition of anniversaries marks an auspicious time for us to begin to explore in earnest this rich heritage of recordings that has deeply affected and continues to enrich our lives.

Notes

1. Pekka Gronow, "Finnish-American Records," *JEMF Quarterly* 7, no. 24 (Winter 1971):176–85, and "A Preliminary Checklist of Foreign-Language 78s," ibid. 9, no. 29 (Spring 1973):24–32.

2. Not incidentally, I also acquired a good and close friend in Myron Surmach, who has taught me a great deal and has been infinitely patient while I learned. The list of people like him whose knowledge and feeling for our ethnic music helped in the preparation of the *Folk Music in America* series is long indeed.

3. *Columbia Record* 12, no. 5 (May 1914):10, reproduced in Pekka Gronow, *Studies in Scandinavian-American Discography*, vol. 2 (Helsinki: Suomen Äänitearkisto [Finnish Institute of Recorded Sound], 1977), p. 8.

4. "Brunswick Co. Broadcasts Polish Hours of Music," *Talking Machine World*, February 1928, p. 99.

5. See Folklyric 9014 and 9015, *Ukrainian-American Fiddle & Dance Music: The First Recordings 1926–1936, Volumes 1 and 2;* the two Polish firms cited are Chicago Polkas and Bel-Aire.

Early Field Recordings of Ethnic Music

Joseph C. Hickerson

Since the late 1880s, an increasing number of interested and dedicated men and women have sought to collect examples of folksong and music in America. Their purposes have been several—documentation, publication, analysis, and enjoyment—and their findings have comprised a vast body of documents in journals, books, published recordings, archives, and private collections.

In 1887, an early group of such scholars and enthusiasts banded with fellow folklorists and anthropologists to form the American Folklore Society. The first page of their *Journal of American Folklore* (April–June 1888) contained this prospectus:

> It is proposed to form a society for the study of Folk-Lore, of which the principal object shall be to establish a Journal, of a scientific character, designed: —
>
> (1) For the collection of the fast-vanishing remains of Folk-Lore in America, namely: (a) Relics of Old English Folk-Lore (ballads, tales, superstitions, dialect, etc.). (b) Lore of Negroes in the Southern States of the Union. (c) Lore of the Indian Tribes of North America (myths, tales, etc.). (d) Lore of French Canada, Mexico, etc.
>
> (2) For the study of the general subject, and publication of the results of special students in this department.

Groups (a) through (c) are then described in some detail, followed by this brief statement: "The fourth department of labor named consists of fields too many and various to be here particularized, every one of which offers an ample field to the investigator."

It is this last "department of labor" that primarily concerns us here. Did many investigators delve into these "many and various" fields? Were any of them successful with the use of sound recordings?

Early meetings of the society and issues of the journal contained but a scattering of offerings dealing with the folklore of ethnic groups, such as the Louisiana French, Pennsylvania Germans, and Spanish in the Southwest, as compared to considerations of "Old English," Negro, Indian, and foreign folklore. To place such ethnic recording activity in perspective, it would perhaps be useful to briefly describe the overall history of field recording in the United States.

The Edison cylinder recordings machine was barely thirteen years old when it was used by Harvard University anthropologist Jesse Walter Fewkes. Fewkes took the device in March, 1890, to record songs and stories of several Passamaquoddy Indians in Calais, Maine. His resultant field recordings were the first made anywhere in the world. Fewkes's venture was an experiment with new paraphernalia; his conclusion, as reported in *American Naturalist, Science, Scientific American,* and the *Journal of American Folklore,* was affirmative. This statement in the May 2, 1890, issue of *Science* best sums up his conclusions:

> The possibilities of the phonograph in these studies indicate one of the great advantages of this instrument. What specimens are to the naturalist in describing genera and species, or what sections are to the histologist in the study of cellular structure, the cylinders made on the phonograph are to the student of language. In the quiet of his study he can hear the song repeated over and over again as often as he wishes, and can, so to speak, analyze it, and in that way separate the constituent sounds. Moreover, these records on the cylinders can be submitted to specialists for study. The collector may not have a musical ear, as in my own case, and may not be able to write out the songs, no matter how many times they are repeated. He can in that case collect the records, and submit them at some favorable time to one who is able to catch the song and set it to music.

Jesse Walter Fewkes admonished his colleagues through his articles and personal presentations (including a paper read before an American Folklore Society meeting in Boston on April 19, 1890) to use the cylinder recorder for all collecting projects involving language and music. It is of interest to observe the responses to this urgings.

Fewkes's fellow ethnologists who dealt with American Indian traditions paid heed from the outset. Several colleagues secured equipment through Harvard's Peabody Museum of American Archaeology and Anthropology. Franz Boas was quick to supply his Columbia University students with the device. Collections amounting to a thousand cylinders or more had been amassed by the time the United States Government began to sponsor field trips with the cylinder machine. Beginning in 1907, Frances Densmore conducted numerous field trips for the Smithsonian Institution's Bureau of American Ethnology. By the early 1930s, she had garnered nearly three thousand of her own recordings, plus close to a thousand by other collectors. Estimates made by the recently established Federal Cylinder Project at the Library of Congress, together with information and collections already processed by the Archive of Folk Song, indicate upward of fifteen thousand American Indian cylinders residing in various locations around the country.

Some Europeans were also quick to heed Fewkes's suggestions. Ethnologists from Berlin, Vienna, and Paris took cylinder equipment to distant countries or recorded musicians visiting from afar. By 1906, collectors (often composers) were busy recording the folk music of their own country; Percy Grainger in England and Béla Bartók in Hungary are two important early examples.

In the United States, however, early researchers into folk music almost totally ignored the recording machine. While their anthropological fellows were energetically capturing the voices of countless Native Americans, the "humanistic" folklorists were by and large content to gather songs and tales in manuscript form. The exceptions during the first two decades of this century are scant. For English-language folksong traditions derived from Europe, one can point to a number of cylinders made by John A. Lomax in Texas before World War I. Black folksong was documented on a few cylinders by Howard W. Odum and Guy B. Johnson of the University of North Carolina and by Natalie Curtis Burlin at Hampton Institute. The current whereabouts of these early efforts are largely unknown.

Mountain Chief of the Blackfoot Tribe listens to a cylinder recording and translates the song into sign language for Frances Densmore, Washington D.C., 1906. Courtesy of the Smithsonian Institution.

The 1920s saw two pioneers emerge in this field. Duke University's Frank C. Brown began recording extensively in North Carolina. Robert W. Gordon collected up to a thousand cylinders in California, North Carolina, and Georgia, before coming to the Library of Congress in 1928 to head the newly established Archive of American Folk-Song. A few other folksong collectors—Phillips Barry, Helen Hartness Flanders, Eloise Hubbard Linscott—took to the cylinder machine in its latter days and John Lomax returned to the field with cylinder equipment in 1932; but a new technology was developing. In 1931, Robert W. Gordon began his experiments with a portable disc apparatus and made his first foray into the field with a disc machine during the winter of 1931–32. A year and a half later, John and Alan Lomax began a career of disc recording for the Archive of Folk Song that sparked several agencies and numerous individuals to take up the disc machine for folksong fieldwork.

The 1888 design of the American Folklore Society referred in (1)(d) to the "lore of French Canada, Mexico, etc." That "etc." is of particular concern to us here.

Robert W. Gordon, head of the Archive of American Folk Song at the Library of Congress, with part of the cylinder collection and recording machinery, about 1930. Archive of Folk Song, Library of Congress.

As early as 1916, C. Marius Barbeau was recording French-language folksong on cylinders in Canada. A corresponding interest in French-American songlore was less evident until a decade or more later, when Joseph M. Carrière made cylinders of French musical traditions in Louisiana and Missouri. The Lomaxes were recording Cajun music by the mid-1930s, and Herbert Halpert followed suit shortly thereafter. (A checklist of French-American holdings in the Archive of Folk Song is appended to this article.) The following report by John Lomax from the 1935 annual report of the Librarian of Congress constitutes an early document for these recording activities:

> During the latter part of July and through August of last year, we again visited southern Louisiana and with headquarters at New Iberia continued the recordings among the French "Cajuns" of that section. As heretofore reported, these descendants of the French, particularly those who live in remote country districts, still preserve French speech and the custom of group singing, led by semiprofessionals, at weddings or other public festivals. Also drinking parties are always singing parties, where old songs survive and where perhaps the newer ones, through the years, have been originated and passed along.

Spanish-language song traditions were recorded relatively early, beginning in 1903, by Charles F. Lummis of the Southwest Museum in Los Angeles. Lummis's research included Mexican and Indian traditions of the

Recording equipment used by John and Alan Lomax, transported in the trunk of their car. Archive of Folk Song, Library of Congress.

Sound recording truck purchased by the Library of Congress for field recording folk music. Archive of Folk Song, Library of Congress.

Southwest, and numbered well over two hundred cylinders. Much later, the Lomaxes recorded numerous examples of Mexican-American songs. (Subsequent efforts are detailed in an appended checklist.) John Lomax's paragraphs in the 1936 Librarian's annual report describe their findings in Texas:

Almost a quarter of the vast territory of Texas is thickly populated with Mexicans, most of them being of mixed Indian and Spanish blood. Nearly all are Catholics. One-half the school population of San Antonio is Mexican. In the early efforts to Christianize the Indians the Franciscan Friars brought over with them from Spain a miracle play called "Los Pastores." Handed down orally for more than 300 years by the working class who are usually without education, the text and the music have undergone many changes.

I spent some weeks in making plans for recording the music of "Los Pastores." The ceremony is sacred, the people timid and suspicious. Given in the open at night, the singers moving about as they sang, it seemed an impossible task. However, through the kind help of Father Tranchesi, Pastor of Our Lady of Guadalupe Church in San Antonio, I finally succeeded in making records of the best of the duets and other group singing. Then I journeyed to Houston, Tex., where I again recorded the play, this time not all of the singers being men.

I also secured records of "Los Posadas," the singers coming from the guild of San Antonio Mexican midwives.

Another interesting type of Mexican sacred folk music is the Natachines dance, said to be Indian or Aztec in origin. Of these I

A file card at the Archive of Folk Song describing the contents of documentary film footage made by Alan Lomax in 1938.

[THE ARVHIVE OF FOLK SONG] (MOTION PICTURE) (CARD 3)

16. WISCONSIN LUMBERJACKS FILMED BY ALAN LOMAX IN ODANAH, WIS., OCT. 1938. 19. THE DETROIT GUSLA PLAYERS ARE SERBIANS PLAYING THEIR INSTRUMENTS AND SINGING, AND THEY WERE FILMED BY ALAN LOMAX IN DETROIT IN 1938. 20. SERBIANS FILMED AGAINST SCENERY IN 1938. 21. JOHN FREDERICKSON PICKING FRUIT AND TAKING WATER FROM THE WELL, FILMED BY ALAN LOMAX IN CALUMET, MICHIGAN, 1938. 22. MR. FREDERICKSON AND SON. MR. FREDERICKSON WAS AN ACCORDION PLAYER, AND HE WAS FILMED BY ALAN LOMAX IN CALUMET, MICHIGAN, 1938. 23. HAITIAN GROUP SINGING AND DANCING, FILMED IN HAITI IN 1937 BY ALAN LOMAX.

1. FOLK-SONGS - AMERICAN. 2. DANCING - FOLK AND NATIONAL. 3. MUSICAL INSTRUMENTS. I. LOMAX, ALAN, 1915 -

Library of Congress   Motion Picture Collection   C

secured a dozen or more of the better known and most popular tunes. An old Mexican couple at Crystal City, near the Rio Grande, sang for me several beautiful hymns of the people—brooding, sad, reflecting the loneliness of their lives in the desert country of central Mexico. The revolution of Villa had exiled them from their ranch home far back in a cove of the mountains. Their songs seemed to reflect the dreamy sadness of their longing for their lost country as they looked across the river at the hills of their homeland.

Every night on the Mexican market square in San Antonio are many small groups of public singers and guitar players plying their trade. Selecting the most skillful group, I made records of the most appealing examples of their songs, including four different ballads about their most popular hero, Villa. The words of one give, from the Mexican angle, many details of the invasion of General Pershing.

Reports of early field recording among German speakers in the United States are sparse. A survey of private and archival collections of Amish materials, for instance, is sorely needed. Perhaps the 1938 field recordings made by Alan and Elizabeth Lomax in northern Indiana were a pioneer effort. In that year Alan Lomax reported: "Dr. Umble, of Goshen College, introduced us to Jonie Easch and Eli Bontreger, two of the singing leaders of the large and flourishing Amish community near Goshen [Indiana]. These two singers recorded the tunes of thirteen traditional Amish hymns and thus opened the way for valuable studies in the traditional religious music of the Amish settlers in America."

Apart from the Indian, English, French, and Spanish song traditions described above, field recordings of other ethnic groups are virtually impossible to locate prior to 1937. It would seem that subsequent fieldwork in these areas was preceded, and perhaps encouraged, by the presentation of such music at folk festivals. Exemplified by Sarah Gertrude Knott's National Folk Festival, which began in 1934, these events frequently celebrated the music and dance of a variety of native and transplanted traditions in America, including occasional ethnic groups. These festivals were infrequently recorded before the 1950s, but we can look to at least two exceptions that pertain to this article.

In May, 1935, George Korson mounted the first annual Pennsylvania Folk Festival in Allentown. Disc recordists George Hibbit and Walter Garwick recorded much of the proceedings for Columbia University, including a number of songs by Pennsylvania Germans. Similarly, the May 1937 National Folk Festival in Chicago was recorded by Sidney Robertson Cowell of the Special Skills Division, Resettlement Administration, for a project headed by Charles Seeger. Cowell's disc machine documented Norwegian, Finnish, Swedish, Polish, and Lithuanian performances at the event.

In August and September 1937, Sidney Robertson Cowell journeyed to Minnesota to record folksongs for the Resettlement Administration. Through the auspices of Margorie Edgar, whom she had met in Chicago, Cowell recorded a number of ethnic songs sung primarily by Finnish-Americans, with additional selections by singers of Swedish, Serbian, and Gaelic extraction.

By May 1938, Cowell was recording for the WPA California Folk Music

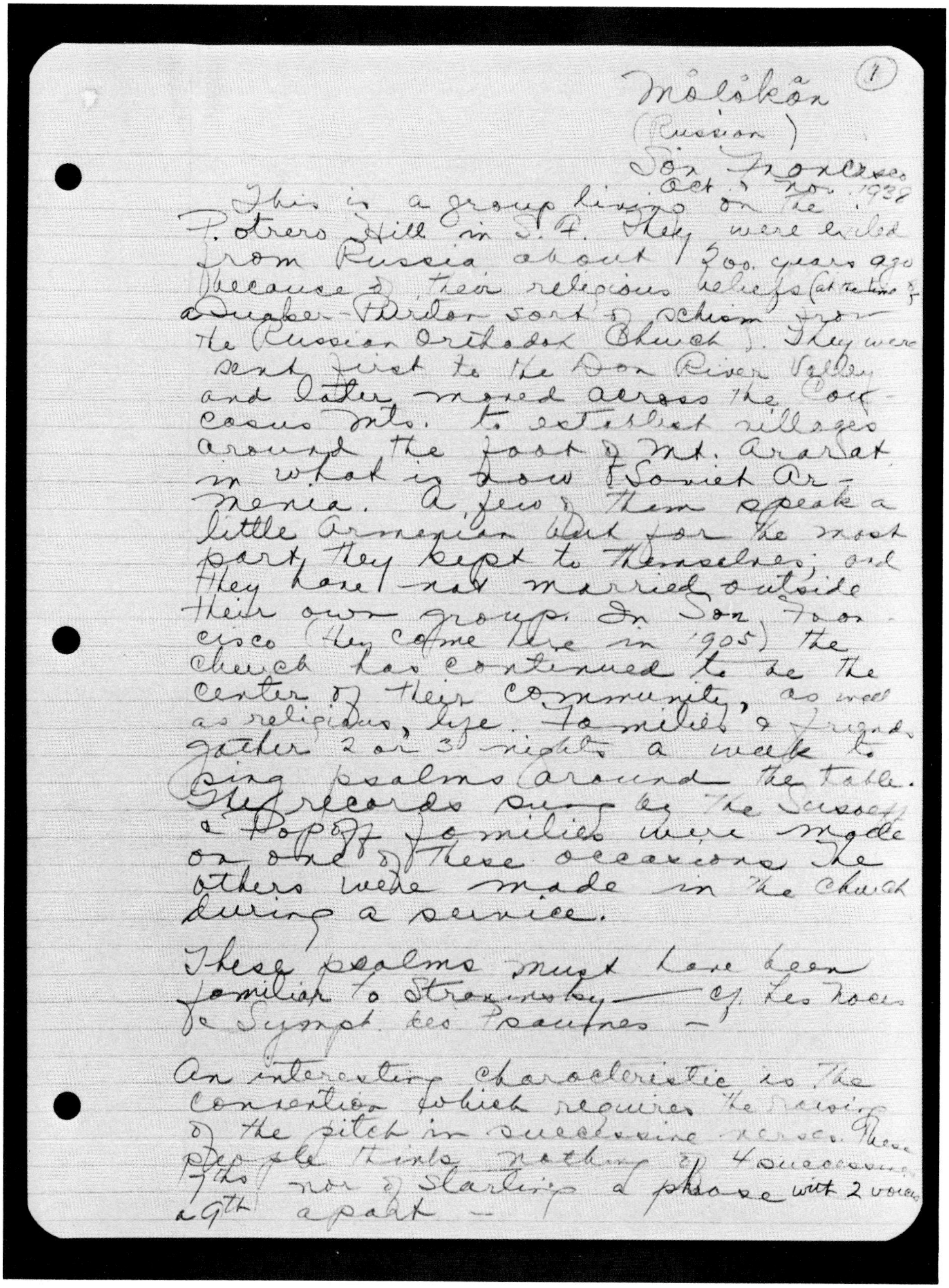

Mălăkăn
(Russian)
San Francisco
Oct. & Nov. 1938

This is a group living on the
Potrero Hill in S.F. They were exiled
from Russia about 300 years ago
because of their religious beliefs (a sort of
a Quaker-Shaker sort of schism from
the Russian Orthodox Church). They were
sent first to the Don River Valley
and later moved across the Cau-
casus Mts. to establish villages
around the foot of Mt. Ararat
in what is now Soviet Ar-
menia. A few of them speak a
little Armenian but for the most
part they kept to themselves; and
they have not married outside
their own group. In San Francisco (they came there in 1905) the
church has continued to be the
center of their community, as well
as religious, life. Families & friends
gather 2 or 3 nights a week to
sing psalms (around the table.
The records sung by the Sussoff
& Popoff families were made
on one of these occasions. The
others were made in the church
during a service.

These psalms must have been
familiar to Stravinsky — cf. Les Noces
& Symph. des Psaumes —

An interesting characteristic is the
convention which requires the raising
of the pitch in successive verses. These
people think nothing of 4 successive
7ths nor of starting a phrase with 2 voices
a 9th apart —

Project operating out of the University of California at Berkeley. Her forays into ethnic traditions were extensive, as were the reports generated by the project. The following is taken from the project's "Statement of Accomplishment" (January 1940):

> . . . the plan for this first year was to take a rapid cross-section of traditional music in the state, exploring the minority groups as well as the folk of Anglo-Saxon antecedents. It was expected that valuable illustrations of the process of acculturation would be found side by side with examples of "Old Country" music as yet unadulterated by contact with other musical cultures in the United States.

Notes on file at the Archive of Folk Song written by Sidney Robertson Cowell describing her fieldwork in California in the 1930s.

Peter Boro, an immigrant from Yugoslavia, playing the *gusla* in San Mateo, California, 1939. The photo is included in "A Study of California Folk Music," a manuscript report from the Department of Music of the University of California and the California Works Projects Administration, 1940. Archive of Folk Song, Library of Congress.

Since Anglo-Saxon culture in California is not yet a hundred years old, it was not surprising to find that Spanish-California music has still survived. Most of this material recorded consists of songs which were probably popular ditties of known authorship as late as 1870. A few, however, have an older folk history and are of great interest. Among these is a single melody still sung among Spanish-speaking Indians on Pala Reservation in San Diego County. This melody is said to have been taught the early Mission Indians at Pala by the Mission Fathers from San Luis Rey who established the assistencia at Pala in 1812. There is also in California Portuguese folk music in quantity, most of it of real interest, still associated with Portuguese folk instruments not very different from those which came with Cabrillo when he discovered California in 1542. Most of the Portuguese here came from the Azores Islands, where singing and dancing are still vital parts of the folk culture. In California the tradition is attenuated somewhat; but it is possible to unearth material of great beauty and interest which seems never to have been studied in Portugal proper, such as the old dances which were carried from Portugal to Brazil, modified there, carried back to the Azores and from there to California. The Portuguese have been established in California longer than the Americans, and nearly as long as the Spaniards. There are seventy titles in the Spanish-California group and eighty in the Portuguese.

The Gaelic recordings of singers from the Hebrides Islands are extremely rare and very beautiful, as are the few recordings of Armenian folksongs from the mountains of Van, which are free of Turkish influence.

In addition to the items mentioned above, the minorities series includes some instrumental music of great interest from the

Scale drawing of a Yugoslavian *lirica* included in "A Study of California Folk Music," a manuscript report from the Department of Music of the University of California and the California Work Projects Administration, 1940. Archive of Folk Song, Library of Congress.

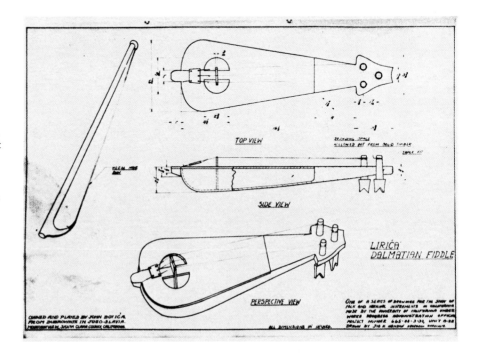

Balkans, and a little Sicilian, Norwegian, Finnish, Spanish (from the Asturias), Costa Riqueño negro, Magyar, and Mexican music. There are also religious folk songs by Russian Molekani and some Icelandic hymns and boat songs.

On the federal level, there was some reluctance at first to publicize the recordings of foreign-language singers in the United States. Congressional philosophy was not strongly pluralistic, and the melting-pot persuasion was prevalent. However, by the 1939 annual report of the Library of Congress, Alan Lomax was commenting on this sphere of activity by a few collectors, and he described at length his own successes in Michigan beginning in August 1938:

> Not only has the Archive grown in sheer size and in terms of improved recording technique, but the range of its material has been greatly expanded. Sidney Robertson, Alan Lomax, John Lomax, and Herbert Halpert have explored fields of foreign minority music with recordings of Finnish, Serbian, Russian, Polish, Portuguese, Cuban, and Mexican songs and dances. . . .
>
> A two and a half month reconnaissance survey of folk-music in Michigan brought into the Archive a group of about a thousand songs, lumberjack, lake sailor, Irish, Southern Negro, Finnish, Serbian, Polish, Canadian French, German, Hungarian, and Croatian. Dr. Ivan Walton of the University of Michigan, Dr. E. C. Beck of the Michigan State Teachers College, and Mr. Howard Newsome, Director of the Federal Writers' Project of Michigan, were of assistance in locating singers.

Mrs. Otto Rindlisbacher (left) and her Swiss bells, with Helene Stratman-Thomas (center), Rice Lake, Wisconsin, 1941. Courtesy of the State Historical Society of Wisconsin, Helene Stratman-Thomas Collection.

Adam Bartosz, who performed Polish, Kashubian, and Ukrainian songs. Stevens Point, Wisconsin, August 11, 1941. Courtesy of the State Historical Society of Wisconsin, Helene Stratman-Thomas Collection.

After ten days spent in Detroit recording a few of the many types of foreign minority music still orally current there, notably records of Serbian diple and douduc players. . . .

A visit to Posen, Michigan, brought the Library an interesting collection of Polish ballads and fiddle tunes. Many of the latter had been learned from local fiddlers when the Polish settlers arrived and now among young people are passed under Polish names as Polish tunes. Here, as all over Michigan, even including Detroit, a great revival of interest in old dance forms was in evidence. Local bands were expected to be able to play national music, jazz, and American square-dance music.

The Upper Peninsula of Michigan proved to be the most fertile source of material. After six weeks of recording a mass of lumberjack, Finnish and French folk-songs, I felt that there was material enough in the region for years of work. Near Newberry, Munising, Greenland, and Ontonogan, it was comparatively easy to find lumberjack singers. Everywhere through the Copper Country and south of it, Finnish singers generously furnished me with more material than I had time to record. And in Champion and Baraga I found French ballad singers who still enjoy ballad fests that lasted all night long.

Subsequent prewar ethnic fieldwork included Florida WPA Federal Writers and Federal Music Projects recordings of Greeks, Slovaks, Czechs, Puerto Ricans, Cubans, and Arabs; and the University of Wisconsin Project recordings of Swedish, Finnish, Swiss, Welsh, Czech, Croatian, Norwegian, Polish, Belgian, and other immigrant traditions. Also at this time, Thelma James was beginning her long-term collection of ethnic folklore in the Detroit area, aided by contacts provided by her students at Wayne State University.

This article has pinpointed some of the known examples of field recordings of ethnic music that American Folklorists made during the discipline's first few decades. It is to be hoped that similar early collections of these multifarious traditions still exsit, and that they may be made available both to scholars and enthusiasts and to the communities whose musical heritage they document.

French-American Folksong and Music on Field Recordings in the Archive of Folk Song

AFS Accession Numbers	Description of Collection
11–17, 20–21, 24–43, 79–83, 85, 111–113	38 discs recorded by John A. Lomax in the South, 1934. Includes some Cajun music from New Iberia, Kaplan, Crowley, and Erath, Louisiana.
889–893, 939, 944	6 discs recorded by John A. Lomax in New Orleans, Louisiana, 1937.
1757, 1761–1762	3 discs recorded by Alan and Elizabeth Lomax in Fort Wayne and Vincennes, Indiana, 1938.
2425–2430, 2435–2438, 2440, 2445–2466	13 discs recorded by Alan Lomax in northern Michigan, 1938.
3119–3134	16 discs recorded by Herbert Halpert, 1938. Includes some French music from New Orleans, Louisiana.
3990–3991	2 discs recorded by John A. and Ruby T. Lomax, 1940. Includes some Cajun music from Shreveport and New Roads, Louisiana.
4998, 4999	2 discs recorded by Robert Draves in Wisconsin for the University of Wisconsin, 1941.
8388–8393, 8446–8449A	10 discs recorded by Aubrey Snyder, Phyllis Pinkerton, and Helene Stratman-Thomas (Blotz) in Wisconsin for the University of Wisconsin, accessioned 1948.
9092	23 12'' discs recorded by the New York Public Library Recording Project in the New York City area, accessioned 1948. Includes some French songs.
9590–9595	6 16'' discs of Cajun music recorded by William A. Owens in southwestern Louisiana, 1948 or earlier.
9974–9978	5 7'' tapes of a traditional French New Year's Eve ceremony recorded by John W. Allen for the Southern Illinois University Museum, accessioned 1950.

10,494	1 7'' tape of French voyageur songs recorded by Mary Agnes Starr, accessioned 1952. Sung by Reuben Valley (at age 100) of Prairie du Chien, Wisconsin.
10,942	1 7'' tape of Cajun folksongs from Louisiana sung by John Dubois, recorded at the Library of Congress, accessioned 1956.
12,594	1 7'' tape of Negro-French folksongs from Louisiana recorded by Harry Oster, 1963.
13,681–13,702	22 10'' tapes recorded by Ralph Rinzler, accessioned 1969. Includes some Cajun music from Louisiana.
13,992–14,021	Includes 31 items in French from the National Federation of Music Clubs Collection recorded by Mary Agnes Starr in Wisconsin, 1963.
15,075–15,076	2 10'' tapes recorded by Ralph Rinzler, ca. 1964. Includes Negro-French music from Louisiana.
15,110	1 7'' tape of Old Christmas, "Song of the Three Kings," recorded by John W. Allen in Illinois, accessioned 1960.
15,402	1 7'' tape of Cajun folksongs sung by John Dubois with Bunyan Webb on guitar, accessioned 1973.
16,984–16,994	11 10'' tapes of fiddle tunes recorded by Chris Delaney in Louisiana, Kentucky, Missouri, Nebraska, Oklahoma, and West Virginia, accessioned 1973. Includes some Cajun music.
17,473	1 7'' tape of the Jolly Boys of Lafayette [Louisiana], Decca 542, accessioned 1975.

Mexican-American Folksong and Music on Field Recordings in the Archive of Folk Song

AFS Accession Numbers	Description of Collection
1–10, 84	11 discs recorded by John A. and Alan Lomax in Texas, 1934.
560–562, 564–566, 568, 571–574, 581–582, 585–593, 607, 609, 624–639, 663, 666–667, 675–678	47 discs recorded by John A. and Alan Lomax in Texas, 1936.
3316, 3318, 3321, 3333	4 discs recorded by Margaret Valiant in the Southwest, 1939.
3809, 3825, 3830, 3832–3833, 3836–3839, 3879–3885, 3889	17 discs recorded by Sidney Robertson [Cowell] in California for the University of California and the Archive of Folk Song under the WPA, 1938-39.
3905–3940	36 discs recorded by Juan B. Rael in Colorado and New Mexico, 1940.
3962–3963, 3965–3967	5 discs recorded by John A. and Ruby T. Lomax in Texas, 1940.
4194–4325	132 discs recorded by Sidney Robertson [Cowell] in California for the University of California and the Archive of Folk Song under the WPA, 1940. Includes some Mexican-American selections.
5145–5146	2 discs of migrant workers recorded by Charles Todd and Robert Sonkin in California, 1941.
5620, 5625–5629, 5631–5636	12 discs recorded by John A. Lomax in Texas, 1941.
6144–6151	8 discs recorded by J. D. Robb in New Mexico, 1942, 1944.
6742–6766	25 discs recorded by Brownie McNeil in southern Texas, 1942.
8018–8023	6 discs of Mexican workers in a Pennsylvania Railroad camp recorded by Charles Seeger in Maryland, 1948.

9300-9306, 9313-9323, 9329-9330, 9345-9348	23 discs recorded by Frances Gillmor for the University of Arizona Recording Project, 1948.
9612-9616, 9626-9627	7 discs recorded by J. D. Robb for the University of New Mexico Recording Project, 1949-50.
9629-9658, 10,119-10,131	43 discs recorded by Arthur L. Campa for the University of New Mexico Recording Project, 1950.
11,307-11,309, 11,338, 11,340	5 10'' tapes recorded by Sidney Robertson Cowell in California, ca. 1957-58.
11,861	1 10'' tape recorded by Wayland D. Hand and students in California for the UCLA Recording Project, 1960.
12,336, 12,338-12,339	3 7'' tapes recorded by J. D. Robb in New Mexico and Arizona, 1950s.
14,015	1 3'' tape recorded by Mrs. T. A. Mitchell in Texas for the National Federation of Music Clubs, 1962.
15,459-15,523	63 7'' tapes and 2 5'' tapes recorded by J. D. Robb, primarily in New Mexico, 1939-72. Includes a large number of Mexican-American songs.
17,114	1 10'' tape of migrant worker songs from California recorded by Mike Heisley, Joseph C. Hickerson, Robert B. Carneal, John E. Howell, and Ed Tittel at the Library of Congress, 1974.
17,607	1 10'' tape recorded by Judy Crane for the College of Idaho Folklore Archive, 1971.
18,712-18,721	10 7'' tapes recorded at the San Diego Folk Festival, April 16-20, 1975. Includes some Mexican-American selections.

VICTOR RED SEAL RECORDS

McCORMACK, JOHN, Tenor

Born in Athlone, Ireland, John McCormack early learned to sing the songs of his native land, but he had no reason to suspect that the voice he loved to use was exceptional. Induced to compete at the Dublin Musical Festival, however, he met with such success as enabled him, with the proceeds of a few other concerts, to go to Italy to study. After a successful début, followed with numerous other operatic appearances in Italy, he was engaged for Covent Garden, London, on October 15, 1907. His succeeding triumphs in America are well within memory. He has traveled the length and breadth of the land, and is everywhere received with tumultuous enthusiasm. Now an American citizen, John McCormack has come to be something of an "institution" in America, and he undoubtedly interprets in song the heart of the

McCORMACK

American people in a way peculiarly his own. Gifted with a voice of superb beauty, he can turn lightly from the most exacting of operatic airs to simple, haunting melodies that linger in the memory with the most treasured experiences of a lifetime.

THE McCORMACK RECORDS

		No.	Size	List p.
Adeste Fideles (Oh, Come, All Ye Faithful) *Latin*	with Trinity Choir	6607	12	$2.00
Allerseelen (All Souls' Day) (Op. 10, No. 8)	R. Strauss	1660	10	1.50
★Angel's Serenade *(Violin by Kreisler)*	Braga	8033	12	2.00
Annie Laurie	Douglass-Scott	1305	10	1.50
Auld Scotch Sangs (O Sing to Me the Auld Scotch Sangs)	Bethune-Leeson	1305	10	1.50
★Ave Maria *In Latin (Violin by Kreisler)*	Bach-Gounod	8032	12	2.00
★Ave Maria *(Violin by Kreisler)*	Schubert	8033	12	2.00
★Berceuse from Jocelyn *(Violin by Kreisler)*	Godard	8032	12	2.00
Bless This House	Brahe	1625	10	1.50
Charm Me Asleep	W. Sanderson	1649	10	1.50
Christ Went Up Into the Hills	Adams-Hageman	6708	12	2.00
Dear Old Pal of Mine	Robe—Gitz-Rice	1321	10	1.50
Garden Where the Praties Grow	arr. Liddle	1553	10	1.50
Hark! Hark! the Lark—Who Is Sylvia?	Shakespeare—Schubert	6926	12	2.00
Harp That Once Thro' Tara's Halls	Moore	1553	10	1.50
Hedge Roses	Goethe—Schubert	6926	12	2.00
Holy Child, The	Luther-Martin	1281	10	1.50
Holy Night (Schiller) The Trout—Impromptu—To the Lyre	Schubert	6926	12	2.00
I Hear You Calling Me	Harford-Marshall	1293	10	1.50
Ireland, Mother Ireland (From "Song O' My Heart")	O'Reilly—Loughborough	1452	10	1.50
Is She Not Passing Fair?	Elgar	1649	10	1.50
Just for Today	Partridge-Seaver	1281	10	1.50
Kathleen Mavourneen	Crawford-Crouch	6776	12	2.00
Little Boy Blue (from "Song O' My Heart")	Field-Nevin	1458	10	1.50
Love's Old Sweet Song	Bingham-Molloy	6776	12	2.00
Maison Grise, La (The Grey House) (from "Fortunio")	Messager	1660	10	1.50
Marchéta (Love Song of Old Mexico)	Victor L. Schertzinger	1247	10	1.50
Minnelied (Love Song) *German*	German Folk Song	1272	10	1.50
Moonlight and Roses	Black-Morét	1092	10	1.50
Mother Machree	Young-Olcott-Ball	1293	10	1.50
None But a Lonely Heart	Tschaikowsky	1306	10	1.50
Palms The (Les Rameaux)	Faure	6607	12	2.00
Panis Angelicus (Oh Lord Most Holy) *Latin*	Franck	6708	12	2.00
Prayer to Our Lady	Ford	1625	10	1.50
Rosary, The	Rogers-Nevin	1458	10	1.50
Roses of Picardy	Weatherly-Wood	1321	10	1.50
Rose of Tralee (from "Song O' My Heart")	Spencer-Glover	1452	10	1.50
Schlafendes Jesuskind (Sleeping Christ-Child) *German*	Morike-Wolf	1272	10	1.50
Schubert Album with Victor Salon Group and Orchestra Album C-3 (6927, 6928, 9307, 9308) List Price $7.00				
Silver Threads Among the Gold	Rexford-Danks	1173	10	1.50
Somewhere a Voice is Calling	Newton-Tate	1247	10	1.50
Sweetest Call	Troon-Morrow	1092	10	1.50
★Wearing of the Green	Old Irish Air	788	10	1.50
★When Irish Eyes are Smiling ("Isle of Dreams")	Olcott-Graff-Ball	788	10	1.50
When You and I Were Young, Maggie	Johnson-Butterfield	1173	10	1.50
Who is Sylvia?	Shakespeare-Schubert	1306	10	1.50

★ Indicates old acoustical method of recording.

Irish Ethnic Recordings and the Irish-American Imagination

Mick Moloney

Irish ethnic recordings have been made in America since the beginning of this century. Since they reflect the changing musical tastes of Irish-Americans, they offer useful insights into the changing shape of Irish-American identity and concerns between 1900 and the present time.

Irish commercial recordings can be conveniently divided into four major separate, though overlapping, categories that encompass both musical genre and performance style. The first category is represented by the body of song composed by nineteenth-century Anglo-Irish songwriters, who usually had been trained in the European classical traditions. The most prominent performer of this material in the twentieth century was the famous Irish tenor John McCormack. While Irish tenors had been performing in America for more than a hundred years prior to McCormack's emergence as a concert artist and recording star between 1904 and 1941, he represented the pinnacle of this tradition.[1] He was trained in bel canto in Milan and achieved eminence in Europe and America after his spectacularly successful concert tours between 1909 and 1912. His performances of Irish material were viewed with some disdain by his classically trained contemporaries, but it is for these that he is best remembered. He packed concert halls all over America with Irish and non-Irish audiences, singing a mixture of operatic selections along with songs like "Danny Boy," "The Kerry Dances," "The Rose of Tralee," "Mother Macree," and the beautiful lyrical creations of Thomas Moore.

Moore (1779–1852) has been one of the most influential of all Irish songwriters over the past two centuries. He wrote plaintive lyrical verses, mostly to ancient harp tunes notated by Edward Bunting from the playing of the last great Irish harpers.[2] His verses, characterized by Michael Turner as "the foundation stone of Victorian balladry,"[3] lamented the plight of the Irish nation, but in a very genteel and nonmilitant fashion. Paddy Galvin has described the tone of his protestations as a "great wail,"[4] and William Hazlitt remarked that Moore had "converted the wild harp of Erin into a musical snuff box."[5] His songs were indeed performed in genteel settings for the Anglo-Irish aristocracy, but through John McCormack they reached the Irish people as never before. "The Minstrel Boy," "The Harp That Once through Tara's Hall," "Dear Harp of My Country," "The Meeting of the

A description of one of McCormack's new recordings in the March 1920 *New Victor Records* illustrates the company's awareness of the Irish immigrant's nostalgia for the homeland. Music Division, Library of Congress.

John McCormack was born within 100 yards of the Castle and Bridge of Athlone

McCORMACK, JOHN

64837 That Tumble-Down Shack in Athlone   Pascoe-Carlo-Sanders
10-in. list price $1.00

John McCormack sings once more, this month, of his Irish homeland, in a song which carries with it the very spirit of desire for the things on "the other side of the world"—the long road of white cobblestones, gleaming pale in the night, and at the end of the road the tumble-down shack, with the single lamp in its window, lighted by the old mother to welcome the returning pilgrim. The song has a pleasant, flowing melody, gathering strength and beauty toward the close of each stanza, when there is a long, clear upper note of unusual sweetness and purity. Between the stanzas there is an exquisite violin obbligato as an interlude. This is one of the songs which have endeared Mr. McCormack to so many thousands on both sides of "the water," and contributed so to his fame as one of the great singers of modern times. Its peculiar significance to the artist lies in the fact that Athlone was his own birthplace, and that today, in the midst of his world-triumphs, he somehow yearns back to it every time its name reopens for him the rainbow gates of memory. And if memory cannot be shared with the singer by those who hear him, at least the inner vision can—the town and the bridge, beneath whose arches, without ceasing, the "River Shannon flows"; the castle, with its records and traditions, and, almost within the very shadow of its historied walls, the "tumble-down shack" itself.

8

Waters," "Oft in the Stilly Night," and "Believe Me If All Those Endearing Young Charms," became household songs both in Ireland and among the Irish in America. His composition "The Last Rose of Summer" sold more than one and a half million copies in America alone. Because McCormack was the first internationally recognized Irish tenor to perform Irish songs, he was instantly acceptable to all strata of the Irish-American communities.[6] His songs became a vital part of the cultural expression of an Irish population in America that was uneasily consolidating its position in American society, after the turbulent experience of adaptation from a rural to a hostile urban environment in the New World.

The second category of Irish-American recordings can be broadly described as the "Stage Irish" variety. The Stage Irishman, honed during two centuries in the English theater, had been readily incorporated into the burgeoning New York stage and music halls in the nineteenth century. The prototypical Stage Irishman is described by Maurice Bourgeois as the one who

> habitually bears the general name of Pat, Paddy or Teague. He has an atrocious Irish brogue, perpetually jokes, blunders and bulls in speaking, and never fails to utter, by way of Hibernian seasoning, some wild screech or oath of Gaelic origin at every third word: he has an unsurpassable gift of blarney and cadges for tips and free drinks. His hair is fiery red: he is rosy-cheeked, massive, and whiskey loving. His face is one of simian bestiality with an expression of diabolical archness written all over it. He wears a tall felt hat (billicock or wideawake), with a cutty-clay pipe stuck in front, an open shirt collar, a three caped coat, knee breeches, worsted stocking, and cockaded brogue-shoes. In his right hand he brandishes a stout blackthorn, or a sprig of shillelagh, and threatens to belabour therewith the daring person who will tread on the tails of his coat. For his main characteristics (if there is any such thing as psychology in the Stage Irishman) are his swagger, his boisterousness and his pugnacity. He is always ready with a challenge, always anxious to back a quarrel, and peerless for cracking skulls at Donnybrook Fair.[7]

This character was, in large part, the product of combined fear, suspicion, and ridicule. Given the anti-Irish climate so prevalent in mid-nineteenth-century urban America, it is not surprising that this grotesque stereotypical character should find an accommodating environment. Indeed, such was the position of the Irish in the social structure at the time when Edison made his first recordings that there were few other roles open to the Irish on the American stage. In his recent study of the Irish character in nineteenth-century American fiction, Stephen Garret Bolger concludes that because of the cumulative effects on public consciousness of the stereotyping of the Irish in English and American drama and fiction, the Irishman in the second half of the nineteenth century was "simply ineligible to become the hero of the novel." [8]

A glance at the published sheet music from 1850 onward shows that the Stage Irishman became quickly established here as well. Songs such as "Finnegan's Wake," "Lannigan's Shillelagh," "Gilhooley's Out of Jail," "Murphy's Wife," "No Irish Need Apply," and, of course, the creations of Harrigan and Hart have blundering Pat as the central character with shillelaghs, fisticuffs, and whiskey bottles in plentiful supply. The following text of "Paddy Miles" is a good illustration of the genre:

> From the big town of Limerick lately I came,
> I left Ireland solely bekase of my name,
> For if anything wint wrong, or a mischief 'twas done,
> Shure they'd have all the blame on my mother's own son

So my name now is Paddy O'Connor,
'Pon as Irishman's thrue word and honor,
Oh misfortune my curse light upon her,
'Twas she christened me Paddy Miles.

If a windy was broke, or a house robbed of tiles,
And you'd ax who done that, shure they say Paddy Miles,
Who was it set fire to his reverence's wig,
And cut the tail of Pat Flanigan's pig,
    Who called Mishes Muloney a scollop,
    And gave Biddy McGee's cat the jallop,
    Some blackguards would hit me a wollop,
    And say it was you, Paddy Miles.

I worked in the bogs and behaved as I thought,
From my master, Mick Flynn a character I brought,
But it done me no good and I thought that was odd,
So I made up my mind for to leave the ould sod,
    For the devel a wan would employ me,
    The girls there they would annoy me,
    They threatened at once to destroy me,
    All bekase I was called Paddy Miles.

Who cut off one of the tails of Pat Finegans coat,
And who broke the left horn of Ned Shoughnessy's goat,
Who through the back door to the chapel got in,
And drank all the wine, blood and ounds what a sin,
    Who half murdered a poor house inspector,
    And fired at a police detector,
    When Miss Fagan they tried to eject her,
    Who was it, but you, Paddy Miles.

I trotted to Dublin to look for a place,
Tho' they'd ne'er saw me there, faix, they all knew my face,
The jackeens kept calling meself to annoy,
There goes Paddy Miles, he's a Limerick boy,
    Till I flouished my sprig of shillely,
    An' smattered their gobs so genteely,
    When the blood it began to flow freely,
    Said I how do you like Paddy Miles.
In short before long, to this country I came,
An' found Paddy Miles here was the same,
If my name wasn't changed I was likely to starve,
For bad luck to the master could I sarve,
    So Paddy O'Connor it is made sir,
    An' if you want to get a smart blade sir,
    Be my soul then you need not be afraid, sir,
    For to hire me, I'm not Paddy Miles.[9]

The large number of Stage Irish songs that were recorded between 1900
and 1940 and subsequently incorporated into the song repertoire of hundreds
of Irish-American performers indicates that many of the Irish enjoyed this
kind of material. The fact that the central characters in songs like "Finne-

gan's Wake" clearly were not representative Irishmen did not appear to bother most of the Irish-Americans I have interviewed who sing these pieces. One singer, whose repertoire included two burlesque songs, "Finnegan's Wake" and "Johnny McEldoo," said, "Everyone knows that [the central characters] aren't real. . . . It's just a bit of fun." [10] The trickster element in these characters and the prevailing twinkle in the eye are perhaps what appeals most to the singers of these songs. We can view the buffoonery as a set of role expectations consciously acted out by Mick, Pat, or Tague with tongue very much in cheek.

Acceptance of this material was by no means unanimous among Irish-Americans, however. Gene Kelly, a seventy-one-year-old accordion player from County Kilkenny, now living in retirement on Long Island, tells how he used to take part in vigilante-style activities designed to stop Stage Irish productions, causing loud disruptions in theaters where they took place. He maintains that many of his contemporaries shared the same feelings and participated in the disturbances.

The third major category of Irish ethnic recordings is the body of traditional dance music played on instruments such as the fiddle, uilleann pipes, concertina, accordion, flute, tin whistle, tenor banjo, piano, and combinations thereof.[11] Some of the first recordings of this music in America were home cylinder recordings by the legendary Galway-born piper Patsy Touhey. Touhey made more than one hundred cylinders for private sale to pupils and enthusiasts, and the several that still survive in private collections form a priceless testimonial to his remarkable skills. Touhey was also the first Irish-born traditional musician to record commercially. Four of his best pieces were issued by Victor.[12] John J. Kimmel, an American-born accordion player of German ancestry, also made several fine recordings of Irish dance music for Columbia. However, it was not until 1913 that Columbia issued its first recordings of traditional music played by native Irish musicians. At the time, Irish communities clearly felt the need for such material. Justus O'Byrne DeWitt remembers the Irish musical scene in New York City then:

> My mother owned a record store in Manhattan, and Irish people were always coming in and asking for old favorites, like "The Stack of Barley." Well, she'd no records to give them because there weren't any. So she sent me up to Gaelic Park in the Bronx to find some musicians. There was always music there on Sundays. Well, I found Eddie Herborn and John Wheeler playing banjo and accordion, and they sounded great. So my mother went to Columbia, and they said that if she would agree to buy five hundred copies from them they would record Herborn and Wheeler. She agreed, and they both recorded "The Stack of Barley," and the five hundred records sold out in no time at all.[13]

The 1920s and 1930s saw the issuing of hundreds of traditional instrumental recordings by Victor, Columbia, and several minor companies. This era was most notable for the landmark recordings of the great trio of County Sligo fiddlers, James Morrison, Paddy Killoran, and Michael Coleman.

Morrison was born in Ballymote around 1891 and came to America in the 1920s. He lived in Boston for some years before moving to New York, where he made most of his recordings. He died in 1947.[14]

Patrick J. (Patsy) Touhey. From Capt. Francis O'Neill's *Irish Folk Music: A Fascinating Hobby* (Chicago: Regan Printing House, 1910).

Killoran was born in 1904, also in Ballymote, and emigrated to America in 1925. He worked as an elevator operator for several years and later ran a very successful bar in the Bronx. He founded his own orchestra, the Pride of Erin, and played in numerous Irish dance halls in the 1930s and 1940s. It was then that he made most of his recordings, both solo and with the band.[15]

The Classic Recordings of

Michael Coleman

Masterpieces by the Greatest Irish Fiddler of Our Time

A recent issue of Michael Coleman's recordings by the Shanachie Record Company. Courtesy of Richard Nevins.

Coleman, the most famous of the three, was born near Ballymote in 1891. He came to America in 1914. During his years in New York City, where he also was based, he recorded more than eighty sides for several companies, including Columbia, Victor, and Decca.[16] Since his death in 1945, his reputation has assumed heroic dimensions; stories and anecdotes about his exploits, musical and otherwise, abound in America and Ireland.

The recordings of these men, the finest Irish musicians of their time, and of some of their contemporaries, such as fiddler Paddy Sweeney, piper Tom Ennis, flute players John McKenna and Tom Morrison, and Dan Sullivan's Shamrock Band in Boston, had a profound influence on Irish traditional music both in America and back home in Ireland. They helped maintain and expand repertoires and created stylistic models that were emulated faithfully by new generations of musicians. John Vesey, a fine Sligo fiddler now living in Philadelphia, recalls that the arrival in his township of every new recording made by any of the great trio was eagerly awaited. When news came about a new record, John would travel into Tubercurry with his father on a cart carrying turf (peat) to market, buy the record, take it home, and, after listening to it several times, try to reproduce every nuance in the musician's playing. The influence of the recordings in America can be illustrated by an afternoon of music I recorded in Chicago in 1977, by fiddler Johnny McGreevy and uilleann piper Joe Shannon. At the end of the session I asked both men where they learned the tunes they had been playing. No fewer than 75 percent of the tunes, it turned out, had been learned from 78 rpm recordings. In addition, their playing style was very closely modeled on that of the musicians whose records they had listened to. Johnny, who was born in Chicago, was heavily influenced in his youth by the recordings of James Morrison. Joe, who was born in Ireland and came to Chicago at the age of nineteen, learned to play by listening to the Victor releases of Patsy Touhey. He would shut himself in a room alone for hours trying to figure out exactly what Touhey was doing on the pipes. With no piper to teach him in person, Joe developed some strikingly original methods of producing the same musical effects. He is now the last living exponent of the Touhey style (known in Ireland as "the American style"), and a constant stream of young pipers and enthusiasts visits him to marvel and learn.

The fourth and last category of Irish ethnic recordings can be loosely described as a hybrid, characterized by a mixture of elements from the other three categories, with a large dose of the popular American music of the day thrown in. This category is perhaps the most fascinating of all for the social researcher, in that the multifaceted strands of Irish-American[18] musical taste are clearly illustrated by the wide cross-section of material that was popular through the years. The musical arrangements were usually the product of performers who earned their living or supplemented their wages by playing for money at taverns, dance halls, weddings, parties, and concerts. Hundreds of groups were formed, with a wide range of vocal and instrumental lineups. I talked at some length with three musicians, Ed Reavy, Tommy Caulfield, and Gene Kelly, who performed in such ensembles in the 1930s and 1940s. All agreed that a band playing for money had to give the audiences "a little bit of everything." As Gene Kelly put it, "If you didn't, you weren't asked back the next night."[17] Thus it was not uncommon to see bands with an instrumental lineup that combined fiddle, flute, and accordion with saxophone, tuba, cornet, and drums, and a repertoire that could include such songs as "A Nation Once Again," "Danny Boy," "Did Your Mother Come from Ireland," "The Dear Little Shamrock," "Sweet Rosie O'Grady," "Daisy, Daisy," and "When Irish Eyes Are Smiling."

Many traditional musicians played in these bands, usually supplying the instrumental music for dancing—jigs, reels, hornpipes, polkas, and square dances—and playing a relatively minor role in the more popular material. Some good early examples of the music of these bands can be heard in the Victor recordings of John McGettigan and his various orchestras, and the Four Provinces Orchestra; the Columbia and Decca recordings of the Paddy Killoran Orchestra; and the Columbia recordings of O'Leary's Irish Minstrels.

The songs recorded by bands like these and by other Irish entertainers, such as John Griffin (the Fifth Avenue Busman), Patrolman Frank Quinn, the Flanagan Brothers, and tenors Shaun O'Nolan, Seamus O'Doherty, Michael Ahern, and George O'Brien, became the staple repertoire of three generations of Irish-Americans raised between the 1920s and 1950s. My cousin Kay Touhey, born in Boston, gave me a list of seventy Irish and Irish-American songs in her repertoire, fifty of which I was able to trace to Irish commercial recordings. She and her family and friends sang these songs at home, at parties and weddings, in the car traveling, and at all sorts of other social occasions where Irish people gathered. For her, the Irish songs of the era have always been a vital mechanisms for expressing her "Irishness." Like many of her contemporaries, she makes no distinction between native Irish and Irish-American songs; they are all simply "Irish."[18] Indeed, many Irish Americans have been extremely upset at hearing that such "Irish" songs as "I'll Take You Home Again, Kathleen," "If You're Irish Come into the Parlor," "My Wild Irish Rose," and "To-Ra-Loo-Ra-Loo-Ra" were composed in America, and by non-Irish composers at that! I saw one delightful fourth-generation Irish-American woman reduced to tears at a party when an

Paddy Cronin. From the jacket of "Kerry's Own Paddy Cronin," a 1977 reissue by Outlet Recording Co., LTD, in Belfast. Courtesy of Richard Nevins.

earnest young Celtophile pointed out how mistaken she was in thinking all those years that "Galway Bay" was an Irish song. This typical anecdote illustrates how potent this material is in the lives of hundreds of Irish-Americans I have come to know in the course of five years' research within Irish-American communities.

The major recording companies ceased putting out Irish ethnic recordings in the 1940s. Decca was the last company to pay them serious attention. A strong preference was shown for the commercial hybrid material represented by performers like the McNultys, a New York-based family, whose recordings have had a profound effect on New World Irish song repertoires in the 1950s, extending as far as the fishing villages of Newfoundland.[19]

Justus O'Byrne DeWitt sought to fill this gap in the Irish record market by founding the Copley Record Company in Boston in the late 1940s. During the next ten years, Copley issued a wide range of Irish and Irish-American material aimed mainly at the more commercial Irish market. Also featured on DeWitt's recordings were several fine pieces by Kerry fiddler Paddy Cronin, who emigrated to Boston in 1949. Interestingly, DeWitt decided to record Cronin, not because he thought his records would sell widely, but because "Cronin was the finest fiddler I heard since Coleman."[20] Though very little data is available, it is likely that over the years several A & R (artist-and-repertoire) men, or their prime contacts in the ethnic communities, shared DeWitt's concern for quality as well as for commercial appeal. Otherwise, it would be hard to explain why so many great musicians who played infrequently to a minority audience were recorded.

In the early 1960s, a new dimension was added to Irish recordings in America—one that has since had profound consequences for the development of Irish folksong performance. Three brothers from County Waterford named Clancy, and a friend from County Armagh named Tommy Makem, all actors by profession, were losing money on a small theater in New York City. The American urban folksong revival had produced a thriving coffee-house concert and folk club scene in New York at that time, and the young Irishmen hit upon the idea of running Irish folksong evenings at the theater in order to raise funds. They all remembered songs from their childhood, and since they came from musical families, they had no trouble getting a program together. They sang in unison, with occasional harmony, and this approach caught on immediately. Before long they had made their first LP, produced by Kenneth S. Goldstein and Diane Hamilton for Tradition Records, and were appearing on an ever-widening circuit of folk clubs and colleges. Prominent American musicians, such as Pete Seeger, Bruce Langhorne, and Eric Weissberg, joined them in sessions and on subsequent Columbia recordings, and their musical and singing arrangements improved rapidly. An appearance on the Ed Sullivan Show cast them into the national spotlight; according to Liam Clancy, only then did Irish-American audiences accept their music.[21]

Their style was characterized by a lusty, lively delivery, and the songs they chose were all Irish or Scottish folksongs or songs written by British and Irish composers in the folk idiom. This material was largely unfamiliar to Irish-Americans from the second generation onward, whose concept of Irish music had been developed largely by commercial Irish-American recordings and particularly the nostalgic, sentimental material made popular by singers like Bing Crosby and Dennis Day. However, as soon as the Clancy Brothers and Tommy Makem achieved national prominence, Irish-Americans began to take an active interest in these "new" songs, and in the men singing them. They were handsome, clean-cut Irish lads the likes of whom no respectable Irish-American could possibly object to; and here they were, the first Irish-born entertainers since John McCormack to achieve international recognition.

Columbia issued their records back in Ireland, and the new, vital, fresh approach to familiar folksongs caught on immediately. On their first tour of Ireland they played to packed houses everywhere and were greeted, as Liam Clancy recounted, with a hysteria akin to Beatlemania.[22] Their skill as actors enabled them to fashion a highly sophisticated, yet thoroughly informal, stage performance, which was likely to appeal to any audience.

Within months of their first tour, a whole folk music industry had been generated, centered in Dublin. Mirror-image groups mushroomed and found ready part-time employment in bars, belting out third-rate copies of Clancy Brothers songs, with untuneful guitar and banjo accompaniment. Many of these groups recorded with small local record companies or with Irish subsidiaries of the big international companies.

By the early 1970s, audiences in Ireland had begun to tire of the "ballad groups," who kept singing the same rehashed verisons of songs recorded by the Clancy Brothers or by the Dubliners, a colorful Irish group who combined personality, verve, and instrumental virtuosity with a unique singing style. By then, however this form of entertainment was catching on in America, and a stream of groups began coming over from Ireland, either on tour or to stay. They have found ready employment in Irish bars in New York, Boston, Chicago, and elsewhere, singing mainly a mixture of Irish rebel songs, drinking songs, and country-and-western pieces, the latter being ex-

The Molly Maguires on the AVOCA label. Motion Picture, Broadcasting, and Recorded Sound Division, Library of Congress.

An Irish rebel song from the 1920s. Courtesy of Pekka Gronow.

tremely popular in Ireland. The rebel songs all have one thing in common, a clearly expressed desire to rid Ireland forever of the British forces of occupation. Most of these songs are extremely militant—a quality that distinguishes them from the plaintive complaining of Thomas Moore's patriotic compositions. The most popular rebel repertoire is drawn from songs composed in the mid-nineteenth century, those written around the time of Ireland's fight for independence between 1916 and 1921, and recent compositions about the struggle in Northern Ireland. Even the recent pieces are written in the folk idiom, and many use familiar airs and formulaic textual devices common to the older body of rebel songs.

Much of this category of material is readily available to Irish-Americans through Avoca and REGO records distribution outlets in New York City. These companies, both formed in the 1960s, carry in stock a wide range of Irish material, mainly aimed at a general Irish-American audience. By contrast, two other Irish record companies formed in recent years, Schanachie (and its sister label, Morning Star) in New York and Innisfree/Green Linnet in Connecticut, have catalogs devoted almost entirely to traditional Irish music and song. The formation of these companies has coincided with a massive revival of interest in Irish traditional music in America. The impetus for this revival can be traced in part to the success in Ireland of a strongly nativistic musical organization called Comhaltas Ceolteoiri Eireann (the Musicians' Association of Ireland).

The Irish Tradition, one of the traditional Irish bands performing in the Washington, D.C. area, on the Innisfree/Green Linnet label. Motion Picture, Broadcasting, and Recorded Sound Division, Library of Congress.

Comhaltas was founded in 1951 by a small group who sought to revive interest and participation in Ireland's traditional music, song, and dance, which they felt to be in grave danger of extinction at the hands of modernization. The efforts of Comhaltas, assisted on one hand by the urban folksong revival boom sparked by the Clancy Brothers and Tommy Makem, and on the other by the pioneering musical arrangements of Sean O'Riada, a classically trained folk music arranger, met with spectacular success. By the late 1960s, traditional music was being played all over Ireland, including areas where the music appeared to have died out many years earlier. Comhaltas established ties with the traditional musicians' organizations in America, and before long the revival had spread to the United States. At present, according to older Irish-Americans, more musicians are playing Irish music in America than ever before.

The musicians playing Irish music can be divided into roughly three categories. First, there are the first-generation Irish immigrants, many of whom played infrequently for years, but who are now playing again with renewed vigor and skill. Second, there is a large group of young American musicians, with no Irish ancestry at all, who have been drawn to Irish music by hearing visiting Irish musicians at folk clubs and festivals or on recordings. The third and largest category is represented by young Irish-Americans who learn their skills in organized Irish music schools from older, usually Irish-born, traditional musicians. This method of transmitting skills arose because of the dispersion of Irish communities in the major metropolitan areas since the 1950s; the Old World method of learning from family, friends, and neighbors in one's community is generally no longer possible in this new situation. There are thousands of such young musicians, mostly distributed around the suburbs of New York and Chicago.

The three groups together form a network of musicians across the United States. Given the vast distances involved, it is not surprising that transmission of tunes and songs is effected almost entirely by published tune collections, by phonograph records, and, most of all, by cassette recordings. The cassette recorder has revolutionized the process of acquiring repertoires and styles and has contributed more than any other technological phenomenon to the emergence of the new breed of young "super musicians" playing Irish material. Practically every session of Irish music I have attended or participated in during the last four years in America has been punctuated by the clicking of cassette recorder buttons. One consequence has been that the average Irish musician now has a repertoire that older musicians, who had to learn by ear (and more often than not had perhaps only one or two opportunities to learn an unfamiliar tune played by a visiting musician), consider massive. The mobility of these cassette recordings is astonishing. In spring, 1974, I made a friend a cassette copy of a recording that Kenneth S. Goldstein and I had made in Ireland of two outstanding young musicians. By autumn of the same year I had personally come across sixteen copies, all originating from that one cassette, and I have since heard of numerous others from Boston to San Francisco. There is also a brisk trade in cassettes between musicians in Ireland and in America, and word of a promising young musician usually spreads like wildfire across the Atlantic.

The generic divisions I have made in this overview should not be considered discrete categories. There has always been an overlap, and a number of recordings could be considered as belonging to two or more categories.

However, viewing them as basically separate domains helps us understand the changing patterns in Irish-American musical taste. To understand the symbolic importance of music, song, and dance in Irish-American life, it is necessary to look at the history of the Irish peasantry, living in dire poverty for several hundred years under conditions of colonial exploitation and repression that effectively denied education and upward social mobility. In that context only certain kinds of cultural expression were possible. The graphic arts, for example, which flourished so magnificently in ancient Celtic society, were not part of Irish cultural expression under British colonial rule. Ecological and political conditions militated against anything more than stark simplicity in folk architectural forms and other aspects of material culture.

It is not surprising, therefore, that the creative genius of the Irish peasantry found expression through such cultural vehicles as folktales, instrumental music, song, and dance. The richness of these traditions is well illustrated

A cassette recorder documents Kevin Henry offstage at the 1977 Annual Midwest *Fleadh Cheoil* Music Competition at a Chicago high school. Photograph by Jonas Dovydenas, American Folklife Center, Library of Congress.

by the vast holdings in the archives of the Folklore Department of University College, Dublin, and the folk music archives of Dublin's Department of Education.

The same pattern has manifested itself among the Irish in America. Though little real ethnography has been done in Irish-American communities, recent research and many discussions with older Irish immigrants indicate that traditional Irish crafts and foodways have not survived in the New World. Yet music, song, and dance *have* survived, and the continued strength and vitality of these traditions indicate a powerful symbolic function in the overt expression of Irishness in America. The complex historical and contemporary relationship between choice of song material and Irish-American social structure is something we know little about, simply because it is an area of the Irish-American experience that has not been addressed by scholars. The fact that there is such a wide spectrum of Irish music popular among different strata of the Irish in America is highly significant. It is hardly surprising that large numbers of immigrant Irish at the turn of the century,

Without a language barrier, Irish records always had appeal for the general audience. *Talking Machine World*, March 1928, page 26. Motion Picture, Broadcasting, and Recorded Sound Division, Library of Congress.

Push Irish Records

When this issue of The Talking Machine World is received by dealers but two days remain to make preparations to increase record business by featuring Irish records, taking advantage of the occasion of St. Patrick's Day. Of course, to secure the greatest benefits dealers should have started their campaigns to sell these records weeks before, but if, for some reason or other, this has been neglected, repair the damage as much as possible by dressing your window in an appropriate manner with records of Irish songs, by Irish artists, featured. That there is a tremendous market for music of Ireland is well evidenced by the fact that practically every record manufacturer has a special catalog of Irish recordings and that advertisements and display matter featuring this type of music are used regularly. The music of the Gael has an appeal that is international, for the lilting strains are known and loved not only by Irish-born and their descendants but by all races.

who were striving to better their lot, should reject a traditional music that was associated with a low-status, poverty-stricken peasant environment. That they should accept with open arms the crafted performances of John McCormack seems perfectly understandable, as was their subsequent gravitation toward a body of nostalgic sentimental song that painted a rosy, romantic scenario of a little green haven nestling in a corner of paradise. The eclectic, hybrid range of Irish ethnic recordings between the 1920s and 1950s is placed in cultural context when one looks at the heterogeneity of Irish communities in this period. First-generation Irish immigrants lived beside third- and fourth-generation Irish-Americans; and, aided by a combination of political, religious, fraternal, and social institutions, they gradually achieved access to more and more avenues of upward and lateral social mobility.

The revival of the older Irish traditional instrumental music in America in the 1970s assumes added significance when one discovers that the thousands of Irish-American youngsters involved in learning this music are the sons and daughters of first-generation Irish-Americans who came here mainly in the late 1940s and early 1950s. The majority of these later immigrants retain very strong contacts with Ireland. For the most part, they were not driven out by the dire poverty that forced their forebears to leave Ireland, but came by choice, "to better themselves." Many intended to go back, but, once they had found work, married, and begun to raise a family, they found it impossible. Cheaper air-charter travel, higher incomes, and the availability of more leisure time, however, have enabled these immigrants to make regular visits back to Ireland. Most have close relatives still living here, so all in all, their relationship to Ireland is markedly different from that of previous generations of immigrants who never went back. Many of these first-generation Irish-Americans feel it absolutely crucial that their children retain their Irishness, and they see in music a powerful mechanism for doing this. Noel Rice, who is president of the Francis O'Neill School of Music in Chicago, and has two children who are learning the fiddle, describes the music as "the mortar that holds [Irish culture] together."[23] It seems fitting that many of the contemporary canons of excellence should have been forged in America and carried back to Ireland by the recordings of the great emigrant musicians.

It may be useful, then, to look at the various categories of Irish ethnic recordings as affording a unique insight into the concerns and values of successive generations of Irish-Americans who adapted to changing conditions in America in the twentieth century. No other symbolic domain throws more light on the complex process of identity management among the Irish in America. I have suggested some general relationships, but they are more in the nature of hypotheses than conclusions. A thorough treatment would need to draw upon the field and library research of social, ethnic, and urban historians, as well as sociologists, folklorists, musicologists, anthropologists, and popular culture scholars. This research is in its infancy.

Notes

1. For biographical information, see *John McCormack: His Own Life Story*, ed. John Scarry (1918; reprint ed., New York: Vienna House, 1973), and Leonard Alfred George Strong, *John McCormack: The Story of a Singer* (New York: Macmillan, 1941).

2. See Edward Bunting, *The Ancient Music of Ireland* (1796; reprint ed., Dublin: Waltons, 1969).

3. Michael R. Turner, *The Parlour Song Book* (New York: Viking, 1972), p. 216.

4. Patrick Galvin, *Irish Songs of Resistance* (New York: Oak Publications, 1962), p. 81.

5. Quoted in ibid., p. 77.

6. For a complete listing of McCormack's records, see Leonard F. McDermott Roe, *The John McCormack Discography* (Lingfield, England: Oakwood Press, 1972).

7. Maurice Bourgeois, *John Millington Synge and the Irish Theatre* (London: Constable, 1913), quoted in George Chester Duggan, *The Stage Irishman* (Dublin: Talbot Press, 1937), pp. 288–89.

8. Stephen Garret Bolger, "The Irish Character in American Fiction 1930–60" (Ph.D. diss., University of Pennsylvania, 1971), quoted in Denis Clark, "The Irish in the Movies: A Tradition of Permanent Slur," in *Ethnic Images in American Film and Television* (Public Committee for the Humanities in Pennsylvania, 1978).

9. Broadside, H. DeMarsan, New York, reprinted in Robert L. Wright, ed., *Irish Emigrant Ballads and Songs* (Bowling Green, Ohio: Bowling Green University Popular Press, 1975), pp. 587–88.

10. John Rooney, personal communication, Sept. 16, 1977, Philadelphia.

11. For a good historical overview of the development of this music see Brendan Breathnach, *Folk Music and Dances of Ireland* (Dublin: Talbot Press, 1971).

12. A reissue of Touhey's "Morning Star," "Miss McLeod," "Main on the Green," "Jackson's Jig," and "A Drink of Water" can be heard on *The Wheels of the World*, Shanachie SH 33001.

13. Justus O'Byrne DeWitt, taped interview with Mick Moloney, Apr. 4, 1977, Dedham, Mass.

14. Some of Morrison's recordings are reissued on *The Pure Genius of James Morrison*, Shanachie 33004.

15. Some of Killoran's recordings are reissued on *Pady Killoran's Back in Town*, Shanachie SH 33003.

16. For reissued Colemand material, see *The Legacy of Michael Coleman*, Shanachie SH 33002; Michael Coleman and the McNulty Family, *Irish Dance Party*, Ace of Hearts AH 95; *Irish Jigs and Reels*, Ace of Hearts AH 56; *The Heyday of Michael Coleman*, Intrepid Records [no number; matrix C3RM 0459–0450 SP]; *The Musical Glory of Old Sligo as Interpreted by Michael Coleman*, IRC 3327; *Irish Popular Dance*, Folkways FW 6818.

17. Gene Kelley, taped interview with Mick Moloney, Mar. 10, 1978, Ronkonkoma, Long Island, N.Y.

18. Kay Touhey, taped interview with Mick Moloney, Apr. 11, 1978, Hackensack, N.J.

19. Wilf Wareham, personal communication, 1975, St. John's, Newfoundland.

20. DeWitt, interview, Apr. 11, 1978.

21. Liam Clancy, taped interview with Mick Moloney, June 24, 1978, Leeds, N.Y.

22. Ibid.

23. Noel Rice, interview with Mick Moloney, May 23, 1977, Chicago.

LIDYA
(GUAPANGO)

HOMENAJE A LA SRITA.
LIDYA MENDOZA
POR EL
DIRECTOR DEL CUARTETO
MICHOACANO,
AGUSTIN MENDOZA

Ni muy alta, ni bajita,
soy de un cuerpo regular
Soy sencilla, visto humilde
y mi trato es siempre igual.

Soy de rango muy humilde
más alegre en mi cantar.
Y yo canto a todo mundo,
la canción del arrabal.

Mal hombre, que no tiene ..
Todos dicen: quién es Lidya?
Todos hablan, quién será?
Mas yo d'go, no soy nadie,
No presumo y nada más!

Cancionera de los pobres,
Cancionera nada más,
Mi guitarra, compañera
de mis cantos de arrabal.

Mal hombre!
Mi voz no es de lo más linda,
ni estudié a cantar con nadie
sólo canto porque quiero
expresar lo que yo siento.

Mi madre me dió la vida,
y por ella es por quien canto,
con sonrisas o con llanto,
con sonrisas o con llanto!

Cancionera de los pobres,
cancionera nada más,
mi guitarra, compañera
de mis cantos de arrabal.
Mal hombre.....

Me despido sin recelos,
me despido con amor,
y el aplauso más sincero,
lo guardo en mi corazón.

CUARTETO MICHOACANO

Agustin Mendoza

Cruz Arizmendiz

Manuel Orozco

Heriberto Campos

Lydia Mendoza: An Enduring Mexican-American Singer

James S. Griffith

Cancionera de los pobres

Cancionera nada más

These words were used in the mid-1930s to describe a remarkable woman who was then well embarked upon a career that has lasted for more than forty years and that shows no real signs of slowing down. More than four decades later, Lydia Mendoza of Houston, Texas, remains as she was described in Augustin Mendoza's "Lydia Huapango": "Singer for the poor people / Just a singer, that's all." Many folk and ethnic artists of the 1920s and 1930s have experienced new careers in recent years thanks to the heightened interest in our vernacular music. Others can claim the same audience—and in some cases, the same individual fans—after a fifty-year career. Lydia Mendoza belongs to this latter group. To be sure, she has also played and sung for young Anglo-American audiences at folk festivals; her reactions to that experience appear below. Her real audience remains, however, what it apparently was in San Antonio in the early thirties: la gente humilde—the Mexican-American working people. When she visits southwestern towns outside her native South Texas, the first reaction is often the same as it was in California in 1947—surprise that she is still alive. After that, the crowds turn out in large numbers. Her rapport with her público is just what one would expect after reading her statements in this article. I have heard her give a show in Tucson during which she sang one song of her own choosing and then honored requests for half an hour.

The story that follows, then, is that of a still-active historical figure in the world of Mexican-American popular entertainment. May her perspective contribute to the understanding of one fascinating aspect of cross-cultural interaction in the United States, the Mexican-American entertainment industry.

In this article Lydia Mendoza tells her story in her own words and in her own language. As she remarks at the end, she has given us just a bare sketch. I was primarily concerned with taking down the details of her career as she sees it, rather than as I might wish to hear about it in my roles as scholar, fan, or record collector. I did ask a few questions and suggest a few topics; her responses follow the main narrative and are concerned with Lydia's perception of her music and her audience.

The account raises several fascinating questions that it does not pretend to answer. For example, Lydia Mendoza's memory that her first great hit,

A song written in honor of Lydia Mendoza by a fellow musician. Courtesy of James S. Griffith.

"Mal Hombre," was recorded at her first Bluebird session does not agree with the available data from the Victor files, which show it to have been recorded at a second session, later in the same year. However, it was apparently the first of her records to be released. Such details, fascinating and important though they may be, do not really matter in this particular context. This is an exercise in the art of artistic autobiography; it is Lydia Mendoza's story.

Before embarking upon the narrative, it might be useful to outline Lydia's career:

1916	Lydia Mendoza is born in Houston, Texas.
1926	The Mendoza family is in Monterrey, Mexico.
1927-28	The Mendoza family, calling itself "El Cuarteto Carta Blanca" at times, performs professionally in the lower Rio Grande Valley.
1928	El Cuarteto Carta Blanca makes ten records for OKeh in San Antonio.
1928-30	The Mendozas live in Detroit, Michigan, working as professional musicians.
1930-34	The Mendozas return to Texas, eventually coming to San Antonio and playing in the Plaza del Zacate, or public market. Lydia starts singing solo and appears on radio.
1934-40	Lydia Mendoza cuts just under 200 sides for Bluebird and tours extensively in the Hispanic Southwest.
1940-47	Lydia lives in semi-retirement in San Antonio.
1947-77	Lydia's career enters its second phase, with more touring, work in Mexico, and recordings on the Falcon, Ideal, Victor, and Columbia labels.
1971	Lydia makes her first folk festival appearance, at the Smithsonian Festival of American Folklife in Montreal, Canada.
1977	Lydia appears as a performer and panelist at the Library of Congress conference Ethnic Recordings in America.
1979	Lydia gives concerts in Alaska and Columbia.

La Alondra de la Frontera

Lydia Mendoza

Bueno, comenzaré con decirle que casi yo creo desde que yo nací, nací con la vocación de la música. Porque me recuerdo que tendría exactamente como unos cuatro años cuando yo ya empezaba sentir el impulso para le música. Tomando en cuenta que mi madre tocaba la guitarra y siempre en la casa después de la cena, después de que ella y mi papá ya descansaban, siempre agarraba mi madre su guitarra y empezaba a tocar y a cantar, porque desde luego ella también tenía una voz muy preciosa. Personas que la conocieron a ella ahora me dicen que yo heredé su timbre de voz. En aquellas familias, digamos principalmente de allá de México, porque mi madre era de San Luís Potosí, siempre querían que las niñas aprendieran algo, y mi abuela—la madre di mi mamá—tocaba la guitarra. La mamá de mi abuelita enseñó a mi abuelita, y mi abuelita enseñó a mi mamá. Ella no tuvo maestros, no fué al colegio ni nada de eso, sino que supo tocar guitarra porque mi abuelita le enseñó. Y yo sé tocar la guitarra porque mi madre me enseñó a mí.

Como yo le decía antes, yo no más oía pulsar la guitarra y si andaba jugando, corría y me sentaba a sus pies. Era tanto que me gustaba la música que yo quería—en ese edad yo ya quería tocar la guitarra y se lo decía a mi madre que yo quería tocar como ella, y me decía que cuando mis manos me crecieran entonces ella me iba a enseñar—¡y así fué! Pasaron los años y cuando tenía unos—no tenía los siete años cuando empecé otra vez a insistir con mi madre que me enseñara. Ella creía que eran cosas de niños, ya ve—un chamaquito ve una guitarra y quiere sonarle las cuerdas—pues que yo sentía que yo quería tocarla. Y Diosito me lo concedió, porque ella me empezó a poner clases de guitarra, a enseñarme lo poco que sabía. Cuando ya tenía unos ocho, nueve años, ya tocaba perfectamente la guitarra.

No vivíamos de eso cuando la familia estaba mas chica (porque fuimos diez de familia). Mi padre trabajaba y todo. Pero al correr del tiempo, pues yo fuí el eje principal para la música porque como a mí me gustaba, pues yo quería que todos mis hermanos supieran también. Empecé a enseñar a mi hermana María a tocar la guitarra. Entonces yo hice por aprender el violín— bueno, primeramente la guitarra, y luego la mandolina y después el violín. Entonces yo fuí inculcando en el corazón de mis hermanas la música también. Y a ellas, pues yo creo que también les gustaba porque todas aprendieron a tocar instrumentos, y entre ellas formamos un grupo. Mi madre tocaba la guitarra, yo tocaba el violín, y una de mis hermanas la mandolina, y uno de mis hermanos un triangulito, y mi papá tocaba una pandereta. Así es que formamos un grupo y entonces ya nos dedicamos de lleno a vivir la vida de la música. Empezamos en todo el Valle de Texas, y luego fuimos hasta Detroit, Michigan, siempre con la música.

Vivimos un año en todo el Valle de Texas—en McAllen, en Wéslaco, en Edinburg, en Kingsville. Vivíamos una temporada en un pueblito—allí estábamos y luego nos íbamos a otro y así. En aquellos años no habían cantinas, no había cerveza, no había nada de eso. Tocábamos en restaurantes, en las barberías. Llegaba mi papá y pedía permiso—los sábados principalmente que estaba la gente—que había gente nos sentábamos y cantábamos y . . . lo que regalaron la gente! Y luego, pues que venían los tiempos de las piscas cuando nos íbamos a los pueblitos donde estaban los piscadores, donde había reuniones así de mexicanos, y allí cantábamos y allí juntábamos nuestros centavos.

En aquellos años, a la edad que yo tenía, pues para mí todo estaba bien, verdad, pues yo no más pensaba en que tuviéramos el medio para vivir y para comer y . . . Sí, me daba mucha vergüenza ir a las barberías, principalmente porque habían muchos hombres—me daba pena. Y los restaurantes no. Pues fué dura la vida. Afanamos mucho así. Por eso ahora digo yo, ya comencé mi carrera desde muy abajito, muy abajo, con muchos afanes, mucho sufrimiento. A veces no teníamos para comer y nos teníamos que esperar hasta juntar los centavos para ir a comernos una taza de café en aquellos años. Así pasé yo mi niñez. Y luego mi juventud fué lo mismo. Claro que ya cuando yo grabé mi disco y que empezó gustar mi nombre y que empezamos a tener muchos buenos contratos, pues ya cambió nuestra vida y modo de vivir. Pero al principio siete años afanamos mucho. Sufrimos mucho. Pedíamos favores que nos llevaran a otros pueblitos a trabajar y había veces que fracasábamos.

Primeramente después de que ya formamos ese grupo nos gustó a todos la música, entonces ya nos dedicamos por completo a la música. Entonces ya ésto era nuestro vivir. De eso vivíamos, y andábamos cantando en fiestas y en diferentes lugares. Cantábamos canciones de aquella época—"El Rancho Grande," Las Cuatro Milpas," "El Mundo Engañoso," pues muchas canciones. Cantábamos lo que andaba de moda en esa época. Mi mamá cantaba, porque tenía una voz muy bonita, "El Viejo Amor," el "Sole Mio"—canciones muy bonitas. Cuando estábamos en todo el Valle de Texas, una vez salió un anuncio en *La Prensa* de aquel tiempo, que era muy popular aquí. Salió un anuncio que estaban pidiendo artistas que cantaran para grabar en la marca OKeh. Entonces nosotros hicimos el viaje con muchos sacrificios, porque pues no teníamos nosotros carro, ni teníamos manera de viajar, ni dinero, pero buscó mi papá un amigo que tenía un carrito viejo y él fué que nos hizo el favor de traernos a San Antonio, y llegamos y nos dieron diez discos. Entre ellos incluimos "El Rancho Grande," "El Adolorido," "Las Cuatro Milpas." Tengo una copia que me mandó el Dick Spottswood donde está "Las Cuatro Milpas" con "El Corrido de Monterrey." Grabamos las grabaciones y luego nos fuimos para el norte y no duramos aquí arriba de tres semanas. Nunca los oímos nosotros. Tenía diez años. Por las diez grabaciones nos dieron $140. Por diez discos, que son veinte canciones. No era mucho dinero pero para nosotros lo más grande fué la satisfacción de que queríamos grabar el grupito. Fué en un hotel.

Nos fuimos a Michigan en aquellos años—fué por el año de 1928. Toda

El Cuarteto Carta Blanca in 1928. Left to right: Leonor Mendoza (mother), Lydia Mendoza with mandolin, Francisco Mendoza (father), and Francisca Mendoza, Lydia's younger sister. Courtesy of Lydia Mendoza.

aquella gente que vivía por allá pues estaba deseosa de oír algo mexicano. Cuando nosotros llegamos al estado de Michigan, hicimos furor la familia, tocando, cantando. Tuvimos mucho trabajo allá, y allá anduvimos por dos años. Estuvimos en Detroit. Y luego ya nos regresamos otra vez aquí a Houston. Y aquí vivimos. En 1930 llegamos aquí otra vez. Pero Houston en aquellos años estaba muy . . . no había mucho ambiente, no habían estaciones de radio, no había nada. Estaba muy triste. Entonces buscábamos siempre donde hubiera ambiente, y nos vinimos para acá, para San Antonio. Aquí en San Antonio empezábamos. Durábamos àfanando dos años, trabajando, cantando, en la Plaza del Zacate, que ya no existe ahora—que ya lo quitaron. Había un mercado muy grande, pero de aire libre. Allá en la noche de las doce de la noche en adelante era el mercado donde llegaban todas las trocas que venían del Valle y donde quiera, que traían verduras. Entonces estaban allí desde las doce hasta como las diez o once de la mañana. Y ya se iban, y quedaba solo aquello. Entonces a las siete de la noche entraban todos los que iban a vender allí—ponían mesas como restaurantes. Cada lugarcito ponía sus mesas y vendían chile con carne, enchiladas, tamales—pero habían muchos. En cada lado habían como unos veinte acá, veinte allá, y quedaban en el medio donde entraban los carros pues a comer o a oír canciones, porque habían muchos grupos que cantaban allí en aquellos años. Y allí fué donde hicimos nuestro vivir.

Y ya por ese tiempo entonces ya empezaba yo cantar sola. Allá era cuando dije a mi madre "Déme la guitarra" y cantaba yo aunque no me pidiera la gente. Pero empezaban a oír mi voz y me puso a gustarles y ya casi en grupo ni cantábamos. Y así fué como me escuchó un señor de radio de aquí. Era el unico programa que había en San Antonio, Texas, en aquellos años—"La Voz Latina," no más media hora.

Entonces ya mi nombre empezó a popularizarse primero. En la estación de radio empezaron a oírme. Ya para cuando vino una compañía a grabar que yo ni sabía me llevaron, y me dieron dos discos. Fué mi bandera, "Mal Hombre." Fué la primera grabación, "Mal Hombre," que hasta la fecha—han pasado más de cuarenta años, y esa canción vive en el corazón del público. Porque no hay noche que yo me presente que no la pidan. "Mal Hombre," "Al Pie de tu Reja," y luego "El Pajarito Herido" y "Mundo Engañoso"—fueron no más dos discos.

No sé de quien es ["Mal Hombre"] y hasta la fecha no ha aparecido el compositor. Mucha gente cree que es mía, pero no. Pues, ¿porqué decir, "Sí, es mía," si no es? Me acuerdo que yo creo que me la aprendí de unas chicles que vendían en Monterrey. Venía en cada chicle una canción y a mí me parece que allí venía esa canción. Y así la aprendí. Eso fué en 1926. Y yo la aprendí como cualquier canción y cuando fuí a grabar, pues la grabé. Dije "Bueno, yo voy a grabar esta." Porque desde el momento que empecé a cantar esta canción al público, le empezó a gustar.

Me dieron dos discos y me pagaron $15—$7 por cada disco. Yo, encantada de la vida. Y ya grabé y me fuí par mi casa. Pero a los tres meses, bueno cuando salió el disco, fué un impacto. Fué un éxito grandísimo. Y luego, luego a los tres meses ya estaban en la casa donde vivía con mi papá porque yo estaba señorita—todavía no me casaba. Hicieron contrato. Entonces le dijeron que querían agarrarme con contrato para que no fuera yo a grabar con nadie. Que me daban $40 y dos centavos de regalía o me pagaban $50, y no me daban regalía. Y mi papá dijo que no, que mejor me pagaban $50 no más y que estaba bueno. Oh, ¡si hubiera grabado a regalías, "Mal Hombre" me hubiera hecho muy rica!

Seguí grabando con ellos. Entonces pasé el año de 1934, y nunca recibimos nada de reporte. Pasó el año y yo me casé en marzo de 1935. Como a dos semanas de estar yo casada fué cuando fueron a mi casa una que trabajaba en la casa de música [San Antonio Music Company], la señora T——, y él que había venido a grabarnos, que se llamaba M——. Ella fué el intérprete de todas las artistas y todo . . . Y vinieron que como yo ya me había casado que ahora le pertenecía firmar el contrato a mi esposo, porque ya estaba casada. Y entonces, bueno, firmamos, ni yo no me fijé, ni mi marido, pues él no hablaba inglés. Firmamos y lo que sí noté cuando acabamos de firmar nos dieron $10, que porque habíamos firmado fué todo. Resulta que ellos hicieron mal—el contrato que traían no era tal contrato como me habían dicho porque me había casado, sino que yo les cedía las primeras regalías. Que yo y mi esposa estábamos de acuerdo en cederles los dos centavos que me habían dado por "Mal Hombre" y la otra canción al Sr. M—— porque él me había grabado por la primera vez. El fué que se quedó con el dinero. Entonces hablé con los de la Victor pero no me hicieron caso. Trataron de buscar a M—; M—— ya no estaba trabajando con ellos. Se había ido para Alemania. Son cosas de la vida. Pues, y han pasado tantos años, pues, ya . . . Probablemente si se hubiera hecho algo pronto, pero pues ya . . . son historias que han quedado, no más.

Seguí con Bluebird desde 1934 hasta 1940. Allá empezaron a salir muchos contratos para afuera, para Corpus, pues luego hasta California y . . . Que por cierto al principio batallé mucho, porque como mi nombre empezó a conocerse mucho entre la gente mexicana y todo. Pero las empresas de los teatros, pues no sabían quien era Lydia Mendoza. Pues, era Lydia Mendoza muy famosa pero ellos pues no sabían quien era. Entonces no nos daban trabajo en los teatros—íbamos y pedíamos que nos dieran y no nos daban. Entonces nos dedicábamos a trabajar en los salones de las iglesias. Y cuando trabajábamos—no, ¿pues para que negar?—no más era de llegar a un pueblito y agarrar dinero. Teníamos mucho éxito en todo donde nos presentábamos. Y ya fué corriendo el tiempo—entonces, llegamos hasta El Paso, Texas. Pues también la primera vez que trabajé en El Paso fué en un salón de un iglesia. Entonces, fuimos a saludar al Sr. Calderón que era de los que tenían los teatros en aquellos años—El Teatro Colón. Y fuimos a saludarle y el señor, pues, me apreciaba muy bien—ya había oído mis discos. Y él sí no hizo el favor de darnos oportunidad en el teatro. Y luego, él dijo que me iba a ayudar mucho, y a él le debo de que siguiéramos nosotros nuestras giras en teatros, porque él fué que les hablaba de mí. Y me ayudó mucho en El Paso, Texas, en 1936. A puros cines, a Las Cruces y todo anduvimos porque un empresa se reportaba el show de Lydia Mendoza y pues decía que tuviera buenas entradas, y entonces todos nos fueron abriéndonos puertas—todos los cines y así fué como comenzamos. Yo mi carrera casí la dediqué pues a este lado. En México sí, he visitado México, he estado en México también trabajando, pero más aquí en los Estados Unidos.

Radio publicity photograph taken in 1938 in Cuidad Juarez, Chihuahua, Mexico. Courtesy of Lydia Mendoza.

Bueno, en esos años yo estuve grabando con la Victor—la Bluebird que era la Victor—hasta 1940. En 40, me mandaron un nuevo contrato porque yo estaba así a un año, y un año de opción, y ya no más iba a llegar el año de opción y me mandaban los contratos para que los firmara para seguir trabajando. Entonces, ya el último año que grabé fué el 40. Me mandaron decir que lo sentían mucho pero ya se iban a parar las grabaciones por cuestiones de la guerra. Que ya no iban a poder seguir grabando por los materiales y muchas cosas que se escasiaron. Pero ellos estaban muy agradecidos y muy contentos pero que terminándose que si acababa podía entonces volvernos a comenzar de vuelta. Y así fué. Terminé de grabar con ellos. Entonces, seis años estuve . . . no inactiva, digamos, porque aquí en San Antonio me radicaba, me señor y mis niñas chiquitas. Y ya pues me dediqué a mi hogar, y cantaba en festividades así que habían, verdad, pero no salí afuera. Giras no hice. Y yo pensaba que ya mi carrera ya había terminado y ¿porqué? pues seis años ya sin salir en giras y todo eso y sin hacer grabaciones. Entonces, yo estaba muy tranquila en mi hogar.

Pero, en 47, viene una persona, un empresario de California y andábamos yo y mi madre en el pueblo y me encontró. Y luego me dijo pues "¿Porqué no comenzamos a hacer una gira otra vez?" Entonces, ya le dije yo que no, que, "ya . . . habían pasado muchos años y . . ." Dijo "Yo me voy a volver a revivir a Lydia Mendoza"—y así lo hizo. Me sacó un contrato en California que por cierto ya ni lo creían que era Lydia Mendoza. Pues, habían pasado seis años . . . creían que hasta me había muerto. No, pues, fué un éxito. Comenzó mi segunda época otra vez, del 47 y hasta la fecha.

Empecé a grabar de nuevo precisamente en 1947 cuando yo llegé a esa presentación que me presentaron en el Cine California en Los Angeles. Pues luego, luego en aquel tiempo estaban grabando mucho los discos Azteca en California, y luego, luego me fueron a ver que fuera a grabar. Entonces fué cuando empecé a grabar otra vez—con ellos, con contrato. Entonces a mí ya me daban contrato. Y después, la Victor vinieron aquí a San Antonio, a mi casa, que pues ya querían volver otra vez a comenzar a grabarme, pero yo, pues, ya no podía—tenía contrato. Entonces, empecé a grabar con la Azteca. Después grabé con Falcón, Ideal, y luego también fuí a grabar a México, a la Columbia.

Fuí a México, a la capital, al Teatro Iris por dos semanas en 1953 o 54. Pues, fuí por dos semanas y me quedé seis meses. Pero no en la capital. Casi en la capital no más trabajé las dos semanas, y luego me agarró un empresario que sacaba artistas así a toda la república de México, y así fué como anduve viajando. No yo sola, sino que una gran caravana de todas figuras de México. Un artista como yo, que soy de disco, tiene que hacer muchas presentaciones y giras, para que sus discos se promuevan más. En México son conocidos, sí, pero no con el auge de aquí.

Le voy a platicar un detallito de cuando yo fuí a México, la primera vez que me presenté en el Teatro Iris. Nos citaron a todos artistas para el ensayo, que tenemos que ensayar o ver lo que íbamos a hacer. Pues ya a las diez de la mañana estábamos todos, y dije al director de escena que yo casi nunca iba a los ensayos porque yo me acompañaba yo sola, y había llevado mis números. Y dijo "No, pero aquí en México es distinto—aquí tienen que estar todos los artistas." Bueno, pues, y llegamos allí, se presentaron todos, ya los bailarines, y los que iban a cantar, y todo. Y luego, pues "Lydia Mendoza a escena," a presentarme yo. Pues entré con mi guitarra y luego se

Mendoza family handbill, ca. 1935. Left to right: Panchita, Juanita, Leonor (Lydia's mother), Manuel, and Maria. Courtesy of Lydia Mendoza.

Teatro SALON

Antonio Montes, Representante

Hoy · . Hoy

Unica presentacion a las 8 p. m. del cuadro de váriedades modernas

"MENDOZA"

Los cancioneros mas populares de las estaciones de radio y de los discos Pajaro Azul y Decca.

8

8 ARTISTAS 8
CANCIONES BAILES
TRUCOS . . . COMEDIA
NO FALTE, SOLAMENTE HOY

DOS HORAS DE ALEGRIA

PRECIOS: ADULTOS · NIÑOS

queda viéndome el director de ese ensayo.

"Y Vd., ¿Que va a hacer?"

Yo creo que él no me conocía. Le dije, "Pues, yo voy a cantar."

"¿A cantar con qué?"

Le dije "Pues, con esa guitarra."

"Si Vd. cree," dice, "que yo voy a presentar una artista aquí no más con guitarra, nos agarrán con tomatazos," dice.

"Pues señor," le dije yo, "soy Lydia Mendoza y así me he presentado. No es el primer teatro en que yo me presento. Me presenté en Nueva York, en California," ya le dije, "en grandes ciudades."

"Oh no," dice, "pero aquellos públicos son muy distintos. Aquí el público es exigente. Y aquí no vamos a presentarle una artista, aunque sea una estrella, no más con un instrumento."

Dije, "Bueno, pues, así me contrataron."

Dice, "No, aquí tenemos que rodearla de un mariachi. Vd. al frente, pero el mariachi con Vd. también."

Dije, "Bueno, pues, como Vd. guste."

No, pues, en este momento lo consiguieron al mariachi—un mariachi de México. Y llegaron allí los muchachos y todo. "¿Que va a cantar, Lydia?" Pues, "Besando la Cruz" fué la primera y los otros dos, tres números que ellos ya conocían. La noche del debut pues ya que se presentaron todos los números y luego ya se llega Lydia Mendoza. Entonces, es que en el foro aparecía el mariachi y, detrás de la cortina, yo. Y cuando empezaba a tocar el mariachi la canción, entonces salía—se abría la cortina y salía yo al frente con mi guitarra, cantando. Oh, pues me aplaudieron mucho, muy bonito. Pues para no alargarle, no más esa canción me acompañaron. Porque después empezaron pues—que el "Mal Hombre." Eso, yo no había esperado nada de eso. Y además, ellos no las conocían. Pues, empezaron "Que el 'Mal Hombre' Lydia Mendoza—que el 'Pajarito Herido,'" y todas canciones— grabaciones mías. Pues el mariachi no más me miraba, pues, ellos parados detras de mí, y yo cantando con mi guitarra sola, y el público, oye, encantado de la vida—nada de tomatazos, ni nada de lo que me platicó él de escena. Pues, bueno—así me la pasé la semana. No más la primera canción y esa, pues, ahorcados la agarraban.

Bueno, a la semana me dice el director de escena: "¿Porqué estamos haciendo estos gastos de oquis? Los muchachos no tocan."

Dije, "Bueno, ¿qué quiere Vd.? Dijo que quería mariachi; pues, páguelo."

Dice, 'No, yo creo que lo vamos a quitar—pues, de veras Vd. sola puede."

La siguiente semana yo me levanté con la pura guitarra. Allí les probé yo que—pues, yo tengo mi público; y él, pues, yo no sé que se imaginó. Que el público no me iba a aceptar no más con la pura guitarra. Y después . . . en todo México me presenté no más con la pura guitarra. Y bien aceptada!

Ultimamente, hace como unos cinco-seis años para acá, he tenido muchas solicitudes para ir a presentarme a festivales y lugares así. La primera vez que me hablaron para que fuera a Canadá, yo me sentí muy feliz porque era un gran festival donde iban a presentar artistas de todo el mundo. Cuando me escribieron diciéndome que si me gustaba ir, bueno, desde luego que para mí siempre fué algo duro porque, pues, sí era un país que nunca había ido yo. En mi larga carrera . . . siempre me dediqué a aquí en los Estados Unidos. Entonces cuando me solicitaron de por allá, ¿como no? sí lo acepté. Y así estuve en Washington, y he estado en varios lugares así.

Me siento mal en este sentido. No es porque no quiero estar con ellos, sino que me figuro que como yo no canto en inglés—canto en español—pues se me hace que no me entienden. Igualmente me pasó hace como dos años que estuve en San Diego, también una gran festividad que fuí para allá. Y allí había algunos otros latinos que hablaban español—no eran mexicanos, pero hablaban español. Y entonces, sí pues, actué para ellos—pura juventud, ¿verdad? Desde luego noté el entusiasmo que hay entre los chamacos jóvenes en saber la música mexicana—parece que les emociona—les gusta cuando oyen algo de corridos. Quisieron saber que dice aquella, pero pues no la entienden, ¿verdad? Entonces ya cuando terminé, se arrimaron algunos que hablaban español allí, y decían todos que les había gustado mucho. Entonces fué cuando yo les dije que yo me sentía muy mal porque yo no cantaba en inglés, que yo no más español.

¿"Para qué cantar en inglés? Pues, hay muchos que vinieron a cantar en inglés. Nosotros vinimos a oír lo que es cantar en español," dice. "Nos gusta la música mexicana aunque no la entiendo mucho," dice. "Pero nos gusta oirla. Es como ir a oír una canción japonésa . . . pues no sabemos la pieza pero queremos oír la música. Así estamos dentro de lo mexicano—aunque no lo entendemos." "Tu," dice, "tu nos gusta como tocas tu guitarra."

Bueno, se expresaba muy bonito. Y bueno, me he convencido un poco que probablemente aunque no me entiendan, pues les gusta. Pero siempre me siento mal porque como se me hace que no me entiendan, pues, a lo mejor no les gusta . . . pero . . . sí les gusta.

El público siempre quiere oír la guitarra. Si no toco la guitarra, no soy Lydia Mendoza. Ultimamente estoy grabando con la pura guitarra, y hemos tenido mucho éxito. Es una guitarra exactamente de doce cuerdas. La que traigo actualmente es una guitarra española. Ya tengo con ellas desde 1937. La primera vez que fuí a Los Angeles fué cuando yo compré una guitarra de ésas. Anteriormente, bueno, como le decía antes, en la Plaza del Zacate habían muchos grupos que anadaban tocando allí, eran tres, cuatro guitarras. Y muchos traían bajos y las guitarras les habían hecho de doce cuerdas. Entonces, pues yo quería tener una guitarra de ésas, pues pero no teníamos con que comprarla. Y entonces, alguna vez le dije a mi papá que yo quería un guitarra doble. Dijo, pues, que no tenía con que comprar una; guitarras estaban muy caras. Entonces se fué a una segunda mano—un Monte Pío que se le dice, en donde venden cosas de segunda. Que allí me compró un bajo viejo. Bueno, lo llevé a una casa de música y me le hicieron guitarra. Y en ése empecé yo a grabar mis primeras grabaciones. Y ya últimamente, no, pues traigo una guitarra Valenciana, pero de doce cuerdas. De ésas no más las venden en Los Angeles. El bajo sexto tiene la misma cabeza que una guitarra de doce cuerdas, de manera que se adoptó muy bien, no más cambiándole las cuerdas. Porque ni se toca igual al bajo que la guitarra ni las cuerdas son iguales. Mucha gente me alega que es bajo . . . no—no es bajo, es guitarra.

Siendo músico, todo me gusta de música, pero la música que me gusta más a mí es por ejemplo muy romántica, de mucho amor. Por ejemplo allí tiene Vd. "Nocturno a Rosario," no sé si lo conociera Vd. Era una poesía de Manuel S. Acuña, de México, un gran compositor que hubo. El se la compuso a una novia que quería mucho. Es una canción hermosísima en la letra. Bueno—de esa clase de canción—es un enamorado que hasta se quita la vida por aquel amor imposible—eso es que a mí me gusta . . . cariño grande. Hay otra de Guti Cárdenas que se llama "Para Olvidarte a Ti." Esta es una canción también muy romántica, muy bonita. Y esa clase de música que tiene mucho amor, mucha historia es lo que a mí me impresiona. Que desde luego, toda clase de música, siendo músico, todo me gusta. Pero me gusta más lo más romántico.

Bueno, tengo algunas canciones que he compuesto. Ultimamente es cuando me ha dado más por componer—como una composición que se la compuse a mi esposo que se llama "Amor Bonito." Una cancioncita muy sencillita, pero creo que está bonita porque le ha gustado mucho. Y así tengo varias composiciones mías, pero casi no me he dedicado de lleno a ello. Sí, una o dos veces puedo componer alguna cancioncita, pero no mucho.

¿Cuando aprendo mis canciones? Bueno, siempre estoy dentro de lo que el público pide, ¿verdad? Empiezan a pedirme corridos y canciones que andan de moda, pues como estoy dentro del ambiente de la música tengo que aprenderlas. Porque no me gusta que me digan "Lydia, ¿sabes esta?" "Pues no. No la sé." "¿Sabes esta otra?" "Pues tampoco, no." No me gusta— para mí es muy, mucha satisfacción que, si me dicen, "¿Sabes este corrido o canción?" "Sí, como no," y les canto, ¿ve? Siempre estoy dentro de lo que está actual.

La hora mas propicia para aprender yo una canción es en la mañana, muy temprano. Por ejemplo, mi esposo se va al trabajo a las seis de la mañana. No más se va él . . . que quiero aprender algo nuevo, entonces . . . me agarro mi guitarra y aprendo de cuatro a cinco canciones. Me las aprendo—se me meten aquí ¿ve? [dentro de la cabeza]—y ya de aquí, ya no salen. Me pongo a estudiarla, la doy dos o tres pasadas, y luego la estoy mirando. Y luego hago a un lado la letra, me pongo a cantarla, no más memorizandola, y ya la sé. A así la hago a un ladito y luego veo otra— cuatro, cinco canciones en un día yo me las aprendo. Y de memoria.

Yo no leo música. No, pues, yo no fuí ni a la escuela. Mi papá no nos mandó a la escuela a las mujercitas. Decía mi papá que no—que para qué— al cabo crecían y se casaban. Los hombres sí, pero las mujeres no. Si no más crecen y se casan—no, así es que mejor ayudan a la mamá aquí en la casa y ya. Y a mí no me mandó a la escuela. Desde luego, digo yo, estoy contenta con lo que la vida me dió, con el don que Diosito me dió de la música y que pude aprender algo y llegar a—pues a ser algo en la vida digamos—por lo menos divertir al público con mi música y mis canciones. Pero si yo hubiera ido a la escuela, creo yo que hubiera aprendido más, hubiera sabido más. A mí me gustaba mucho—desde que era niña también me gustaban mucho los libros . . . leer, saber, aprender. Pero como ni fuí a la escuela entonces en mi casa mi madre fué la que nos enseñó las primeras letras—enseñó a leer, y a escribir. Nos compraba cuadernos y libros y ella nos enseñaba en la casa. Y luego ya empecé a crecer más y empecé a comprar . . . compraba el libro del arte de escribir cartas, la aritmética, geografía, todo eso compraba. Tenía todos esos libros yo—yo estudiaba; lo poquito que yo sé lo aprendí por libros que compraba. Pero a escuela pues nunca fuí. Si hubiera ido a la escuela, yo cantaria en inglés también. Pero de todas maneras—pues para qué me lamento, para qué estoy pensando. Lo que pasó, pasó con que sé, y Dios me ayudó. Feliz! Aunque no haya ido a escuela . . . no le hace.

Cuando canto, me voy a otro mundo. Me voy a otros mundos. Yo cuando estoy en mi casa, en mi hogar, haciendo mi que hacer—yo soy una mujer casada que tengo mi obligación de mi hogar y no tengo sirvientes, no tengo nadie—no más somos yo y mi esposo; podía tener uno o dos sirvientes, pues que a mí no me gusta hacerlo, verdad, me gusta hacer mis cosas en mi casa. Y no más somos dos. Bueno. Pero ya se llega el día de mi trabajo, yo

A handbill from about 1948-50 describing Lydia Mendoza as "Lark of the Border," "Singer of the Home," "The Humblest of Singers," and "Singer of a Thousand Legends." Courtesy of Lydia Mendoza.

me arreglo, me alisto, me voy a donde voy a trabajar. Yo ya saliendo de mi casa y yendo al lugar donde voy a trabajar, allá es otro mundo para mí. Allí estoy no más para el público y cantando, y me fuí para la luna, o para Marte, yo no sé para donde, pero yo me fuí ya.

Yo no sé porqué es eso, si yo canto una canción que es un corrido, digamos, que "Juan Charrasqueado" o que "Gabino Barrerra" no sé porqué estoy—me siento adentro de aquel ambiente, dentro de aquella. Hay corridos que me impresionan mucho, por ejemplo hay un corrido que me gusta tanto que es "El Lobo Potro Gateado"—es un corrido de un caballo. Pero no sé porqué me gusta tanto. Hay otro corrido que canto también acerca de Arturo Garza Treviño. No sé porqué ese corrido me impresiona cuando lo canto. Todo me gusta mucho y los canto con mucho gusto, pero hay, hay corridos que me impresionan. Igualmente si estoy cantando una canción con mucho sentimiento—no sé porqué—mi alma siente aquella canción. Y si es de desprecio, la misma cosa. Vivo aquella canción que yo canto. No sé porqué.

Para mí es un placer cantar lo que el público me pide. Si ellos me piden una canción yo me siento muy feliz y contenta. Es como le digo, más de cuarenta años de haberlo grabado "Mal Hombre" y no hay noche que no me piden esa canción. Siempre la piden. Y yo—no me fastidio, no me canso.

Pues, lo que pienso y digo es que no sé como pagarle a ese público que a pesar de que en cuarenta años han surgido muchas figuras del canto—tantas cancioneras y buenas y todo—y aun sin embargo yo vivo con ese público todavía. Siempre prefieren mi música y les gusta, y—pues—yo no hallo como pagarles más que complaciendoles hasta aquellos quieran. Como cuando me voy a presentar en un lugar me dicen "¿Cuántas canciones va a cantar?" Les digo, "Las que el público pida." No digo que yo no más voy a tocar tres canciones o cuatro. Si hay veces que me presento así en un baile y—pues—si no me dejan, y "Otra" y "Otra" y "Otra" estan pide y pide hasta que yo les digo, "¿Es que pues vinieron a bailar, o no más a oírme cantar?" "Oh, no queremos bailar—queremos oírte cantar." "Bueno, pues . . ." y yo puedo cantar toda la noche si quieren. Yo soy feliz con mi música, y mientras Dios me de licencia y yo pueda hacerlo, y mi público me aguante, pues aquí voy a andar.

Pues, puedo grabar con mariachi porque hay públicos que también quieren oírlo con mariachi. Grabé con mariachi como cuando fuí a México—grabé en la Victor con el Mariachi Vargas de Tecalitlán—famoso. Grabé con ellos, grabé un LP y luego he grabado con conjuntos. Pero resulta una cosa últimamente, porque yo cuando me presento así siempre llevo mis grabaciones para anunciar al público las últimas novedades y todo. Entonces, empecé yo a notar que vendo más discos con pura guitarra que con acompañamiento de otros instrumentos.

Tocante a mi voz, yo no podía decir porqué, pues . . . Yo el único que saco es que Dios me conserva todavía con la fuerza para cantar, y mientras yo tenga gusto y sentimiento y todo eso, pues yo creo que tendré voz. Porque cuidados no los he tenido—que ando yo haciendo gárgaras o que cuidándome de los aires, no. Yo puedo cantar mucho y todo y tomar algo frío y no me afecta. Lo que sí me puede afectar es una corriente de aire. Es lo que me puede afectar, pero de allí más no. Yo puedo cantar dos turnos—ocho, diez horas y . . . Por ejemplo, comienzo un turno de las seis de la tarde, de seis a diez, y luego voy tocando de diez hasta las dos de la mañana. Ocho horas, y no soy de esas que agarran *breaks* y que van a descansar—yo lo agarro seguido, seguido, seguido. Claro, en la mañana, ya al último día, el domingo, ya me siento afónica un poco, pero no se me quita que yo me ando curando—no se me quita. Con que los dos, tres días descanse mi voz, que no cante, ese es el alivio mío. Se me pone mi voz otra vez limpia.

No, pues, yo soy la que . . . estoy ideando siempre, pues, para arreglarme mis trajes porque una cosa me gusta a mí—no es vanidad ni nada—es ponerme un traje y que nadie lo traiga. Por ejemplo, yo me hago un vestido y me dicen que "¡Que bonito!"—quieren ir a comprar uno—¡pues no pueden ir a comprarlo porque no hay! Y pues, yo diseño a mi gusto a lo que yo quiero hacer y como yo quiero hacerlo. Mi idea más grande es irme a las tiendas donde hay materiales—telas que tengan flores, tengan dibujos bonitos. Entonces, yo compro aquellas yardas de ese trapo y yo los dibujo, los pongo *sequins*, o cuentas . . . los adorno. Y luego que ya los arreglo, los recorto, y más luego los pongo en mis trajes que yo hago.

De esto apenas tendré como unos quince años—que empecé idear a hacerlo mi traje. Antes me los traían de México, pero, pues, muy caros. Carísimos, que no llevaban gran cosa. Una ranchera me las traían de México, me las daban por $150, cuando yo con $30, $35 yo me las hago. Porque no tiene más que una falda y puros listones y el encaje y es todo. Entonces, dije pues "¿Porqué voy a pagar tanto si yo me la puedo hacer más bonita?" y luego, pues, ya empecé a hacerme mis vestidos así de flores y de todo eso. Yo los adorno.

Pues, fíjese no más que ese nombre [La Alondra de la Frontera] no sé quien fué, pero tengo un idea que alguien le nació ponerme ese nombre porque cuando yo empecé a grabar, era de este lado—Bluebird—discos Americanos, ¿verdad?. Entonces, no muy fácil pasaban las grabaciones para el otro lado. Sí

Lydia Mendoza at the 1976 Tuscon Meet Yourself Festival. She designs and makes her own costumes. Photograph by Woody Wooden.

pasaban, pero no tan fácil como los que estaban aquí hechos. Entonces todas las fronteras como Matamoros, Reynosa, Piedras Negras, pues sí allí para California, en todas las estaciones de radio tienen los discos de Lydia Mendoza. Entonces, algún locutor probablemente se lo ocurrió ponerla "La Alondra de la Frontera," porque claro, no más en las puras fronteras me oían. Mis discos no estaban en México. Cuando yo comencé apenas no más de este lado, pero los oían en las fronteras de México. Se refería a las fronteras mexicanas, no de este lado. Por eso, a algún anunciador se le ocurrió decir "La Alondra de la Frontera," porque no más en las fronteras me escuchaban. Mis discos no se conseguían, digamos al principio—después, claro, empezaron a pasar para el otro lado.

También me pusieron "El Jilguero del Valle." Pero el que más se quedó fué "La Alondra de la Frontera."

"Cancionera de los Pobres" se deriva de un huapango que me compusieron aquí en San Antonio precisamente. Cuando yo principié a cantar hubo un compositor de aquí de San Antonio. Que no sé si estará retirado o todavía existirá, no sé. Pero en ese tiempo, él componía canciones y tenía un trio. Y él, fué él que me compuso "Lydia Huapango." Y en ese huapango dice:

Cancionera de los pobres
Cancionera y nada más.

Por eso, de allí deriva esa palabra "Cancionera de los Pobres."

En mi larga carrera son tantas cosas que habría de platicar que sería imposible. Necesitaremos un libro muy grande para expresar todo lo que el público quiere saber. Mi idea es, si Dios me conserva, si no me muero, escribir algo de mi historia, porque familias estan interesadas en saber como comencé yo, y detallito tras detallito, pero para eso es como le digo, se necesita escribir un libro. Creo que con la que acabamos de platicar es más que suficiente para enseñar lo que fué mi carrera. Que tengo cincuenta años cantando. Porque yo comencé mi carrera artística—digamos sin hacer nombre todavía—desde 1927. Eso quiere decir que son cincuenta años que ya uso mi voz y que he estado dentro del ambiente artístico, primero por necesidad y ya últimamente porque, pues, me gusta hacerlo. Que ya, pues ya naturalmente yo quisiera hacer mucho, mucho, mucho, pero pues ya los años ya estan encima de una persona y pues no se puede hacer mucho, pero el gusto, el deseo de cantar y todo eso no se me quita a mí todavía.

The Lark of the Border

Lydia Mendoza

Well, I'll begin by telling you that I believe I've had a vocation for music almost from the time I was born.[1] I remember clearly that I began to feel drawn towards music when I was about four. You must realize that my mother played guitar, and at home after dinner, after she and my dad had rested up, she would always pick up her guitar and begin to play and sing. Of course, her voice was lovely, too. People who knew her tell me that I inherited the timbre of her voice. These older families, especially back in Mexico (my mother was from San Luis Potosi), always wanted their daughters to learn some kind of music, and my grandmother—my mother's mother—played guitar. Her mother taught her, and she taught my mother. Mother didn't have real teachers, she didn't go to school or anything like that, but she could play guitar because my grandma taught her. And I can play because my mother taught me.

As I said earlier, whenever I'd hear her strum the guitar, if I was playing I'd stop and run over and sit at her feet. I liked music so much that even then I wanted to play guitar, and I told my mother that I wanted to play like her, and she told me that when my hands got big enough she'd teach me—and that's the way it happened. A few years went by, and when I was only seven I started pleading with mother again to teach me. She thought that it was just childishness—you know how a kid will see a guitar and try to strum it—but I knew I really wanted to play it. And God allowed it to happen, because she started to give me guitar lessons and teach me what little she knew. When I was about eight or nine, I could play perfectly well.

We didn't live off our music when the family was smaller (there were ten of us in all). My father worked and all that. But as time passed, I was the prime mover of music in the household. I liked it, so I wanted my brothers and sisters to play, too. I started teaching my sister Maria the guitar. Then I picked up violin—well, first I learned guitar, then mandolin, then violin. Then I tried to get my sisters' hearts set on music, too. And I guess they liked it, because they all learned to play instruments, and we got a group together. Mother played guitar, I played violin, one of my sisters the mandolin, a brother played the triangle, and father played tambourine. So we got up a musical group, and then we dedicated our lives to music on a full-time basis.

We started off all over the Lower Rio Grande Valley, and later on we got as far as Detroit, Michigan, always with our music.

We lived one year in the Lower Rio Grande Valley—in McAllen, Weslaco, Edinburg, and Kingsville. We would stay a while in one little town—we'd be there a while and then we'd go to another, and so on. In those days there weren't any cantinas, or beer or anything like that. We would play in restaurants and barbershops. Dad would go in and ask permission to play—mostly on Saturdays, when there would be lots of people—and then if folks were there we'd sit down and sing, and people would give us tips. And later on, when harvesting season came along, we'd go to the little towns where the workers were, where there would be gatherings of Mexican people. We'd sing there and get some pocket money.

In those years, at my age, well, as far as I was concerned everything was all right, because I only worried about having enough to eat and live on. Yes, I was embarrassed to go into the barbershops because there would be so many strange men there—I was ashamed. The restaurants didn't bother me. But life was hard. We struggled a lot. That's why I can say that I started off at the bottom, with a lot of toil and suffering. At times we didn't have anything to eat, and we'd have to scrape some pennies together to get a cup of coffee. That's the way I spent my childhood. My youth was about the same. Of course, when I made my big record and folks began to know my name, we started to get lots of nice contracts and our life changed. But for the first seven years we struggled. We suffered a lot. We would beg rides to towns for work, and there were times when we weren't a hit.

After we got the group going and found that we really liked music, we became full-time musicians. And so that was our life. And we went around singing at fiestas and different places. We sang the songs of that day—"El Rancho Grande," "Las Cuatro Milpas," "El Mundo Engañoso," lots of songs. We sang whatever was popular in those days. Mother sang "El Viejo Amor" and "El Sole Mio" because she had a lovely voice—they're pretty songs. When we were in the Lower Rio Grande Valley an announcement came out in *La Prensa*,[2] a very popular paper in those days. There was an announcement to the effect that they were looking for singers to record on the OKeh label. We made the trip with a lot of hardships, because we didn't have a car, we had no means of getting there, and no money. However, dad found a friend who had a little old car, and he gave us a ride to San Antonio, and we got there and they let us make ten records. Among them were "El Rancho Grande," "El Adolorido," and "Los Cuatro Milpas." I have a copy of "Cuatro Milpas" and "El Corrido de Monterrey" that Dick Spottswood sent me. We cut the records, and then we went up north—we didn't stay there more than three weeks. We never heard our records. I was ten. They gave us $140 for the ten records. That's twenty songs. It wasn't a lot of money, but the big thing for us was that we had wanted to record the group. It took place in a hotel.

At that time we went to Michigan—it was in 1928. All those people who lived up there really wanted to hear some Mexican music. When we got to Michigan, our family really made a hit, singing and playing. We had a lot of work there, and we stayed two years. We were in Detroit. Later on, we returned down here to Houston, and lived there for a while. We came back in 1930. But Houston in those days wasn't much—there was no atmosphere, there weren't any radio stations, there wasn't really anything. It was a pretty dull place. And so we kept looking for some place with atmosphere, and we came up here, to San Antonio. We really got started here in San Antonio. We kept on struggling two years, singing in the Plaza de el Zacate. That place doesn't exist any more—they tore it down. It was a huge open-air market. In the evenings from midnight on it was the market where all the produce trucks from the valley and everywhere would arrive. This went on from midnight until about ten or eleven in the morning. Then they'd leave, and the market would stay empty a while. Then around seven in the evening all the folks who were going to sell food there would come in and set up restaurant tables. Each stand would set up its tables and sell chile con carne, enchiladas, and tamales—there were lots of them. There would be about twenty on each side, with a space down the middle where cars would come with people wanting to eat or to hear songs, for there were a lot of groups singing there in those years, too. That was where we made our living.

It was about this time that I started to sing solo. That's when I asked my mother to give me the guitar, and I'd sing even if nobody had asked me to. But folks started to hear my voice and like it, and we hardly sang as a group any more. That's how a local radio announcer came to hear me. It was the only program they had in San Antonio, Texas, in those days—"La Voz Latina," just a half-hour show.

Publicity photograph, ca. 1932, San Antonio.

Well, my name started getting known. People started to hear me over the radio. Then a company came to record and before I'd even heard about it they came and got me, and let me cut two records. The first was my theme song, "Mal Hombre." It was my first record—"Mal Hombre"—and after more than forty years this song still lives in the hearts of my audience, because there's not a night when I'm singing that someone doesn't ask for it. "Mal Hombre," "Al Pie de tu Reja," and then "Pajarito Herido" and "Mundo Engañoso"—just two records.

I don't know who wrote "Mal Hombre," and the composer still hasn't shown up. Lots of people think its mine, but it isn't. And why say it is if it isn't? I think I remember learning it from a chewing-gum wrapper that they sold in Monterrey (Mexico). Each piece of gum had a song with it, and I think that's where this song came from. That's where I learned it. That was in 1926. I just learned it like any other song, and when I went to record, well, I recorded it. I said, "I'll just record this one." Because from the moment I started to sing that song to my audiences, they loved it.

I cut two records and they gave me fifteen—seven dollars for each record. I was thrilled. I made the records and went home. But about three months later, when the record came out, it was a hit. It was a huge success. And later on, three months after that, they came to the house where I was living with my father (because I was still unmarried). They made a contract. They said they wanted to sign me up so that I wouldn't record for anyone else. They'd give me forty dollars and two cents royalties, or they'd give me fifty dollars and no royalties. And dad said no, it was better to give me the fifty dollars and that was fine. Oh, if I'd only recorded for royalties, "Mal Hombre" would have made me rich!

I kept on recording for them. By the end of 1934, we still hadn't heard anything. The year passed and I got married in March of 1935. I'd been married for about two weeks, when a woman who worked with the San Antonio Music Company, Mrs. T——, came to our house with Mr. M——, the man who had recorded us. She served as interpreter for all the musicians. And they came because now that I was married, my husband had to sign the contract. And then, well, we signed it, and I didn't pay much attention to what it said, and my husband didn't speak English, so he didn't either. We signed it and I did notice that they gave us ten dollars for having signed it and all. It turned out that they had done wrong—what they had us sign wasn't what they had told us about me being married, but it was a paper ceding away the first royalties. My husband and I agreed to let Mr. M—— have the two cents royalties on "Mal Hombre" and the other song because he had helped me make my first record. It was he who got the money. Later I talked with the Victor people about it, but they didn't pay attention to me. They looked for Mr. M——, but he wasn't working for them any more. He had gone to Germany! These are facts of life. Well, it's so many years ago, now. Probably if I'd done something right away, but now . . . It's just a story that's stayed with me, that's all.

I kept on with Bluebird from 1934 till 1940. At that time we started getting lots of jobs away from San Antonio—to Corpus Christi, later on even to California. Of course, I struggled a lot at first, but my name started to get known among the Mexican people. But the theater managers, they didn't know who Lydia Mendoza was. Well, Lydia Mendoza was pretty famous, but they didn't know who she was. Therefore they didn't let us work in their theaters—we went and asked but they wouldn't let us. So we played in church halls. And there's not much point in denying that we'd just arrive in a town and rake in the money. We were very successful wherever we went. Well, time passed, and we arrived in El Paso, Texas. The first job I played in El Paso was in a church hall. Then we went to visit with Mr. Calderon, who was one of the theater owners of those days—he had El Teatro Colon. And we went to see him, and, well, he really liked me; he'd heard my records. And he helped us by giving us a chance in his theater. And later on, he said he was going to help me out, and it was due to him that we continued our tour in theaters, because he recommended me to them. He was a great help. That was in El Paso, Texas, in 1936. We played in movie houses, in Las Cruces and all, and one owner would pass the word about the Lydia Mendoza show and that he had had a good gate, and then everyone would open their doors to us, and that's how we got started. My career has been pretty much in the United States. Sure, I've visited Mexico and worked there, but mostly it's been up here.

Well, now, in those years I was recording for Victor, or for Bluebird, which is the same thing, until 1940. In '40 they sent me a new contract, because I was working on a year's contract with a year's option, and as soon as the year would end they'd send the new contracts for me to sign, so I could keep on working. So the last year I recorded was '40, and they sent me a letter saying that they were very sorry but they had to stop making records because of the war—that they couldn't keep on recording because of materials and a lot of things that were scarce. But they were pleased with my work, and when it was all over they would like to come back and start up again. And so it was. I stopped recording with them. So I spent six years . . . not really inactive, because I was here in San Antonio with my husband and my little girls. I stuck close to home and sang at a few parties and all, but I didn't go out of town, on tours or anything. I thought my career had ended, because I spent six years without going on tour or making records. So I was content at home.

A handbill from mid 1930s advertising Lydia Mendoza's show, with Lydia at upper left and her sister, Maria, at lower right. The show included dancing as well as music. A pencilled "parroquial" suggests that it was held in a church parish house. Courtesy of Lydia Mendoza.

TEATRO - SALON

Parroquial

Representante y Director Artístisco
ANTONIO MONTES
HOY   HOY
A LAS 8 DE LA NOCHE

UNICA PRESENTACION del Notable
Cuadro de REVISTAS Y VARIEDAI

LYDIA MENDOZA

Lydia Mendoza

La Cancionera más Popular de toda la
América Latina

Figurando además ELEMENTOS ARTISTICOS DE FAMA, tan
por el RADIO cómo por los DISCOS.

ELENCO ARTISTICO
LYDIA MENDOZA
CANCIONERA Y GUITARRISTA DE FAMA INTERNACIONAL
MARIA DEL JESUS . . . Dama Joven
PAQUITA . . . Coupletista y Bailarina
LEONOR-MARI . . Duetistas de Guitarra
TITA-MANOL   ANTONIO MONTES
PAREJA DE BAILE y CANCIONEROS   TANGUISTA DE MODA
y el popular CUARTETO MENDOZA con sus canciones populares
No deje de ver y oir a LYDIA MENDOZA en PERSONA en su única presentación
¡JUVENTUD!   ALEGRIA!
Canciones, Sketchs, en fin un Programa que Ud.
NO OLVIDE SOLO ESTA NOCHE

However, in 1947, a person, an impresario from California, arrived, and he met me when I was downtown with my mother. Later he said, "Why don't we put together a new tour?" "No," I said, "a lot of years have gone by, and . . ." He said, "I'm going to revive Lydia Mendoza . . ." and that's what he did. He got me a contract for California, even though they didn't believe it was really Lydia Mendoza. Well, it had been six years, and they thought I might even be dead. Well, it was a success. I started on the second part of my career, from 1947 up to the present.

The Lark of the Border   123

I started to record again in 1947, when I gave a show in the Cine California in Los Angeles. The Azteca company in California was making lots of records, and they came to see me and get me to record. That's when I started to cut records again, under contract with them. So they gave me a contract. And later on, Victor came to San Antonio to my house, wanting to record me, but no, I couldn't, I was already under contract. So I started to record for Azteca. Later I recorded for Falcon, Ideal, and later still I recorded as well in Mexico for Columbia.

I went to Mexico City, to the Teatro Iris for two weeks in 1953 or '54. Well, I went for two weeks and stayed six months. But not in the capital. I only worked two weeks in Mexico City, and then an impresario who took performers all over Mexico contacted me, and that's how I went touring. Not alone, but in a big road show with lots of the celebrities of Mexico. A recording artist like me has to make a lot of personal appearances and tours, to promote her records. My work is known in Mexico, to be sure, but not as universally as here.

I'll tell you a story that happened to me in Mexico, the first time I appeared at El Teatro Iris. They gave us all a rehearsal call. Well, we were all there at 10:00 A.M., and I told the stage manager that I hardly ever went to

Lydia (second from left) with sister Maria and comedians Tin-Tan and Marcello at the Million Dollar Theater in Los Angeles, California, 1950. Courtesy of Lydia Mendoza.

rehearsals because I did my own accompaniment, and knew all my numbers. And he said, "No, but it's different here in Mexico—all the artists have to show up here." Well, fine, so we got there, and everyone showed up—dancers and singers and all. And after a while it was "Lydia Mendoza on stage," to do my turn. Well, I came in with my guitar, and the stage manager stood looking at me.

"And you—what are you going to do?"

I thought he didn't recognize me. "Why, I'm going to sing."

"To sing with what?"

I told him, "Why, with my guitar."

"If you think," says he, "that I'm going to present a singer here with just a guitar—why, they'd throw tomatoes!" he says.

"Well, sir," I said, "I'm Lydia Mendoza, and that's my act. This isn't the first theater I've worked in. I've been to New York, to California—to the big cities," I said.

"Oh no," he said, "but these audiences here are different. Here they're demanding. And we're not about to put an artist on stage here, even a star, with just one instrument."

I said, "Well that's the way my contract reads."

He said, "No, we'll have to put you on with a mariachi. You'll be in front, but the mariachi will be there with your, too."

I said, "Fine, just as you please."

They went right out and got a Mexico City mariachi group. And the boys got there with their instruments and said, "What are you going to sing, Lydia?" Well, "Besando la Cruz" was the first number, and two or three others that they knew already. Opening night the show went on, and finally they got to Lydia Mendoza. Well, the mariachi was at the rear of the stage, and I stood behind the curtain. As soon as the mariachi started playing our first number, the curtains opened and I came out with my guitar, singing. Oh, they gave me a nice round of applause. Well, to make a long story short, they just accompanied me on that one song. Because after that the audience started off crying "Mal Hombre." They hadn't practiced that or anything. And furthermore they didn't know it. Well, the audience started off, "Play 'Mal Hombre,' Lydia Mendoza—play 'Parjarito Herido' "—and all the songs from my records. And the mariachi just watched me—they standing behind me, and me playing my guitar alone, and the audience loving it all—no flying tomatoes, or anything of what the stage manager had been talking about. Well then, that's the way the week went. Just the first number with accompaniment, and then they stood silent.

Well, at the end of the week the stage manager said, "Why are we paying all these expenses for nothing? The boys aren't working."

I said, "Well, what do you want? You said you needed a mariachi—pay them."

He said, "No, I guess we'll stick with just the guitar—you really can do it alone."

And the second week I went up alone with my guitar. I showed him that, well, I have my fans, and he just couldn't imagine it—that the audience would accept me with just my guitar. And after that, I went all over Mexico with just the guitar. And well received, too!

Recently, for the past five or six years, I've had lots of requests to go and play at festivals and that sort of event. The first occasion was when I was asked to go to Canada—that pleased me because it was a big festival where they were going to present artists from all over the world. When they wrote me saying that they really wanted me, it was a little hard for me, because I'd never been there before. In my long career I've always stayed here in the United States. But when they asked me to go over there, why not? Of course I accepted. And after that I went to Washington, and lots of other places.

I worry about it in this sense: It isn't because I don't want to be with those people, but that I feel that because I don't sing in English—I do all my singing in Spanish—they aren't going to understand me. The same sort of thing happened when I went to San Diego two years ago, to another big festival over there.[3] There were a few Latin Americans who spoke Spanish—they weren't Mexicans, but they spoke Spanish. And well, I performed for them—they were all kids, you understand. I noticed how eager some of those youngsters are to understand Mexican music—it appears to move them—they really like it when they hear *corridos*.[4] They wanted to know what the words meant, because of course they couldn't understand. Well, when I was finished, some of the Spanish-speaking ones gathered around me and they all said they had liked it a lot. That's when I told them I felt sorry for not being able to sing in English, just in Spanish.

"Why sing in English? Lots of people come here who can do that. We came to hear you sing in Spanish," he said. "We like Mexican music, even though we don't understand it very well," he told me. "We like to hear it. It's like listening to a Japanese song—we don't know the song, but we like listening to the music. That's the way we feel about Mexican music, although we don't understand it, and," he said, "We like the way you play guitar."

Well, he expressed himself very nicely, and I'm convinced somewhat that they probably enjoy me even though they don't understand me. But I still feel bad because it seems to me that most of them won't like what they can't understand—but they do like it.

The audiences always want to hear my guitar. If I don't play guitar, I'm not Lydia Mendoza. Lately I've been recording with just the guitar, and it's been very popular. It's a twelve-string guitar. The one I use now is from Spain. I've been using that kind since 1937. The first time I got one was in Los Angeles. Before that—well, as I told you before, there used to be a lot of groups wandering around the Plaza de el Zacate, playing three or four guitars. A lot of them used basses, and had twelve-string guitars. Then of course I wanted to have a guitar like that, but we didn't have the wherewithal to buy one. I told my father once that I wanted a double guitar. He said that we didn't have the money to get one—guitars were very expensive. Finally he went to a secondhand store—what we call a *Monte Pio,* where they sell used things. There he got me an old *bajo sexto.*[5] Well, I took it to a music store and they converted it to a guitar. That's what I used for my first recordings. (And now I use a twelve-string Valenciana. They only sell those in Los Angeles.) The *bajo sexto* has the same peghead as the twelve-string guitar, so it was easy to adapt—we just changed the strings. It's strung and played differently from a guitar. Lots of people think I play a *bajo sexto,* but it isn't—it's a guitar.

Being a musician, I like all kinds of music, but the kind I like most is the very romantic kind, with a lot of love interest. For example, take "Nocturno a Rosario"—I don't know if you're acquainted with it. It was a poem by Manuel S. Acuña, a great Mexican composer. He wrote it for a sweetheart of his—someone he was very much in love with. It has really beautiful words. Well, it's the kind of song—it's about a lover who almost kills himself over his impossible love affair. That's what I really like—songs of strong love. There's another by Guti Cardenas called "Para Olvidarte a Ti." It's a very romantic, lovely song as well. And that kind of music that has a lot of love, a strong story—that's the kind that really moves me. Of, course, I like all sorts of music—I'm a musician. But I like the romantic kind the best.

I've written a few songs. I've done most of my composing recently—like the song "Amor Bonito" that I wrote for my husband. A simple little song, but I think it's nice because he's liked it a lot. And I've got a few of my own songs, but I really haven't tried to devote myself to writing full time. Yes, I've composed a song or two, but not many.

How do I learn my songs? Well, I'm always wrapped up in what my public asks for, don't you see. They start to ask for popular *corridos* and songs; well, I have to learn them. Because I don't like it when they say, "Lydia, do you know this one?" "No, I don't know it." "How about this one?" "No, I don't know it either." I don't like that—what I really enjoy is when they ask, "Do you know such-and-such a *corrido* or song?" and I answer, "Of course," and I sing it to them. I always like to stay up to date.

The best time for me to learn a song is in the morning, very early. For example, my husband goes to work at 6:00 A.M. As soon as he leaves, if I want to learn some new material, well, I pick up my guitar and learn four or five songs. I learn them—I get them up here (gestures: in my head) and once here, they never leave. I start studying one, I go over it two or three times, and then I look at the words. Then I put the words to one side and start to sing it, committing it to memory, and then I know it. Then I put that to one side and start on another, and in one day I learn four, five songs. They're memorized.

I don't read music. Why, I never even went to school. My father didn't send us girls to school. He said, "No—why? After all, they just grow up and get married. The boys yes, but the girls no. They'll just grow up and marry—better stay home and help mother around the house." And he never sent me to school. Of course, I'm contented with what life has given me, with the gift of music God gave me, and that I've been able to learn something and make something of my life—at least to amuse the audiences with my music and my songs. But if I had gone to school, I believe I could have learned more, have been more. I really like to read—I've liked books since I was a child—and to read and find out about things. But since I never went to school, my mother was the one who taught us our letters at home—she taught us to read and write. She bought us notebooks and books and taught us at home. And later on I began to grow up more and started to buy . . . I bought the book on the art of letter writing, and an arithmetic book, and a geography, and all that. I had all those books, and I learned the little I could learn from the books I bought. But I never went to school. If I'd gone to school, I'd be able to sing in English as well. But why am I complaining or worrying about it? What has happened, happened with what I know, and God has helped me, and I'm happy. Even though I never went to school, it doesn't matter.

When I sing, I go to some other world. I go somewhere else. When I'm at home, in my household, doing my chores—I'm a married woman, and I have my obligations to the home, and I don't have servants, I don't have

128   Lydia Mendoza

help. (It's just me and my husband living at home, and I could have a servant or two, but I don't want to—I like to do my own things in my own house. And we're just two. And that's fine.) But when a working day comes around, I get ready, I get changed, and I go to wherever it is I'm going to work. And when I leave home and get to the place where I'm going to work, that's another world for me. There I exist only for my audience and for singing . . . I'm on the moon, I'm on Mars, I don't know where I am, but I'm really there.

I don't know why it is, but if I sing a song—a *corrido*, let's say, like "Juan Charrasqueado" or "Gabino Barrera"—I don't know why it is, but I'm really in the song. There are *corridos* that affect me a lot; for example, there's one I really like called "El Lobo Potro Gateado"—its about a horse. But I don't know why I like it so much. There's another about Arturo Garza Treviño. I don't know why that one makes such an impression on me when I sing it. I like them all and I like to sing them all, but there are some *corridos* that move me. In the same way, when I'm singing a song with a lot of sentiment, I don't know why, but my soul feels that song. And if it's about a rejection in love, the same thing. I live the song I'm singing, I don't know why.

For me it's a joy to sing what the audience asks for. If they ask for a song, I feel happy and content. As I told you, I cut "Mal Hombre" more than forty years ago, and not a night passes that someone doesn't ask for it. They always want to hear it. And me—I'm never bored or tired of it.

Well, I tell you that I don't know how to repay this audience that's still with me, in spite of the fact that over the past forty years a lot of singers—good ones, too—have come up. They still prefer my music and they like it, and—well, I can't think of any way to repay them except by singing whatever they want to hear. Like when I go to sing somewhere, they ask me, "How many songs are you going to sing?" and I say, "However many the audience wants to hear." I say I'm just going to play three or four. And there are times when I get up like that at a dance, and, well, they don't let me stop—they call out "Another," "Another," 'Another," and they beg until I finally tell them, "Did you come here to dance, or just to hear me sing?" "Oh no, we don't want to dance—we want to hear you sing." "O.K., then," and I can sing all night if they want it. I'm happy with my music, and while God allows me and I'm still able to do it, and my fans like me, that's where I'll be.

Now, I can record with mariachis because there's a part of my audience who wants to hear that. I recorded with a mariachi group when I went to Mexico—I recorded on Victor with the Mariachi Vargas de Tecalitlán, a famous outfit. I've recorded with them, I've recorded with conjuntos. [6] But one thing has turned up recently. Lately when I make a presentation I always take my records along to let the audience know what's new and all. Well, I started to notice that I sold more records that just had guitar on them than I did ones where there were a lot of other instruments.

Concerning my voice, I just can't say . . . the only thing I've thought is that God has still preserved me with a singing voice, and while I have the desire and feeling and all, well, I guess I'll have a voice. I haven't taken precautions like gargling or watching out for the bad air or anything like that. I can sing a lot and drink something cold, and it won't hurt me. What can affect me is a draft. That does do some harm, but the rest doesn't. I can

Lydia rehearsing in the Coolidge Auditorium of the Library of Congress for her concert at the 1977 Ethnic Recordings in America Conference. Photograph by Carl Fleischhauer, American Folklife Center, Library of Congress.

sing two sets—eight, nine hours, and . . . for example, start a set at 6:00 P.M., from six to ten, and then do a job from ten until 2:00 A.M. Eight hours, and I'm not one of those people who takes breaks or takes a rest—I just keep on and on and on. Certainly on Sunday morning after a long stint I am a bit voiceless, but it doesn't really disappear, and I cure myself. With two, three days of resting my voice, of not singing, I'm cured. My voice is clear again.

No, I'm one of these people who . . . I'm always planning ways to fix up my costumes, because one thing I like—it's not vanity or anything of that sort—is to wear clothes that nobody else has. For example, I'll make myself a dress and they'll say, "How pretty"—they'll want to buy one, but they can't because there aren't any for sale! Well, I design what I'm going to make and how I'm going to make it, all to my own taste. I really like to go to stores where there's material—cloth with flowers, with pretty designs. Then I'll buy enough yards of the stuff and, well, I'll draw on them, I'll put sequins, I'll draw little scenes—I'll decorate them. And after I've fixed them up, I'll cut them out and put them on the clothes I make.

I've been doing this for about fifteen years. That's when I started dreaming up my own costumes. Before that they'd bring them to me from Mexico, but they'd be terribly expensive. A *ranchera* costume they brought from Mexico cost $150.00, when I could make it myself with $30, $35. It's just a skirt and some ribbons and appliqué work, that's all. Well then, I said, "Why should I pay so much if I can make it myself, prettier?" And so I started making my own clothes with flowers and all. And I decorate them myself.

Well, you've got to realize that I don't know who gave me this name *(La Alondra de la Frontera)*, but I've got an idea that someone thought it up because when I started to record, it was on this side [of the border]—on Bluebird . . . American records, you know. Well, it wasn't very easy for records to get across the line. Yes, they crossed, but not as easily as those made over there.[7] So in all the border towns like Matamoros, Reynosa, Piedras Negras, even over in California, on all the radio stations, they would have Lydia Mendoza records. So some announcer probably had the idea of calling me "The Lark of the Border" because you could only hear me right on the border. My records weren't in Mexico. When I started off, it was just over here, but you could hear them in the Mexican border towns. The name refers to the border from the Mexican side, not this one. It must have occurred to some announcer to call me "The Lark of the Border" because you could only hear me in that area. You couldn't get my records over there—at first, that is, because later on they started to cross the border.

They also called me "The Linnet of the Valley." But the one that took was "The Lark of the Border."

"Cancionera de los Pobres" (The Poor People's Singer) comes from a *huapango* that was composed for me right here in San Antonio. I don't know if he has retired or if he's still around.[8] But in those days he composed songs and had a trio. And it was he who composed "Lydia Huapango" for me, and in this *huapango* it says:

Singer for the poor people
Just a singer, and that's all.

That's where the name "Poor People's Singer" comes from.

There's so much to talk about in my long career that it would be impossible. We would need a really big book to tell all that the public wants to know. My idea is, if God preserves me and I don't die, to write something of my story, because some families are very interested in knowing how I got started, and all the little details, but in order to tell that, it's like I said—I'd need a book. I think that what we've said here is more than enough to give some idea of what my career has been like. Because I started my artistic career—without making a name for myself—in 1927. That means that I've been using my voice, I've been in the world of entertainment for fifty years, out of necessity at first, and now lately because, well, I like it. Oh, of course I'd like to do lots and lots and lots, but the years do get on top of a person, and you can't do much. However, the joy, the desire to sing hasn't left me yet.

Notes

I am indebted to various people for their valuable help with this project. First and foremost, of course, is *La Alondra de la Frontera*, Lydia Mendoza herself. She graciously consented to be interviewed at her daughter's home in San Antonio, lent illustrative material for copying, and offered every possible assistance. I am honored by her kindness, and I hope she enjoys the results. José Ramón of Houston, Texas, offered his hospitality, his car, his assistance, and his deep affection for and understanding of Lydia Mendoza and what she has accomplished; I could have done little without his help. Back in Tucson, Claudio Jimenez of station KXEW spent many hours helping me with the difficult task of transcribing a language not my own. Any errors in the translation are, of course, mine. Judy Spencer assisted with the photography.

1. Portions of the English translation of Lydia Mendoza's statement appeared as liner notes to Folklyric 9023 and 9024. These albums, volumes 15 and 16 of the series *Una historia de la musica de la frontera*, comprise reissues of her early recordings. They include two sides from the 1928 Cuarteto Carta Blanca sessions as well as many cuts from the 1930s.

2. A San Antonio newspaper.

3. The 1975 San Diego State University Folk Festival.

4. I.e., ballads.

5. A bass guitar with twelve strings.

6. Norteño, or Tex-Mex, accordion bands.

7. This appears to be Lydia Mendoza's meaning.

8. Agustín Mendoza, director of the Cuarteto Michoacano.

The Sajewski Story: Eighty Years of Polish Music in Chicago

Richard K. Spottswood

When Władysław H. Sajewski first opened the doors of his business on Chicago's North Side in 1897, he was in no position to see the opportunities technology would hold in store for him, and still less the directions his modest business would take. Meat packing and other booming industries had already begun to lure immigrants from the old country in addition to Polish-Americans from the eastern mining districts seeking improvements in their lives and working conditions. Polish communities formed in both the South Side and the North Side, centered around employment areas and church parishes, the latter providing outlets for worship, education, and social activities. Sajewski's original operation was small, financed only by profits and family savings, but as further immigration brought more Poles to Chicago in the decades before World War I, the Sajewskis and their store became an indispensable element of their community's life.

Władysław's son Alvin has worked continuously in the store since 1914, when he was a boy. As Alvin describes the early days, the operation began as a kind of urban general store. It was

> a little bit of everything. If you needed a spool of thread or a needle or pins or stockings, there wasn't a tremendous variety, but you would be able to have something—photographic supplies, sewing machines, religious art, musical instruments, guns, and records. Of course, there was the language barrier: People spoke Polish only, most of them, and so naturally when they needed something and couldn't find it or didn't know how to ask for it, they would come to you. They'd say, "Do you know where I might be able to find one" or "Can you find one for me?" "Well, we don't have it, but I think we'll be able to find one for you." We would always try to get it for them, but it would take a little time.

Early undated catalogs printed by Władysław advertise the wares of the original store at 218 Blackhawk Street, at first called the Columbia Supply House (following the famous 1893 Columbian Exposition). Almost immediately he began mailing these catalogs wherever he could, and advertising

Władysław Sajewski in front of his store in 1911. Courtesy of Alvin Sajewski.

Sajewski's first published catalog, 1910–1914. Courtesy of Alvin Sajewski.

One of Władysław Sajewski's early publications. Courtesy of Alvin Sajewski.

them in the Polish press. The store itself was small, and advertised items were often not stocked, but bought from others and resold on demand. Thus the business grew, aided by a climate of opportunity and even more by Władysław's ability to exploit it.

Music was an important element of life in Chicago, as it had been in the old country. It was (and is) important in the church, for social ceremonies like weddings and engagement parties, and in the education of children. During the Sajewskis' first decade, demand for printed music, instruments, and accessories grew as the demand for other wares slackened.

When did it become clear that music would dominate your activities?

That was just a matter of elimination. You eliminated the things people could purchase elsewhere and tried to specialize. Other businesses opened which carried the same things.

Jania Terley: Dad probably diverted his attention to musical instruments and music accessories and music books because there were none, and there was tremendous demand for them. There were teachers teaching piano and violin but there was no source for music in their own language. He could get someone the right instrument at the right price. There wasn't anyone else in the city who could do that, and so his business grew.

By 1910 the store had turned almost exclusively to music, supplying phonographs, records, and printed music as well. Edison and Columbia cylinders, and Columbia and Victor flat discs all were available with increasing quantities of Polish music on them, making both record and phonograph sales profitable. Only a limited selection of Polish sheet music was available in the early 1900s. Much of it was the classical music of established Polish composers like Chopin and Wieniawski, which had only limited appeal to the Sajewski clientele. Since there were no other sources for the kind of music Władysław wanted, he began to publish music himself. He was an accomplished amateur violinist, and a keen enough student of public tastes that his sheet music operation began to flourish. Almost immediately, it became necessary to place a full-time person in charge of publications.

This was Frank Przybylski, a quiet, studious man, who was at first commissioned to write songs for school use, including suitable arrangements of Polish folksongs. His duties soon expanded to preparing full-scale orchestrations for small and large ensembles and for military bands, writing original compositions, and arranging those of others. He was a versatile composer and a good bandleader. Later, as we shall see, he even turned his efforts to recording.

Because Władysław Sajewski was an early publisher of sheet music, he was aware of the protection offered by copyright laws. Though physical publication is a less important part of the Sajewski business today, as a publisher Alvin owns an important catalog of copyrighted compositions, which are regularly licensed through SESAC.

Frank Przybylski. Courtesy of Alvin Sajewski.

At what point did you need to start getting your music copyrighted?

Just as soon as the copyright laws were enacted in 1909. A lot of songs expired, and we didn't renew them because there wasn't any demand for them. We tried to renew on anything that was popular. There were times when we slipped up, and by the time we sent a renewal notice in, they would write and very, very nicely told you how sorry they were that they couldn't renew it for you, but that the copyright laws are made for everybody.

Did anyone ever challenge you when you copyrighted a folksong?

From time to time we get letters where someone says they have written this or that. We'd find that his mother or someone had sung it for him and that he'd written it out. He'd say he'd written it out in 1949 or 1951. We'd write back and say that we'd copyrighted it in 1927 and that it had been already renewed, and send him a photostatic copy of it so he could compare it.

We still have boys come in and ask, "Why do we have to pay a royalty on this? That's old stuff. My grandmother used to sing that." I say, "Yes, but don't forget those copyrights were made for twenty-eight years and twenty-eight years after that. Maybe your grandmother was just a little baby at that time. You don't have to pay anything until you sell the records. You can print 5,000, and when you sell the records you've got the money, and they're entitled to their two cents per copy." "But we got our own arrangement, and it's altogether different." "You may have your own arrangement, but it's still someone else's number." "But we've changed it!" "Well, change it and change the name, so it doesn't sound like it at all."

Still, not all of the store's early publishing was devoted to music. Polish culture had many facets, and since people wanted other outlets for themselves and their children, plays soon became another element of the Sajewski publishing activity. According to Alvin, the plays were an important part of educational programs:

We published dramas, comedies, and historical plays of all kinds. We have quite a collection of plays for graduation. We have three-act, four-act, some short sketches, plays for children, Mother's Day, everything in Polish. We have plays for graduation, we have very very heavy dramas. A lot of 'em are with music. A lot of them are for amateurs. That was one of the musts as we went along.

When the immigrants were coming in and settling, the first thing they would do is see that they had a church they could go to. They would all live as close as possible to the church so the children could go to school, and it was usually the center for all activities then.

Were the children in church or public schools then?

Parochial schools immediately. They had one room for the mass and the other rooms for the classrooms. They would have half a day of Polish language reading and writing, Polish geography and history. In the afternoon they would have English reading, writing, and arithmetic, and United States history and geography.

So the sisters decided that the children should have something for a play, for mother superior, for father rector or the pastor. So there was always something they were preparing. Or for May 3, which is the Polish Constitution Day—Poland had a constitution before the United States, and May 3 is usually a big holiday. You always had songs or a play of some kind.

The plays for mother superior or father rector would be on their name days. So they would want a few little playlets. Father rector would come in and they would have a chair for him. Some children would recite poems or sing a little song, and there was always a play of some kind. Or the girls would have one play and the boys another. We were getting some plays from Poland, but it was hard for these children to memorize these things, and if you skipped one word you were lost.

Several plays were about classrooms, and one of the girls would dress up as a teacher or sometimes in a sister's habit. The boys would all want to play in that. They'd have tricks of all kinds. One of them would have a piece of sausage, and when the sister wasn't looking they'd take a bite of it and put it away. They enjoyed those things.

Is that still going on?

No. That was gone twenty years ago. It slowly, slowly stopped. There are so many Polish schools that are closing and don't have any attendance. But then it was very, very big. But television took quite a bit of that away. These plays were always written with a little moral to them—to respect your parents or something. They

Polish MINSTREL SHOW

Published By
W. H. SAJEWSKI
1817 MILWAUKEE AVE.   CHICAGO, ILL.

A comic skit in Polish compiled by J. S. Zielinski in 1940, described on the title page as "A Full and Complete two and half hour Show with Clean, Catchy, Sure-Fire Songs, Dances, Jokes, and Slap Happy Comedy. Ready for Performance."

were very pretty and there were so many of them. To this day, every now and then, somebody'll write in that took part in one when they were small, and wondering whether they can still get a book that we had put out. It brings a lot of memories back.

The Sajewski family was close knit. Alvin, the third child, developed a keen interest in the business while he was still young. In 1914, when he was nine years old, he began coming home most afternoons straight from school to help in the store, starting at first with simple chores like stamping and folding catalogs. His abilities grew with added responsibilities, which became equally shared between father and son after Alvin's graduation from high school.

Edison's Polish recording activity diminished as the popularity of the early cylinders waned. By 1908, Columbia had eliminated cylinders, and thereafter both it and Victor began to rapidly expand ethnic music elements in their catalogs. By the time young Alvin began working, sales of records rivaled those of sheet music and demanded considerably more staff involvement in merchandising them:

We had two big booths in the store that would hold between fifteen and twenty people each, and a long counter. Now, at the end of the counter we had a phonograph. In the back we had all the records in racks. One booth had all the Columbia records, and the other had all the Victor records. Down below we had special things we didn't keep numerically, like Caruso or Paderewski records, things like that. So there'd always be two of us. If customers came in for records, we'd put them into the first booth. On Saturday you'd have twelve or fifteen people in a booth, and when somebody came and asked for numbers, you'd play them. All these other people would be listening, and someone would say, "Oh, that's a good number, give me one of those!" And along that long counter we'd put records here for one man or over here for another, and they'd be building up stacks of records for themselves.

The hardest part was changing needles for every record. They were steel needles and only good for one record. If you didn't change the needle the man would say, "Don't give me that one. That's all worn out. I want another one." You'd just pick up the tone arm and give it a twist and put another needle in there. The machine would be going and you had to wind it up, and sometimes if you got stuck while you were looking for a record, the record that was on the machine would start slowing down—you had to be able to turn around fast enough to wind up. Because if the customer reached over, I've had it happen that he'd knock the whole machine right off the counter, just trying to be nice and crank it up for you.

You had a strong right arm in those days, didn't you?
Oh yeah. And the skin on your two fingers was like shoe leather. The screw [for securing the needle] had the ridges in it; I could take a needle and put it through my skin. When more people came in we'd put them in the other booth. On our side of the counter we had a door in between, so if I needed a Columbia record and I was working the first booth, I would go over and get it. Of

course, we'd always keep the door closed so that . . . one booth wouldn't interfere with the other. But if you took a record off and the machine was playing, someone would say, "Hey that's a real good one, why don't you play that one? They got all the good ones over there!" One of my brothers would be working the other booth. Later on when the piano rolls came out and we had a player piano about twenty-five feet away from these booths, there was another brother that had to sit and play these rolls over there, or whoever got stuck. Or you could say to a customer, "Look around and find something you like and sit down and play if for yourself." That saves you the job, see? But if somebody got on there and started to play, then you had a little switch where you could make it louder or softer, so they'd get extra loud and pump away over there, and you could hardly hear the records.

This account of the hectic pace required by early record retailing operations is both amusing and significant. These records contained a reaffirmation of Polish music and Polish culture, and they were a solid hit with their intended customers, who, like all other Americans who could afford the price, were buying this new mechanically reproduced music in greater and greater quantities.

By the war years (1914–18) acoustical recording and reproduction methods had improved significantly. Record surfaces were quieter, a greater part of the sound spectrum was reproducible, and two-sided records retailing at seventy-five cents were only ten cents more than one-sided records had been. Even modern ears that are used to extended-frequency-range recordings can readily discern the differences between the 1905 and 1915 products.

Still, it was obvious that records were a long way from being accurate reproductions of musical performances. So, while the phonograph was increasing in popularity, people were also buying bellows-operated player pianos (or pianolas), whose forerunners were the nineteenth-century music boxes and barrel organs. "Records" for the player piano came in the form of cylindrical rolls of perforated paper whose holes activated the piano keys. These reproductions involved mechanical rather than sound recording, making it possible to repeat on one piano what had been played on another, with comparatively lifelike results. The Sajewskis were perceptive enough to see that a potential market for piano rolls of Polish music existed among their clients:

> When player pianos came out, they didn't have any rolls [of Polish music]. There were just classical things. So what we had to do, we supplied them with the music, and by that time we had quite a good catalog. But we had a problem with piano rolls, they wouldn't make them. So dad finally went down to the U.S. Roll Company and made arrangements with them to have the rolls made for him. Mrs. Brown, I guess, was in charge of the United States Music Roll Company at that time, and she said, "Well, who's going to buy them? Pianos are very expensive, and who's going to buy them?" And dad said, "You just make them, and people will buy them."

Did he have to underwrite them himself?

Yes, he had a contract with them for several years. They weren't allowed to make Polish rolls for anybody except for him. They didn't want to make them at their own expense because they'd never be able to sell enough of them. So Dad put out the Sajewski Special rolls, and that was before the word rolls [piano rolls with printed song lyrics beside the punched holes] were out.

What year did he put piano rolls out first?

About 1917, between 1916 and 1917. That goes back a long way; I have to try to think how big I was. I know I was big enough to play the damn thing.

Who cut the rolls?

I guess Mrs. Brown. We supplied her with the music we wanted. They were made in Chicago, right up on Lake Street. I was there with Dad when he was arguing about the rolls. They had rolls recorded by artists, like Paderewski and all those people, but Mrs. Brown was the pianist for us. Later on when the QRS Company came out with word rolls, the U.S. Company came out with word rolls for us. Later on we released U.S. from the contract, and they began making Polish rolls for the general market. U.S. made Polish rolls first, then QRS, which is still in business, but they don't make the Polish rolls any more. In 1924 or 1925 Przybylski and several others organized a factory where they manufactured rolls. They called it the Victor Roll Company.

Listing of foreign player piano rolls published by U.S. Music Company. From *Talking Machine World*, September 15, 1925, page 225. Motion Picture, Broadcasting, and Recorded Sound Division, Library of Congress.

REGULAR ROLLS—MUSIC ONLY
Air Mail—March ....W. Wirt Parks

FOREIGN WORD ROLLS
Graj Mam—Waltz (Winc. Baluta)—Polish.
Aroma Tropical—Danson (Bolisario De J. Garua)—Spanish.
La Provinciana—Tango (Romero-Joves)—Spanish.
Una Mas—Tango Cancion (Viergol-Joves)—Spanish.
Internacijonalas—Lithuanian.
1. "Ant Barikadu," 2 "Darbininku Marselicte—Lithuanian.
Varsavieto—Lithuanian.

FOREIGN ROLLS—MUSIC ONLY
Carmulinda—Valtzer (Luigi Tutela)—Italian.
Czarodziejeki Taniec—Polka (Win Baluta)—Polish.
I Primi Albori—Masurka (Alfred Longo)—Italian.
Stizzosetta Polka (Marco Longo)—Italian.

DUO-ART
(These Rolls for Standardized Reproducing Tracker Bar)

INSTRUMENTAL ROLLS—MUSIC ONLY

Title	Composer	Played by
Badner Mad'ln—Viennese Waltz		McNair Illgenfritz
Zephyrs—Valse Graceouse		McNair Illgenfritz
Study on the Minute Waltz (Fr. Chopin),		McNair Illgenfritz

LIBRARY EDITION—WORD ROLLS
Roamin' in the Gloamin'—Scotch Song.....Robert Billings
She Is Ma Daisy—Scotch Song...........Robert Billings
Blue Bells of Scotland—Scotch Song.....Robert Billings
Campbells Are Coming—Scotch Song......Robert Billings

Demand for the Sajewski rolls decreased after the introduction of electrical recordings in 1925, when it became possible to record the piano more accurately. By 1930 the piano roll industry was all but extinct. The Sajewskis were joined by at least one other colleague: Myron Surmach began to have Ukrainian rolls produced by QRS in the mid-1920s, and by 1927 was offering over fifty selections. Undoubtedly other foreign language retailers followed the Sajewskis' example, though no other series are known of at this time.

The Sajewskis carried one other nonmusical line—postcards and form letters with preprinted messages. Alvin Sajewski remembers them with a mixture of amusement and poignancy:

> We carried postcards. Postcards were a very big thing in those days. They were big all the way up to 1925 or 1926. We carried printed letters from a man who was putting them out. A letter would be printed with some beautiful flowers for somebody who wanted to write home. It might be difficult for them to write a letter, so they would get these printed letters. We had different form letters to Dear Father, Dear Mother, or for the young lady who left a sweetheart behind, or for a young man who left *his* sweetheart behind. They were written very nicely: "My beloved, here I am in this Land of Lincoln working hard, but my thoughts are always of you. I hope that someday you will be able to come to America or that I will be able to come back to Poland to marry you and bring you here." They were very endearing letters, and after you got through with the schmaltz, you had the inside pages to add something to it. People who came in had to remember which ones they'd already sent so they wouldn't send the same one twice. So there were always new ones. The man who was printing them had some for Easter, Christmas, always something pretty. In between the pages the senders would put in a paper dollar or whatever they could afford. That was quite a popular thing.

Advertising was an important function from the earliest days. There was an active Polish press by the time Władysław Sajewski went into business, and he used it regularly to announce specific items and the availability of free catalogs—at first of general merchandise and later of the sheet music and records.

> We'd advertise in the Polish papers; they were published in Chicago, but they sold throughout the United States. We advertised in the oldest Polish paper that was published in Stevens Point, Wisconsin, the *Gwiazda Polarna (Morning Star)*. It had the biggest circulation of them all.

After records became a major commodity, advertising was carried out by cooperative agreements with local distributors:

> What we used to do, Columbia used to run an ad in the Polish papers from time to time, especially at Christmas. It depended on the distribution which was changing, and some young blood would come in and say, "We have to have a little more publicity. Let's run an ad." So the newspaper would call me up and say they were running a two-column ad, ask if we'd want to put our name on it.

We'd say sure, and take one inch for fifteen dollars or whatever. Columbia would pay for the whole thing, and down at the bottom we'd put "Biggest Supplier of Polish Records—Sajewski Music Store." We'd just pay for the strip down below, and Columbia'd pay for the rest of it.[1]

By the 1910s, the production of Polish-language records was hitting its stride, but the predominance of trained singers and more-or-less formally arranged orchestrations was beginning to leave some record buyers wanting more. Most of the Sajewskis's customers were not from the wealthy or educated classes, and Victor and Columbia were not producing the music they could hear casually in their neighborhoods, or the music they remembered from the rural villages and countryside of their homeland. Since country people in Poland were generally too poor to constitute an audience for their music on records, little attention was paid to recording it there either. As Alvin Sajewski describes the problem:

> The companies didn't know what to make. That was their big problem. They had the material and they had the money. We had people with money in their hand and they wanted to buy a phonograph, but only if they could have some good records to play. There were a few that were good, but not too many. What we had were some waltzes, some marches and band arrangements, but they wanted folksongs. The records featured people who had been on stage, comedians or singers. Some of the comedians talked too fast, and you couldn't understand, and when the punchline came you couldn't catch it. The records were by people from the city who liked the classical singers, the high-pitched soprano solos. Each singer had to show how loud he could sing or how high he could go. People wanted simple pretty melodies, but they would buy these records because there was at least something in Polish on them. And that went on up to 1917 or 1918.

"Hey! Hey! Hey! They're Taking Me Away" by the Polish Merry-Go-Round Orchestra. Motion Picture, Broadcasting, and Recorded Sound Division, Library of Congress.

In 1915, Columbia made its first Chicago recordings, and a group led by Frank Przybylski recorded "Laughing Polka" (Sieszmy Się) (Columbia E-2221); on the other side was "Dziadunio Polka," which was the ancestor of "Clarinet Polka." He also recorded two marches with a big band on Columbia E-2220. These were released simply as the "Orkiestra Columbia."

The Przybylski records were a step in the right direction, since they at least were locally produced and were intended to respond to what the Sajewskis and their customers wanted. But Frank Przybylski was a trained musician, and his musicians played from the orchestrations he supplied. Nevertheless, he consciously relied on folk materials, and the quality of his records was such that his orchestras and arrangements were in demand by Columbia for more than thirty years. Along with the Sajewskis, he actively recruited talent for the label that by the 1920s was trying to adjust its foreign-language program more closely to the tastes of local markets.

> The salesman would come in, and phonographs and records—Victor and Columbia—were the two main lines. Each one was watching the other; if one had a hit, the other wanted somebody like that.

Frank Przybylski's Orchestra in Columbia's 1930 Polish catalog. Music Division, Library of Congress.

We were always interested in folksong records. The company would tell us to find somebody and they would record them. Then you would have to find somebody, and then be able to sell the records. So naturally we were always on the lookout. People would come in and ask for a song they knew on a record. They might sing it, and we would find somebody to write it down, Mr. Przybylski was a capable man. He knew how to arrange these things. We would then find an artist who would be able to sing the song in that type of way that the people wanted—not a concert singer, but a person with an ordinary voice. Often people would come in to the store and would sing a song just in that way that you wanted. Then we would have to get Mr. Przybylski or somebody to accompany him.

And you would put that person on a record, somebody who walked into the store?

Oh, absolutely. That's how we found a lot of our artists. The record companies didn't care who they were; all they wanted to know was how many we could sell. They didn't care what language it was or how it sounded. They left it up to who was in the control room. As a rule it would be somebody who was selling those records, because the company representative didn't know what it was all about. He'd ask you, "What do you think? You think you'll be able to sell 'em?" If you went to a record company and said you had somebody who was good, they'd ask how good was he? You'd say, "Oh, he's good. Everybody likes him." Well, they'd turn around and say, "Well, how many will you be able to sell?" And you'd have to be able to say you could sell 500.

Following World War I some vernacular material slowly began to appear. In 1917, Victor released some tasteful accordion solos by Jan Wanat.

Frank Dukla in Victor's 1931 Polish catalog. Courtesy of Richard K. Spottswood.

Shortly after that, an Odeon release (11055) featured solos by an unidentified *kobza* (bagpipe) player, recorded in Poland. In 1923, Columbia recorded a *duma* and a waltz by a fine old-time fiddler named Henryk Landowski and released them on Columbia 18005-F, one of the first records in their new, specially numbered Polish series. The newer orchestras were beginning to play polkas and other polish dances in a livelier and less formal fashion. Just as the Ukrainian records of Pawlo Humeniuk seem to have been the turning point for record company attention to folk music in natural settings, the village *(wiejska)* music of Chicago's Franciszek (Frank) Dukla seems to have been the first recorded dance music in a real village style, using lead fiddle, a clarinet, two harmony fiddles, and bowed cello or bass. He recorded for Victor for only two and a half years, beginning in December, 1926, but his performances had a genuine excitement and an authentic touch, and many stayed in the catalogs for years.

> *Frank Dukla's music sounds older than other music that was on records at that point.*
>
> Well, yes, it was. After all, they were all old musicians, and they all played by ear. None of 'em played from music. Maybe some of them did, but they didn't have any arrangements or anything. They just went in, sat down, and said, "Well, what are we going to play?" It was like when we were with the Highlanders: "Well, this one or this one?" "You start, ok?" And there they'd go. That's the way they'd record also. Sometimes they weren't sure when to finish, and they'd start over again. Sometimes you couldn't get a better take than that, so you kept it. Then they'd play it back and say, "Do you think you can do a better one?" "Yeah, maybe we can do a better one." "Well, we'll hold this one and start over again."
>
> Now that they have tape, they can cut the pieces together. But when you had the needle cutting, you couldn't do that. When it was spoiled it was spoiled.
>
> Dukla had a kind of bass that really came out beautifully on [early electric phonographs].

Dukla's was exciting country music, and it paved the way for other good village music groups, such as those of Józef Brangel, Józef Kmiec, Karol Stoch, and John Wyskowski, who followed on Victor. Columbia released somewhat less material of this type, relying primarily on Pawlo Humeniuk (Paweł Humeniak) and another Ukrainian group, the Orchestra Bratia "Holutiaky-Kuziany," or the Wiejska Czwórka "Bracia Kuziany," as they were credited in the Columbia 18000-F series. In nearly all cases, their Polish releases were not duplicated from the Ukrainian series. Humeniuk employed Polish singers; the Bracia Kuziany (Kuziany Brothers) Polish records were all instrumentals.

The accordionist Jan Wanat first appeared on Victor in 1917, and his records as soloist and leader continued to sell through the 1930s.

Jan Wanat possibly holding the modified accordion used for recording in Victor's 1931 Polish catalog. Courtesy of Richard K. Spottswood.

> Victor has an old artist Jan Wanat, he played an accordion. His records always sold. Whenever a new record of his came out, almost everybody bought it. He had a style all of his own; he had a way of getting right up to that horn and getting the bass in there.

People like that bassing. In fact, there was a story around that he had a special accordion with a special pedal put on the bottom to let him play the bass with his foot. Now, I never saw the accordion or had the opportunity to meet Mr. Wanat. He would be a very old man, if he's living.

Two of the most popular Polish singers of the day were not folk artists in any sense. Władysław Ochrymowicz appeared on Victor, Columbia, OKeh, Brunswick, and Vocalion and recorded some interesting topical material, including "W Suchym Kraju," which concerned Prohibition (Vocalion 60155); "All Right," a song about learning English (Brunswick 60029); "Bolszewik" (Bolshevik) (Victor 79139); and "Bolszewiczka" (a female Bolshevik) (OKeh 11396). Paweł Faut worked exclusively with Victor, and his records remained popular through the 1930s. His polish versions of pop hits were quite successful.

Władysław Ochrymowicz in Victor's 1927 Polish catalog. Courtesy of Richard K. Spottswood.

Władysław Ochrymowicz was a popular singer. His wife went by her stage name, Theodosia Wandycz; they were often on records together. They were one of the first entertainers to come to the United States after the First World War. He had a popular program and was very active out east. He had radio programs, and in the earlier years he had stage plays, comedies, and dramas.

One of the biggest hits Victor had was the one about the two Polish flyers who were going to fly across the Atlantic right after Lindbergh made his trip. It was called "The Polish Eagles" (Polskie Orly, Victor V–16058). It was one of the biggest sellers they had by Paweł Faut, one of the outstanding vocal artists that Victor had. He had a very pleasant voice, and he picked out some of the most beautiful songs. In fact he made a beautiful recording of "Ramona" (Victor 81339) when it was popular [1928]. He hit his stride, and for a couple of years the things he made were very big hits.[2]

His voice is more like a crooner's, isn't it?

Yes, like Bing Crosby, a very pleasant voice. He's still alive. I spoke to him about two years ago. He looked very well. In fact, he's still very popular up east. He has a Polish program somewhere up there.

Paweł Faut in Victor's 1931 Polish catalog. Courtesy of Richard K. Spottswood.

Of greater interest are recordings by the singers Bruno Rudziński, Władysław (Walter) Polak, and Stanisław (Stanley) Mermel. Rudziński, who still lives in Chicago, recorded for Victor, accompanying himself on a concertina. He played and sang with abandon, often singing wordless vocals in a Polish approximation of scat singing. One song, "Paweł Walc" (Paul's Waltz) (Victor V–16114), is the melody later claimed by Tex Fletcher, who popularized it in the 1930s (as did Eddy Arnold again in the 1940s) as "The Cattle Call." Polak's Victor records included good humorous and topical material. He played his own accordion accompaniments and performed in a style only slightly more formal than Rudziński's. Mermel, like Ochrymowicz appeared on a number of labels, including Victor, Columbia, Brunswick Vocalion, and OKeh. He was usually accompanied by good village groups, including those of John Wyskowski, Anton Labucki, and Jan Kapalka. My own high regard of Rudziński and Polak is not shared by Alvin Sajewski, but we do agree on Mermel:

> Both Rudziński and Polak, you would have to consider them a novelty. It was something unusual, their style and their singing. They weren't trained singers or anything. They just had a gimmick, a self-made style. Walter Polak kept changing from one time [signature] to another. Bruno Rudziński kept repeating himself. Then he'd forget something, so he'd start over. It was a novelty, like Spike Jones or something. If they'd make a dozen, only the first two or three would sell. After that they'd get monotonous.
>
> Stanley Mermel was very popular, a typical old-fashioned singer. He was self-made, not a concert singer. But he knew all the songs, and he sang them the way that people liked to sing themselves. That was the type of singer the companies wanted, the type they were looking for.

Perhaps the most exciting single discovery I made among Polish records from the 1920s was the music of the Polish Highlanders, or *górale*. Elsewhere I have recounted what I have been able to learn about this ancient and lovely

Publicity photograph. Left to right: Josef Nowobilski, second violin; Karol Stoch, leader; Stanisław Bachleda, singer; Stanisław Tatar, cello-bass; Francisek Chowaniec, second violin. Courtesy of Richard K. Spottswood.

singing and fiddle music.[3] Of particular interest is the music of fiddler Karol Stoch, who recorded twenty-eight sides for Victor between June, 1928, and November, 1929, and for Columbia with the visiting Polish scholar, actor, and singer Stefan Jarosz for Columbia in April, 1927.

> Karol Stoch's records sold only to a limited group of people, the Highlanders only. They're the only ones who would buy those records, because the music was typically theirs. There was no written music, and no two groups would play . . . they would play the same melodies, but they would play them altogether differently. They had trouble getting them on records, because the union was so strong. Anybody that came to record had to be a union musician or he wouldn't be let into the studio. Or if he got into the studio, then the engineers would walk out. You'd have to file with the union when you planned to record, and they'd look to see if the musicians were in good standing, and when they'd come to record the engineer would already have a clearance for them.
>
> When Stefan Jarosz came to America, he tried to get musicians, but he couldn't find any. At the time I wasn't so well acquainted with that type of music. We called Mr. Przybylski again—the old reliable—and asked him if he would be able to muster up the musicians. They got together and he sang his songs. They were strange to Przybylski, even. He listened and listened and said he couldn't write it that way. He said, "You sing, I'll write it out, and we'll see how it works out." He wrote them out according to the measures, and then he started to play. But the emphasis was all wrong. The records were a failure. When the Highlanders heard them, they said, "That's not our music." It was like somebody trying to play hillbilly music that wasn't familiar with it. You gotta have that feeling. But the record company didn't care. All they wanted to know was how many we could sell?

Stefan Jarosz

Początkowe dzieje Związku Podhalan w Ameryce Północnej są nierozłącznie związane z pobytem w Stanach Zjednoczonych p. Stefana Jarosza, obecnie profesora uniwersytetu, a naszego podróżnika i prelegenta tak w Ameryce jak w Europie. Wprawdzie z akcją organizacyjną Związku nie miał p. Jarosz nic wspólnego, jemu jednakże zawdzięczyć można powstanie Towarzystwa Tatrzańskiego, z którego wyłonił się Związek Podhalan.

Pan Jarosz przez swe odczyty i prelekcje o góralszczyźnie, Tatrach i Podhalu rozbudził w ludzie góralskim, zamieszkałym w Ameryce akcję w kierunku pracy nad podtrzymaniem tradycyj podhalańskich. Rozbudził on w tym ludzie przywiązanie do ziemi ojców i dawnych zwyczajów i obyczajów, podnosząc w nim świadomość, że być góralem, to nie tylko nie ujma, ale przeciwnie chluba. Dzięki tej rozbudzonej świadomości łatwiej już było powołać do życia samoistną organizację podhalańską, do czego pośrednio bardzo się przyczynił p. Stefan Jarosz, mający zamiar znowu nas odwiedzić.

A brief encomium; from *Pamiętnik 2-go Sejmu Związku Podhalan w Północnej Ameryce, 1933* (Polish Highlanders' Yearbook). Courtesy of Richard K. Spottswood.

The Columbia files indicate that Jarosz first recorded with Stoch, and subsequently made ten sides with Przybylski in January and April, 1928, the reverse of the sequence Sajewski outlines. Perhaps Stoch and his musicians, lacking union cards, were unable to gain entry to Columbia more than once, but had ample time to secure them during the year between the Victor and Columbia dates. Sajewski's assessment of the records with Przybylski are correct: His musicians were unable to play in the choppy rubato style of the *górale*, and his orchestrations are conventional.

Stefan J. Zieliński (d. 1953) was a multi-talented artist who recorded frequently in the 1920s and 1930s. He performed both songs and skits, recorded in conjunction with bandleader Jan Kapalka, and others. His association with the Sajewskis lasted for many years:

> When he came to the United States he had already been on the stage. He had a theater here on Milwaukee Avenue for many years. He wrote all the plays and directed them and made all the big signs. He made all his own stage decorations—it was a one-man thing.
>
> When the schools started, the nuns and the organist would come to dad asking him for something for the children to sing, something for the organist to use in church. Whatever we could get

from Poland we got, but they wanted something simpler that would fit the children here. When we couldn't find anything, dad would have Mr. Zieliński, Mr. Przybylski . . . there were a lot of songs Mr. Zieliński wrote the words for and Mr. Przybylski the music.

Zieliński studied drama in Europe. He died just as he was about to establish a Polish theater. He had remodeled a building, made all his scenes by himself, it was all in place and the opening date was set. And he got a heart attack and passed away.

There isn't any other book in the whole world like [Zieliński's *Dances of Poland* (Chicago: W. J. Sajewski, 1953)]. It has all the figures and music. We were looking for something like this for many, many years. We had written to Poland, we'd written to libraries asking if there was anything. We wrote to publishers, too, but there was nothing in Polish dance. So when dad was in Europe, he went to the Library in Kraków and then in Warsaw, and he looked all over. He found books on Polish dances but they weren't instruction books. So finally dad commissioned Mr. Zieliński to do something. It took him several years, even with the help of a man at the Polish Museum here in Chicago. It's one of the finest there is even today.

Stefan J. Zielinski. From his *Instruction for Dances of Poland*, 1953. Courtesy of Alvin Sajewski.

When radio arrived in the 1920s, record sales slowly went into a general decline, though not so rapidly for ethnic dealers as for the general trade. While thorough study of foreign-language broadcasting in the United States has yet to be made, we know that in the early days, at least, radio did not provide serious competition. To the contrary, Zieliński and the Sajewskis for a time saw the new medium as an opportunity to expand their operations and get into something that seemed to offer as much entertainment for producers as it did for listeners.

In 1927 or '28, one of the first Polish programs on the air, on WKBI, had Mr. Zieliński as the announcer. It was on twice a week. He got some very good talent, and he did some singing.

The radio station was just starting. The studio was on top of a big bank building. Fred Shanewell, who owned the station, the bank gave him the top floor, where the elevator mechanism was. They told him he could use all that space up there for his controls and everything.

He didn't know how far he was going to go with it, because he was working on a shoestring. I went up to see him one time, when I was looking to buy a radio station, about 1927. I was commissioned by a big packing company which had several hundred thousand dollars ready. I went to several stations, but nobody wanted to talk about it at all. So I heard about Fred, so I thought here's a chance, so I went up to see him. We struck up a very nice acquaintanceship. He said it was something he had to try himself, but he invited me to sit down. We talked and talked, and finally he said, "Why don't you come over Wednesday? We're going to broadcast the fights from a little arena over here." So I went down with a friend and heard them broadcast, and he said, "You got anybody that wants to put on a Polish program? I won't charge them anything for it. Just let 'em come in and put on a program."

So I got ahold of Zieliński and said, "Look. Get yourself ready and you can have a Polish program." And it worked out good. It wasn't the first Polish program, but there wasn't anything earlier that was an established program.

Rudy Patek and Ben Ray, two concertina players, used to come up there, and they'd open up their concertina cases, take the concertinas out, sit on the cases and play. And no preparation: "And now they will play 'Edelweiss Waltz,' " and they would play "Edelweiss Waltz." "And now they will play 'First Waltz' " or something. "And now this is a polka, . . .Well, that's all today." Ben would say, "Hey Rudy, whatcha playing?" "Oh, I don't know, 'Kelma Polka.' " "Is that the name?" "No, but that's a good name for it." It was so amateurish, but it was a beginning.[4]

Sajewski store in 1920. Note the early electric violin-shaped sideboard. Courtesy of Alvin Sajewski.

One other potential area of expansion did not work out so well. The 1926 Brunswick Panatrope phonograph was the first to reproduce records electrically, and the difference in both the quality and volume of sound prompted the Sajewskis to consider new uses for it.

> One time I tried to have records made for mortuaries. When the Brunswick Panatrope came out, we needed records for undertakers. The Panatropes were installed in their chapels so you could hear soft music during the visting time when people came to pay their respects. The only trouble was, they wanted some organ records when some people objected to singing. But if you had soft music going it would be fine. They found a few things in the Victor and Brunswick catalogs, but there was nothing in Polish. I went to Columbia and told them I had an organist who would make records for me. We had arranged a whole series of Polish religious hymns he could have played on maybe a dozen records.
>
> But the first thing they asked was, "How many will you be able to sell?" Well, I started figuring how many undertakers we had in Chicago and then figured how many I thought would have Brunswick Panatropes. We, I found out there was maybe a dozen in Chicago, one or two in Gary, another in south Chicago or someplace. I could have sold fifty of them, but there were Polish communities in Detroit, Toledo, Hamtramck, Buffalo, Worcester, Massachusetts, Bridgeport, Connecticut. They asked, " Well how many do you know up there?" I said I didn't know any of them, but I knew there were a lot of Polish churches, and where there are Polish churches there's Polish undertakers. But they said that unless I could take a thousand that it wouldn't pay for itself. And that was the end of it.

After the October, 1929, crash, the record business suffered more than most. Columbia had purchased the General Phonograph Corporation in 1926; in 1930 it stopped production of most foreign-language records on OKeh and Odeon. A few OKeh artists had subsequent releases on Columbia, but most did not have the chance to record again. The Brunswick company kept releasing Polish records on its Vocalion label until 1931, but the better Vocalion Polish artists were also making records for other companies, and the Vocalion 60000 Polish series sold poorly. Not only did the Sajewskis' trade dwindle, but people were forced to return the phonographs purchased on installment because they could not meet their payments.

If the decline in business was gradual, the resurgence was abrupt. Juke boxes were already in evidence during the 1920s, following the development of electric phonographs. They continued to appear during the Depression, replacing live musicians in many areas. Juke boxes reinforced a process radio had begun, standardizing tastes as they offered familiar popular tunes by prominent artists.

I do not know when "Beer Barrel Polka" by Will Glahé's Musette Orchestra was recorded in Germany, or the exact date it was released here. Victor numbered it V–710 in its V–700 series, advertised as "especially adapted for coin machine operators," [5] and released it in 1935 or 1936.

> And when the "Beer Barrel Polka" came out, things never stopped again until the war. It was the first thing like that that ever

"Beer Barrel Polka," released by Victor around 1935. Courtesy of Pekka Gronow.

came out. There were instrumentals before that, but not anything unusual, unless it was in the popular field. But "Beer Barrel Polka" really started things going, and they never slowed down after that. It started the whole polka thing.

It was just as the juke boxes were coming out. The juke boxes were in the taverns. "Beer Barrel Polka" came out in the spring, so all the doors were open, and all the taverns with juke boxes put them right in the door and blasted away. That was a shot in the arm. People were getting jobs, and all of a sudden there was new life completely. You could get a big twenty-six-ounce stein of beer for a dime, and things were really rolling.

"Beer Barrel Polka" suited everybody's mood exactly. Not only was it possible to buy full-strength beer legally again, but more and more people had the means to do so. The tune was simple and catchy, and Glahé's recording of it was loud and forceful enough to be easily heard over the din in a noisy tavern. In popular locations the record had to be replaced frequently because copies rapidly wore out. Sales of the record spiraled; it appealed to many national groups, and "Beer Barrel Polka" soon became successful in the popular field, too. When the Andrews Sisters brought out a version with English words for Decca, it became one of the company's biggest sellers and rivaled the success of the original.

From that time onward, polkas were big business on records, either as instrumentals that could easily cross language barriers or as vocals with English lyrics. The Andrews Sisters compounded their success with tunes like "Pennsylvania Polka" and "Deep in the Heart of Texas." A host of new polka bands sprang up, each vying for another hit record. Among them were the Skertich Brothers (Serbo-Croatian), "Whoopee John" Wilfahrt and Lawrence Duchow (German), the Plehal Brothers and Jerry Mazanec (Czech), Wasyl Gula (Bill Gale) (Ukrainian) the Bonetti Brothers (Italian), and Eddie Terley (Edmund Terlikowski), Bernie Wyte (Bernard Witkowski), Edward Królikowski, and Joe Łazarz (all Polish). These and others all had successful polka records, spelled by an occasional waltz for relief. Titles appeared more and more often in English, and like the polkas, they were snappy and ephemeral: "Kicking Up," "Nickel in the Slot," "Hy'a Susie," "Elmer the Milkman," "Nosy Rosie," "Pound Your Table," "Fly a Kite," "Charlie Was a Boxer," "Rookie Playing Hookey," "Let's Try a Jumpka." [6] As swing music swept the country after 1935, the hot music of Benny Goodman and Count Basie, and the Lindy, Big Apple, and other new dances found their counterpart in the revitalized polkas. If the polka bands did not swing in the conventional sense, the brillance and energy of their music made up for it.

Earlier it had taken a depression to slow the Sajewskis' momentum; the next obstacle they faced was another war. Record production was hampered because the raw materials were needed for defense. Difficulties were compounded when the American Federation of Musicians declared a strike that kept union musicians from recording for nearly two years, from 1942 to 1944. Record companies attempted to keep their best-sellers in print, and a system evolved by which one record was turned in and melted down for every new one sold:

In World War II we had to turn in old records for every new

record, and that's where we lost a lot of the good records that we had. When the time came that I had to go and pick up records, they would call me and say they had 150 or 200 records for me, but in order to get them I had to take a bushel basket with old records in it. We would advertise in the paper that we were paying five cents apiece for old records. People would bring them in; they could be cracked, broken, damaged, it didn't make any difference. It got to the point where there wasn't any old records to be had any more. So if they had 200 records for me, I would go to the shelf and dump records into a box or bushel basket and save sleeves. They just dumped them into barrels. First of all we took the popular English records, and when I didn't have any more of them, I started to reach into the Polish records.

But the polka bands' popularity remained strong. Following the war new labels like Harmonia, Rondo, Sonart, Dana, and Continental quickly formed and brought out records as soon as they could. Of the big labels, only Columbia remained genuinely active. Like Victor, it kept its older popular ethnic records in print, and established favorites like Bill Gale and Edward Krolikowski kept new releases coming. But Columbia wanted some new talent as well. Alvin Sajewski had worked briefly with the Rondo label, suggesting songs and musicians for recording, until a young organist named Ken Griffin made a hit version of an old German waltz called "You Can't Be True, Dear" ("Du Kannst Nicht Treu Sein"). Rondo had its hands full keeping track of both the record and the artist and as a result stopped making Polish records. When Columbia sent an executive to consult with Alvin Sajewski, he was ready to help out.

I had switched from Rondo when Sandor Porges came in. Rondo had been a little hesitant about Polish music and didn't want to get too many records out. Sandor Porges came in from the Columbia office in Bridgeport, Connecticut. He was a new man, so he came to see us in Chicago. He introduced himself and told us what he was looking for. He had Edward Królikowski's band from Bridgeport, and Królikowski suggested that he come to see me. Królikowski had already made "Clarinet Polka" and "Julaida Polka," and other instrumentals.

So Mr. Porges wanted some polkas. I told him, "Fine, fine, how many do you want?" He said he was going to have a Slovenian band come in and a German band from Wisconsin, and he wanted one session with four selections. So I got John Niemiński and Fred Drzewicki to do some vocals, and I got Ed Terlikowski to back 'em up with the music, and they were tremendous hits. Mr. Porges called me and said, "Alvin, I want you to get me another band and another singer."

Was he paying you at the time?

Oh no, I did that for gratis. I was glad to do it because I knew what I wanted. I knew that if I had those records that I could sell them. And Li'l Wally was just starting out, and I saw that he had good possibilities. So I got ahold of Li'l Wally, he was only about eighteen or nineteen, and I had Ed play for him again. And Li'l

One of Li'l Wally's first recordings, 1949. Motion Picture, Broadcasting, and Recorded Sound Division, Library of Congress.

Wally did OK. He went big. So they were happy with that and said, "Alvin, we need more." By that time I had just gotten hold of Joe Durlak. He did "Whose Girl Are You?" and that one just busted wide open. In the meantime I had also gotten Anna Malec, who was a very fine singer with a beautiful voice, and we made several sessions with her.

Then Mr. Porges switched from Columbia to Capitol Records, which were going big. They had just organized, and he was put in charge of the foreign records.

Did he organize their foreign-language program?

Yes, he did the whole thing. All they had was Johnny Mercer and a few others. They were just starting. So I got him Marisha Data. I got Eddie Zima, Steve Adamczyk, and Jania sang for him. Then he may have retired, I'm not sure. But there was a change of organization or something, and Mr. Porges left them. When he left, they discontinued their foreign catalog.

The Columbia releases sold well, aided not a little by the company's maintaining a fifty-three-cent retail price while its smaller competitors were forced to sell at seventy-nine cents. But as its strength grew in the popular field, records in the foreign-language area accounted for a smaller percentage of profit. Finally Columbia withdrew, as Victor was also doing, and left the field to the new entrepreneurs.

Predominant among these was Walt Dana, a talented musician with classical training who had directed some choral records for Victor before the war. By 1950 his catalog could boast several dozen records, including a number of popular tunes recorded twice, once with Polish and once with English vocals. His records sold well in the East, but like Porges, Dana realized that there were other regional music styles. A short time after Porges left Capitol, Dana came to Alvin Sajewski for help in breaking into the midwestern market.

He had several records; he had Ray Henry and Gene Wiśniewski and a few others, but they were all eastern bands, which didn't have our style of playing; they were too fast, and we couldn't do much with 'em.

Was that always the case, that the eastern bands played too fast?

Yes. The eastern bands referred to the Chicago style as "hillbilly." Now they've forgotten their style, and they all follow the Chicago style.

So Mr. Dana came in and wanted to record some Chicago bands. So I game him Marisha Data and Steve Adamczyk, Johnny Bomba, the Polkateers. He was a nice man to get along with. He needed somebody over here, and I happened to be here and it worked out very nicely. Whatever you suggested, he was happy with it.

Who supervised his Chicago recordings?

Oh, he did. He came to Chicago. Mr. Dana was a very accomplished musician. He was a pianist, a composer, and a great jazz enthusiast. He knew what the people wanted, too. The nice part of it was that some of these musicians, if they couldn't get something straight, he would just take a pencil and change this or that and say, "Now try it." And there it was. If they were lacking something he would find where there was an empty spot where they could use a little something, and there it was.

In 1948, Władysław Sajewski died suddenly while attending a play. He and Alvin had been inseparable, both personally and professionally. Alvin was henceforth responsible for the store, its staff, and its merchandise. Though he remained actively involved with Walt Dana for several years, Alvin was eventually forced to withdraw from the promotional actvities that kept him away from the business, which was still expanding and requiring greater amounts of time.

Those were some very, very beautiful years. I had about eight or nine years of it. They closed Dana because he had overextended himself. Fiesta Record Company took it over. That was the end of it. The musicians I knew were getting old, and by that time there were already so many young groups coming up and they were doing very well.

The younger musicians still had great respect for Alvin Sajewski's opinion and counsel. The store had been a major retail music outlet for more than two generations. His experience in music and close contacts with customers made him an excellent arbiter of tastes.

They would come over when they put out a new record and say, "Well, what do you think of it, Mr. Sajewski, how does it sound?" I'd say, "It sounds pretty good. Leave me about twenty-five, and if I need more next week I'll call you again." It helped them; if Sajewski was selling it, it must be good. So I never discouraged them. If they came to me and asked what to record, I would tell them.

Someone would come in and say, "Hey, we got a band. We sound just like Frankie Yankovic. Boy of boy, are we ever good!" And I'd say, "Well that's fine. What are you going to do?" "Well, we want to make some records." I'd answer, "I don't know if anyone needs a Frankie Yankovic band because they got one already. One Frankie Yankovic is enough. Why don't you go out and make your own style?

"And don't be afraid to play what people want. When they come to you and say, 'Play that one that you played before,' don't tell them, 'Whaddaya mean, play that? We just played it. Whaddaya think, that's all the songs we know? We'll play you some songs you didn't hear yet.' " I said, "Don't ever do that to people. You know why they asked you to play that song? Because they liked it."

I said, "If you want to know how much people like you, get yourself at least five thousand printed cards. Give each guy a whole pocketful. After you play for about an hour and a half or so, have all the musicians go pass them around. After the dance is over, if

Władysław Sajewski, Alvin's father, died in 1948. Courtesy of Alvin Sajewski.

Album cover from Bel Aire, Eddie Blazonczyk's own record label. Courtesy of Richard K. Spottswood.

Advertisement in International Polka Association *News*, May 1978. Courtesy of Pekka Gronow.

you see a lot of your cards on the floor, change your style. It's the only way you can ask people; they won't tell you to your face."

Although there was a flurry of recording activity in the United States for many national groups following the war, by the end of the 1950s much of it had come to an end, and many of the retail stores that stocked such discs closed down or relied in greater degrees on imported music. Television, Top 40 radio, and the increasing standardization of tastes in music are probably among the factors in the change. An exception to the rule is Alvin Sajewski, whose business has prospered. The Polish community in Chicago is still large and self-reliant, and one can easily hear the new bands and singers on radio, on television, and in person. There are still active recording studios in the city that specialize in Polish music, and at least two (those of Chet Schafer and Eddie Błazonczyk) are currently involved in reissuing important music from 78s.

Błazonczyk, an energetic and multi-talented individual, is of *góral* descent, the son of musical parents. As Eddie Bell and the Bel-Aires he toured with a rock group in the late 1950s before returning to Chicago to form a Polish band which today is one of the best. As Alvin Sajewski indicates below, the modern bands tend to be eclectic, and Błazonczyk is especially so. He is an active fan of rock, country, bluegrass, and Cajun music and likes to incrorporate them, when appropriate, into his own music. From his headquarters on West Forty-seventh Street he also runs an active record label (Bel-Aire), a distributorship for his own and other labels, and a recording studio. Błazonczyk's band, the Versatones, play a memorable mixture of old and new songs, which Eddie sings in Polish, English, or sometimes both. A fiddler and concertina provide traditional elements, balanced against two precision trumpeters who also double on clarinet. The lead instruments are heavily underscored by Błazonczyk's own booming electric bass and by a good drummer, who plays a polka beat as loudly as would a rock drummer. This successful formula keeps the band busy touring and their 45s, LP albums, and eight-track tapes selling rapidly. And Błazonczyk is far from being the only active producer.

Our record business has improved every year since the war. It's bigger now than it ever was. Now you have mostly LP records, they're all $4.98, $5.98. So before, when you sold four or five records it took you a heck of a long time. Now the volume is much bigger. You sell records faster for more money.

These new bands, the Dynatones and Dynaswings and Dynasties, Versatones, they all mix 'em up. They have a little Polish, a little English. Some of these boys don't even know what they're singing. They write the words out phonetically and sing them as well as they can. But people don't mind as long as the rhythm is there and the song is there, they sell.

Who are the biggest artists today?

We have Little Richard, Li'l Wally's still holding his own. We must have gotten six or seven hundred LPs this month from him. Of course, there's a lot of Christmas records there, but with his polka records he has quite a catalog. On Monday I'll probably call him in Florida and ask him to send me a few more. We have to consider Eddie Błazonczyk's Versatones, and Chester Schafer's records. About 25 percent of our records come from Poland, and that's quite a bit.

The eastern bands make about 15–20 percent of our sales. Eddie Błazonczyk's Bel-Aire label has some eastern bands. He has Wanda and Stephanie, those two concertina players, those two girls; they sell very well. Then Chet Schafer's Chicago Polkas label has that Forty-seventh Street Concertina Band; that's selling real big. Marion Lush sells real well, too.

On May 18, 1977, a large banquet was held in Chicago to celebrate the eightieth year of the Sajewski Music Store, an event that testified to the importance of the cultural role it has played both in the community and in the lives of many individuals. A year later, Alvin Sajewski was elected to the Polka Music Hall of Fame; he was cited as a "pioneer music publisher, former talent scout and A & R [artist and repertoire] man for major record labels." He was the first nonperformer to win election to the Hall of Fame, a creation of the eight-year-old International Polka Association, with headquarters in Chicago.[7] In addition to commemorating the accomplishments of Władysław and Alvin Sajewski, these events also celebrated the fact that Polish music in America is alive and flourishing. As long as it remains so, the last chapter on the Sajewskis will not be written for quite a while.

Mr. and Mrs. Alvin Sajewski by an exhibit case for the 1977 Ethnic Recordings in America Conference at the Library of Congress. Photograph by Carl Fleischhauer, American Folklife Center, Library of Congress.

Notes

I first met Alvin Sajewski in September, 1975, when my friend and colleague Marianne Kozlowski of the Fine Arts Library at Southern Illinois University suggested we visit him. If Alvin was nonplussed to meet a young easterner who was not of Polish descent, who had never been to Chicago before, and who could only claim he was there because he had heard Polish music recently for the first time and liked it, he did not show it in the least. He greeted us cordially and took several hours away from his busy schedule while we talked, examined old record catalogs and sheet music, and ate a delicious Polish lunch together.

We became good friends quickly, and Alvin has since generously given several hundred Polish 78s to the Library of Congress, and swelled my own collection with some catalogs and beautiful recordings as well; these form the basis for much of my own discussion in this article.

Mr. and Mrs. Sajewski's participation in the Library of Congress conference on ethnic recordings made many people aware of his extensive knowledge and experience, as well as his deep feelings for the music that has formed the backdrop for his life. A number of people have visited him since then with cameras and tape recorders to learn his story. Nevertheless, when I asked for the chance to interview him again on December 8, 1977, he graciously consented, even though it would take him away from his business during the busy Christmas season.

Since this article is based on our discussion that day, I have quoted Alvin Sajewski extensively, with minimal editing. The interview and this article cannot of course cover eighty years of the Sajewskis' business, much less its community background, in extensive detail. Nevertheless, many points were brought out as we talked—enough, I hope, that the reader can grasp some of the flavor and intrinsic interest of the Sajewski story.

I would like to give special thanks to Alvin's sister Jania Sajewski-Terley, who is directly quoted once, and whose work forms a part of this history. She is an excellent singer in her own right and in recent years has lent her expertise to the operations of the store, continuing to keep it a family business. During this interview, as on other occasions, she came to my assistance by amplifying and reinforcing a number of facts and details.

1. At the Ethnic Recordings in America conference, January, 1977, Myron Surmach described his arrangements with Columbia. It involved a simple fifty-fifty split of his Columbia advertising costs with the company, which made it slightly less complicated, though certainly less economical, then the Sajewskis' arrangement.

2. "The Polish Eagles" was released Sept. 13, 1929, under the title "Polski Ory," Victor V-16058. "Ramona" appeared on Victor 18-81339.

3. "Karol Stoch and Recorded Polish Folk Music from the Podhale Region," *JEMF Quarterly* 13, no. 48 (Winter 1977): 196-204.

4. Rudy Patek was one of the earlier Chicago Polish artists to record. Beginning in 1923, the General Phonograph Corporation released a number of concertina duets by Patek and Charles Blim on its OKeh and Odeon labels.

5. *Victor International Records ("V" Series): Complete Alphabetical Catalogue of All Languages* (?New York: Standard Phonograph Co., 1940).

6. Titles from ibid.

7. *IPA News*, May, 1978, front page.

Stylistic Change in Recorded Polish Music

At present we can make only rather general statements about the whole range of Polish music on record. To trace the history of Polish recording activities both here and abroad, we will ultimately need access to a far greater number of recordings from all eras. Unfortunately, there is no public or private archive posessing Polish recordings in any significant number. Early and modern catalogs do exist, and this helps considerably. But even these often do not contain enough information to let us draw accurate descriptions of a given performance. Nevertheless, since the Sajewski operation spanned eighty years and has paralleled virtually the entire history of Polish recording, both here and abroad, to place it in perspective it is useful to recount what *is* known, paying specific attention to artists and styles of particular interest to students of folklore.

The earliest American Polish-language recordings, by a tenor with piano, were made for the Berliner Company around 1897, the year Władysław H. Sajewski opened up shop. During the following decade, the acoustical process was improved enough to allow small instrumental ensembles to back singers, and this format dominated until electrically processed records were first issued in 1925. Baritones, contraltos, tenors, and sopranos were recorded in New York and Europe. Fred Gaisberg (not always a reliable chronicler) mentions a recording trip made for the Gramophone and Typewriter Company, Victor's English affiliate, to Warsaw prior to April, 1901, where he recorded several members of the Polish National Opera.[1]

We can consider the Victor Polish-language recording program in some detail, since we have more complete sources of documentation for that firm, which issued annual numerical lists for dealers from the mid-1910s through 1932, and numerous foreign language catalogs afterward. Victor's primary rival, Columbia, tended to follow many of the same patterns. The only other companies with Polish catalogs of any size were the General Phonograph Corporation (which became the OKeh Phonograph Corporation after 1926, when it became a subsidiary of Columbia), whose labels were OKeh and Odeon; and the Brunswick-Balke-Collender Company, which released Polish material on Brunswick and Vocalion between the mid-1920s and 1931.

The 1921 list shows a preponderance of trained singers, performing material ranging from grand and light opera to popular, comic, standard, and patriotic songs.[2] There are vocal trios, quartets, and choral groups offering primarily religious material. Spoken word items include comic monologs, recitations, or small skits—and it is in this area that we encounter some topical material. There are performances by instrumental soloists, small groups, and orchestras, but not in great quantities. Records by the Kapel "Victor" (Victor Military Band) and Kapela Konwej'a (Patrick Conway's Band) attest to Victor's use of studio musicians to make special records for the foreign catalogs. Other recordings with vague artist credits, like the Orkiestra Warszawa (Warsaw Orchestra) or the Orkiestra Wiejska (Village Orchestra), are possibly by studio groups as well.

Two releases by the Sycylijski Kwartet (Sicilian Quartet) indicate that polkas and mazurkas from other national groups had some appeal. Within a few years Victor expanded its practice of reissuing, as Polish numbers, recordings from other language series, often disguising both title and artist credits. Eventually, records from Italian, Lithuanian, Slovak, Ukrainian, Finnish, French-Canadian, and German series were marketed to Polish customers.

Those artists enjoying the greatest popularity (or at least the highest number of releases) in the acoustical era include comics Antoni Fertner, M. Domosławski, and Wincent Rapacki; tenors Jan Sztern, Józef Kallini, and Karol Wachtel; soprano Wiktorja Kawecka; baritones Tadeusz Wroński and Norbert Wicki; accordionist Jan Wanat; the Orkiestra Włościańska directed by Karol Namyslow; and, of course, concert pianist Ignacy Jan Paderewski. Though other language series had twelve-inch releases in some quantity (especially German and Italian), Polish releases (with the exception of those by Paderewski, marketed to a general audience) were virtually all ten inch. One interesting pair of ten-inch records is by Henryk Czaki, whose "Spórki Wojskowe" (Victor 65566, 65567) is described as singing with violin accompaniment; the discs were listed 1914 and may contain genuine vernacular music.

By 1931 the Victor Polish catalog had changed radically.[3] Only one artist from the 1921 offering, Jan Wanat, was still making records. All acoustical records (those made before May, 1925) were deleted, and the percentage of trained singers is much smaller. In December 1928, Victor began issuing records intended for minority groups in special numerical series whose numbers were preceded by V–. The V–16000 ten-inch series and V–66001 twelve-inch series were reserved for Polish records; by February, 1931, the series had reached V–16169 and V–66008, respectively. These releases may be divided into a far greater number of categories, many of them interesting as folk music. A rough breakdown reveals the following:

VICTOR
POLSKIE REKORDY
(Victor Polish Records)

KAWAŁKI PATRJOTYCZNE
(Patriotic Selections)

J. S. ZIELIŃSKI Z ORKIESTRĄ J. KAPALKI
80328 | Boże Coś Polskę
10"-75¢ | Jeszcze Polska Nie Zginęła

POLSKA KAPELA WOJSKOWA
68844 | Marsz Narodowy Polski
12"-$1.25 | Marsz Piłsudskiego

ORKIESTRA WITKOWSKIEGO
78887 | Marsz Tadeusza Kościuszki
10"-75¢ | Mazur Po Komendzie Kościuszki

PIEŚNI KOŚCIELNE
(Religious Songs)

WYKONAŁA GRUPA ŚPIEWAKÓW
V-66006 | Procesja na Boże Ciało—Część 1, 2
12"-$1.25 |

WYKONAŁ ZESPÓŁ PIELGRZYMÓW
59001 | Pielgrzymka na Jasną Górę
12"-$1.25 | Powrót z Jasnej Góry

An example of topical categories for record listings in Victor's 1931 Polish catalog. Courtesy of Richard K. Spottswood.

Village orchestras: 38 (primarily by Frank Dukla)

Popular/standard vocals: 35 (primarily by Paweł Faut, including some skits)

Skits (usually with village music): 14

Singers with village orchestras: 13 (primarily by Stanisław Mermel)

Singers with accordion or concertina: 12 (primarily by Władysław Polak)

"Legitimate" (nonvillage) orchestras: 12

"New-wave" polka bands: 12 (primarily by Ignacy Podgórski)

Instrumental duets, trios, quartets: 11 (primarily featuring accordion and violin)

Podhale (Góral): 10 (all by Stanisław Bachleda and Karol Stoch)

Accordion solos: 9

Vocal quartet or choral: 6

Pipe organ solo: 1

Whistling solo: 1

Street organ solo: 1

Military band: 1

The predominant musical unit by this time was the village (*wiejska*) orchestra. There was increased interest in a variety of Polish dances. Polkas were available in much greater numbers, but so were *obereks*, mazurkas, *kujawiaks*, *krakowiaks*, waltzes and góral dances. Much of this music was played by *wiejska* orchestras, usually string groups whose sound bore more than a faint resemblance to the string-band music heard in the American South and Southwest. Frank Dukla's records featured lead clarinet and violin, backed by harmony violins and bowed cello. Others followed this pattern or occasionally augmented it with extra brass or reeds. Several singers recorded with village orchestras, especially Stanisław Mermel, who had a fine, natural untrained voice. Village orchestras were almost always included on recorded skits as well.

The skits themselves are of interest, since they often deal with topical material. Józef Kmiec's records are particularly intriguing, and include one about moonshining ("Munsiajni Agenci," Victor V–16112), a drunkard's dream ("Sen Pijaka," V–16093), a silver wedding party ("Srebne Wesele," V–66003) and an Old Country festival ("Odpust w Odpoyszowie," V–16118).

I have coined the term "new-wave" polka bands to distinguish the music of Ignacy Podgórski, Edward Królikowski, and others from that of their predecessors. Their groups blended brass, accordion, and violin, combining the energy of the village orchestras with a smoother, more emphatic melodic line; their music also had greater speed and a brighter edge. Podgórski, from Philadelphia, and Królikowski, from Bridgeport, Connecticut, continued to enjoy great popularity in the 1930s and 1940s.

Of interest are several records drawn from other national groups, including the whistling solo by the Italian Guido Gialdini (V–16089), who had several releases in the early acoustical period, and a French-Canadian accordion-bones duet credited to Latrowski and Ryandowski on V–16084. The names were almost right; the original

Listing of comic skit recordings in Victor's 1931 Polish catalog. Note the top illustration depicting a moonshiner's encounter with the law. Courtesy of Richard K. Spottswood.

Canadian release on Victor 263626 was by Joseph Latour and Charles Riendeau. Two good German records by Die Sechs Hungrigen Musikanten (The Hungry Six, V–6002, V–6023) appear on V–16005 and V–16097 as by Pięć Glodnych Muzkantów (The Hungry Five). A mazurka and polka were drawn from two separate Ukrainian releases (V–21047 and V–21062) by the Ukrainska Selska (Village) Orchestra of Philadelphia, and released as V–16134, recredited under the fiddler's name, M. Slobodian, as the Wiejska Orkiestra Slobodziana. One item, the street-organ solo by Katrynka, is suspicious. The organ is of the nineteenth-century barrel type, but the melodies on V–16155, though given other titles, turn out to be "O Sole Mio" and "La Paloma."

A sixteen-page Polish catalog issued in January, 1940, reveals further changes which took place in the 1930s.[4] Its only categories are dance music (8½ pages), vocal music (2 pages), and marches (½ page). Smatterings of the 1931 offerings remain, including a few old records by Stoch and Bachleda, Frank Dukla, and the ubiquitous Jan Wanat, who was still recording for Victor in the 1930s. But by 1940 the offerings concentrated on dance bands. Leading the list is Bernard Witkowski i Jego Orkiestra "Srebne Dzwony" ("Silver Bell" Orchestra), who is given a full page advertising twenty-five releases. Bernard, who is still active in music, was the nephew of Leon Witkowski, referred to earlier as the leader of a more standard orchestra of the early 1920s. Bernard's music was bright and snappy, and the momentum created by his "Beer Barrel Polka" (to which he added a Polish vocal) assured him of a long career. Also popular were the orchestras of Edmund Terlikowski, Ignacy Podgórski, and Walter Dombkowski, and the Makowska Orkiestra of Chicago, led by G. Dzialowy. The latter was close to the village music of the 1920s. The first Makoswka records were made for Vocalion around 1928, and the group became even more popular when Victor began recording them four years later.

Of the thirty-eight singers, M. Fogg leads the list, with six releases. Half of his songs are tangos, for which he perhaps enjoyed a personal vogue. Following him is Paweł Faut, the Chór Arfa (Arfa Choir), and the Chór Dana, led by the same Walt Dana who worked with the Sajewskis in the 1940s and 1950s.

V–16606, released in December, 1942, and V–16607, released in November, 1943, were the last Victor Polish records made before the war brought production to a close. Production resumed in 1946, when 170 old releases were reinstated in a new 25–9000 series, along with some new ones by younger bands like the Polish Mountaineers and Walt Ossowski's Orchestra. Releases following 25–9170 were newly made, and the series continued until all Victor Polish recording activity was dropped.

Columbia's activities closely parallel Victor's. Columbia recorded for the Polish audience from the earliest days (the Sajewski store still has some discs made in 1902 and possibly earlier). During the acoustical period, both companies recorded many of the same artists, like Tadeusz Wrónski and Leon Witkowski's Orchestra. In 1924, Columbia began its 18000–F series (ten-inch) and 63000–F series (twelve-inch) devoted to Polish releases. Like Victor, it began recording electrically in May, 1925, and soon dropped most of its earlier records from circulation, though in 1930–31 the company remastered a number of acoustical releases and brought them out again as new releases, advertising them as "Electrically Recorded" on the labels.

Some of Columbia's best village music was recorded by various groups under the leadership of the Ukrainian fiddler Pawlo Humeniuk, whose name was changed to Paweł Humeniak for Polish purposes. Some of his best-selling Ukrainian releases were skits built around ceremonial occasions; many of these were re-recorded with singing and speaking in Polish. Thus, his successful "Ukrainske Wesilie" (Columbia 70002–F) was transformed into "Polskie Wesele" (63005–F), which sold nearly as well as the original. Humeniuk continued making Polish records until 1936; Alvin Sajewski considers him one of the company's most popular artists of the period. Humeniuk's "Polka 'Kanarek' " (18257–F), released in 1928, was one of the Sajewskis' biggest sellers. It proved so popular with Polish audiences that it was re-released twice in the Lithuanian and Slovak series (16191–F and 24202–F, respectively), with new titles and fictitious artist credits. Nearly as popular was the Wiejska Czworka Bracia Kuziany (Kuziany Brothers' Village Group), another Ukrainian group from the New York area. Their Polish releases were exclusively instrumental and featured the usual clarinet and four violins, somewhat in the style of Frank Dukla. Other popular artists of the 1925–35 period included the singer-comedian Ignacy Ulatowski, various ensembles directed by Frank Przybylski, the opera tenor Marek Windheim, Stanisław Mermel (who recorded for Columbia as frequently as he did for Victor), Fabian Okulski (who specialized in songs like "Halleluja Jestem Bom" and "Wesoly Kawaler"—"Hallelujah, I'm a Bum" and "The Gay Caballero," respectively—and other translations of pop song hits), violinist and bandleader Edward Mika, and accordionist Bruno Kamiński.

Heading a Columbia list in the late 1930s[5] was the Ukrainian bandleader Wasyl Gula, who earlier had directed the Trembita Orchestra that recorded for Victor's Ukrainian series. Like other bands of his time, Gula's offered the newer bright polka tempos, and his records sold well. Following the success of "Beer Barrel Polka," Gula's group became known as the Bee Gee Tavern Band, Brunek Grabówski's Orchestra, and even the Orqestra El Salon Columbia (for Hispanic audiences) on the Columbia and OKeh labels before World War II. Following the war Gula led a group known as Bill Gale's Trotters. His recording activities did not slacken until the 1950s.

Gula leads this eight-page Columbia listing, printed around 1937, with thirty-nine releases (including fifteen credited to Brunek Grabówski). All but five are instrumentals, which made it possible for his records to be marketed in the Ukrainian, Lithuanian, and other series. Gula is followed by other bands, like those of Paweł Humeniak (Pawlo Humeniuk) with twelve releases, and Ignacy Podgórski with eleven.

Earlier in this article, Alvin Sajewski referred to the aggressive activities of Sandor Porges in Columbia's behalf after 1945. Porges was indeed responsible for an enormously popular foreign-language program. For several years, with artists like the Orkiestra Polskiej Karuzeli (Polish Merry-Go-Rounders Orchestra), the Windy City Five, Juke Box Serenaders, Edward Królikowski, and Frankie Yankovic, Columbia competed successfully with the smaller polka companies during most of the polka fad of the later 1940s.

The postwar period and more recent decades are dealt with earlier in this article by Mr. Sajewski, and there is little I can add to his discussion.

Notes

1. F. W. Gaisberg, *The Music Goes Round* (New York: Macmillan, 1942), p. 16.

2. *1921 Numerical List of Victor Records Including All Records Announced Prior to January 1921 Supplement* (Camden, N.J.: Victor Talking Machine Co., 1920).

3. *1931 Numerical List of Victor Records Containing All Records Announced Prior to and Including the February 1931 Supplement* (Camden, N.J.: RCA Victor Co., 1931), pp. 257–61, 343–44, and *passim*.

4. *Victor International Records Kompletny Spis Rekordów Polskich* (Complete list of Polish records) (?New York: Standard Phonograph Co., 1940).

5. *Polskie Recordy, Columbia Polish Records* (Bridgeport, Conn.: Columbia Recording Corp., n.d.).

Artists Promoted and/or Recorded by the Sajewskis

The following list was compiled from a souvenir booklet distributed at the Sajewski testimonial banquet in Chicago, May 18, 1977, and from additional information supplied by Alvin Sajewski.

1920–40

Artist	Label
Chór Noew Lycie, choir	Victor
Niuta Gutowska, singer and actress	Victor
Stefan Jarosz, singer	Columbia
Władysław (Walter) Jonas, singer and accordionist	Victor, Polonia
Jania Kapalka, orchestra leader	Victor, Brunswick
Kipkowski Brothers Orchestra	Columbia
Władysław (Walter) Polak, singer and accordionist	Victor
Frank Przybylski, band and orchestra leader	Columbia
Bruno Rudziński, singer and concertina player	Victor
Stefan J. Zieliński, singer and actor	Victor

1945 to the present

Artist	Label
Steve Adamczyk, orchestra leader	Capitol, Dana, Rondo
Ampol-Aires, orchestra	Ampol
Johnny Bomba, orchestra leader	Dana
Marisha Data, singer and monologist	Capitol, Chicago, Dana, Harmonia, Rondo
Fred Drzewicki, singer	Columbia
Joe Durlak, singer	Columbia, Rondo
Harmony Kings, orchestra	Chicago
Gene Heir, orchestra leader	Rondo
Hi Notes, orchestra	Chicago
Alice Kusek, singer	Rondo
Li'l Wally (Jagiello), singer and orchestra leader	Columbia, Jay Jay
Mattie Madura, singer and orchestra leader	Chicago
Anna Malec, singer	Columbia, Vita-Tone
Naturals, orchestra	Chicago
Jan (John) Niemiński, singer and orchestra leader	Columbia, Vita-Tone (his own label)
Joe Pat (Paterek), accordionist and orchestra leader	Chicago, Melodia, Vita-Tone
Rudy Plocar, orchestra leader	Rondo
Polish Merry-Go-Rounders Orchestra (Orkiestra Polskiej Karuzeli)	Columbia
Polka All Stars, orchestra	Chicago

1945 to the present—continued

Artist	Label
Polkateers, orchestra	Dana
Frank Przybylski, orchestra leader	Rondo, Capitol, Columbia
Jania Sajewski, singer	Capitol, Credo
Stan-Lee (Lyskawa), singer and orchestra leader	Chicago
Kaz. Stefaniak, singer	Rondo
Edmund Terlikowski, violinist and orchestra leader	Columbia, Victor
Windy City Five, orchestra	Columbia
Casimir Zieliński, singer	Capitol
Eddie Zima, orchestra leader	Capitol, Dana, Rondo, Victor

Appendix III *Selected Discographies*

Franciszek (Frank) Dukla

Frank Dukla's recordings were all made for Victor. They appeared with numerous small variations in the credits, such as Orkiestra Dukli, Fr. Dukli Wiejska Banda (Frank Dukla's Village Band), and Fr. Dukla Wiejska Orkiestra. Polish nouns and proper names change endings according to case, the use of which is often unclear on old record labels; however, *Dukla* seems to be the nominative form of his name.

All recordings I have heard feature a lead fiddle (Dukla), two harmony (or second) fiddles, clarinet, and bowed cello or bass. I do not know the identities of any of the supporting musicians, except the singers. English titles are taken directly from record labels as available.

The numbers given in the left-hand column are the master numbers assigned to each selection, with the issued takes (–1, –2) where known. The numbers in the right-hand column indicate one or more release numbers for each selection.

All recordings were made in Chicago, Illinois.

December 7, 1926

BVE 37200-1	"Na Około Czarny Las" (A Dark Forest Around)—Polka Singing by Stefan J. Zieliński	79268, V-16203, 25-9023
BVE 37201-2	"Uparta Dziewczyna—Oberek" "Singing by Stefan J. Zieliński	79138, Bluebird B-2629
BVE 37202-1	"Icek Rekrut" (Isaac the Recruit)—Polka	79203, V-16164, Bluebird B-2628, Library of Congress LBC-4 (33⅓)
BVE 37203-2	"Obertas z Dukli" (Obertas from Dukla)	79268, V-21063
BVE 37204-1	"Polka z Pod Krakowa" (Cracow Polka)	79138
BVE 37205-2	"Bukowina—Mazurek"	79203, V-16164, V-21063, Bluebird B-2628

June 17, 1927

BVE 39013-1	"Kukłeczka Polka" (Cuckoo Polka)	80146
BVE 39014-1	"Taniec Poślubny" (After the Wedding)	80146
BVE 39015-1	"Polka z Dębowca" (Polka from Debowca)	80051, 25-9304, 53-9304 (45), Bluebird (?) B-0061-1
BVE 39016-1	"Na Wykretke—Oberek" (Twisting Oberek)	80051, 25-9304, 53-9304 (45), Bluebird (?) B-0061-1
BVE 39017-2	"Pomalusku Nawracajcie—Obertas" (Slowly Return) Singing by Jan Kapalka	79445, V-16203, 25-9023
BVE 39018-1	"Na Boisku—Polka" (In the Barn)	79445

November 6, 1927

BVE 40814-2	"Walc z Podgorza"	80301
BVE 40815-1	"Walc z Lwowa"	18-80642[a]
BVE-40816-1	"Zawzieta-Dziewczyna—Polka" (Stubborn Girl) Singing by Jan Kapalka	80301, New World NW 283 (33⅓)
BVE 40817-2	"Wesola Dziewczyna—Oberek" (Happy Girl) Singing by Jan Kapalka	18-80719
BVE 40818	"Mazur—Dworski"	18-80719
BVE 40819-2	"Drobno Tańcuj—Polka"	18-80642

[a] The "18-" prefix before a release number indicates that the record is Polish. This system was used briefly prior to the introduction of Victor's V-16000 Polish series in 1928.

November 13, 1927

BVE 40859-2	"Smutna Dziewczyna—Polka" (Sad Girl) Singing by Jan Kapalka	80372, V-16561, 25-9135
BVE 40860-2	"Polka Wirzbickiego"	80372, V-16561, 25-9135
BVE 40861-2	"Nik to Nam Niemoźé—Mazur" (Nobody Can) Singing by Jan Kapalka	18-80589
BVE 40862-2	"Polka z Góry Marcina"	18-80589
BVE 40863-2	"Polka z Krosna" (Polka from Krosna)	80477
BVE 40864-2	"Waltz z Wiednia" (From Vienna)	80477

June 17, 1928

BVE 45393-1	"Uwiedziona Dziewczyna—Polka" (The Cheated Girl) Singing by Paweł Faut	V-16051, 25-9003
BVE 45394-2	"Dziewczyna w Zielonem Ogrodzie—Polka" (A Girl in a Green Garden) Singing by Paweł Faut	V-16051, 25-9003
BVE 45395-1	"Polka z Lublina" (Polka from Lublin) Singing by Paweł Faut	V-16003, V-16331
BVE 45396-1	"Pierwsza w Ameryce—Polka" (First in America)	18-81449
BVE 45397-1	"Polka z Bochni" (Polka from Bochni)	18-81449
BVE 45398-a	"Polka z Dębicy" (Polka from Debicy)	18-81669, 25-9298 53-9298 (45)

June 24, 1928

BVE 45968-1	"Chłopak Jedzie po Dziewczynie" (The Boy is Riding for his Girl) Singing by Paweł Faut	18-81512
BVE 45969-1	"Zalotna Dziewczyna (Flirting Girl) Singing by Paweł Faut	18-81512
BVE 45970-1	"Dziewczyne Odprowadzil" (He Escorted His Girl) Singing by Paweł Faut	V-16003, V-16331
BVE 45971-1	"Mazur z Sonoka" (Mazur from Sonoka)	18-81669, 25-9298 53-9298 (45)
BVE 45972-1	"Wesele z Wojtowy" (Wedding from Wojtowy)	V-16034
BVE 45973-1	"Wesele w Ogrodzie" (Wedding in the Garden) Talking by Paweł Faut	V-16034, Folk Lyric FL9026 (33⅓)

July 24, 1929

BVE 55484-1	"Weselny Krakowiak" (Wedding Krakowiak)	V-16119
BVE 55385-1	"Polka z Harklowy" (Polka from Harklowy)	V-16119
BVE 55486-2	"Sztajerek Dukli" (Dukla's Sztajerek)	V-16082
BVE 55487-1	"Sztajerek od Gorlic" (Sztajerek from Gorlic)	V-16082
BVE 55488-	"Na Weselu w Harklowy—Część 1" (At a Wedding in Harklow—Part 1)	V-16063
BVE 55489-1	"Na Weselu w Harklowy—Część 2" (At a Wedding in Harklow—Part 2)	V-16063
BVE 55490-1	"Weselny Marsz" (Wedding March)	V-16147[a]
BVE 55491-1	"Polka Wegierka" (Wengerka Polka)	V-16147

[a] The titles on V-16147 seem to be reversed; the march side is actually a polka, while the polka side seems to be a march.

Recordings by Jōzef Kmiec's Orchestra (V-16096, V-16189) and by Walter Dombkowski groups (V-16205, V-16214) were credited to Dukla also.

Paweł Humeniak (Pawlo Humeniuk)

Only Humeniak's Polish recordings are listed here. All releases are on Columbia except as indicated. As with Frank Dukla, no supporting musician's identities are known; instrumentation is given, when known, following each session. All recording were made in New York City.

January, 1927

w107530-2	"Zaręczyny, Część 1"	18182-F
w107531-2	"Zaręczyny, Część 2" Odegrał Skrzypce Solo Paweł Humeniak Singing by Ewgen Żukowsky Violin and accordion	18182-F

Dates unknown

w107885-1	"Poprawiny, Część 1"	18202-F
w107886-2	"Poprawiny, Część 2" Ułożył I Odegrał Z Orkiestrą Paweł Humeniak Singing by Ewgen Żukowsky and Nasza Roza Krasnowska Two violins, accordion, and trombone	18202-F
w107887-3	"Oberek pod Stodoła"	18221-F
w107888-1	"Oberek na Przedmiesciu" Odegrał Z Orkiestrą Paweł Humeniak Two violins, accordion, and trombone	18221-F
w205554-6	"Polskie Wesele, Część 1"	63005-F (12")
w205555-5	"Polskie Wesele, Część 2" Ułożył I Odegrał Z Orkiestrą Paweł Humeniak Singing by Ewgen Żukowsky, Nasza Roza Krasnowska, and others Two violins, accordion, and trombone	63005-F (12")
w108009-2	"Tance w Karczmie, Część 1"	18207-F

Dates unknown—continued

w108010-2	"Tance w Karczmie, Część 2" Ułożył I Odegrał Z Orkiestrą Paweł Humeniak Singing by Ewgen Żukowsky, Nasza Roza Krasnowska, and others Two violins, accordion, and trombone	18207-F
w205598-1	"Huczne Chrcziny, Część 1"	63007-F (12")
w205605-2	"Huczne Chrcziny, Część 2" Ułożył I Odegrał Z Orkiestrą Paweł Humeniak Singing by Ewgen Żukowsky, Nasza Krasnowska, and others Two violins, accordion, and trombone	63007-F (12")

Fall, 1927

w108537-1	"Tańce w Lesie"	18236-F
w108538-1	"Krakowiak Górala" Odegrał Z Orkiestrą Paweł Humeniak Singing by Stanisław Grazda Three violins, flute, and bowed cello or bass	18236-F
w108539-1	"Oberek na Trzy Mile"	18242-F
w108540-2	"Sztajerek" Ułożył I Odegrał Z Orkiestrą Paweł Humeniak Three violins, flute, and bowed cello or bass	18242-F

Ca. March, 1928

w108883-1	"Weselne Czasy, Część 1"	18255-F
w108884-2	"Weselne Czasy, Część 2" Ułożył I Odegrał Z Orkiestrą Paweł Humeniak Singing by Antoni Antoniewski Two or three violins, two clarinets, trumpet, and bass saxophone	18255-F
w108885-2	"Oberek Mieszany"	18257-F
w108886-1	"Polka 'Kanarek' " Ułożył I Odegrał Z Orkiestrą Paweł Humeniak Two or three violins, two clarinets, trumpet, and bass saxophone 16191-F is a Lithuanian issue. Title: "Paukštužis." 24202-F is a Slovak issue, as by "Slovensky Hudba." Title same.	18257-F, 16191-F, 24202-F, Surma SU 141

August, 1928

w205989-1	"Jaselka, Część 1"	63008-F (12")
w205990-1	Jaselka, Część 2" Orkiestrą Pawła Humeniuka Singing by two unidentified men Violin, clarinet, flute, trombone, and bowed cello or bass	63008-F (12")

December, 1928

w110133-3	"Dwa Szczygle, Polka"	18303-F

December, 1928—continued

w110134-2	"Nie Żeń Się Góralu, Krakowiak" Ułożył I Odegrał Z Orkiestrą Paweł Humeniak Two or three violins, clarinet, and bowed cello or bass	18303-F

March, 1929

w110433-4	"Polka 'Wiesniaczka' "	18321-F, 16194-F Library of Congress LBC-4 (33⅓)
w110434-5	"Oberek z pod Babiej Gory" Ułożył I Odegrał Paweł Humeniak Violin solo, accompanied by two violins and bowed cello or bass 16194-F is a Lithuanian issue. Title: "Kaimetè."	18321-F, Folk-Lyric FL9015 (33⅓)

Ca. March, 1929

w110453-2	"Polka 'Marianna' "	18332-F, 27307-F
w110454-2	"Oberek 'Po Robocie' " Ułożył I Odegrał Z Orkiestrą Paweł Humeniak Two or three violins, clarinet, and bowed cello or bass 27307-F is a Ukrainian issue. Title: "Dobra Hospodynia, Jak Powna Skrynia, Polka."	18332-F

March, 1929

w206198-2	"Ślub Janka z Heleną, Część 1"	63010-F (12")
w205199-2	"Ślub Janka z Heleną, Część 2" Ułożył I Odegrał Z Orkiestrą Paweł Humeniak Singing by two male voices, one female voice Three violins, clarinet, bowed cello or bass, and organ	63010-F (12")

June, 1929

w110824-1	"Oberek na Bosaka"	18337-F
w110825-1	"Polka 'Figuranta' " Ułożył I Odegrał Z Orkiestrą Paweł Humeniak Two or three violins, clarinet, and bowed cello or bass 27307-F is a Ukrainian issue. Title: "Polka 'Pocilnuok.' "	18337-F, 27307-F

Summer, 1929

w110959-1	"Oberek Krakusa"	18340-F
w110959	"Nowe Krakowiaki" Ułożył I Odegrał Z Orkiestrą Paweł Humeniak Two or three violins, clarinet, and bowed cello or bass	18340-F

September, 1929

w111091-1	"Polka 'Farmerka' "	18354-F
w111092-1	"Jestem Imigrantka, Walc" Odegrał Z Orkiestrą Paweł Humeniak	18354-F

Early 1930

w111485-2	"Imieniny Marysi, Część 1"	18378-F
w111486-1	"Imieniny Marysi, Część 2"	18378-F
w111487-2	"Kłótnia Matki ze Synowa"	18381-F
w111488-1	"Odjazd Rekruta do Wojska" Ułożył I Odegrał Z Orkiestrą Paweł Humeniak Two male and two female singers Violin, trumpet, accordion, and piano	18381-F

Fall, 1930

w112199-2	"Polka 'Figa z Makiem' "	18409-F
w112260-1	"Chodzym do Karczmy, Oberek" Ułożył I Odegrał Z Orkiestrą Paweł Humeniak	18409-F

March, 1931

w112844-2	"Dalej Chłopcy Dalej Nasy"	18446-F
w112845-2	"Oberek Komiczny" Ułożył I Odegrał Paweł Humeniak violin, accordion, guitar, bowed cello or bass.	18446-F

June, 1931

w113044-1	"Icek we Lwowskiem Więzienieu"	18460-F
w113045-2	"Oj Nie Żeń Się Synu" Ułożył I Odegrał Z Orkiestrą Paweł Humeniak Singing by Stanisław Grazda Clarinet, accordion, piano, and whistling; no violin audible.	18460-F

September, 1931

w113126-1	"Jak to Przykro Zyk Sanemu"	18471-F
w113127-1	"Jak Się z Kejda Wie Ozenie" Singing by Stanisław Grazda Credit uncertain; two or three violins, clarinet, piano and bowed cello or bass.	18471-F

1934

w113924- (w131247-1)	"Gosc z Ameryki w Stary Kraju, Część 1"	18571-F
w113925- (w131248-1)	"Gosc z Ameryki w Stary Kraju, Część 2" Credit and instrumentation unknown	18571-F

November 7, 1935

CO 18243-	"Taniec na Zareczynach"	18599-F

November 7, 1935—continued

CO 18244-	"Hasia Basia Polka"	18599-F

December 13, 1935

CO 18377-1	"Krakowiak Górala" (Mountaineer Krakowiak)	18600-F
CO 18378-1	"Polka Kukułka" (Kuku Polka) Credit and instrumentation unknown	18600-F

January 30, 1936

CO 18606-	"Stukaj Pukaj Polka" (Treat 'em Rough)	18601-F
CO 18607-	"Wokolo Wesolo Oberek" (Everybody's Happy)	18601-F
CO 18608-1	"Z Gory na Doł Polka" (Down the Hill)	18602-F
CO 18609-1	"Kujawiak na Wiosce" (Village Kujawiak) Ułożył I Odegrał Z Orkiestrą Paweł Humeniak Violin, clarinet, accordion, and bowed cello or bass	18602-F

May 12, 1936

CO 19232-	"Matula"	18613-F
CO 19233-	"Oberek Mlynarza"	18613-F
CO 19234-	"Jagusia Polka"	18616-F
CO 19235-	"Krakowiak Ulana" Credit and instrumentation unknown	18616-F

Other Humeniuk records in the 18000–F Polish series are reissues of Ukrainian releases, and are not listed here.

Władysław Polak   All recordings are on Victor, except as indicated, and all were made in Chicago, Illinois. Unless otherwise noted, all feature singing with accordion.

December 4, 1927

BVE 41306-2	"Lament Pijaka"	80410
BVE 41307-2	"Krakowiaki Makowiaki"	80410
BVE 41308-1	"Żonka Piła, Chłop Orał" (The Wife Drinks, While Husband Works)	V-16002
BVE 41309-2	"Ruru Piesa Nie Pasowal" (The Stove Pipe Did Not Fit)	Unissued
BVE 41310-1	"Niestały Kawaler" (Wandering Sheik)	18-80590
BVE 41311-1	"Żal Kochanski" (Lover's Fate)	18-80590

June 8, 1928

BVE 45320-2	"Polska Dziewczyna" (Polish Girl)	18-81338
BVE 45321-1	"Gdy Byłem Młody" (When I was Young)	18-81338

June 8, 1928—continued

BVE 45322-1	"Złamane Przyrzecenie" (Broken Promise)	V-16013
BVE 45323-2	"Śpiew Młodego Więźnia" (Song of a Young Prisoner)	V-16013
BVE 45324-1	"Rozmaite Krakowiaki" (Variety—Krakowiaks)	V-16020

July 10, 1928

BVE 46087-1	"Ze Starej Wsi" (From the Old Village)	V-16002
BVE 46088-1	"Dzieci w Krateczki" (Children in Squares)	V-16020, Library of Congress LBC-6 (33⅓)
BVE 46089-1	"Dobry Apetyt" (Good Appetite)	18-81513
BVE 46090-1	"Ostatnia Wola Pijaka" (The Drunkard's Last Will)	18-81513, Library of Congress LBC-9 (33⅓)
BVE 46091-1	"Niewierz Kobiecie" (Don't Believe a Woman)	V-16044

Decembers 3, 1928

BVE 48648-1	"Żony z Pieniądzamy" (Women With Money)	V-16073
BVE 48649-2	"Rada Sasiada" (Neighbor's Advice)	V-16073
BVE 48650-1	"Tak To Bywa na Tym Świecie" (It Happens on This Earth)	V-16115
BVE 48651-1	"Serce Samo Kocha" (The Heart Loves)	V-16115
BVE 48652-	"Sąd Nad Rozwódkami" (Judgment Day for the Widows)	V-16044
BVE 48653-	"Kochanie Się w Strach Zmienło" (Love Turned into Hate)	V-16039
BVE 48654-	"Zstanej Strony Wody" (From the Other Side of the River)	Unissued
BVE 48655-	"Śpiewki Przed Muzyka" (Songs before the Orchestra)	V-16039

July 15, 1929

BVE 55412-1	"W Amerykańskiem Miśscie" (In an American City)	V-16091, Library of Congress LBC-10 (33⅓)
BVE 55413-2R	"Prędkie Ożenienie" (Quick Marriage)	V-16091
BVE 55414-1	"Polka Samohód" (Automobile Polka) Accordion solo	V-16130
BVE 55415-2	"Djabeł w Niewoli" (Devil in Jail) Accordion solo	V-16130
BVE 55416-1	"Polka Lucyja" Accordion solo	Unissued
BVE 55417-1	"Pijany Władek" (Drunken Walter)	Unissued

Bruno Rudziński

All recordings are on Victor, except as indicated, and were made in Chicago, Illinois. All feature singing with concertina.

July 9, 1928

BVE 46071-2	"Przysezedł Chłop do Karczmy" (A Man Came to the Saloon)	V-16114, Library of Congress LBC-11 (33⅓)

July 9, 1928—continued

BVE 46072-1	"Skoczmy—Polka" (Hopping—Polka)	V-16008
BVE 46073-1	"Francuska—Polka" (French—Polka)	18-81522
BVE 46074-1	"Na Obie Nogi—Polka" (On Two Feet—Polka)	V-16008, New World NW-283 (33⅓)
BVE 46075-1	"Tramla Polka"	18-81522
BVE 46076-1	"Paweł Walc" (Paul's Waltz)	V-16114, Folk Lyric FL 9026 (33⅓)

Recorded Ethnic Music: A Guide to Resources

Norm Cohen and Paul F. Wells

The readers of this book have now been introduced to the careers of several persons—artists and businessmen—who have been involved in the recording of America's ethnic music; they have followed the history of ethnic recordings in this country; they have learned about the role of ethnic music today in various American communities. The goal of this final chapter is to tell them where they can obtain examples of ethnic music, and where they can turn for more information about it.

Although this book, *Ethnic Recordings in America*, is subtitled *A Neglected Heritage*, there is a great deal of relevant material that can be considered under the heading of resources. Ethnic recordings have been neglected only in a special sense: They have not, in general, been neglected within the ethnic communities; rather, they have been neglected by the outside scholarly community. Furthermore, even this statement is not entirely correct. The literature dealing with Amerindian music, Hispanic music, and Jewish music, for example, is in each case vast; we would have no trouble listing several hundred references in each of these three areas. In the spirit of our volume's subtitle, then, we have allowed considerable bias in our survey of resources. We have been very restrictive in the cases of those musical traditions for which the literature is extensive; at the other extreme, we have tried to comb all likely sources for information about those traditions that truly have been overlooked. Apart from the three areas just specified, another body of ethnic music has received considerable scholarly attention; this includes the English-language ethnic music traditions: Anglo-American (in particular, the music called "hillbilly") and Afro-American (in particular, "blues" and "gospel" music). Our coverage in these areas, therefore, is also very cursory. We stress that our treatment does not result from any arbitrary decision of what constitutes "ethnic" music, but follows directly from a desire to focus our efforts where the least amount of work has been done. However, we have tried not to slight Irish and Scottish material, particularly to the extent that they represent traditions distinct from the English.

Within the above framework, we still found it necessary to draw our boundaries more restrictively than the material at hand allowed for; and here we discuss in more detail the limits of our coverage. In the first place, that this volume is titled *Ethnic Recordings* rather than *Ethnic Music* directs attention to the mechanical medium of recordings. Therefore, in citing printed references we have paid particular attention to those that are concerned with recordings. Furthermore, the medium of recordings does admit nonmusical genres, such as drama, comedy, and monologues, and we have tried to take this into account.

A second question of scope concerns the distinctions between folk, popular, and classical music, all of which can still be subsumed under the heading of "ethnic" music if a foreign language and culture are involved. Are we to include Indian ragas? Armenian operas? Hebrew cantorial music? Taking our cue from the fact that this study was carried out under the auspices of the American Folklife Center of the Library of Congress, we concluded that folk music was the genre of primary interest, and accordingly devoted most of our coverage specifically to folk music. Classical and pop music are surveyed only to the extent that they are related to or derived from a folk tradition.

Now, there are admittedly areas where a clear-cut distinction between folk and pop music is not possible. A common phenomenon in Western musical culture is the commercialization of what once was local folk tradition and its escalation into a product of the mass media. In this country it has happened several times: in the evolution of hillbilly music into country-and-western music; "downhome" blues into rhythm-and-blues; midwest Polish-American dance music into the ubiquitous polka parades; regional music of the Caribbean (calypso, reggae) into a national phenomenon; *norteño* music of the Texas-Mexican border into a hybrid that is currently having considerable impact on country-and-western. In every case, one can observe the same general trends as the music is transformed: The initial performers are semi-professionals or nonprofessionals to whom music is only a casual pursuit; the music is intended for local consumption; the performances are rough and unpolished. As the genre becomes popularized, the professionals take over; the music becomes polished and slick; the industry undertakes to broaden the appeal as widely as possible by obliterating the strongly regional characteristics. The music moves toward the mainstream of American popular music. While the transformation that thus takes place does not necessarily make the music any less interesting to, or viable within, the ethnic community, it does move it toward a product that is more readily and widely obtainable today, and therefore less interesting to us in terms of the kinds of criteria we have already described as guiding our attentions. We stress early, "folksier" recordings, therefore, at the expense of later, more polished and sophisticated ones. In particular, we have looked for noncommercial field recordings made by folklorists and ethnographers not intended for consumption within the ethnic community, because these often are able to present the precommercial roots of the musical idioms.

For this reason, we are particularly interested in the early commercial foreign-language recordings of the 78 rpm era, the history of which has been documented earlier in this volume by Pekka Gronow. In their often indiscriminate efforts to provide foreign-language recordings for domestic consumption, the large record companies were as likely to turn up vigorous but unpolished bands of street folk musicians as operatic singers who rendered folksongs from sheet music arrangements. The record labels are generally no guide to which extreme is being presented (though the designation "folk song" on a 78 rpm record label is more often than not the clue to a concert-hall style of presentation), and the record catalogs are still less helpful. Furthermore, it is often presumptuous to assume that the inexperienced listener will be able to classify a Serbo-Croatian accordion player or a Hopi chanter as performing in the folk rather than the concert-hall style (if indeed these are meaningful distinctions in every musical culture). Consequently, our efforts to note every recent LP reissue of 78 rpm recordings may, in the light of later knowledge, have led us further afield than we had hoped; but at this point we can do no better.

Another type of restriction has been found necessary to make our task manageable, and that is the exclusion of all recordings that originated outside North America. In several senses this is an artificial distinction, justifiable only in terms of the space and time available to us. For example, what intrinsic difference is there between a recording made of a Norwegian fiddler while he was still living in Norway and one made of him a few years later, after he emigrated to the New World? Or, why should we take into account commercial recordings of Lithuanian artists recorded and issued in the United States, but not recordings (often issued in the same numerical series, and often not distinguished on the label) made by Lithuanian singers in the old country that were pressed and offered for sale in the United States? Both were purchased by the Lithuanian-American community, and both had the potential for influencing the course of music within that community. (To emphasize our point we have stressed in the latter example the frequent interchangeability of the domestic and the foreign-originated recordings when offered for sale in this country; in fact, there was often a certain prestige value attached to the foreign recordings; labels never specified United States–originated recordings, but occasionally did note recordings that were imported. The arbitrariness of this limitation is further evident to anyone who wishes to pursue in depth any questions about the nature or background of American ethnic music. How can one study the ballads of Sephardic Jews of Seattle or Atlanta without having at hand the materials pertaining to Sephardic balladry in Turkey, Salonica, Spain, and other Old World regions whence the immigrants came?)

Finally, we have neglected material that is "American" in a broader context but comes from outside the fifty states of the union. Thus, in particular, music in Puerto Rico is not included—but Puerto Rican music by immigrants in New York is.

So much for the scope of our focus. We have tried to gather information on resources, written and recorded, that are relevant to the ethnic recordings that fall within the outlined limits. But resources for whom? For those within the ethnic communities or those outside them? For the most part, the members of the communities, who partake of an active and continuing musical tradition, do not need to be directed to resources. Our intended audience, rather, consists of outside scholars and enthusiasts—those who wish to study the traditions, and those who wish to recreate them. For these reasons we are particularly interested in articles that provide broad surveys and introductions to the music, and in albums that are accompanied by informative liner or brochure notes and are particularly useful for demonstration and educational purposes.

Following a brief general section of references that apply to ethnic music in general, our survey is broken up into divisions that have proven useful to us but are admittedly inconsistent in mixing linguistic and regional groups. The sequence is as follows:

I. Native American
   A. Amerindian
   B. Hawaiian
II. European and Eurasian
   A. English
      1. Celtic (Irish, Scottish, Welsh)
      2. Anglo-American and Afro-American
   B. Hispanic
   C. French (Canadian French, Louisiana French, Missouri French)
   D. Scandinavian
   E. Germanic
   F. Baltic (Lithuanian, Latvian)
   G. East European
      1. North Slavic (Polish, Czech, Slovak, Slovenian, Ukrainian, Russian)
      2. Serbian and Croatian
      3. Other Balkan
   H. Other European (Italian, Hungarian, Portuguese, Miscellaneous, Gypsy)
III. Asian
   A. Armenian
   B. Middle Eastern
   C. Oriental
IV. Jewish
   A. Hebrew (Liturgical, Hassidic, Zionist)
   B. Yiddish (Folksong, Art Song and Theater Music, Dance Music)
   C. Judezmo
   D. Nonmusical
   E. General

Within each of these sections we include a general discussion followed by references to significant printed and recorded sources. These in turn are followed by lists of the record companies and archives included in the appendixes at the end of this chapter that are relevant to the musical traditions under discussion. Often we are aware of other companies, archives, and collections, which did not, however, respond to our questionnaires (discussed further in the appendixes). In many such cases, we have tried to provide useful finding information elsewhere in the chapter.

We are deeply grateful to several friends and colleagues who read all or parts of the manuscript and offered many helpful suggestions for additions and revisions. Philip Sonnichsen, in particular, undertook to rewrite the section on Hispanic music completely, including a lengthy and fascinating section on the history of Latin American musical influences in the United States. His full essay was too long for inclusion here; it is being published separately in the *JEMF Quarterly*. Judy Tiger and Meredith Wright reordered our Balkan material. Christina Niles made several additions to the

Baltic section, as did Barbara Kirshenblatt-Gimblett to the Jewish section. Richard K. Spottswood and Pekka Gronow read the entire manuscript and offered numerous emendations. Our thanks to all of them.

General References

Surprisingly little has been written about the many facets of the traditional American musical heritage. Until very recently, almost all scholarship has focused on the Anglo-American, the Afro-American, and the Native American traditions. The best general guide to the literature dealing with other genres published up to mid-century is Charles Haywood's *Bibliography of North American Folklore and Folksong*, 2 vols. (1951; reprint ed., New York: Dover Publications, 1961). Part 3 (pp. 429–607), subtitled "Ethnic Bibliography," deals mostly with black American folklore, but also with non-English-speaking groups. All of volume 2 is devoted to Native American peoples.

There are very few general texts on American folk music; of them, only Bruno Nettl's *Folk Music in the United States: An Introduction*, 3d ed., revised and expanded by Helen Myers (Detroit: Wayne State University Press, 1976), has much that pertains to what we are calling ethnic music, for instance, in the chapters "Hispanic-American Folk Music" and "Folk Music in the City." A pioneering work, then, is Theodore C. Grame's *America's Ethnic Music* (Tarpon Springs, Fla.: Cultural Maintenance Associates, 1976), a 232-page survey of the various kinds of music found in America, arranged by type rather than by national origin.

None of these, however, deals at any length with the specific subject of *recorded* ethnic music; on this topic the essay by Pekka Gronow, "A Preliminary Checklist of Foreign-Language 78s" (*JEMF Quarterly* 9, no. 29 [Spring 1973]: 24–32), is indeed groundbreaking; that essay is revised and expanded considerably in this book. The primitive state of scholarship in this field reflects the general low esteem in which sound recordings have been held until quite recently. It would seem obvious that there should be some publication—or at least some archive—to which one could turn for a complete listing of all recordings made by a given record company in a given time period, but such is far from the case. In this matter, scholars in all fields can look to the jazz discographers, who were decades ahead of everyone else in setting standards for the information science of discography. Today, only blues and gospel music has been comparably well served. For example, one of the most important recent discographical publications is Brian Rust's *Victor Master Book, Volume 2 (1925–1936)* (Hatch End, Middlesex, England: By the author, 1969), a comprehensive guide to recordings by the Victor Talking Machine Company (and its successor, RCA Victor) during a ten-year period. Yet this book specifically excludes all recordings made "for nationals in America speaking other than the English language" and all classical recordings. One cannot fault Rust, however, for being guided by what were clearly the dominant interests of record collectors a decade ago (or even today, for that matter). We can think of few effects a publication such as this might have that would be more far-reaching than the undertaking of a similar discography for non-English-language recordings.

Native American Traditions

For purposes of this directory, we have stretched the term "Native American," which is usually applied to North American Indians (including Eskimos), to cover natives of Hawaii as well. Although Hawaiians did not actually become "Americans" until statehood was achieved in 1959, we feel that this is the most sensible way of treating their music in this directory.

Amerindian

There has been a vast amount of American Indian music recorded for both commercial and scholarly purposes. The first ethnomusicological field recordings of any type were those made by American anthropologist J. Walter Fewkes of the music of the Zuni and Passamaquoddy Indians in 1889. Fewkes later became director of the Bureau of American Ethnology and sponsored or encouraged other field recording of Indian music, including the work of Frances Densmore (see Densmore bibliography, cited below). Much of this early material is now housed in the Library of Congress.

Although commercial recordings of American Indian music were issued prior to 1910, little discographic research in this area has been attempted. Two articles from *Talking Machine World* of June 15, 1926 (reproduced in *JEMF Quarterly* 9, no. 29 [Spring 1973]:32) suggest that the division between commercial and scholarly recordings was not a strict one. The articles describe how the Starr Piano Company recorded Hopi music (for their Gennett label), and note that the Starr representatives were working in conjunction with Dr. Fewkes. Masters of these recordings were to be deposited in the Smithsonian Institution. Although the discs were designed to be sold throughout the country, particularly through the tourist trade in the Southwest, one of the articles notes that "records of this sort do not appeal strongly to those who are interested chiefly in record sales volume, but they have importance from a historical standpoint that should not be underestimated."

Currently active companies, such as Canyon and Indian House, are also operated in the spirit of preservation and documentation of Indian traditions, rather than strictly as commercial ventures. Canyon has recorded contemporary performances of Indian rock and country-and-western music as well as traditional tribal music. They have also released records of the Mexican-influenced *waila* music of the Papago, Yaqui, and Pima tribes.

As noted above, little discographic research has been conducted on American Indian music. However, James Griffith is currently compiling discographies of *waila* music and of Yaqui music. Few LP reissues of early commercial recordings of American Indian music have appeared. The only one of which we are aware is *Hopi Katcina Songs and Six Other Songs by Hopi Chanters* (Folkways FE 4394), which is compiled from Gennett and Victor 78s of the 1920s; see Evans for a review of this disc.

Noncommercial field recording of Indian music certainly did not cease with the work of Fewkes and Densmore, as can be seen by the number of archives that list holdings of this sort. Ethnomusicologists David P. McAllester (Wesleyan University, Middletown, Connecticut), Charlotte Heth (UCLA), and Bruno Nettl (University of Illinois) are among the leading researchers in the field of American Indian music.

Although the published literature that deals specifically with recordings of Indian music is small, that dealing with the music in general is vast. Interested readers are urged to consult the Hickerson thesis and other bibliographic works cited below for leads to further printed sources. The Archive of

C-8031

PARKER SINGERS
Rocky Boy's Reservation, Montana
Cree Pow-Wow Songs Vol. II

SIDE 1
War Dance Song ● Owl Dance Song ● Pow-
Wow Song ● Pow-Wow Song ● Pow-Wow
Song ● Owl Dance Song

SIDE 2
Pow-Wow Song ● Pow-Wow Song ● Owl
Dance Song ● Pow-Wow Song ● Pow-Wow
Song ● Pow-Wow Song

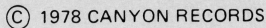

© 1978 CANYON RECORDS

Current Native American recordings on a cassette produced by Canyon Records. Motion Picture, Broadcasting, and Recorded Sound Division, Library of Congress.

Folk Song at the Library of Congress also distributes brief bibliographies relating to the music of various tribal and/or geographical areas. For a general introduction to American Indian music, see Nettl.

Printed References

"American Indian Music." In *The Folk Music Sourcebook,* edited by Larry Sandberg and Dick Weissman, pp. 149–50. New York: Alfred A. Knopf, 1976. Annotated bibliography.

"Bibliography [of Frances Densmore's writings]." *Ethno-Musicology Newsletter,* no. 7 (April 1956): 13–29. Additions, no. 10 (May 1957): 15. Corrections, *Ethnomusicology* 2 (January 1958): 26. Additions by Frank Gillis, ibid. 2 (September 1958): 131–32.

Cavanaugh, Beverly. "Annotated Bibliography: Eskimo Music." *Ethnomusicology* 16 (September 1973): 479–87.

Evans, David. "North American Indian Music." *Journal of American Folklore* 90 (July-September 1977): 364–71. Record review essay.

Fewkes, J. Walter. "A Contribution to Passamaquoddy Folk-Lore." *Journal of American Folk-Lore* 3 (October-December 1890): 257–80.

———."On the Use of the Phonograph among the Zuni Indians." *American Naturalist* 24 (1890): 687–91.

Guédon, Marie-Francoise. "Canadian Indian Ethnomusicology: Selected Bibliography and Discography." *Ethnomusicology* (September 1972): 465–78.

Hickerson, Joseph Charles. "Annotated Bibliography of North American Indian Music North of Mexico." Master's thesis, Indiana University, 1961.

———."History of Field Recording of North American Indian Music." *Phonographic Bulletin* (Utrecht) 9 (August 1974): 6.

Howard, Helen Addison. "A Survey of the Densmore Collection of American Indian Music." *Journal of the West* (April 1974): 83–96.

Isaacs, Tony. "Traditional American Indian Music on Record." *Sing Out!* 24, no. 5 (November-December 1975): 20–22. Survey of current companies and available material.

Korson, Rae, and Joseph C. Hickerson. "The Willard Rhodes Collection of American Indian Music in the Archive of Folk Song." *Ethnomusicology* 13 (May 1969): 296–304.

McAllester, David. "North American Indian Music." In *The Folk Music Source Book,* edited by Larry Sandberg and Dick Weissman, pp. 40–44. New York: Alfred A. Knopf, 1976.

Nettl, Bruno. *North American Indian Musical Styles.* Philadelphia: American Folklore Society, 1954. General survey of musical styles; brief history of scholarship.

Robb, J. D. "The J. D. Robb Collection of Folk Music Recordings." *New Mexico Folklore Record* 7 (1952–53): 6–20. List of 1,090 items, mostly Indian and Mexican; material presently located in the Archives of Southwestern Music, Albuquerque, New Mexico.

Roberts, Don L. "The Archive of Southwestern Music." *The Folklore and Folk Music Archivist* 9 (Winter 1966–67): 47–52.

Schultz, Henry. "Some American Indian Music on Records." *American Record Guide* 15, no. 9 (May 1949): 259–62; 15, no. 10 (June 1949): 291–96; 15, no. 11 (July 1949): 329–34; 16, no. 1 (September 1949): 7–10.

Watkins, Frances E. "The Charles F. Lummis Collection of Spanish California and Indian Songs in the Southwest Museum, Los Angeles." *California Folklore Quarterly* 1 (January 1942): 99-101. Description of early collection of sound recordings.

White, Glenn H., Jr. "Canyon Records." *American Indian Crafts & Culture* 7 (January 1973): 14-15.

Record Companies

Kay C. Bennet	Folkways	Salt City
Canyon	Indian House	Taos
Chinle Galileans	Indian Records	Waltiska
Dine	Iroqrafts	University of
Dineh	Library of Congress	Washington Press
Everest	Navajo Serenaders	Zuni Midnighters
Fenders	Request	

Archives

Arizona
    Arizona State Museum
California
    Ethnomusicology Archive, UCLA
    Lowie Museum of Anthropology
Colorado
    Southwest Folklore Collection
    State Historical Society of Colorado
Connecticut
    Laboratory of Ethnomusicology, Wesleyan University
District of Columbia
    Archive of Folk Song
Idaho
    Idaho State University Archives
Illinois
    University of Illinois Archives of Ethnomusicology
    Northwestern University Music Library
Kansas
    Sioux-Dakota Indian Oral Narrative
Massachusetts
    Peabody Museum of Archaeology and Ethnology
Michigan
    Ethnomusicological Audio-Visual Lab, University of Michigan
New Mexico
    Archive of Southwestern Music
    Mary Cabot Wheelwright Research Library
New York
    Center for Studies in Ethnomusicology, Columbia University
Utah
    University Archives, Brigham Young University
Washington
    Archives of Ethnic Music and Dance, University of Washington

Wisconsin
Mills Music Library
State Historical Society of Wisconsin
Alberta
Provincial Museum and Archives of Alberta, Human History Division
Ontario
Canadian Centre for Folk Culture Studies
Edward Johnson Music Library and Recording Archives

Hawaiian

Hawaiian music has also had a long history of commercial recording, reaching back at least to 1901 when Columbia issued two cylinders of Hawaiian music by uncredited performers (see Gronow). Hawaiian music became popular in the continental United States in the second decade of this century, and many companies began to issue Hawaiian records. Today, there are numerous companies producing Hawaiian records; many labels are available on a mail-order basis from the House of Music (1450 Ala Moana Boulevard, Ala Moana Shopping Center, Shop 1116, Honolulu, HI 96814) or from Harry's Music Store (3457 Waialae Avenue, Honolulu, HI 96816).

The Kanahele and Tatar works cited below will guide interested persons seeking to learn more about Hawaiian music in general. *Ha'ilono Mele*, the monthly publication of the Hawaiian Music Foundation (P.O. Box 10293, Honolulu, HI 93616), is devoted to Hawaiian music.

At least four reissues of early steel guitar playing, featuring mainland as well as Hawaiian performers, have been produced: Rounder 1012: *Hula Blues*; Rounder 1024: *Sol Hoopii*; Folklyric 9009: *Hawaiian Steel Guitar, 1920s–1950s*; and Folklyric 9022: *Early Hawaiian Classics*.

Printed References

Gronow, Pekka. "When Was Hawaiian Music First Recorded?" *Ha'ilono Mele* 2, no. 1 (January 1976): 1.

Kanahele, George S., ed. *Hawaiian Music and Musicians: An Illustrated History*. Honolulu: University of Hawaii Press, 1979.

Kasher, Robert Kamohalu, and Burl Burlingame. *Da Kine Sound: Conversations with the People Who Create Hawaiian Music*. Kailua, Hawaii: Press Pacifica, 1978.

Tatar, Betty. "Annotated Bibliography of Hawaiian Music." *Ha'ilono Mele* 1, no. 12 (December 1975): 4–6; 2, no. 1 (January 1976): 6–7; 2, no. 4 (April 1976): 6–7; 2, no. 5 (May 1976): 4–7; 2, no. 6 (June 1976): 5.

Todaro, Tony. *The Golden Years of Hawaiian Entertainment, 1874–1974*. Honolulu: Tony Todaro Publishing Co., 1974.

Recordings

Folklyric 9009: *Hawaiian Steel Guitar, 1920s–1930s*. Reissued from 78s. Various artists, both Hawaiian and mainland performers. Liner notes by Chris Strachwitz.

Folklyric 9022: *Early Hawaiian Classics: Kalama's Quartette*. Edited by Chris Strachwitz. Reissues of 78s from 1927–30.

Rounder 1012: *Hula Blues*. Reissued from 78s. Various artists, both Hawaiian and mainland performers. Liner notes by Robert F. Gear.

Rounder 1024: *Sol Hoopii: Master of the Hawaiian Guitar*. Reissue LP edited by Robert Gear.

Victor 1916 Hawaiian catalog. Courtesy of Pekka Gronow.

Topsoil TSR-7046: *'Auhea 'oe e Sanoe: Field Recordings of Hawaiian Slack Key.* Recordings made in 1975. Various artists. Liner notes by Mike McClellan.

Record Companies

Alshire	Folkways	Topsoil Music
Folklyric	Rounder	

Archives
California
     Eugene W. Earle
Hawaii
     Bernice Pauahi Bishop Museum
     Hawaii Archives of Ethnic Musics
Utah
     University Archives, Brigham Young University

European and Eurasian Traditions

English: Celtic

While Irish and Scottish musical traditions have, of course, contributed a great deal to mainstream Anglo-American folk music, there are many Irish and Scottish communities where traditional music, and other aspects of culture, have been maintained apart from the dominant culture. Additionally, there are a few Welsh communities in this country, and although information about Welsh-American music is slight, it deserves separate mention. We include it here, even though we realize that most of the recordings are in the Welsh (Cymrn) rather than the English language.

Irish

Much of the Irish-American population came to the United States in the wake of political and economic turmoil in Ireland in the 1840s. Irish communities were formed in many cities, including Boston, New York, Philadelphia, and Chicago. Although these communities are not so strong today as a few generations ago, they still support many musicians. Commercial recording of both traditional and popular Irish music began around the turn of the century. John J. Kimmel, a German accordion player who played Irish music, was a prolific recording artist who waxed a few popular airs along with a great quantity of dance music. He began his career around 1904 and eventually recorded for Columbia, Victor, Edison, and other labels. A few other traditional musicians appeared on record throughout the second decade of the century, but, as with most other types of ethnic recordings, the 1920s saw the real blooming of Irish recordings. Columbia instituted its 33000–F Irish series in 1926; it eventually ran to more than 500 releases (some of these were reissues of earlier recordings). Decca began a 12000 series devoted to Irish music in the 1930s. Victor, OKeh, and Gennett also offered many Irish discs. Columbia discontinued the 33000 series in 1937, having reached 33562, but revived it in 1947, starting again at 33500. Many items in this later series were reissued from the earlier line.

Although there is, as yet, little published material relating to Irish discography, the present high level of interest in Irish music indicates that such work will certainly appear. One recent contribution is a numerical listing of the Columbia 33000–F and OKeh 84000 series, prepared by Pekka Gronow and jointly published by the John Edwards Memorial Foundation and the Finnish Institute of Recorded Sound. Also in preparation is a master's thesis on

A reissue of Paddy Killoran's recordings on Shanachie Records. Courtesy of Richard Nevins.

early commercial recordings of Irish-American instrumental music, being written by William M. Healy in the folklore program at UCLA.

Similarly, although few reissues of Irish 78s have thus far appeared, many more will undoubtedly be released in the near future. Companies that have produced reissue LPs include Shanachie, Folkways, and Folklyric. Of these, Shanachie is most actively pursuing a reissue program. Two privately produced reissues of the work of fiddler Michael Coleman have appeared, one on the I.R.C. label and one on Intrepid, but both are now out of print. Most in-print records of Irish and Irish-American music are obtainable by mail order from Shanachie Records.

Printed References

Ferrel, Frank. "The Heyday of Michael Coleman." *Seattle Folklore Society Journal* 5, no. 3 (March 1974): 3-4.

Gronow, Pekka. *The Columbia 3300-F Irish Series.* JEMF Special Series, no. 10. Los Angeles: John Edwards Memorial Foundation, 1979.

Hall, Reg. "Peter J. Conlon Discography." *Traditional Music,* no. 6, (1977), pp. 9-10. Discography of an Irish-American accordionist.

MacCullough, Lawrence. "Michael Coleman, Traditional Fiddler." *Eiré-, Ireland* 10, no. 1 (1975): 90-94.

Ward, Alan. "Review: *Irish Dance Music.*" *Traditional Music,* no. 2, (1975), p. 23. Review of Folkways FW 8821, a reissue album, followed by a reply from Reg Hall, compiler of the album, giving a brief survey of early Irish recording activity in America and Ireland.

Recordings

Folklyric 9010: *Irish-American Dance Music and Songs—The Late 1920s.* Various artists. Liner notes by William M. Healy.

Folkways FW 8821: *Irish Dance Music.* Various artists. Brochure notes by Reg Hall.

Folkways FS 3517/3521: *Irish Music from Cleveland,* Vols. 1 and 2. Instrumental music recorded in 1977-78 by Richard Carlin and Mike Comer. Brief four-page brochures include biographical notes and comments on the selections.

Library of Congress LBC 4: *Folk Music in America, Volume 4: Dance Music—Reels, Polkas & More.* Includes four Irish-American items by various artists. Brochure notes by Richard K. Spottswood.

Shanachie 33001 (originally issued as Morning Star 45001): *The Wheels of the World: Classics of Irish Traditional Music.* Various artists. Liner notes by Barry O'Neill.

Shanachie 33002: *The Legacy of Michael Coleman.* Reissue of twelve sides by the legendary and influential Sligo fiddler. Liner notes by Rob Fleder.

Shanachie 33003: *Paddy Killoran's Back in Town.* Reissue of fourteen sides by an important fiddler, long resident in New York City. Liner notes by Barry O'Neill.

Record Companies

Avoca	Folkways	Shanachie
Biscuit City	Philo	Standard-Colonial
Folklyric	Rex	

Archives
California
    UCLA Folklore Archive
District of Columbia
    Archive of Folk Song
Florida
    SCAMP

Scottish

Scottish communities also exist in many American cities. The most visible form of Scottish music is, of course, bagpipe music, and many pipe bands are to be found in the United States and Canada. Recordings of pipe music can be found in the international section of nearly any record store, and readers of this directory need no further assistance in locating such material.

A very strong tradition of Scottish fiddling exists on Cape Breton Island, Nova Scotia, and in the communities formed by Cape Breton emigrants in Boston, Toronto, and Detroit. Much Cape Breton music has been issued in Canada on the Celtic label, which is now owned by Rodeo Records in Ontario. Angus Chisholm, A. A. Gillis, and Dan J. Campbell were the first Cape Breton fiddlers to record for this label, beginning in 1936. Prior to this, however, Colin J. Boyd recorded some Scottish music for Brunswick in Montreal in 1932, and two discs (Brunswick 533 and 534) were released in the United States in Brunswick's 100 "Songs from Dixie" series. Decca maintained a 14000 series devoted to Scottish music, but this apparently ran to only thirty-three releases (in contrast with close to 300 releases in Decca's 12000 Irish series). A few items that originally appeared on the Celtic label were also issued in the 14000 series.

Rodeo has continued to issue Cape Breton music on LPs (on the Rodeo, Celtic, and Banff labels), but the present availability of this material is unknown. A few of the LPs on Celtic were compiled from material originally issued on 78s. However, these repackagings have not been accompanied by any annotation. One very interesting reissue is Celtic CX 1: *Cape Breton Violins,* an anthology of several different musicians, including such great fiddlers as Angus Chisholm, Winston "Scotty" Fitzgerald, Little Jack MacDonald, and A. A. Gillis. Rounder Records has recently become very active in issuing Cape Breton fiddle music, primarily through the efforts of Mark Wilson. Beginning with the recording of Cape Bretoners resident in Boston, Wilson has expanded his activities and made recording trips to Cape Breton.

In addition to the Cape Breton Scots, there is also a strong center of Scottish culture in parts of Ontario Province. Although we are unaware of any commercial recordings from this area, see Proctor for a discussion of fiddling in Ontario.

Albums of Scottish music can be obtained by mail from Shanachie Records, Roundup Records (see Rounder Records), and the Celtic Music Store (P. O. Box 154, Antigonish, Nova Scotia, Canada).

In addition to fiddle music, there is also some Gaelic singing performed on Cape Breton. Most of the archives listed below contain holdings of vocal rather than instrumental music.

Printed References

Garber, Jim. "The Glendale Festival of Scottish Fiddling." *Sing Out!* 26, no. 2 (July-August 1977): 32–33.

"Lee Cremo Speaks." *Cape Breton's Magazine,* no. 1 (1973), pp. 3–4, 24. Interview with a Micmac Indian fiddler who plays some Scottish music.

Proctor, George A. "Old-Time Fiddling in Ontario." In *National Museum of Canada Bulletin,* no. 190, Contributions to Anthropology, pt. 2, Anthropological Series, no. 60, pp. 173–208. Ottawa, 1960. Descriptive article with musical transcriptions.

Wells, Paul F. "Canadian and Canadian-American Music." *Journal of American Folklore* 91 (July-September 1978): 879–84. Review article.

Wilson, Mark. "South West Bridge Reel." *Sing Out!* 26, no. 2 (July-August 1977): 34. Short note about fiddlers Joe Cormier and Dan R. MacDonald, with a printing of a tune composed by MacDonald. Brief comments on playing style.

Recordings

Celtic CX–1: *Cape Breton Violins.* Reissued from 78s. Various artists. Brief liner notes.

Celtic CX 34: *Winston "Scotty" Fitzgerald and His Radio Entertainers.* Reissued from 78s. This is one of five albums featuring the playing of one of the best, most widely known, and most influential Cape Breton fiddlers.

Rounder 7001: *Joe Cormier.* New recordings of a Scottish-style fiddler of French descent now living in the Boston area. Autobiographical liner notes. A second disc of Cormier's playing, Rounder 7004: *The Dances Down Home,* has also been issued.

Rounder 7003: *John Campbell.* New recordings of a Boston-area resident, son of pioneer fiddler and recording artist Dan J. Campbell.

Rounder 7008: *Jerry Holland.* New recordings of young American fiddler (of Canadian parentage) who plays in Cape Breton style.

Record Companies

| Banff | Rodeo |
| Celtic | Rounder |

Archives

Florida
    SCAMP
New York
    Archive of Folklore, Traditional Music, and Oral History
Newfoundland
    Memorial University of Newfoundland Folklore and Language Archive
Nova Scotia
    Angus L. MacDonald Memorial Library
Ontario
    Canadian Centre for Folk Culture Studies

Welsh   Although no Welsh series were established by any of the companies who produced ethnic records, a few individual Welsh discs were issued. *Talking*

Machine World, February 15, 1925, p. 153, noted the sales success of a Gennett release, "A Welsh Courtship" (Gennett 5519). Sales of this disc were particularly strong in the mining district of Pennsylvania. Notice reproduced in *JEMF Quarterly* 9, no. 29 (Spring 1973): 31–32.

Academic investigation of Welsh music in America has also been quite limited. The Jones article and Philips thesis listed below are the only references we have discovered. No body of field recordings has come to our attention; the holdings claimed by SCAMP consist of commercial 78s.

Printed References

Jones, Wynn. "Welsh Folksongs." *Tennessee Folklore Society Bulletin* 9, no. 4 (December 1943): 1–7. Music and text transcriptions of four Welsh songs.

Philips, Mary K. "A Study of the Sources of Welsh Music in America and an Analysis and Evaluation of the Welsh-American contribution to the Folk and Art Music of This Country." Master's thesis, Claremont College, 1948.

Archives

Florida
  SCAMP

English: Anglo-American and Afro-American

Given the limitations set forth in our introduction, recordings of Anglo-American folk music and Afro-American blues will receive only cursory treatment here. Neither type of music has been "neglected" by scholars; and, although the study of Anglo-American traditions ("hillbilly music") is not yet on a par with blues research, discographic work in both cases is quite well advanced.

The two standard sources of discographic information for blues are John Godrich and R. M. W. Dixon, *Blues and Gospel Records, 1902–1942* (London: Storyville Publications, 1969), and Mike Leadbitter and Neil Slaven, *Blues Records: 1943–66* (London: Hanover Books, 1968). Interested readers should also consult the bibliography "Black Music" in *The Folk Music Sourcebook,* edited by Larry Sandberg and Dick Weissman (New York: Alfred A. Knopf, 1976), pp. 150–56, for leads to other printed sources.

Although no complete discography of white traditions yet exists, one covering the early years of hillbilly recordings is being prepared by Tony Russell in conjunction with the Country Music Foundation in Nashville, Tennessee. Many biographic/discographic articles appear in *JEMF Quarterly* (John Edwards Memorial Foundation, at the Folklore and Mythology Center, University of California, Los Angeles, CA 90024), *The Journal of Country Music* (Country Music Foundation, 4 Music Square East, Nashville, TN 37203), and Old Time Music (22 Upper Tollington Park, London N43EL, England). Separately published bio-discographies on a number of artists are also available from these sources.

Hispanic

A recently published survey of Chicano music by Philip Sonnichsen gives a rather complete overview of available commercial recordings from the southwestern United States. Rather than cover the same material as that article, here we concentrate on bringing it up to date, repeating only a few particularly significant references. At the same time, we include a survey of the major field collections and archives, which were not part of Sonnichsen's earlier article. We conclude with just a few references to the Hispanic traditions at the eastern end of the country, where it is mainly the Puerto Rican and Cuban traditions that are influential, rather than the Mexican.

One of the first individuals to systematically collect traditional Spanish-American religious and folk music in the American Southwest was the journalist, traveler, and founder of the Southwest Museum in Los Angeles, Charles F. Lummis, whose efforts began in the late 1890s. Lummis's field collection of some 350 cylinder recordings has been copied for the Library of Congress Archive of Folk Song. A number of transcriptions were published by Lummis in his *Land of Poco Tiempo*.

In Texas, some of the most important pioneering work was done by John Lomax and, later, Alan Lomax. Their collection has been deposited with the Library of Congress; samples have been issued on the album *Bahaman Songs, French Ballads and Dance Tunes, Spanish Religious Songs and Game Songs* (Library of Congress Archive of Folk Song L 5).

Another pioneer was Aurelio M. Espinosa, the Stanford University linguist and folklorist. His collecting forays in New Mexico, Colorado and California produced some of the earliest ballad fragments to come down to us. Unfortunately, music was not Espinosa's prime concern; apparently at no time did he ever use cylinder, disc, or tape machines to record his informants. He was reputed to have an excellent memory, and would simply memorize the ballad and then repeat it for his music transcriber. Some of these songs, with musical notation, were published in *El Romancero de Nuevo México*. His son, J. Manuel Espinosa, has completed a bibliography of his father's writings for publication in a forthcoming issue of *The Americas*, and he is presently working on a book documenting the work of this pioneer in Hispanic music.

A succeeding generation of scholars did avail themselves of recorders. The now-retired Stanford professor Juan B. Rael collected between fifty and seventy-five different works, all of which have been deposited with the Library of Congress. His article "New Mexican Wedding Songs" documents one aspect of his collection; his *New Mexican "Alabado"* and *Sources and Diffusion of the Mexican Shepherds' Plays* document other aspects.

John Donald Robb and Rubén Cobos have done considerable collecting, primarily in the New Mexico area. As retired University of New Mexico professors (Robb in music and as Dean of Fine Arts, and Cobos in Spanish), both men have deposited their collections with the University of New Mexico library and duplicate copies have been made for the Southwestern Studies Program at Colorado College, Colorado Springs. Robb has listed his collection in two articles (1952–53 and 1976–77), a collection that served as the basis for his *Hispanic Folk Songs of New Mexico* and his more recent *Hispanic Folk Music of New Mexico*. In addition, the Folkways record album *Folk Music of New Mexico* presents a variety of material recorded by Robb between 1946 and 1951. The Cobos collection is presently being indexed by Colorado College and will soon be available.

Another important collection is that of Arthur Campa, professor emeritus of modern languages at the University of Denver. Presently housed at the Library of Congress, the collection serves as the basis for several articles and monographs, including *The Spanish Folksong in the Southwest* and *Spanish*

Folk-Poetry in New Mexico. From his extensive bibliography Arno Press has republished his Hispanic-related material in *The Hispanic Folklore Works of A. L. Campa.* His most extensive work, based on a lifetime of study, is *Hispanic Cultures of the Southwest.*

Mexican immigrants to the United States were of great interest to Paul S. Taylor, who reprinted a number of the songs and ballads he collected in "Songs of the Mexican Migration." His notes and other material are on deposit at the Bancroft Library, University of California, Berkeley. Brownie McNeil was another collector of border material. In his "Corridos of the Mexican Border" McNeil told of his experiences and printed the music and texts to several ballads. His collection is housed at the Library of Congress.

The dean of Texas collectors is University of Texas professor Américo Paredes, whose most active collecting occurred between 1951 and 1956. His collection of variants of the ballad "Gregorio Cortez" inspired his doctoral dissertation and, in revised form, his book *"With His Pistol in His Hand."* His more recent *A Texas-Mexican* Cancionero: *Folksongs of the Lower Border* is a well-documented study of sixty-six songs of the Texas-Mexican border.

In addition to his own early collecting and extensive writing, Paredes has also inspired a number of students. They include Jerry Abrams, Rumel Fuentes, Jose Limon, Inez Cardoza Freeman, Jennifer Sookne, Kay Scott, Felix Pena, and Dan Dickey. To Parades, the senior scholar in Texas-Mexican folklore and folk music, the renewed interest in the ballad tradition and other musical traditions of his native border land is gratifying, if somewhat late in coming.

Two large collections besides that of J.D. Robb have been described in print: Roberts has summarized the holdings of the Archive of Southwestern Music, and Robertson has catalogued the relevant holdings of the Indiana University Archives of Traditional Music.

Of the several bibliographies on Spanish-American music that have been published, the most comprehensive seems to be that of Heisley, which lists nearly 250 books, articles, and dissertations dealing with music-making traditions. A useful guide to sources of commercially available discs as well as field recordings has been published by Chavez.

In the area of Hispanic-American music the commercial tradition has been vigorous; *norteño* (more recently also called "Tex-Mex") music from north of the Mexican border has been recorded in great quantities since the late 1920s. Chris Strachwitz, whose own personal collection of commercially issued discs is extensive, has produced sixteen outstanding reissue albums of border music on the Folklyric label; he asserts that the surface has barely been scratched. This series provides an excellent introduction, with informative annotations, to the music.

The contemporary music market is blossoming with many small regional labels, mostly centered around Albuquerque, but also elsewhere in the Southwest. Many of the labels are owned by Mexican-Americans and aim their product at that segment of the population. Albuquerque labels include Hurricane, MORE, Christy, Casa Nova, Alta Vista, Pueblo, and RJG. The leading artists on record include Al Hurricane, Tiny Morrie, Baby Gaby, Gloria Pohl, and Miguel Archibeque (Hurricane); Debbie "La Chicanita" Martínez and Lorenzo Martínez (MORE); Bennie Martínez and Nick and Jane (Del Norte); Los Chavos (Alta Vista and Christy); and Robert Griego

A reissue of early Texas-Mexican border music on the Folklyric label. Motion Picture, Broadcasting, and Recorded Sound Division, Library of Congress.

(RJG). Recordings of Hispanic-oriented popular music in Colorado remain somewhat limited. Infal Records in Denver has released or distributes Clem García, Baltazar López, Lusia Mendoza, Eulogio Montoya, Los Populares del Norte, Charlie Sauceda, Edelmiro Zuniga, and Los Alvarados. Rayo Records, also in Denver, is a house label for Rudy García.

The Cantemos and Taos record labels in Taos, New Mexico, represent the most extensive efforts to document musical folk traditions in that state. Previous titles include: *Buenos Dias, Paloma Blanca: Five Alabados of Northern New Mexico* and *New Mexico Alabados*, both sung by Cleofes Vigil; *Meliton M. Trujillo Sings Taos Spanish Songs, Bailes de Taos*, and *Taos Matachines Music*, all on the Taos label. On the Cantemos label Jenny Wells Vincent has released *Spanish Folksongs of the Americas, Folksongs for Children of All Ages*, and most recently *Music for a Fiesta*, mainly folk dances with mandolin, guitar, accordion, and vocals.

Lydia Mendoza, the subject of a separate chapter in this volume, has become something of an institution on the lower border. Her recording career began in 1928 when she and her parents sang as the Cuarteto Carta Blanca and subsequently as the Cuarteto Mendoza. Examples of her early work may be found on reissues in the Folklyric series mentioned above and also on Library of Congress LBC 2: *Songs of Love, Courtship, and Marriage*. Her more recent work may be found on the Arhoolie *Chulas Fronteras* album and on the Norteño label.

Although this review is primarily concerned with the recorded tradition, we must mention the film *Chulas Fronteras*, since it is both a musical and a cultural documentary of Mexican-Americans in south Texas. Filmed in 1976 by Les Blank and Chris Strachwitz, the film deals with the lives of many of the most significant musical personalities along the Texas-Mexican border. The film (58 minutes, color, 16 mm) is available from Brazos Films (10341 San Pablo Avenue, El Cerrito, CA). A companion recording with the complete text of film has been released on Arhoolie 3005. Strachwitz has also issued, on his Arhoolie label, several other albums of *norteño* music, all with informative liner notes aimed at the general Anglo consumer. These include *Los Pinguinos del Norte* (3002); Conjunto Trio San Antonio, *Viva El West Side* (3004); and *Flaco Jimenez and His Conjunto* (3007).

The growing interest in Tex-Mex music, partially inspired by the successful crossovers of such artists as Freddy Fender and Johnny Rodriguez, has prompted a rash of articles, mostly of the public relations type, in a variety of publications. The musicians most widely discussed include Flaco Jimenez (the man most responsible for broadening the *conjunto* tradition musically, largely through jazz techniques), Tony de la Rosa, Steve Jordan, Wally Gonzales, Conjunto Cuatro Espadas de Mingo Saldivar, and Freddy Fender. This aspect of Hispanic-American music deserves much more intensive study than can be accorded here.

We conclude this section with two albums that offer important surveys of eastern United States Hispanic-American traditions. An interesting and unusual documentary recording of Puerto Rican life in New York is Tony Schwartz's album, Folkways FD 5559; *Nueva York*, recorded between 1948 and 1956. Very different in content is the 1977 New World Records album NW 244: *Caliente = Hot: Puerto Rican and Cuban Musical Expression in New York*. The informative liner notes describe the various musical styles and include a selected discography.

New recordings of "Latin Music" on New World Records. Motion Picture, Broadcasting, and Recorded Sound Division, Library of Congress.

Printed References

Campa, Arthur. *The Hispanic Folklore Studies of A. L. Campa.* Compiled by Carlos E. Cortés. New York: Arno Press, 1976.

———. *Spanish Folk-Poetry in New Mexico.* Albuquerque: University of New Mexico Press, 1946.

———. "The Spanish Folksong in the Southwest." *University of New Mexico Bulletin* 4, no. 1 (1933).

Chavez, Alex. "Recommended Sources for Commercially Available Discs and Field Tape Collections of Chicano Music." *MLA Newsletter,* no. 14 (September-October 1973).

Espinosa, Aurelio. *El Romancero de Nuevo Mexico.* Madrid: Consejos Superior de Investigaciones Científicos, 1953.

Espinosa, J. Manuel. "Spanish Folklore in the Southwest: The Pioneer Studies of Aurelio Espinosa." *Americas* 35 (October 1978): 219-37.

Heisley, Michael. *An Annotated Bibliography of Chicano Folklore from the Southwestern United States.* Los Angeles: Center for the Study of Comparative Folklore and Mythology, UCLA, 1977. An annotated bibliography of 1,028 items, arranged by genre, with indexes.

Lummis, Charles F. *The Land of Poco Tiempo.* 1893. Reprint ed., Albuquerque: University of New Mexico Press, 1952.

McNeil, Brownie [Norman Laird]. "Corridos of the Mexican Border." In *Mexican Border Ballads and Other Lore,* edited by Mody C. Boatright, pp. 1-33. Publications of the Texas Folk-Lore Society, 21. Austin: Texas Folk-Lore Society, 1946.

Paredes, Américo. *A Texas-Mexican* Cancionero: *Folksongs of the Lower Border.* Urbana: University of Illinois Press, 1976.

———. *"With His Pistol in His Hand."* Austin: University of Texas Press, 1958.

Rael, Juan B. *The New Mexican "Alabado."* Palo Alto: Stanford University Press, 1951.

———. "New Mexican Wedding Songs." *Southern Folklore Quarterly* 4 (June 1940):55-72.

———. *Sources and Diffusion of the Mexican Shepherds' Plays.* Guadalajara, Mexico, 1965.

Robb, John D. *Hispanic Folk Music of New Mexico.* Norman: University of Oklahoma Press, 1979.

———. *Hispanic Folk Songs of New Mexico.* Albuquerque: University of New Mexico Press, 1962.

———. "The J. D. Robb Collection of Folk Music Recordings." *New Mexico Folklore Record* 7 (1952-53): 6-20 and 14 (1976-77):11-23. "A listing of 1,096 items with title, performer, and place and date of recording. This collection is housed in the Library of the University of New Mexico . . ." (From Heisley, no. 419, about the 1952-53 installment.)

Roberts, Don L. "The Archive of Southwestern Music." *Folklore and Folk Music Archivist* 9, no. 2 (1966-67):47-52. "A description of the holdings and facilities of the folk music archive at the University of New Mexico at Albuquerque . . ." (From Heisley, no. 423.)

Robertson, Carol E., comp. *Catalogue of Latin American Music and Oral Data Holdings.* Bloomington: Indiana University Archives of Traditional Music, 1971. "Catalogues as of May 1971 of the Archives' sound recordings pertaining to all of Latin America and Spanish-speaking areas of the United States. Provides accession numbers, recording data, and description of each recording's contents." (From Heisley, no. 424.)

Sonnichsen, Philip. "Chicano Music." In *The Folk Music Sourcebook*, edited by Larry Sandberg and Dick Weissman, pp. 44–51. New York: Alfred A. Knopf, 1976.

Taylor, Paul S. "Songs of the Mexican Migration." In *Puro Mexicano*, edited by J. Frank Dobie, pp. 221–45. Publications of the Texas Folk-Lore Society, 12. Austin: Texas Folk-Lore Society, 1935.

Puerto Rican music from Chicago produced on the Ebirac label. Motion Picture, Broadcasting, and Recorded Sound Division, Library of Congress.

Recordings

Folklyric 9003/9004/9005/9006/9007: *Texas-Mexican Border Music, Volumes 1–5*. Reissues of commercial recordings. Volume 1 serves as introduction to the series, with recordings from 1930 to 1960; brochure notes include text transcriptions and translations, artist biographies, a "selected discography of currently more-or-less available" albums of Texas-Mexican border music, and a list of producers and record companies. Volumes 2 and 3 are devoted to *corridos* recorded between 1929 and 1936; a thirty-two-page brochure by Philip Sonnichsen provides extensive background on the songs. Volumes 4 and 5 are devoted to accordion and stringband music, respectively.

Folklyric 9011/9012/9013/9016/9017/9018/9019/9020. A continuation of the above reissue series. Titles include: *Cancioneros de Ayer, Parts I/II/III/IV*; *Narciso Martinez, "El Huracan del Valle": His First Recordings (1936–1937)*; *El Ciego Melquiades (The Blind Fiddler)*; and *Norteno Acordeon, Parts II/III*. All albums include informative liner notes.

Folkways FA 2204: *Spanish Folk Songs of New Mexico.* Sung by Peter Hurd. Recorded and with an introduction by J. D. Robb. Brochure includes Spanish and English texts.

Folkways FE 4426: *Spanish and Mexican Folk Music of New Mexico.* Various artists. Recorded in 1946–51 by J. D. Robb. Brochure notes. Includes dance music, *corridos, decimos, matachinas,* etc.

Folkways FD 5559: *Nueva York.* A tape documentary of Puerto Rican New Yorkers, recorded and edited by Tony Schwartz (1956).

New World Records NW 244: *Caliente = Hot! Puerto Rican and Cuban Musical Expression in New York* (1977). Produced by Rene Lopez, with brochure notes by Roberta Singer and Robert Friedman giving general background, discographic data, comments on the music, glossary, selected bibliography, and selected discography.

Record Companies

Alta Vista	Foy Lee Productions	L & M
California Artists	Folklyric	Luna
Corporation	Folkways	MORE
Casa Nova	Hurricane	New World
Christy	Infal	Norteño
Del Valle	Joey	Sombrero
Discos Azteca	Key Loc	Taos
Falcon		

Archives

California
    Ethnomusicology Archive, UCLA
    Chris Strachwitz
    UCLA Chicano Studies Research Library
    UCLA Folklore Archive
Colorado
    Southwest Folklore Collection
District of Columbia
    Archive of Folk Song
New Mexico
    Archive of Southwestern Music
New York
    Archive of Folklore, Traditional Music, and Oral History

French

The French, along with the English and Spanish, were among the first Europeans to explore and colonize North America; their music has been played on American soil for more than three centuries. While the major concentration of the French-speaking population is in Quebec and the Maritime Provinces of Canada, many French-Canadian emigrants live in New England, and there are also areas of French culture in Louisiana and Missouri—although the Louisiana and Missouri French settlements are ultimately the result of emigration from Canada.

Canadian French

It could be argued that the French in Canada should not be included in this directory as an "ethnic group" because they are neither "newly arrived immigrants" nor, in Quebec at least, a minority group—two conditions by which ethnicity is usually defined. However, we have chosen to include them for two reasons. First, if all of Canada is taken into consideration, French people do constitute a minority (28.7 percent of the population in the 1971 census). Second, it would be highly artificial to include the music of French-Canadians living in New England but exclude that of people—sometimes in the same family—living a short drive away north of the Canadian border.

The pioneer in recording French folk music in Canada was the late Marius Barbeau. He recorded several thousand songs and instrumental tunes in the course of a long career. His own account of his activities has been presented in disc form as Folkways FG 3502: *My Life in Recording Canadian-Indian Folk-Lore.* The Fowke and Cass-Beggs bibliography cited below lists Barbeau's publications. The material he gathered forms the basis of the collection at the Canadian Centre for Folk Culture Studies. A second major archival center in Canada, Les Archives de Folklore, was established at Laval University in Quebec in 1944; it is based on the field collection of Luc Lacourcière.

Commercial recordings of Canadian French songs were made around the turn of the century, but recording of traditional music apparently did not begin until about 1920. Although discographic research on French-Canadian music is in its early stages, Moogk, Coltman, and Labbé provide a considerable amount of basic information. It is unfortunate, but not particularly surprising, that Canadian folk music scholars, have, in the past, overlooked the value of commercial recordings as source material. A wealth of traditional material, primarily instrumental music, has been issued. One can assume that the same sorts of prejudices that prevented United States folklorists from accepting early hillbilly records as valid documentation of folk music were at work.

Very little early French-Canadian material has been reissued on LP. The major Canadian labels that hold the rights to early recordings occasionally do repackage older material, but these offerings seem to come and go as quickly as do major-label reissues of early country and jazz records. Philo Records has released, under license from MCA Canada, Philo 2009, *La Bolduc,* a reissue of twenty songs by Madame Edouard Bolduc, a popular French-Canadian vocalist of the 1930s. French performers are, of course, still being recorded by Canadian companies. In the United States, Philo has produced several albums of contemporary performers (both United States and Canadian residents), including fiddlers Jean Carignan, Henri Landry, and Louis Beaudoin, accordionist Philippe Bruneau, and vocalist Jeanne d'Arc Charlebois. Folkways Records has produced a few French-Canadian albums, while Fiddler Records and Voyager Records have released one album each of French-Canadian fiddlers resident in New England (Tom Doucet and Gerry Robichaud, respectively).

French-Canadian records may be obtained on a mail-order basis from Shanachie Records and Roundup Records (see Rounder Records for address).

The well-known French-Canadian fiddler Louis Beaudoin of Burlington, Vermont, on Philo Records. Motion Picture, Broadcasting, and Recorded Sound Division, Library of Congress.

Printed References

"Canadian Folk Music." In *The Folk Music Sourcebook,* edited by Larry Sandberg and Dick Weissman, pp. 51–55. New York: Alfred A. Knopf, 1976. List of current albums.

Coltman, Bob. "Habitantbilly: French-Canadian Old Time Music." *Old Time Music,* no. 11 (Winter 1973–74), pp. 9–13; no. 12 (Spring 1974), pp. 9–14.

D'Harcourt, Marguerite Bedard. "La Chanson francaise au Canada." *Revue Musicale*, February–March 1940, pp. 82–97. Discussion of Barbeau's collection of French-Canadian folksongs.

Evans, John. "Jean Carignan: Traditional Fiddler." *English Dance and Song* 32, no. 4 (Winter 1970):125–26. Brief article about this performer and recording artist.

Ferrel, Frank. "Tom Doucet." *Old Time Music,* no. 22 (Autumn 1976), pp. 19–20. Interview with a Nova Scotia–born fiddler, now living in eastern Massachusetts, who has one album on Fiddler Records.

"The Folk Music of Canada." In *The Folk Music Sourcebook,* edited by Larry Sandberg and Dick Weissman, pp. 157–59. New York: Alfred A. Knopf, 1976. Annotated bibliography.

Fowke, Edith, and Barbara Cass-Beggs. *A Reference List on Canadian Folk Music.* Rev. ed. Toronto(?): Canadian Folk Music Society, 1973.

Krassen, Miles. "An Analysis of a Jean Carignan Record." *Canadian Folk Music Journal* 2 (1974):40–44.

Labbé, Gabriel. *Les Pionniers du disque folklorique Quebecois, 1920–1950.* Montreal: Les Editions de l'Aurore, 1977.

Moogk, Edward B. *Roll Back the Years: A History of Canadian Recorded Sound and Its Legacy: Genesis to 1930.* Ottawa: National Library of Canada, 1975. General history of Canadian recording. While not specifically dealing with folk or ethnic music, does contain listings of most recordings, of all types of music, made in Canada prior to 1930.

Page, Ralph. "Vignette of a Fiddler." *Northern Junket* 10, no. 2 (April 1970):22–24. Brief article on fiddler Jean Carignan.

Wells, Paul F. "Canadian and Canadian-American Music." *Journal of American Folklore* 91 (July-September 1978): 879–84. Review article.

Recordings

Carnaval C–412: *Swing la Baquese avec J. O. LaMadeleine.* Reissue of recordings by a French-Canadian fiddler.

MCA (Canada) Coral CB 37004: *Collection Quebecoise, Isidore Soucy, 20 Grands Succes d'Hier.* Reissue of work of pioneer fiddler and recording artist.

Philo 2000: *Louis Beaudoin.* New recordings of a French-Canadian fiddler resident in Vermont. Liner notes by David Green.

Philo 2003: *Philippe Bruneau.* New recordings by a professional accordionist.

Philo 2009: La Bolduc. United States release of a reissue album that originally appeared on MCA Records (Canada). Material from 78s, probably on the Starr label. Vocalist with varied accompaniment. Brief biographical liner notes.

Philo 2012: *Jean Carignan rend hommage à Joseph Allard.* New recordings by a virtuoso fiddler in tribute to his mentor.

Philo 2022: *La Famille Beaudoin/The Beaudoin Family.* Second album featuring fiddler Louis Beaudoin (see Philo 2000, above), with members of his family contributing singing, harmonica playing, and dance calling. Liner notes by Paul F. Wells.

Record Companies

Banff	Philo	Voyager
Folkways	Rodeo	

Archives
California
    Eugene W. Earle
District of Columbia
    Archive of Folk Song
Maryland
    Richard K. Spottswood
Alberta
    Provincial Museum and Archives of Alberta, Provincial Archives
    Division
Newfoundland
    Memorial University of Newfoundland Folklore and Language Archive
Ontario
    Canadian Centre for Folk Culture Studies

Louisiana French

The music of the Louisiana Acadians, or Cajuns, descendants of the settlers who were evicted from Nova Scotia by the British in 1755, is probably the most well-known type of French music in the United States. Cajun music has had a long, if spotty, association with country-and-western music, resulting in a certain degree of nationwide exposure. Cajun fiddler and bandleader Harry Choates had a regional hit in the late 1940s with a traditional Cajun waltz, "Jole Blon," which became a national hit when it was "covered" by pianist Moon Mullican. Some Cajuns such as Jimmy C. Newman and Doug Kershaw have become established as minor country stars and have brought at least a semblance of traditional Cajun music to a national audience. In the past few years traditional Cajun musicians have appeared at folk festivals throughout the country. Through their performances at such events, the Balfa Brothers and Marc Savoy, for example, have emerged as articulate spokesmen for traditional Cajun music, thus winning many new fans of the music among people who have never been to Louisiana.

Cajun music on Floyd Soileau's Swallow label, Ville Platte, Louisiana. Motion Picture, Broadcasting, and Recorded Sound Division, Library of Congress.

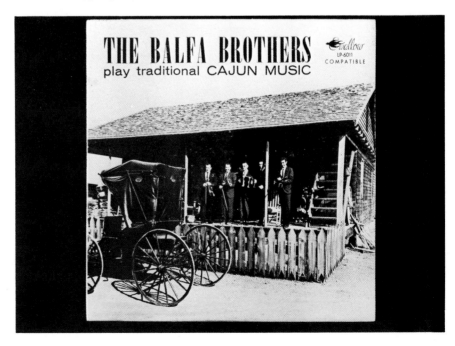

An intriguing offshoot of Cajun music is *zydeco* or *zodico* music played by French-speaking blacks in southwest Louisiana. It can be loosely described as a cross between Cajun music and blues.

Commercial recording of Cajun music began in 1928 with the waxing of "Allons à Lafayette" and "The Waltz That Carried Me to My Grave" by Joseph C. Falcon, accordion and vocal, and Cleoma Breaux, guitar. Originally issued on Columbia 15275-D, these pieces have been reissued on Old-Timey X-108, *Louisiana Cajun Music, Volume 1: First Recordings, the 1920s*, and "Lafayette" has also been reissued on RBF 21: *The Cajuns: Songs, Waltzes and Two-Steps*. For an account of this signal recording session see Pekka Gronow's chapter earlier in this book.

The subsequent history of Cajun recording follows a pattern similar to that of ethnic recording in general. The first records were made by major labels seeking to exploit regional or linguistic markets. Columbia, Victor, Brunswick, and Decca were all involved in Cajun recording to varying degrees. When the major labels eventually lost interest in this field, the gap they left was filled by local companies. The Khoury and Lyric labels, both produced by George Khoury, presented much Cajun music on 78s in the early 1950s. La Louisianne and Swallow Records are currently the two most active Cajun labels.

Since the 1960s, companies geared toward reaching a non-Cajun audience have also released Cajun records. Arhoolie has more than a dozen LPs available, while Rounder and Folkways each include several Cajun items in their catalogs. Arhoolie's offerings include some reissues of 78s (see below). Perhaps the earliest reissues and the earliest Cajun items that were presented to a non-Cajun audience (apart from those songs that found their way into country music, as mentioned earlier) are the seven Cajun pieces included in the Folkways *Anthology of American Folk Music* (FA 2951/2952/2953). The appearance of these few songs probably played a large role in the relatively early recognition and acceptance of Cajun music as a distinct and valid form of American folk music by the folk revival audience.

Cajun records are available by mail order from Floyd's Record Shop (P.O. Box 506, Ville Platte, LA 70586) and from the Down Home Music Company (10341 San Pablo Avenue, El Cerrito, CA 94530).

Printed References

"Cajun Music." In *The Folk Music Sourcebook*, edited by Larry Sandberg and Dick Weissman, pp. 55–57. New York: Alfred A. Knopf, 1976.

The Death of Harry Choates." *Old Time Music*, no. 16 (Spring 1975), p. 13. Reprinting of contemporary notices of the death of an important Cajun fiddler and recording artist.

Godrich, John, Bob Dixon, and Paul Oliver. "Cajun Corner." *Blues Unlimited*, no. 8 (January 1964), p. 16; no. 9 (February [issue dated January] 1964), p. 3. Numerical listing of RCA Bluebird Cajun series.

Leadbitter, Mike. "Back to the Bayous: Southern Blues!/Cajun!" *Blues Unlimited*, no. 34 (July 1966), pp. 8–9. Brief survey of independent Cajun record producers.

———. "Cajun Corner." *Blues Unlimited*, no. 42 (March-April 1967), pp. 15,27. Start of series dealing with Cajun recording.

———. *French Cajun Music*. Collectors Classics 12. Bexhill-on-Sea, England: Blues Unlimited, 1968. Separate booklet, essentially a list of Cajun records on the market at time of publication.

———. "Harry Choates, Cajun Fiddle Ace." *Old Time Music*, no. 6 (Autumn 1972), pp. 20–22. Bio-discography of a Cajun fiddler.

———. "Iry LeJune." *Old Time Music*, no. 14 (Autumn 1974), pp. 21–22. Bio-discography of a Cajun accordionist and recording artist.

———. "Khoury's and Lyric Labels of Lake Charles, Louisiana." *Hot Buttered Soul*, no. 22 (September 1973), pp. 2–6.

———. " 'King of the South'—Clifton Chenier, First Time!" *Blues Unlimited*, no. 25 (September 1965), pp. 3–5. Bio-discography of a black *zydeco* musician.

———. "Well, I'm Going to Louisiana." *Blues Unlimited*, no. 47 (October 1967), pp. 3–11; no. 48 (November-December 1967), pp. 3–9; no. 49 (January 1968), pp. 5–8; no. 50 (February 1968), pp. 5–9; no. 51 (March 1968), pp. 11–13; no. 52 (April 1968), pp. 12–13; no. 53 (May 1968), pp. 8–10; index in no. 54 (June 1968), p. 17. Survey of contemporary activities in Cajun music.

——— and Eddie Shuler. *From the Bayou: The Story of Goldband Records*. Bexhill-on-Sea, England: Blues Unlimited, 1969.

O'Neal, Jim. "Louisiana WaxFacts: The Blues and Cajun Record Scene, 1973." *Blues Unlimited*, no. 13 (Summer 1973), pp. 9–12. Survey of current activity.

Paterson, Neil. "Big Morris Chenier." *Blues Unlimited*, no. 25 (September 1965), pp. 5–6. Bio-discography of a black *zydeco* musician.

Post, Lauren C. "Joseph Falcon, Accordion Player and Singer: A Biographical Sketch." *Louisiana History* 11, (Winter 1970):63–79. Interview with and discography of a pioneer Cajun recording artist.

Spottswood, Dick. "Cajun Date at Melodeon." *Blues Unlimited*, no. 37 (October 1966), p. 11. Note about a Cajun group's recording following an appearance at the Newport Folk Festival.

Strachwitz, Chris A. "Cajun Country." In *The American Folk Music Occasional* [no. 2] edited by Chris Strachwitz and Pete Welding, pp. 13–17. New York: Oak Publications, 1970. General article, with some information on Cajun recording artists.

———. "Cajun Music on LP—A Survey." In *The American Folk Music Occasional*, [no. 2] (1970), pp. 25–29. Review article.

———. "Zydeco Music—i.e., French Blues." In *The American Folk Music Occasional*. [no. 2] (1970), pp. 22–24. Brief survey of music of French-speaking blacks in Louisiana and Texas.

Recordings

Arhoolie F1009: *Zydeco*. Half new recordings, half reissues of music by French-speaking blacks. Various artists.

Arhoolie F1024: *Clifton Chenier, Louisiana Blues and Zydeco*. One of many LPs of this black accordionist and bandleader.

Arhoolie 5008: *Cajun Music: The Early 50's*. Reissues from Lyric and Khoury labels. Various artists. Liner notes by Chris Strachwitz.

Arhoolie 5013: *Nathan Abshire and Other Cajun Gems*. Reissues from Lyric and Khoury labels. Various artists. Liner notes by Chris Strachwitz.

Arhoolie 5009/5015: *Folksongs of the Louisiana Acadians, Volumes 1–2.* Field recordings made by Harry Oster, volume 1 originally issued as Folklyric LP A-4. Various artists. Volume 1 contains sixteen-page booklet by Dr. Oster on the history of the Cajuns, plus annotations, text transcriptions, and translations of the songs.

La Louisianne LL-107: *Aldus Roger Plays the French Music of South Louisiana.* Accordion music.

La Louisianne LL-115: *Doc Guidry, King of the Cajun Fiddlers.* Solo album by a fiddler who once played with country singer Jimmie Davis.

La Louisianne LL-139: *Nathan Abshire, a Cajun Tradition.* New recordings by an accordionist of long-standing popularity.

Morning Star 45002: *The Early Recordings of Dennis McGee.* Reissue of 78s by an important early fiddler.

Old-Timey X-108/X-109/X-110/X-111/X-114: *Louisiana Cajun Music, Volumes 1-5.* Reissues of material recorded 1920s-1950s. Various artists. Liner notes by Chris Strachwitz. Text transcriptions and translations by Catherine Blanchet.

RBF 21: *The Cajuns, Songs, Waltzes and Two-Steps.* Reissued from 78s. Various artists. Brochure by Samuel Charters.

Record Companies

Folkways	Morning Star	Rounder
Jin	Old-Timey	Swallow
La Louisianne	RBF	

Archives

California
   Eugene W. Earle
   Chris A. Strachwitz
   UCLA Folklore Archive
District of Columbia
   Archive of Folk Song
Florida
   SCAMP
Maryland
   Richard K. Spottswood
Louisiana
   George Reinecke

Missouri French

At present, there seems to be little material available relating to Missouri French music. A few selections by vocalist Rose Pratt and fiddlers Charlie Pashia and Joe Politte on Missouri Friends of the Folk Arts MFFA-1001: *I'm Old but I'm Awfully Tough* (two-LP set available from MFFA, P.O. Box 307, New Haven, MO 63068) and two selections by Politte on Rounder 6010, *Music of French America*, are the only recordings of which we are aware. According to the annotation on the former album, French culture in Missouri is now limited to a fifty-square-mile region around the community of Old Mines in the northeastern Ozark area. The tradition of French music in the area is not strong.

Scandinavian

For purposes of this directory, the music of Norway, Sweden, Denmark, and Finland is considered together. This is done primarily because many of our sources fail to make any distinction by nationality, but merely refer to their records or archival holdings as "Scandinavian."

Discographic research on early Scandinavian-American commercial records is more advanced than that for other groups, owing to the efforts of Pekka Gronow of the Finnish Institute of Recorded Sound in Helsinki. Thus far, his work has consisted primarily in compiling numerical listings of the Scandinavian-American output of various record companies, for example, Victor, Edison, Columbia, and several smaller labels. Such work provides a basis for more specific studies of individuals, musical style, or repertoire. A list of Gronow's relevant publications appears below.

We have been able to learn very little about field recording of Scandinavian-American music. A few archives list holdings in this area, but we have no information on the circumstances or the personnel involved in the recording.

Printed References

Gronow, Pekka. "The American Columbia Finnish Language 3000 Series." *Record Research*, no. 101 (October 1969), pp. 8–9; no. 102 (November 1969), p. 10. Numerical listing; part 2 indicates that the series is to be continued, but no further installments seem to have appeared.

— — —. *American Columbia Scandinavian "E" and "F" Series*. Helsinki: Suomen Äänitearkisto (Finnish Institute of Recorded Sound), 1973.

— — —. "Finnish-American records." *JEMF Quarterly* 7, no. 24 (Winter 1971):176–85.

— — —. "Recording for the 'Foreign' Series." *JEMF Quarterly* 12, no. 41 (Spring 1976):15–20. Includes an interview with Swedish accordionist Eddie Jahrl.

— — —. *Studies in Scandinavian-American Discography*. 2 vols. Helsinki: Suomen Äänitearkisto (Finnish Institute of Recorded Sound), 1977.

Recordings

Banjar LP–BR–1825/LP–BR–1830: *Scandinavian-American Folk Dance Music, Volumes 1 and 2*. New recordings of musicians from Minnesota and Wisconsin.

Folkways FW 856: *Tunes and Songs of Finland*. Field recordings of Finnish-Americans John Stark and Aino Karelia. Brief brochure notes.

Love LRLP–17: *Hiski Salomaa*. Reissued from Finnish-American 78s. Salomaa was a popular singer and recording artist. Brief notes by Pekka Gronow.

Love LXLP–505: *Hiski Salomaa*. As above, but this LP also contains the work of several other artists. Liner notes by Lasse Lehtinen.

Mark Custom Recordings MC–6178: *Jarle Foss, Norwegian Emigrant Fiddler*. New recordings of a South Dakota fiddler. Obtainable from Wilbur Foss.

RCA PL 40115: *Siirtolaisen Muistoja: The Immigrant's Memories*. Reissued from Finnish-American 78s by Arthur Kylander, Erik Kivi, Viola Turpeinen, and others. Liner notes by Pekka Gronow.

Rounder 6004: *The American Swedish Spelmans Tio*, New Recordings of fiddlers from Minneapolis. Liner notes by Gordon Ekvall Tracie.

Sävel SALP 662/663: Oi Niitä Aikoja 3/4. Reissued from Finnish-American
78s. Liner notes by Pekka Gronow.

Record Companies

Banjar	Love	Sävel
Cuca	Olle i Skratthult Project	Standard-Colonial
Folkways	Rounder	Viking
Wilbur Foss		

Archives

Florida
    SCAMP
Minnesota
    Collection of Minnesota Ethnic Music
Ontario
    Canadian Centre for Folk Culture Studies
Helsinki
    Finnish Institute of Recorded Sound

Germanic

Rudy Wacek and his hand-
made electric zither on a
Syncro-Tone record pro-
duced in Chicago. Motion
Picture, Broadcasting, and
Recorded Sound Division,
Library of Congress.

German-speaking Americans constitute the second-largest non-English-
speaking group in the United States, outnumbered only by Spanish-speaking
citizens. German immigrants came to this country in two distinct waves. The
earlier, starting with the first wave of Mennonites who established German-
town, Pennsylvania, in 1683, peaked in the early eighteenth century and consisted mostly of splinter religious groups that were seeking religious freedom.
These include the various Mennonite groups, Amish, Dunkards, and Moravians. A second large wave of German immigrants came in the 1850s, largely
as a result of the political upheavals of 1848 and later. Another spurt came in
the 1880s. The Mennonites settled mostly in Pennsylvania, Ohio, and the
Midwest; the Moravians, in North Carolina. Later immigrations have left
large German-American communities in New York, New Jersey, Pennsylvania, Illinois, Wisconsin, Michigan, Minnesota, Ohio, Iowa, Kansas,
Florida, and California.

The religious music of the Amish, Mennonites, and Moravians has
attracted considerable interest on the part of folklorists, and several studies
have appeared in print. The Amish for many years resisted having their
hymns written down, choosing to preserve and transmit them exclusively by
oral means. Joseph W. Yoder was probably the first to notate by hand a
large collection of Amish hymns, many of which appeared in his *Amische
Lieder*. According to Nettl, at that time the only recordings of Amish Hymns
were a series made by Alan Lomax in 1938 near Goshen, Indiana, and three
recorded by Marcus Bach in Ames, Iowa, in 1943. All are on deposit in the
Archive of Folk Song; one has been issued on LP (see below). Of the several
publications on Amish music that have appeared, we note below one dissertation (Hohmann) that involved the use of recordings. We have found no references to recordings of other Germanic religious groups in the United
States. One of the first large collections of secular German-American folksongs was made by Brendle and Troxell. Between 1935 and 1941 they
recorded some 200 songs, almost 30 of which are transcribed in their 1949

article. Boyer, Buffington, and Yoder preserved a large sampling of Pennsylvania German songs in the 1940s on wire recorder; many of these were transcribed in their *Songs along the Mahantongo*.

There is a fair amount of contemporary German-American secular music available on records. Much of it is advertised as beer-drinking songs and polka music. Companies that produce such records include Alcon, Cuca, Delta International, Request, and Standard-Colonial. Folkways has issued an album titled *Pennsylvania Dutch Folk Songs* (FA 2215); the material is traditional, but the performance "city-billy," and some of the songs were learned from secondary sources. One unusual item—we are not sure if it is representative of a widespread movement or is some unique experiment—is an album of German folksongs performed by a German singer, Lieselotte, accompanied by an American rock band (Request RLP 8054: *German Folk Songs—Rocked in U.S.A.*).

Printed References

Boyer, Walter E., Albert F. Buffington, and Don Yoder. *Songs along the Mahantongo: Pennsylvania Dutch Folk-Songs.* Hatboro, Pa.: Folklore Associates, 1964.

Brendle, Thomas R., and William S. Troxell. "Pennsylvania German Songs." In *Pennsylvania Songs and Legends,* edited by George Korson, pp. 62–128. Baltimore: Johns Hopkins University Press, 1949.

Hohmann, Rupert Kar. "The Church Music of the Old Order Amish of the United States." Ph. D. diss., Northwestern University, 1959. "Deals with the history, description, illustration and stylistic analysis of hymns and other tunes taken from literary sources and phonographic recordings." (Reference from *Ethnomusicology and Folk Music: An International Bibliography of Dissertations and Theses.* Compiled and annotated by Frank Gillis and Alan P. Merriam. Society for Ethnomusicology Special Series in Ethnomusicology, vol. 1. Middletown, Conn.: Wesleyan University Press, 1966.)

McCorkle, Donald Macomber. "Moravian Music in Salem: A German-American Heritage." Ph. D. diss., Indiana University, 1958. "Covers all aspects of music in the period 1780–1840" (From Gillis and Merriam.)

Nettl, Bruno. "The Hymns of the Amish: An Example of Marginal Survival." *Journal of American Folklore* 70 (October-December 1957): 323–28.

Yoder, Joseph W. *Amische Lieder.* Huntingdon, Pa.: Yoder Publishing Co., 1942.

Recordings

Library of Congress LBC 1: *Folk Music in America, Vol. 1: Religious Music—Congregational and Ceremonial.* Includes one selection recorded in 1943 by Amish singers of Kalona, Iowa.

Folkways FA 2215: *Pennsylvania Dutch Folk Songs.*

Record Companies

Alcon	Folkways	Request
Cuca	Library of Congress	Standard-Colonial
Delta International		

Archives
Illinois
    University of Illinois Archives of Ethnomusicology
New York
    Columbia University Library
    Archive of Folklore, Traditional Music, and Oral History
Alberta
    Provincial Museum and Archives of Alberta
Ontario
    Canadian Centre for Folk Culture Studies

Baltic

Among Baltic groups, Lithuanian musical tradition has been fairly well represented on disc in the United States; Latvian, much less so. Our awareness of Estonian-American music is confined to the reference to a single archive that reports field recordings on deposit.

Lithuanian

Jonas Balys, in 1949–50, recorded some 1,000 songs on tape from Lithuanian-American folksingers in Gary; Chicago; Brockton, Massachusetts; Elizabeth, New Jersey; Nashua, New Hampshire; Wilkes-Barre, Pennsylvania; and elsewhere. An LP album drawn from his collection was issued by Folkways in 1955. The remainder of Balys's collection is on deposit at the Indiana University Archives of Traditional Music. He has also published two collections of songs from his field tapes. Peacock has published a collection of traditional field recordings of Lithuanian-Canadian songs. The most extensive collection of Lithuanian and Lithuanian-American music in this country is the J. Žilevičius Library of Lithuanian Musicology in Chicago (2345 West 56th St.), containing more than 2,000 records and hundreds of field recordings on tape.

Several Lithuanian communities in America have been musically active in recent years, and many LPs are currently available on the Request and Eurotone labels. (Both labels also import recordings.) These vary from the rather "citybilly" style of the Mothers and Daughters Quartet (Dvi Dukrytes), who sing with accordion accompaniment (Request SRLP 8071 and 8069), to the more formal concert presentation on Eurotone 140: *50th Anniversary of Lithuanian Independence*, recorded at a Newark, New Jersey celebration. Also recorded on the Request label are several other Lithuanian-American groups, including the Ruta Ensemble of Chicago, founded in 1941 by Jack Stukas and originally used principally on the Lithuanian Radio Hour (RLP 8070 and SRLP 8271); and the choir of the Cleveland Lithuanian School (RLP 10061). The Folk Ensemble from the Greater New York Lithuanian-American Community has recorded on the Eurotone label (138).

Latvian

Latvian (and Estonian) immigration to the United States did not take place, for the most part, until after World War II, whereas Lithuanian immigration was heavy early in the century. This distinction, of itself, is not sufficient to determine which nationality will leave the more visible imprint on our musical heritage. We have found no references to field recordings among the Latvian-American community, and only three (possibly four) record companies currently producing Latvian music in this country. Kaibala Records, of Oreland, Pennsylvania, has a catalog of eight albums available, six of which are classical, featuring Latvian artists. One includes a Christmas

Lithuanian folk dance record published by the Foundation for Lithuanian Culture. Courtesy of Elena Bradunas.

cantata and Christmas folk songs (50E02). The eighth is *Latvian Folk Songs* (50E01), beautifully sung and accompanied, but in arrangements reminiscent of Renaissance music. The Latvian Folk Ensemble of New York has recorded two albums on the Monitor label (MF/MFS 466 and MFS [C] 495). The performances, as above, seem urbanely arranged. Not heard is *Latvian Traditional Songs* (Pumpkin Land Records ELA 5957), but this LP is probably of domestic origin. Latvian Music Records and Harmonija Records also issue Latvian recordings, but most, if not all, of their material seems to have originated in Europe.

Printed References

Balys, Jonas. *Lithuanian Folksongs in America. A Treasury of Lithuanian Folklore*, Vol. 5, Boston: Lithuania Encyclopedia Publishers, 1958.

———. *Lithuanian Folksongs in America, vol. 2*. A Treasury of Lithuanian Folklore, vol. 6. Silver Spring, Md., 1978.

Peacock, Kenneth. *A Garland of Rue: Lithuanian Folksongs of Love and Betrothal*. Folk Culture Publications, no. 2. Ottawa: National Museum of Man, 1971.

Viltis [Hope], 1– (May 1942–). A folklore magazine published in Denver, Colorado, with numerous articles on Lithuanian and Latvian folk music activites in America.

Recordings

Folkways FM 4009: *Lithuanian Folk Songs in the United States*. Recorded and annotated by Jonas Balys (1955). Twenty selections recorded in various cities in 1949–50. A twelve-page brochure includes text and tune transcriptions, translations into English, notes on the performers, and a brief general introduction.

Record Companies

Folkways	Kaibala	Request

Archives

California
    UCLA Folklore Archives (Lithuanian)
    UCLA Ethnomusicology Archive
District of Columbia
    Archive of Folk Song (Lithuanian)
Indiana
    Archives of Traditional Music
Minnesota
    Collection of Minnesota Ethnic Music (Estonian)
Ontario
    Canadian Centre for Folk Culture Studies (Lithuanian, Latvian)

East European

Immigration to the United States from the East European countries was greatest in the period 1900–1914, so that by the time the "foreign" record industry was thriving in the 1920s, there was a large potential market for records in those languages. In his introductory chapter, Pekka Gronow cites foreign-language-speaking populations in 1940 and compares those figures with the number of records issued in foreign-language series from the 1920s through the 1940s. The correlation, for most of the East European groups, is very high. Of the foreign-language-speaking populations, the Poles compise the largest East European group, and the third largest foreign-language group in the United States. Polish records, from both Victor and Columbia, were the second-most numerous foreign-language series issued. In decreasing order of numerical strength, according to Gronow's data, are Russian, Czech (Bohemian), Slovak, Slovenian, Serbo-Croatian, and Ukrainian—though the latter were often classed with Russian in both census figures and record series, and thus their ranking is uncertain. (By 1970, the order had shifted somewhat: Slovak, Czech, Russian, Ukrainian, Serbo-Croatian, Slovenian.)

A Folklyric Records reissue of early Ukrainian music recorded in America. Motion Picture, Broadcasting, and Recorded Sound Division, Library of Congress.

Of the early 78 rpm material, none was available on LP until the 1960s, when the Rusalka and Arka labels issued seven albums between them of reissues by Ewgen Zukowsky, Pawlo Humeniuk, and other Ukrainian performers. These albums are now out of print, though two have been reissued on the Request label: SRLP 8168: *Ukrainian Wedding*, and SRLP 8165: *Comic Songs and Dialogs of the Ukraine.* In the past few years, considerably more vintage material has become available, largely through the efforts of Richard K. Spottswood, an eclectic record collector who specializes in blues, jazz, and bluegrass music, and has recently established himself as a leading collector and researcher in the area of commercially recorded Slavic-American music. Since 1976, Spottswood has edited two albums of Ukrainian-American music on the Folklyric label and one of Slavic-American music for New World Records, and has also included eight cuts of Ukrainian, Polish, and Czech music in two albums of dance music edited for the Library of Congress (details are given below).

In the following paragraphs we offer some observations on the individual East European groups in regard to more recent commercial recordings and also activity on the part of scholarly collectors and folklorists.

East European: North Slavic

Polish

The Polish community of Detroit has provided material for two master's theses by students at Wayne State University (Pawlowska [1940], Goranowski), one of which was later used as the basis for a singing collection of Polish songs (Pawlowska [1961]).

One of the most unusual Polish musical traditions is that of the Podhale region of the Tatra mountains. It has been carried to Chicago by immigrants from that region, and several examples were recorded in the 1920s. Spottswood has documented the traditional music of the region as it has appeared on records, and has assembled a complete discography of both American and Polish recordings of Podhale music. It is interesting that Eddie Blazonczyk, descendent of Podhale immigrants and owner of the Chicago-based Bel-Aire Record Company and leader of one of the most popular Chicago-style Polish polka bands, has issued an album of recently recorded Podhale music from Chicago and is planning reissues of Podhale 78s; nothing could be further from polka music than this esoteric mountain style.

The contemporary output of Polish-American music is considerable. In most people's minds, Polish music is almost synonymous with polka music (though in fact the polka was originally a Czech dance), and in most record stores we have visited, the Polish music bins are filled almost exclusively with polka records. Since the 1930s, polka music has been very popular in all regions of America, the Medwest in particular (in this book Gronow has briefly sketched the rise in popularity of this dance music). What is interesting, however, is the existence of many bands and record companies that produce polka music with Polish (or Czech) vocals—records that are thus clearly intended for the ethnic communities.

While the polka craze may have diminished in intensity from the 1940s, there is presently no dearth of record companies involved in the production of such music; between the Polish and the Czech/Slovak companies, there are several hundred LPs of polka, waltz, and oberek music with foreign-language vocals on the market. Rex Records of Massachusetts and Bel-Aire Records of Chicago are two companies with extensive catalogs of music with Polish-language vocals.

Czech, Slovak, and Slovenian

Members of the Bača family produced this Kermit label reissue of old recordings made by the Texas-based band. Courtesy of Carl Fleischhauer.

Folklorists have reported on fieldwork among Czech- and Slovak-speaking residents in Detroit (Nettl and Moravcik), Pittsburgh (Evanson), Masaryktown and Slovenska Zahrada, Florida (Waschek), and Saline County, Nebraska (Babcock). The musical history of the Czechs in Texas is particularly interesting, because here there were definite cross-influences with both the Anglo-American tradition (Adolph Hofner's band played both Czech dance music and western swing) and the Spanish-American, or *norteño*, tradition. There is still a thriving tradition of polka music among the *norteño conjunto* bands of the Texas region. The career of Bačova Česka Kapela, an early Texas Czech band, has been explored in print (Bača), and a reissue LP of their 78s from the 1920s and 1930s appeared at the same time on the Kermit label (*Bača's First Recordings;* now out of print).

There are currently numerous record companies that specialize in Czech- or Slovak-language dance music—polkas and waltzes. Two valuable sources, both of whom sell their own records as well as those of other companies through mail order, are the Nebraska Record Company of Schuyler, Nebraska, and J. J. Recording of Dodge, Nebraska (See Czech Records). Smaller Nebraska Czech record producers are Waverly Records, Rene Sound Studios, and Ray Records (both Czech and Polish). Guide Records of Houston produces contemporary Texas Czech recordings. WAM Records of Youngstown, Ohio, produces Slovak, Polish, and Hungarian records. Delta International of Cleveland distributes mostly Slovenian music. Although Slovenia is a part of Yugoslavia, Slovenian-American music is stylistically closer to Czech and Slovak than to music from other parts of Yugoslavia. There is considerable variety among these various Czech, Slovak, and Slovenian groups: The Oldtimers (Czech SCR 29) play Old World polkas and waltzes on horns at a dignified pace; Spinavy Pepik (Ray RRSLP 4001) sings bawdy Czech songs to his own button accordion accompaniment; Anna Bakova and Pavel Gabor, accompanied by the Jan Berky-Mrenica Gypsy Ensemble (WAM W4014), produce a striking imitation of the highly polished large state vocal and instrumental folk ensembles of Eastern Europe; and so on.

Ukrainian

The extent of early 78 rpm Ukrainian recordings is difficult to determine from superficial data on the number of items in the various foreign-recordings series, inasmuch as Ukrainian material was occasionaly included in the "Russian" series. "Ruthenian," "Lemko-Russian," "Lemko-Ukrainian," and "Carpatho-Russian" were also used as label designations for Ukrainian material. In addition, Ukrainian artists often appeared in Polish and other series. Some important reissues of 78 rpm recordings were discussed at the beginning of this section.

Scholarly work on Ukrainian folklore and music in North America is being carried out by Stefan Maksymjwk of Takoma Park, Maryland, and Roman Sawycky of Cranford, New Jersey. There is also much scholarly activity in Canada, where, especially in the western provinces, there is a large population of Ukrainian extraction. Robert Klymasz has studied and published extensively in this field; some of his publications are listed below. Several Canadian archives have Ukrainian field recordings: the Provincial Museum and Archives of Alberta, The Canadian Centre for Folk Culture Studies, and the Ukrainian Cultural and Educational Centre of Mantioba.

We are not aware of many commercially issued examples of traditional Ukrainian-Canadian folksingers. Two are included in Barbara Cass-Begg's survey, Folkways FE 4312: *Folksongs of Saskatchewan*.

An interesting development has been the emergence of a contemporary "Ukrainian country music" style, blending Old World songs and tunes with characteristically New World—in particular, country-and-western—styles. This genre has been explored by Klymasz. V Records of Winnipeg is among the most active in this field, with catalog of more than 150 albums available.

In both Ukrainian and Russian circles there is thriving tradition of presenting folksongs in formal concert hall fashion, sung by trained singers often well established in opera. Albums of this sort have been imported from Russia in large quantities. Similar presentations have been recorded in this country. The Choir of Saint John the Baptist Ukrainian Catholic Church in Newark, New Jersey, is one of probably many organizations that presents concerts of both religious and folk music in many cities and countries. The choir has recorded at least two albums on the Request label: *Christmas in the Ukraine* (SRLP 8104) and *Ukrainians Sing* (SRLP 8151), the latter a program of folksongs.

This recording of the youth ensemble of the St. Nicholas Ukrainian Catholic Cathedral is sold by the church. Motion Picture, Broadcasting, and Recorded Sound Division, Library of Congress.

Russian

Gronow's census and record-release figures indicate that there should be a good deal of Russian music recorded in this country. To our consternation, we have been able to find little. Since the 1920s, interest in Russian folk music has had political overtones; postrevolutionary songs, in particular, have been favored by musically inclined left-wing social groups for many years. However, as far as we can tell, most of the recordings available here are either imported or else are recorded by politically motivated artists who are aiming their product outside the ethnic community. Since the 1930s such artists as Paul Robeson, Pete Seeger, Theodore Bikel, and Martha Schlamme have included Russian numbers in their concerts and albums, and the great Russian choral tradition has been made available in this country by such long-established groups as the Red Army Chorus, the Don Cossack Chorus, and Piatnitsky Choir. Monitor, Elektra, and doubtless other companies have issued albums of Russian Gypsy music, some recorded abroad, some recorded locally. (Gypsy music is also discussed below.)

Two local Russian groups that have received some attention by folklorists are the Molokans of the western states and the Doukhobors of western Canada. F. Mark Mealing has compiled a discography of Doukhobor LP records that includes thirty-two albums issued by various companies through September, 1976. Two general survey LPs are Folkways FR 8972: *The Doukhobors of British Columbia*, recorded and edited by Barbara

Bachovzeff (1962); and National Museum of Man Bulletin 231: *Song of the Doukhobors*, recorded and edited by Kenneth Peacok (1970). Willard B. Moore of the Minnesota Folklife Center has done fieldwork with Russian Molokans of California, Oregon, and Arizona, and has taped religious musical performances (on deposit in the Indiana University Archives of Traditional Music, Accession number 74–029–F).

East European: Serbian and Croatian

Perhaps it is appropriate to remind readers that present-day Yugoslavia is a post-World War I creation out of the former states of (from northwest to southeast) Slovenia, Croatia, Bosnia, Serbia, Dalmatia, Herzegovina, and Macedonia. Numerically speaking, the important immigrant groups to the United States came from Slovenia and Serbo-Croatia (and in many census figures, the latter term is used interchangeably for Yugoslavia). As noted above, Slovenian music is much closer stylistically to that of Czechoslovakia than to that of the rest of Yugoslavia. According to figures cited earlier in this book by Gronow, Serbo-Croatian-speaking Americans are well down on the list of ethnic groups in terms of population; correspondingly few records were produced in the 78 rpm era by Columbia and Victor. We know of no early material from the 1920s and 1930s that is currently available on LP. However, since World War II, there has been intense activity in the field of Serbian and Croatian dance music; at present there must be hundreds of *tamburitza* bands in Pennsylvania, Ohio, Michigan, New York, Illinois, Arizona, and elsewhere. The popularity of this music among "nonethnic" folk dance groups is discussed in the next section. Most of the articles published on Yugoslav music in America, in fact, have dealt with particular aspects of *tamburitza* bands and *kolo* (dance) clubs. Hoffman has written on the *kolo* club of Steelton, Pennsylvania, and March on the *tamburitza* tradition in the Calumet, Illinois, area; Kolar has written a history of the *tambura* in America, with a discussion of many early commerically recorded bands; Koenig and Raim have discussed briefly the background of the *tamburitza* bands in the United States. Brief articles have appeared on two particular bands: Polavina on the Popovich Brothers of Chicago; and Koenig on the Banat Tamburitzan Orchestra of New York, a group active since 1940.

A record made and sold by members of this South Chicago band. Motion Picture, Broadcasting, and Recorded Sound Division, Library of Congress.

Perhaps the most imposing University-based archive and study program in Yugoslav and other East European traditions is at Duquesne University in Pittsburgh. DUTIFA, the Duquesne University Tamburitzans Institute of Folk Arts, encompasses an academic program leading to a Master of Folk Arts degree; an extensive record, book, tape, and film library and archive; performing folk ensembles active since 1937; community education programs; and a general cultural center. The Duquesne University Tamburitzans have also produced records for many years (some 78 rpm releases presumably from the early 1940s) and have several dozen LPs currently available, featuring a variety of Balkan musical traditions. DUTIFA has produced an educational kit on the Croatian-American heritage, including recordings of folksongs and dances, and film strips.

An excellent source for Yugoslav and other Balkan records is the Balkan Record Distributing Company of Beaver Falls, Pennsylvania. In addition to selling, through mail order, LPs on their own Balkan International Records label, they carry many of the other active labels in this field. They also distribute for many artists who produce their own recordings on their own labels, including the Popovich Brothers, the Balkan Serenaders of Lackawanna, New York, the Lira Tamburitza Orchestra of Detroit, the Duni Vetre Tamburitza Orchestra of Washington, D.C., the Dunav Tamburitza Orchestra of Chicago, the Crlenica Brothers Tamburitzans, the Royal Tamburitzans of St. Louis, and many others.

Kathleen Monahan, who is associated with SCAMP (Study Center for American Musical Pluralism), has written an informative review of some currently available recordings of Yugoslav-American music (1977). More recently, she has compiled a brief history of one contemporary Yugoslav-American record company, Greyko, in the context of ethnic culture in America (1978).

East European: Other Balkan

Interest in foreign folk dances after World War II provided immigrant musicians from Greece, Yugoslavia, Bulgaria, Rumania, and elsewhere with ample opportunity to provide music to nonethnic communities. Initially, dances were learned to a particular recording—often imported—and the demand for the original recording occasionally led to pirated reissues on small domestic labels to assure availability. Eventually, domestic bands learned "original" arrangements, and these were recorded as more and more independent small labels sprang up in the late 1940s and 1950s. Folk dance instructors often worked with particular groups of musicians—sometimes those of foreign extraction, at other times "nonethnic" musicians who learned foreign styles from older records. Consequently, what soon happened was that many labels had mixtures of all kinds of musicians on record. Among the labels that catered to folk and square dance devotees have been Michael Herman's Folk Dancer label of Flushing, New York; Bowery Records of Del Mar, California (now defunct); Sonart (New York); Festival Records and Kolo Festival, produced by Festival Folkshop of San Francisco; and Folkraft of Newark, New Jersey.

Apart from the folk dance–related records, we have found very few examples of Balkan music recorded in the United States since World War II, though during the 78 rpm era most of the countries (except Bulgaria) were extensively recorded. Only Greek-American is represented, by the Grecophon, P.A., and Kallista labels; we have not been able to secure general information about these companies. Our survey has not been very successful in turning up recordings of religious music (apart from the extensive Hebrew cantorial and liturgical material and German-speaking sects discussed below). However, we note one Lyrichord album, LLST 7159: *Music of the Greek Orthodox Liturgy*, featuring the Ascension Choir of the Greek Orthodox Church of Oakland, California.

At the present time, there are a number of "nonethnic" groups in the United States performing East European music, often for "nonethnic" folk dance audiences. They sometimes perform at concerts or festivals, working to build a greater appreciation for East European music within the community at large. Some of these groups (for example, Novo Selo in Philadelphia and Aman in Los Angeles) have produced records.

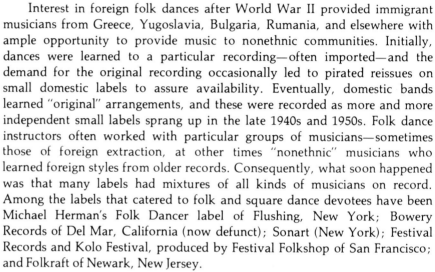

This record of Greek music was produced by the musician in Des Plaines, Illinois. Motion Picture, Broadcasting, and Recorded Sound Division, Library of Congress.

Printed References

Babcock, C. Merton. "Czech Songs in Nebraska." *Western Folklore* 8 (October 1949): 320–27.

Baca, Cleo R. *Baca's Musical History, 1860–1968.* N.p.: *LaGrange Journal,* 1968.

Bennett, Robert J. "The Folk Songs of David Medoff." *Record Research*, no. 90 (May 1968), pp. 3–5. Brief biodiscography of a 1920s singer of Ukrainian and Jewish songs.

Evanson, Jacob A. "Folk Songs of an Industrial City." In *Pennsylvania Songs and Legends*, edited by George Korson, pp. 423–66. Baltimore: Johns Hopkins University Press, 1949.

Goranowski, Helen. "An Analysis of 65 Polish Folk-Songs: with Conclusions Based on This Analysis Concerning the Relation Between Language Rhythms and Music Rhythms: and Concerning the Evolution and Transplantation of These Songs to America." Master's thesis, Wayne State University.

Gronow, Pekka. "Recording for the 'Foreign' Series." *JEMF Quarterly* 12, no. 41 (Spring 1976): 15–20. Includes discussion of activities in recording Ukrainian-American music and the involvement of music store owner Myron Surmach.

Hoffman, D. "The Meaning and Functions of the Kolo Club 'Marian' in the Steelton, Pennsylvania Croatian Community." *Keystone Folklore Quarterly* 16 (1971): 115–32.

Klymasz, Robert B. " 'Sounds You Never Heard Before': Ukrainian Country Music in Western Canada." *Ethnomusicology* 16 (September 1972): 372–80.

———, and James Porter. "Traditional Ukrainian Balladry in Canada." *Western Folklore* 33 (April 1974): 89–132.

Koenig, Martin. Untitled article on the Banat Tamburitzan Orchestra. *Balkan-Arts Traditions* (New York, 1973), n.p.

———, and Ethel Raim. "Tamburashi Tradition in America." *Balkan-Arts Traditions* (New York, 1974), n.p.

Kolar, Walter. *A History of the Tambura, II: The Tambura in America.* Pittsburgh, 1975.

March, Richard. "The Tamburitza Tradition in the Calumet Region." *Indiana Folklore* 10 (1977): 127–38.

Mealing, Francis Mark. *A Doukhobor Discography.* Privately xeroxed and distributed by the author from Selkirk College, Castlegar, British Columbia, Canada.

Monahan, Kathleen. "Yugoslav-American Records." *Journal of American Folklore* 90 (October-December 1977): 497–501. Review Essay.

———. "The Role of Ethnic Record Companies in Cultural Maintenance: A Look at Greyko." *JEMF Quarterly* 14, no. 51 (Autumn 1978): 145–47, 156.

Nettl, Bruno, and Ivo Moravcik. "Czech and Slovak Songs Collected in Detroit." *Midwest Folklore* 5 (Spring 1955): 37–49.

Pawlowska, Harriet M. "Polish Folk Songs Gathered in Detroit, with an Analysis of the Music by Grace L. Engel." Master's thesis, Wayne State University, ca. 1940.

———, ed. *Merrily We Sing: 105 Polish Folksongs.* Detroit: Wayne State University Press, 1961

Peacock, Kenneth. *The Music of the Doukhobors.* National Museum of Man Bulletin 231. Ottawa, 1970.

Polavina, Nada. "Zhiveli Tamburashi." *Balkan-Arts Traditions* (New York, 1974), pp. 35–36.

Proracki, Anthony, and Alan Henderson. "Ukrainian-Canadian Folk Music of the Waterford Area." *Canadian Folk Music Journal* 2 (1974): 19–28.

Spottswood, Richard. "Karol Stoch and Recorded Polish Folk Music from the Podhale Region." JEMF *Quarterly* 13, no. 48 (Winter 1977): 196–204.

Strachwitz, Chris. "Texas Polka Music: Interview with Joe Patek." In *The American Folk Music Occasional* [no. 2], edited by Chris Strachwitz and Pete Welding, pp. 73–75. New York: Oak Publications, 1970.

Waschek, Brownlee. "Czech and Slovak Folk Music in Masaryktown and Slovenska Zahrada, Florida." 2 vols. Ph. D. diss., Florida State University, 1969.

———. "A Study of Czechoslovak Folk Music Transplanted to the Community of Masaryktown, Florida." Master's thesis, Florida State University, 1959.

Recordings

Folklyric 9014/9015: *Ukrainian-American Fiddle & Dance Music: The First Recordings, 1926–1936, Vols. 1/2.* Good general survey of a particular style of Ukrainian-American recordings of late 1920s or 1930s.

Folkyric 9026: *Polish-American Dance Music—The Early Recordings: 1927–1933.* Reissue of fourteen selections originally recorded in Chicago and New York. Brief liner notes.

Folkways FE 4312: *Folksongs of Saskatchewan.* Recorded and edited by Barbara Cass-Beggs (1963). Examples of Welsh-, German-, Ukrainian-, Icelandic-, French-, and Anglo-Canadian and native Indian songs. Brochure notes give song texts and translations and backgrounds on singers, songs, and the ethnic cultures.

Folkways FW 6828: *Ukrainian Christmas Songs.* Recorded by Laura Boulton in Manitoba; sung by choral groups (1956).

Folkways FR 9072: *The Doukhobors of British Columbia.* Recorded and edited by Barbara Bachovzeff (1962). ". . . the largest widely available recording of the songs of Sons-of-Freedom (Svobodniki) Doukhobors. . . . The accompanying folder includes several excellent folklife photographs." (From Mealing discography.)

Krynica XTV 85232/85233: *Lemko Wedding.* Produced by Stephen Skimba. Reissue of Ukrainian-American recordings of late 1920s or 1930s.

Library of Congress LBC 4 and LBC 5. *Folk Music in America, Vol. 4: Dance Music—Reels, Polkas, & More;* and *Folk Music in America, Vol. 5; Dance Music—Ragtime, Jazz, & More.* These two volumes in the series of fifteen edited by Richard K. Spottswood include eight examples of Polish-, Ukrainian-, and Czech-American commercial recordings of the 1920s. Albums are accompanied by very good brochure notes.

National Museum of Man Bulletin 231: *Songs of the Doukhobors.* Recorded and edited by Kenneth Peacock (1970). Publication is accompanied by four flexidisc records of material recorded in 1963–64.

New World Records NW 283: *'Spiew Juchasa/Song of the Shepherd: Songs of the Slavic Americans.* Reissue of seventeen selections originally recorded between 1926 and ca. 1950. Collection edited and annotated by Richard K. Spottswood, with historical background introduction by Andrzej Kaminski.

Polkaland LP 30/33/35/39/40: Roman Gosz and his Orchestra, Vols. 1–5. Five Volumes of reissues of polka music, originally recorded between 1931 and 1939 by a very popular Bohemian-American group from Wisconsin.

Request SRLP 8165: *Comic Songs and Dialogs of the Ukraine.* Reissue of 1920s Ukrainian-American recordings. No substantial liner notes.

Request SRLP 8168: *Ukrainian Wedding.* Reissue of 1920s Ukrainian-American recordings, featuring Pawlo Humeniuk, Eugene Zukowsky, and others. Very brief liner notes.

Record Companies

Alcon (Czech, Yugoslav, Polish)
Ampol (Polish)
Balkan Record Distributing Co.
Balkan Serenaders Record Co.
Becar Tamburitzans (Yugoslav)
Bel Aire (Polish)
Cuca (Polish)
Bill Cvetnic (Yugoslav)
Czech
Delta International (Polish, Yugoslav)
Dyno (Polish)
Du-Tam
Guide (Czech)

Gateway (Polish, Yugoslav)
Goodwill (Yugoslav)
Greyko (Yugoslav)
Guide (Czech)
Folklyric (Ukrainian)
Folkways (Russian)
Heritage (Czech)
K Records (Ukrainian)
Monitor
Marjon (Yugoslav)
Walter Naglich (Yugoslav)
Nikola (Yugoslav)
Olympia (Polish)
Teddy Popovich (Yugoslav)
Ray (Czech, Polish)

Rene (Czech)
Request (Polish)
Rex (Polish)
Royal Tamburitzans (Yugoslav)
Royden (Polish)
Saint Anthony's Tamburitza Orchestra (Yugoslav)
Standard-Colonial (Ukrainian, Polish, Yugoslav)
UK Records (Ukrainian)
V Records (Ukrainian)
Voyager (Russian)
WAM (Czech)
Waverly (Czech)

Archives

California
    UCLA Folklore Archive (Russia)
District of Columbia
    Archive of Folk Song
New York
    Archive of Folklore, Traditional Music, and Oral History (Polish)
Alberta
    Provincial Museum and Archives of Alberta (Ukrainian, Polish)
Manitoba
    Ukrainian Cultural and Educational Centre
Ontario
    Canadian Centre for Folk Culture Studies (Ukrainian, Russian, Czech, Hungarian, Polish, Yugoslav)

Other European Traditions

For several countries and languages not already covered, we have only one or two entries each, and so group them here for convenience, though without any other logical principle.

Italian

While there is a great quantity of imported Italian music available in American stores, we have found very little recorded in this country. Standard-

Colonial lists many LPs in its catalogs, several of which feature the Nordini orchestra. But, as Walter Ericson told the participants at the American Folklife Center's conference on ethnic recordings in January, 1977, that was his own orchestra, recreating Italian standards or creating new "Italian" pieces in the style of the old—thus raising an interesting question about ethnic music and authenticity. As Ericson stressed, his recordings have been well received by the Italian-American community; in fact, many Italians insisted that his created "Italian" melodies were familiar to them from the old country.

One important album of traditional Italian folksongs collected in New York City and Chicago in 1963–64 has been issued by Folkways. The performances are extremely informal; the singers are occasionally rather self-conscious and uncertain; yet the album attests to the survival of a good deal of Old World music representing the domestic tradition—children's songs, lullabies, love ballads, harvesting songs, and so forth. Italian songs have also been collected in the less likely city of Santa Fe, New Mexico (see the January and April 1962 issues of the *Colorado Folksong Bulletin*).

Recordings

Folkways FE 4010: *Italian Folk Songs Collected in Italian-Speaking Communities in New York City and Chicago.* Collect in 1963–1964 by Carla Bianco; edited by Carla Bianco and Alan Lomax (1965). Sixteen-page brochure gives song texts and translations, notes on songs, and on informants.

Folkways FES 34041: *In Mezz' una Strada Trovai una Pianta di Rosa;* and Folkways FES 34042: *Calabria Bella, Dove T'hai Lasciate?* Two volumes of Italian folk music collected in New York, New Jersey, and Rhode Island by Anna L. Chairetakis during 1975–78. Brochure notes include notes on songs and performers, text transcriptions, and translations.

New World Records NW 264: *Old-Country Music in a New Land: Folk Music of Immigrants from Europe and the Near East.* Edited by Richard K. Spottswood. Reissue of sixteen recordings originally made ca. 1916–55. Includes one ca. 1916 Italian-American bagpipe/reed pipe duet recording.

Hungarian   Nearly a half-million Americans speak Hungarian—almost as many as speak Czech—and yet we have found no comparable activity in recorded music. Ware reported on American-Hungarian folksongs more than a half-century ago; more recently, Erdely has discussed the musical activities of the Hungarian community of Cleveland. No archives reported any holdings in Hungarian-American music, though the Canadian Centre for Folk Culture Studies in Ontario has some. Monitor Records imports a considerable quantity of music from Hungary; the only American companies we have found that record Hungarian-American music are Request, WAM, and B & F Record Company.

Portuguese   Portuguese folk music has been reported from Massachusetts (Cuney-Hare) and from California (Purcell, Fontes), and the UCLA Folklore Archive has field recordings on deposit. We have found commercially issued music only on the Standard-Colonial label.

Miscellaneous   Other European language traditions for which archival holdings have been reported are Bulgarian and Austrian, both at the Canadian Centre for

Folk Culture Studies in Ontario. Cowell, in a report on the recording of folk music in California, mentions Spanish, Portuguese, Basque, Italian, Armenian, Hungarian, Finnish, Icelandic, and Norwegian music. Traditions for which there are current commercially available recordings are Swiss and Dutch.

Gypsy   All across Europe, from Russia to England, the gypsies have been marvelous bearers and preservers of musical traditions. The phrase "gypsy music" can conjure up a dozen different images: the sentimental balalaika and violin music and deep coloratura voices of the Russian gypsies; the fiery violins of the Rumanian and Hungarian gypsies; the guitar-based music of the Iberian gypsies (flamenco in Spain, fado in Portugal); the old English and Romany ballads of the "travelers" of England. All of these (except the last named) have served as remarkably successful entertainment in restaurants, nightclubs, and coffeehouses from Paris to New York to San Francisco, and naturally the recording industry has responded to their popularity. This body of "gypsy music" recordings is aimed entirely at a general, non-ethnic audience; gypsies never refer to themselves by that name. Consequently, even though much of this music is recorded in the United States by musicians who have taken up residence here, we are reluctant to treat it as ethnic music, in the spirit in which this entire chapter is being written.

Printed References

Cowell, Sidney Robertson. "The Recording of Folk Music in California." *California Folklore Quarterly* 1 (January 1942): 7–23.

Cuney-Hare, Maud. "Portuguese Folk Songs from Provincetown (Cape Cod, Massachusetts)." *Musical Quarterly* 14 (1928): 35–53. Texts and tunes of fourteen songs.

Erdely, Stephen. "Folksongs of the American Hungarians in Cleveland." *Ethnomusicology* 8 (1964): 14–27.

Fontes, Manuel da Costa. "New Portuguese Ballad Collection from California." *Western Folklore* 34 (October 1975): 299–310.

Purcell, Joanne B. "Traditional Ballads among the Portuguese in California." *Western Folklore* 28 (January, April 1969): 1–20, 77–90.

Hungaria Records, Teaneck, New Jersey. Courtesy of Enikö Molnár Basa.

Ware, Helen. "The American-Hungarian Folk-Song." *Musical Quarterly* 2 (1916): 434–441. Three tunes given.

Record Companies

B & F (Hungarian)	Monitor (Dutch,	Standard-Colonial
Cuca (Swiss)	Hungarian, Italian)	(Portuguese, Italian)
Folkways (Italian)	Request (Hungarian)	WAM (Hungarian)

Archives

California
    UCLA Folklore Archive (Portuguese)
Ontario
    Canadian Centre for Folk Culture Studies (Hungarian, Bulgarian, Austrian)

Asian Traditions

The 1930 census indicated only 32,000 Americans of Armenian birth; the number has grown considerably, however, since then. Until recently, Fresno probably had the largest share of the Armenian population in the United States. In the past few years, there has been a large influx of Armenians from Lebanon (as a result of the civil disturbances there); many of them have settled in Los Angeles. Borcherdt has published a study of Armenian folk songs and dances in Fresno and Los Angeles (1959).

Armenian

Armenian-American music on record seems to be divided between folk and pop dance music and classical music. One example of a small record company that featured fairly traditional music aimed at the ethnic market was Sarkisian, owned by Reuben Sarkisian, then of Los Angeles. Mr. Sarkisian was kind enough to share with us some statistics concerning his company, which was active between 1947 and 1955. Approximately two dozen records were issued, of which some 2,000 copies were sold by mail order and through stores. Sarkisian issued a booklet with the words to the songs on his records; on the first page appeared the notice "For the convenience of our young generation, we were obliged to print the songs in English characters [as well as Armenian], also, so they may be able to read them."

There are several albums of contemporary Armenian-American dance music available. A popular group is Artie Barsamian's orchestra, with several records on the Standard-Colonial and Virgo labels.

At the other end of the musical spectrum is Arka Records of Los Angeles. This firm specializes in classical music, which can include the ballet music of Khatchaturian as well as modern Armenian opera. Most of Arka's material is recorded abroad and leased, or else recorded from visiting Armenian troupes on tour in the United States.

Recordings

New World Records NW 264: *Old-Country Music in a New Land: Folk Music of Immigrants from Europe and the Near East.* Edited by Richard K. Spottswood. Reissue of sixteen recordings origianlly made ca. 1916–55. Includes one selection by Reuben and Vart Sarkisian (Armenian) and one by Nahem Simon (Syrian).

Middle Eastern

In the contemporary mass record market, "Middle East" is practically synonymous with "belly dancing." A substantial number of such albums is currently available, some recorded abroad, others recorded by visiting musicians or those Middle Eastern musicians who have established residence in the United States (not to mention, of course, the recordings by American musicians imitating the "genuine" product). We are hard pressed to distinguish when the antecedents of particular styles or groups are more folk based or art music, though there is little doubt that the domestic albums themselves are firmly in a pop music vein.

In recent years a growing number of albums of genuine Middle Eastern field recordings has become available, but these fall outside the scope of our discussion.

Oriental

We have been unable to find any evidence for commercial recordings representing any of the Far Eastern Asian-American cultural traditions. There have been some published studies that report on musical activities in the Chinese, Japanese, and Korean communities in the United States or Canada, but no references that apply specifically to recordings. Those Asian musical recordings that are available in record stores are invariably imported from abroad, or at least were recorded abroad. Archival reports are also meager. Johanna Spector of New York has done fieldwork in the Indian-, Korean-, and Japanese-speaking New World communities.

Reuben Sarkisian, an Armenian fiddler who issued his own recordings in the 40s and 50s, with other musicians around 1949. Courtesy of Reuben Sarkisian.

Printed References

Borcherdt, Donn. "Armenian Folk Songs and Dances in the Fresno and Los Angeles Areas." *Western Folklore* 18 (January 1959):1-12.

Hofmann, Charles. "Japanese Folksongs in New York City." *Journal of American Folklore* 59 (July-September 1946):324-26.

Jacobs, A. Gertrude, comp. *The Chinese-American Song and Game Book.* New York: A. S. Barnes, 1944.

May, Elizabeth. "Encounters with Japanese Music in Los Angeles." *Western Folklore* 17 (July 1958):192-95.

Riddle, Ronald. "Music Clubs and Ensembles in San Francisco's Chinese Community." In *Eight Urban Musical Cultures: Tradition and Change,* edited by Bruno Nettl, pp. 223-59. Urbana: University of Illinois Press, 1978. Brief mention of recordings available in community stores.

———. "Music in America's Chinatowns in the Nineteenth Century." *Bulletin of the Chinese Historical Society of America,* 12, no. 5 (May 1977):1-5. General survey; no mention of records.

Song, Bang-Song. *The Korean-Canadian Folk Song: An Ethnomusicological Study.* Canadian Centre for Folk Culture Studies, Mercury Series, no. 10. Ottawa: National Museums, 1975.

Record Companies

Arka (Armenian)
Audio-Fidelity
    (Middle-Eastern)
Monitor (Middle-Eastern,
    Armenian)

Saha (Armenian)
Silwani (Arabic)
Standard-Colonial
    (Armenian)
Virgo (Armenian)

Archives

New York
    Johanna Spector (Indian, Japanese, Korean)
Ontario
    Canadian Centre for Folk Culture Studies (Japanese, Chinese)

Jewish Traditions

Jewish music in America encompasses practically every variety of musical genre, from folk to liturgical to popular to classical. In addition, in considering recorded material, a variety of nonmusical forms should be noted: Yiddish humorous monologs and sketches, poetry and literature, and educational recordings for children. Kresh has written an excellent survey of currently available Jewish recordings—the only article of its kind. Two standard general references on Jewish music are Idelsohn and Rothmuller. Extensive bibliographies have been compiled by Sendry and Weisser. Pamphlets by Binder, Heskes (1968), and Eisenstein are additional useful resources. These latter three are all published by the National Jewish Music Council (New York), an excellent source for various educational materials. The following paragraphs offer some general observations on each of the principal categories of Jewish music. The recordings for each category follow the discussion of it; other references are grouped together at the end of this section.

Hebrew
Liturgical
Music

Hebrew has been the traditional language of prayer since biblical times, although today in some congregations there is a tendency toward increasing use of the vernacular language, in both prayer and liturgical music. In modern times it has become the custom for a congregation to have the services of a trained cantor (*hazzan*) to share leadership of the prayer services with the rabbi. Cantorial music is not folk music by most definitions. Though there is a great sense of preservation of tradition, there is much original composition; furthermore, the music is almost certainly passed from one generation to the next via written notation; cantors are generally musically literate.

In America, one often refers to the first decades of the present century as the "Golden Age of Cantorial Music." This is partly because of the influence of the recorded medium on cantorial music. The impact of the phonograph on folk music traditions has been noted in several genres, and cantorial music was no exception. Early in this century the major record companies explored every possible musical genre that could be captured on wax, including cantorial music. Possibly the first cantorial recordings were made by Gershon Sirota in 1903 in Europe; American cantors were being recorded by 1907, if not earlier. In the 1910s and 1920s hundreds of recordings were made by some of the most famous cantors. The availability of records both enhanced the reputations of the cantors who agreed to make the records and provided a convenient medium for their styles to be learned and emulated by other cantors. Some writers at the time criticized cantorial recordings as cheapening the sacred music by crass commercialization.

With the still-current widespread reverential attitude toward the early cantors, it is not surprising that many reissues have appeared in the past few decades. Possibly the best set is RCA Victor VCM-6173: *The Art of the Cantor;* a few others by smaller companies are noted below. Though many of these seem to be authorized reissues (i.e., with the knowledge and cooperation of the company—Victor or Columbia—that made the original recordings), they all lack discographic data, and many lack any but the most sketchy historical information. Currently the most active collector and researcher of early cantorial music is Barry Serota of Musique Internationale, who has reissued numerous albums of cantorial 78s on his own label. A great deal has been written about religious music; it is surprising that there are not companion recordings that survey critically the different cantorial styles, tracing regional and historical influences and trends. Heskes (1966) has compiled a general survey; Rosenblatt has written a biography of one of the best-known cantors. Barry Serota and Joseph Green (formerly Greenberger) are presently at work compiling a complete discography of Jewish liturgical music up to 1948.

Recordings

RCA Victor VCM-6173: *The Art of the Cantor.* Three-LP set issued in 1966, with selections by Josef Rosenblatt (recorded 1925–29), Samuel Vigoda (1929–38), and Moshe Koussevitzky (1947–51). Originally included was a sixteen-page booklet by Samuel Rosenblatt discussing cantorial music in general and the three represented singers in particular; however, more recently the notes have been deleted from the boxed set.

Menorah MEN-213: *Cantor Pinchik Sings.* Seven selections by Pierre Pinchik originally recorded in 1928–30 by RCA Victor. Liner notes include commentary on the selections and a brief biography.

Greater Record Company GRC 84: *A Concert with the Great Cantors.* Ten selections by seven cantors—Hershman, Karpov-Kagan, Roitman, Rosenblatt, Sirota, Karniol, and Rothstein—originally recorded in 1920s. This LP appeared in 1963.

GRC and Collectors Guild have been most active in reissuing old cantorial recordings. Other companies that have produced one or more cantorial reissues are Fiesta, Da Vinci, Metro (now defunct), Scala, and Tikva, but most of these companies are no longer in business. Numerous albums of contemporary cantorial recordings are available.

Hassidic Music

Recording produced by the Nichoach Society of Lubavitcher Chassidim. Motion Picture, Broadcasting, and Recorded Sound Division, Library of Congress.

Hassidism is a still-thriving school of Jewish thought that developed in Poland and Lithuania in the eighteenth century and gradually spread throughout Jewish communities of Europe and then the New World. Music has always played an important part in Hassidic life; many Hassidic leaders believed in and preached the importance of music, and many were musically creative. While the Hassidim did set psalms and prayers to music, more often their music consisted of wordless melodies (*nigunim*). Many Hassidic leaders had an aversion to writing any of their wisdom down on paper; hence sermons, aphorisms, stories, and the like were passed along orally. To the extent that this was true of their music, it fulfills most definitions of folk music (through some modern definitions would not impose this requirement). In the generations after the origins of Hassidism, various schools arose. Many of them have established branches in the New World; each has its own musical traditions. The most extensively represented on records is the Lubovitcher Hassidim of New York, who have issued some ten albums of music, the first in 1960 (they have also published written collections of their tunes). These albums, on the Nichoach label, all provide some historical annotations to the material presented. Taken in chronological sequence, the series exhibits noticeable trends: The earliest albums are less polished and more folksy; the later ones are distinctly more professional, and the music itself shows more modern influences. Other Hassidic schools are also represented on albums, but in most cases these are much more highly polished performances by cantors and/or trained musicians.

There has been some significant scholarly activity in the recording, publishing, and study of Hassidic music in the United States. Ellen Koskoff of Pittsburgh has made extensive field recordings of the Lubovitcher Hassidim in connection with her doctoral dissertation and other publications. Jill Gellerman of New York has videotaped Hassidic dance and music and has subjected her material to detailed analysis. Another New Yorker, Velvel Pasternak, has been studying the idiom for many years.

Recordings

Nichoach N–5720: *Chabad Nigunium.* The first volume of melodies and songs by the Lubovitcher Hassidim, issued 1960. Volumes 2–5 were issued between 1961 and 1964. Later volumes were produced in Israel.

Other Hassidic groups represented on LP include the Gerer Hassidim (Menorah Records), the Modzitzer Hassidim (Collectors Guild; Neginah); and Melitzer Hassidim (Aderet). In addition, Collectors Guild has issued several albums of general selections of Hassidic music. Most of these albums include liner notes that discuss the backgrounds of the selections presented.

Zionist　　　　Zionism—the political movement aimed at the re-establishment of a national Jewish homeland in the territory of Palestine—had its origin in Germany and eastern Europe in the late nineteenth century. Early immigrants to Palestine, and European and American writers and composers in support of them, created a new kind of Hebrew music. The songs were almost entirely about Palestine/Israel and the rebuilding of a Jewish state; the style was based on European music, but modified by the various Middle Eastern cultures that the settlers came in contact with in Palestine. In America, these songs were enthusiastically adopted by Zionist organizations and performed in concerts, at political and fund-raising rallies, and at youth camps. Many of these songs have practically become folksongs, although they are so firmly tied to printed songsters and songsheets and so widely disseminated on recordings that it remains to be seen whether they will have a life apart from the commercial media. While there are innumerable recordings and songbooks available, few take the music seriously enough to trace its backgrounds, cite authors and composers, or comment on styles more than perfunctorily.

Recordings

Numerous albums are available on Tikva, Folkways, Elektra, and several other labels.

Yiddish　　　From the seventeenth century on, Yiddish (a Germanic language written *Folksongs*　　in Hebrew characters, with a large borrowing of vocabulary from Hebrew and smaller borrowings from other languages) was the mother tongue of most East European Jews. It was brought to America by the heavy waves of immigration from East European countries in the late nineteenth and early twentieth centuries. Early in this century Yiddish culture thrived in America through daily newspapers (peak readership of over one million), theaters and concerts, folk choruses, and day schools. These media had a tremendous impact on the American musical and theatrical worlds as well. Yiddish-speaking immigrants brought with them to America Yiddish folksongs of nineteenth-century Eastern Europe—lullabies, love songs, topical songs, songs about life in the *shtetl*. Once in America, the immigrants created new Yiddish folksongs about their experiences in "this golden land."

In recent decades (at least since the 1930s), there have been some efforts to document the Yiddish folksong of America. Probably Ruth Rubin has been the individual most extensively involved in this work. Though best known to a general audience for her books on Yiddish songs and her own recordings, more important in the context of this survey is her extensive fieldwork, both in this country and Canada. A collection of some 850 items she recorded in the 1940s through 1960s is on deposit at the Library of Congress Archive of Folk Song; smaller collections are at the Museum of Man at Ottawa, the Wayne State University Folklore Archive, the YIVO Jewish Institute for Scientific Research, and the Rodgers and Hammerstein Library. The Library of Congress Archive of Folk Song and YIVO both hold another major collection of field recordings—the Ben Stonehill collection, comprising 1,078 items recorded from New York immigrants in 1948 on wire recorder. Also active today in the study of Yiddish folk music in North America are Barbara Kirshenblatt-Gimblett, affiliated with YIVO, who has written a brief survey of scholarship in this field; Beatrice Weinreich, with YIVO; Yosl and

Khane Mlotek, Mark Slobin, and others. To our knowledge, only one commercially available album that includes nonprofessionally performed Yiddish-American folksongs has been issued; it is drawn from Rubin's field tapes. A documentary LP of field recordings made by Kirshenblatt-Gimblett and Slobin is being prepared by them for publication.

Recordings

Folkways FG 3801: *Jewish Life, "The Old Country."* Collected and annotated by Ruth Rubin (1958). The only commercially available album of traditional singers performing Yiddish-American folksongs. Brochure with Yiddish, transliterated and translated texts and notes included.

Numerous other albums by folksong interpreters are available on Folkways, Vanguard, Elektra, Monitor, Tikva, Menorah, Cadence, Capitol and other labels.

Art Song and Theater Music

While the existence of a body of songs that is genuinely folkloric in origin and style cannot be denied, most of the recordings that are casually identified as Yiddish folksongs are better classified as art songs or songs of the Yiddish theater. On records they are generally presented in a formal concert-hall style to the accompaniment of piano, in the manner of lieder. While folksongs of every nationality have been treated similarly, Yiddish folk and art songs are particularly difficult to separate for two reasons: The immense popularity of the theater songs meant that many of them were learned by enthusiastic Yiddish-speaking audiences and sung over and over until they were practically functioning as folksongs; furthermore, many of the writers and composers for the Yiddish stage borrowed heavily from genuine Yiddish folksongs. There is an immense number of recordings of folk and art songs presented in concert style. In most cases, we have made no attempt to provide annotations that separate the contribution of the theater from the anonymous folk poetry of the New or Old World. Mark Slobin of Wesleyan University has been active in the study of this genre.

Recordings

A great quantity of Yiddish art and theater music has been recorded from the 1910s to the present. Of particular historical interest are the several albums of reissues (mostly of material from the 1920s and 1930s) on the GRC label. These include *The Best of Aaron Lebedeff* (GRC 182); *Ludwig Satz at the Yiddish Theatre* (GRC 172); *Molly Picon at the Yiddish Theatre* (GRC 220); and *Leo Fuchs Sings Yiddish Theatre Favorites* (GRC 174). These were among the most popular (and most recorded) artists in the idiom.

Dance (Freilach) Music

Like their non-Jewish neighbors, Jews had ample opportunities when the services of musicians were needed: weddings, festive holidays, circumcisions, and, more recently in America, bar mitzvahs and confirmations. This kind of music—*freilach* or *klezmer* music—is virtually ignored in almost every serious book or article on Jewish music; perhaps it is considered too common or demeaning to receive adequate treatment. It has been recorded in the United States at least since the mid-1920s. There are interesting question concerning *freilach* music that we have not seen explored. For instance, is its frequent similarity to Ukrainian, Polish, or Balkan dance music a result of one-way or two-way borrowing? The influence of Yiddish-American *freilach*

Yiddish music on the Arhoolie label. Motion Picture, Broadcasting, and Recorded Sound Division, Library of Congress.

music on contemporary jazz—Ziggy Elman's 1938 hit "Fralich in Swing" (or "And the Angels Sing") is a well-known example—also deserves investigation.

In recent years, a resurgence of interest in *Klezmer* music has become apparent both by young performers (e.g., the Klezmorim, a Berkeley band) and by researchers. Henry Sapoznik, working at the American Jewish Congress's Martin Steinberg Center in New York has been studying the material issued on early 78s (in particular, its relation to jazz) and is preparing a reissue LP to be released on the Folkways label. Martin Schwartz of Berkeley has a large private collection of 78 rpm klezmer discs and has been studying the relationship of that music to Greek music of the early part of the century. Dave Tarras, a clarinetist who since the 1920s has been one of the leading performers of traditional klezmer music, is the subject of a documentation project headed by Andrew Statman and Zev Feldman of New York. The project will ultimately yield a biography; a carefully produced studio recording of Tarras, backed by a trio, performing traditional East European wedding dance music never previously recorded on field or commercial recordings; and a book-length study (by Statman, Feldman, and Sapoznik) including musical analyses of selected Tarras performances and a complete Tarras discography.

Currently, the most extensive public collections of klezmer music are the YIVO Institute for Jewish Research, the Rodgers and Hammerstein Archive of Recorded Sound, the Judah Magnes Museum in Berkeley, and the Martin Steinberg Center.

Recordings

Folkways FW 6809: *Jewish Freilach Songs.* Played and sung by "Prince" Nazaroff, with octofone and accordion (10" LP). Ten selections by a "street musician" who came to the United States in 1914 and performed for years at dances and weddings, in vaudeville, and on radio and television. Booklet includes Yiddish texts, transliterations and translations.

Unlike the above, most albums of *freilach* music are instrumental only, without vocals. Tikva and Banner have issued several that are still in print that were recorded probably in the 1950s.

Judezmo

Judezmo is a Spanish-Hebrew hybrid vernacular language analogous to Yiddish; it is spoken by Sephardic (literally, Spanish) Jewish communities that are not confined to the Spanish-speaking world, but are scattered throughout the Mediterranean and Middle Eastern countries. (Ladino is the closely related language of biblical translation.) Approximately half of the 2,000 Jews in the American colonies were of Sephardic origin. Their numbers grew gradually in the eighteenth and nineteenth centuries; between the Turkish revolution in 1908 and the fixing of immigration quotas in 1924–25 some fifty to sixty thousand Sephardic Jews arrived in the United States. At present there are Sephardic Jewish communities in more than a dozen American cities. Sephardic Jews, both in the United States and elsewhere, have preserved in oral tradition remnants of Spanish balladry that originated in the late Middle Ages. Folklorists Samuel Armistad and Joseph Silverman have been actively studying this type of material. We know of no commercially available recordings of traditional singers; there are several albums of Judezmo folksongs by folksong interpreters, some of whom grew up at least close to the tradition, and so presumably offer a fairly authentic presentation. One is cited below.

The few Judeo-Spanish titles from commercial records of the 1920s that we have seen were in the Hebrew language, rather than Judezmo. Heskes (1972) has compiled a short general guide to recorded Judezmo music. David M. Bunis, one of the founders of the Judezmo Society of Brooklyn, New York, is compiling data on Judezmo and Sephardic Hebrew recordings released in the United States and abroad, for inclusion in his forthcoming *Sephardic Studies: A Bibliography for Research*, to be published by YIVO.

Recordings

Folkways FW 8737: *Sephardic Folk Songs*. Sung by Gloria Levy (1959). Twenty-one selections by an American singer who learned them from her Egyptian-born mother, who in turn learned them in Turkey from her mother. Brochure notes include a brief sketch, "The Sephardic Song," by H. J. Bernardete, and song texts and translations.

There are a few albums on the Tikva and GRC labels; most other recordings of Sephardic music originated abroad.

Non-musical Recordings

There are several albums of Yiddish humorous material from the Yiddish stage. Some of these, featuring such celebrities as Molly Picon and Leo Fuchs, are obviously reissues from the 1930s and 1940s; others may be more contemporary. The albums we have seen make little attempt to provide any historical background or identify sources of the recordings. Both English- and Yiddish-language material are represented.

Many 78 rpm recordings of the 1910s and 1920s offered "pseudo-Jewish" humor: monologs and dialogs, generally by non-Jews, intended for the general record-buying public, capitalizing on Jewish stereotypes, using Jewish accents. The same type of "ethnic" humor was recorded in this period exploiting Irish, Negro, German, and Italian stereotypes. None of this material has been reissued; and though each recording is bound to offend someone, there would seem to be a great deal of grist here for folklorists, historians, and students of popular culture alike.

There is also a small number of "serious" readings of Yiddish drama, poetry, and literature, some in the original language, some translated into English. A substantial body of recordings is aimed at younger audiences; these are educational records that teach Jewish history, religion, ethics, customs, and Yiddish or Hebrew language.

Recordings

Monitor, Caedmon, and other companies have issued albums of serious readings of Yiddish classical literature (e.g., by Sholom Aleichem, Y. L. Peretz, I. B. Singer), some in Yiddish and some in English.

Banner, Audio Fidelity, Tikva, Rivoli, Madison, and other labels have issued (or reissued) recordings of "Yiddish vaudeville"—humorous monologs, skits, and songs, by famous performers of the Yiddish stage.

General

Finally, there are several albums that combine music with narrative in an attempt to provide a broad survey of all Jewish music, or at least parts of it. We cite below the most successful album of this type that we have heard.

Recordings

Board of Jewish Education (Chicago) BJE 7510: *The American Jewish Experience in Song.* An educational program with more than thirty brief musical selections interspersed with a narrative on the history of the American Jewry. Musical selections by trained singers and a chorus of children. Additional notes in an eight-page brochure. A book, *Songs of the American Jewish Experience,* has also been published as a companion to the record (1976).

Printed References

Agus, Robert. "Hazzanut [Cantorial music]." In *The Second Jewish Catalog,* compiled and edited by Sharon Strassfeld and Michael Strassfeld, pp. 368–76. Philadelphia: Jewish Publication Society, 1976. Includes brief list of recommended LP records.

Armistead, Samuel, and Joseph Silverman. "Hispanic Balladry among the Sephardic Jews of the West Coast." *Western Folklore* 19 (October 1960):229–44.

Binder, Abraham W. *The Jewish Music Movement in America: An Informal Lecture.* New York: Jewish Music Council, 1975. Mimeographed. Following Binder's lecture (an address delivered in 1952 at the Hebrew University in Jerusalem) are resource addenda compiled by Irene Heskes: lists of recordings of Jewish classical music, publishers, record companies, and libraries with pertinent resources.

Eisenstein, Judith K. *The Scope of Jewish Music.* New York: National Jewish Music Council, 1948. Mimeographed. The text of a lecture prepared for nonspecialist audiences. Musical examples (and their source recordings) are indicated.

Greenberger, Joseph. "Cantor Josef Rosenblatt." *The Record Collector* (May 1972), pp. 125–146. Brief biography with complete discography— "the first [and possibly only one] to be published in the field of Jewish liturgical music or cantorial singing." Includes alphabetical title index and index of reissues.

Heskes, Irene. *The Historic Contribution of Russian Jewry to Jewish Music: Supplement.* New York: National Jewish Music Council, 1968. Mimeographed. Includes bibliography, list of suitable recordings, list of compositions by Russian-Jewish composers.

———. *Music of the Sephardic and Oriental Jews: Program Resources.* New York: Jewish Music Council, 1972. Includes selected listings of suitable recordings, names and addresses of record companies, bibliography of published collections of Sephardic music, list of publishers.

———, ed. *The Cantorial Art.* New York: National Jewish Music Council, 1966. Includes a selective bibliography of modern synagogue literature and selective list of cantorial recordings.

Idelsohn, A. Z. *Jewish Music in Its Historical Development.* 1929. Reprint ed., New York: Schocken Books, 1967. An excellent general survey, though it stops a half-century short of the present. Chapter 15 is devoted to synagogue song in the United States; chapters 17–20 deal principally with folksong and folk music.

Kirshenblatt-Gimblett, Barbara. "Yiddish Folksong in Europe and America." In *Balkan-Arts Traditions,* pp. 5–10. New York: Balkan Arts Center, 1974. Includes brief discussion of current research.

Kresh, Paul. "From 'Eli Eli' to Bob Dylan: The Great Jewish Record Hunt." *Present Tense*, Fall 1977, pp. 40–48. Excellent general survey of currently available recordings, shops, and so forth.

Library of Congress Archive of Folk Song. "A Brief List of Material Relating to Yiddish Folk Music." Mimeographed. Compiled in March 1970.

———. "A Selected List of Material Relating to Hebrew and Israeli Folk Music." Mimeographed. Compiled in November 1970, by Leonore E. Weissler.

MacCurdy, Raymond R., and Daniel D. Stanley. "Judaeo-Spanish Ballads from Atlanta, Georgia." *Southern Folklore Quarterly* 15 (December 1951):221–38.

Mlotek, Eleanor G. *A List of 55 Recommended Yiddish Records.* New York: Educational Department of the Workmen's Circle, 1964. Lists 55 LP albums, with descriptive data, arranged according to the following divisions: general (folk, art, popular), children's songs, holiday songs, songs of America, songs of Goldfaden and the Yiddish Theater, songs of the ghettos and concentration camps, sing-along records. An index of 543 song titles, cross-indexed by LP, is included, as well as an index of authors and composers.

Rosenblatt, Samuel. *Yossele [Josef] Rosenblatt.* New York: Farrar, Straus, and Young, 1954. A biography of the famous cantor by his son; includes three pages of very sketchy discography.

Rothmuller, Aron Marko. *The Music of the Jews: An Historical Appreciation.* New and rev. ed. South Brunswick: T. Yoseloff, 1967.

Rubin, Ruth. *Voices of a People: Yiddish Folk Song.* New York: T. Yoseloff, 1963. An important survey of the field; chapters on children's songs, dancing songs, historical and topical songs, songs about America, Hassidic songs, songs of literary origin, and the like. Illustrated with excerpts from some 500 song texts.

———. *The Yiddish Folksong: An Illustrated Lecture.* New York: Jewish Music Council, 1974. Includes text and tunes of twelve musical examples, lists of available Yiddish folksong collections, suggested recordings, and additional references.

———. *Yiddish Folksongs of Social Significance.* New York: Education Department of the Workmen's Circle, 1968. A program prepared and narrated by Ruth Rubin. A tape recording with the full narrative text and the songs used as examples is also available from the publisher.

Schwarzbaum, Haim. *Studies in Jewish and World Folklore.* Berlin: de Gruyter, 1968. Appendix 2 includes a section on Jewish folksong, folk music, and folk dance (pp. 409–17) that surveys recent scholarship in these areas.

Sendry, Alfred. *Bibliography of Jewish Music.* New York: Columbia University Press, 1951. 10,004 individual entries, arranged by subject; of these, fewer than 120 refer specifically to recordings: liturgical, anthropological, folk, art, miscellaneous.

Weisser, Albert. *Bibliography of Publications and Other Resources on Jewish Music.* Rev. and enl. ed. New York: National Jewish Music Council, 1969. Mimeographed. 1,013 entries, divided according to format: books and pamphlets, periodical articles, theses, serials, and so forth. One section, "Accompanying Literature to Records," includes 16 entries. Also of interest is "Libraries Containing Collections of Jewish Music, Books and Materials on Jewish Music" (33 entries).

Record Companies

Aderet	Caedmon	Monitor
Arhoolie	Capitol	Neginah
Audio Fidelity	Collectors Guild	Nichoach
Banner	Elektra	Noam
Board of Jewish	Folkways	Standard-Colonial
Education of Chicago	Greater Recording	Tikva
Cadence	Menorah	Vanguard

Archives

California
    UCLA Folklore Archive
District of Columbia
    Archive of Folk Song
New York
    Rodgers and Hammerstein Archives
    Johanna Spector
    YIVO
Pennsylvania
    Abner and Mary Scriber Jewish Music Library
Ontario
    Canadian Centre for Folk Culture Studies

Record Companies

Information for the following list of record companies was gathered through a variety of means. The primary method was direct solicitation of individual companies. We sent form letters and questionnaires to approximately 175 firms, requesting information on their activities in recording and selling the music of ethnic Americans. We also spent much time browsing in record stores in order to become acquainted with currently available product. In some cases, when a company did not respond to our inquiry but was known to produce recordings of interest, we have presented as much information as could be gleaned. Some other companies that we were unable to canvass have also been listed, if they were given to us by a reliable source. In this regard, we would especially like to thank David P. McAllester for the many sources of American Indian recordings he offered.

The format for the listings is as follows:

Company name, Address

Other labels, if any

Date founded; availability of catalog or other descriptive information; size and activity of product line; product format.

TYPES OF MUSIC PRODUCED

All companies listed are, to the best of our knowledge, still in operation at this time. Most addresses are also known to be current, but many of these firms have a penchant for mobility. Perseverance and detective work are often required in order to obtain desired recordings! A few of the sources listed are individuals who have produced custom or "vanity" records. Such recordings are especially difficult to track down, and there are undoubtedly many more available than we have been able to discover; we apologize for any omissions.

Alcon Recording Studios, 35100 Euclid Avenue, Suite 300, Willoughby, OH 44094

1966; catalog available; ca. 40 titles, with 5–10 new releases per year; LP & 45 rpm discs, 8-track & cassette tapes.

GERMAN; CZECH (including Bohemian); POLISH; YUGOSLAV (including Croatian); SLOVENIAN

Alshire Records, P.O. Box 7107, Burbank, CA 91510

Discos Azteca

1954; catalog available; ca. 400 titles, with 6–12 new releases per year (small percentage of relevant material); LP & 45 rpm discs, 8-track & cassette tapes.

HAWAIIAN; MEXICAN

Alta Vista Records, P.O. Box 6021, Albuquerque, NM 87107
MEXICAN

Ampol Records, *See* Bel-Aire Record Co.

Arhoolie Records, 10341 San Pablo Avenue, El Cerrito, CA 94530
Old-Timey; Folklyric
1960; catalog available ($1.00); ca. 200 titles, with 6–20 new releases per year (not all relevant material); LP discs.
HAWAIIAN; IRISH; LOUISIANA FRENCH; MEXICAN; UKRAINIAN; JEWISH

Arka Armenian Records, 4856 Santa Monica Boulevard, Los Angeles, CA 90029
ARMENIAN

Avoca Musical Industries, P.O. Box 494, Wheatley Heights, NY 11798
1940; catalog available; 85 titles, with an average of 4 new releases per year; LP & 45 rpm discs, 8-track & cassette tapes.
IRISH

Balkan Record Distributing Co., R.D. 2, Concord Church Road, Beaver Falls, PA 15010
Many labels distributed, e.g., Monitor, Greyko, Marjon.
LP & 45 rpm discs, 8-track & cassette tapes.
YUGOSLAV (including Serbo-Croatian); SLOVENIAN

Talking Machine World, August 1928, page 81. Motion Picture, Broadcasting, and Recorded Sound Division, Library of Congress.

Balkan Serenaders Recording Co., P.O. Box 103, North Tonawanda, NY 14120
2 titles; LP discs.
YUGOSLAV

Banff Records, *See* Rodeo Records

Banjar Records, P.O. Box 32164, 7440 University Avenue NE, Minneapolis, MN
    55432
1973; descriptive information available; 6 titles, with an average of 2 new releases per
    year; LP & 45 rpm discs.
SCANDINAVIAN

Banner Records, 68 West Passaic Street, Rochelle Park, NJ 07662
Catalog available; 20 titles; LP discs, 8-track & cassette tapes.
JEWISH

Becar Tamburitzans, 27 Grande Avenue, Stoney Creek, Ontario, Canada
YUGOSLAV

Bel-Aire Record Co., 1740 West Forty-Seventh Street, Chicago, IL 60609
Ampol Records
Catalog available; ca. 300 items; LP & 45 rpm discs, 8-track & cassette tapes.
POLISH

Kay C. Bennet, 6 Aida Street, Gallup, NM 87301
AMERINDIAN (privately produced)

Biscuit City Records, 1106–8 East Seventeenth Avenue, Denver, CO 80218
1971; catalog available; 14 titles, with 8–10 new releases per year (small percentage of
    relevant material); LP discs.
IRISH

California Artists' Corporation, P.O. Box 11474, Fresno, CA 93773
MEXICAN

Cantemos Records, P.O. Box 246, Taos, NM 87571
1957; catalog available; 3 titles; LP discs.
MEXICAN

Canyon Records, 4143 North 16th Street, Phoenix, AZ 85016
1951; catalog available; ca. 300 titles, with an average of 20 new releases per year
    (including "most other available Indian music which is distributed by Canyon");
    LP discs, 8-track & cassette tapes.
AMERINDIAN

Carnaval Records, *See* MCA Records (Canada)

Casa Nova Records, *See* Christy Records

Celtic Records, *See* Rodeo Records

Chinle Galileans, c/o Roland Dixon, P.O. Box 1082, Chinle, AZ 86503
AMERINDIAN

Christy Records, 900 Fourth Street, NW, Albuquerque, NM 87102
Casa Nova Records
MEXICAN

Corona Records, c/o Rangel Distributing Co., 809 Fredericksburg Road, San Antonio, TX 78201
MEXICAN

Cuca Records, American Music Corporation, 123 Water Street, Sauk City, WI 53583
1961; catalog available; over 300 titles, with an average of 15 new releases per year; LP & 45 rpm discs, 8-track & cassette tapes.
SCANDINAVIAN (Norwegian); GERMAN; SWISS; POLISH. Much polka music of unspecified nationality.

Bill Cvetnic, 110 Rockwood Avenue, Pittsburgh, PA 15221
YUGOSLAV

Czech Records, MJ Recording, Dodge, NE 68633, and Nebraska Record Co., Schuyler, NE 68661
Catalog available; ca. 100 titles, with 10 new releases per year; LP & 45 rpm discs, 8-track & cassette tapes.
CZECH

DLB Records, 527 Highway 90 West, San Antonio, TX 78237
MEXICAN

Del Valle–Oro Records, 315 South Seventeenth Street, McAllen, TX 78501
MEXICAN

Delta International Records, 1584 East Thirty-First Street, Cleveland, OH 44114
Catalog available; ca. 35 titles; LP & 45 rpm discs, 8-track & cassette tapes.
GERMAN; POLISH; YUGOSLAV; SLOVENIAN

Dine, P.O. Box 187, Kayenta, AZ 86033
AMERINDIAN

Dineh Records, Tocina Music Enterprises, 900-B Fourth Street SW, Albuquerque, NM 87102
AMERINDIAN

Discos Azteca, *See* Alshire Records

Du-Tam Records, Duquesne University, 1801 Boulevard of the Allies, Pittsburgh, PA 15219
Ca. 20 titles; LP discs
YUGOSLAV

Everest Record Group, 2020 Avenue of the Stars, Century City, CA 90067
1962; catalog available; few releases of ethnic American music.
AMERINDIAN

Falcon Records, P.O. Box 1689, McAllen, TX 78501
Many labels distributed.
MEXICAN

Fama Records, 1445 Knoll Circle, San Jose, CA 95112
MEXICAN

Fenders, c/o Clyde Duncan, P.O. Box 265, Thoreau, NM 87323
AMERINDIAN

Folkraft Publishing Co., 10 Fenwick Street, Newark, NJ 07114
1940; catalog available; ca. 400 titles; LP & 45 rpm discs.
Folk dance music of many different nationalities and ethnic groups.

Folklyric Records, *See* Arhoolie Records

Folkways Records, 43 West Sixty-First Street, New York, NY 10023
RBF Records
1947; catalog available; ca. 1,600 titles with an average of 50 new releases per year
(small percentage of relevant material); LP discs, 8-track & cassette tapes.
AMERINDIAN; HAWAIIAN; IRISH; CANADIAN FRENCH; LOUISIANA
FRENCH; MEXICAN; GERMAN; ITALIAN; LITHUANIAN; SCANDINA-
VIAN; JAPANESE; JEWISH

Wilbur Foss, P.O. Box 629, Yankton, SD
SCANDINAVIAN (1 privately produced disc).

Foy Lee Productions, San Antonio, TX 78200
MEXICAN

Gateway Records, 234 Forbes Avenue, Pittsburgh, PA 15222
Dyno Polkas
YUGOSLAV; POLISH

Goodwill Records, Conshohocken, PA 19428
YUGOSLAV

Greyko Records Co., 4300 Butler Avenue, Pittsburgh, PA 15201
Ca. 30 titles; LP discs.
YUGOSLAV (including Serbo-Croatian)

Guide Records, 1045 Studewood, Houston, TX 77008
CZECH

Heritage Records, *See* Ray Records

Hurricane Records, 1927 San Mateo, NE, Albuquerque, NM 87110
MEXICAN

Ideal Records, c/o Rio Grande Music Co., 119 South Sam Houston Boulevard, San
Benito, TX 78586
MEXICAN

Indian House, P.O. Box 472, Taos, NM 87571

1967; catalog available; 52 titles, with 6–12 new releases per year; LP discs, 8-track & cassette tapes.

AMERINDIAN

Columbia 1918 Greek catalog. Courtesy of Pekka Gronow.

Indian Records, P.O. Box 47, Fay, OK 73646
1964; catalog available; 38 titles, with an average of 5 new releases per year; LP discs, 8-track & cassette tapes.
AMERINDIAN

Infal Records, 2144 Champa Street, Denver, CO 80202
MEXICAN

Iroqrafts, Ohsweken, Ontario NOA IMO, Canada
Founded 1958, incorporated 1972, descriptive information available; 3 titles.
AMERINDIAN (Iroquois)

Jin Records, *See* Swallow Records

Joey Records, San Antonio, TX 78200
MEXICAN

K Records, *See* UK Records

Kaibala Records, P.O. Box 512, Oreland, PA 19075
LATVIAN

Key Loc Records, San Antonio, TX 78200
MEXICAN

L & M Records, P.O. Box 734, Monterey Park, CA 91754
MEXICAN

La Louisianne Records, 711 Stevenson Street, Lafayette, LA 70501
1959; catalog available; 36 titles, with an average of 3 new releases per year; LP & 45 rpm discs, 8-track & cassette tapes.
LOUISIANA FRENCH

Library of Congress, Archive of Folk Song, American Folklife Center, Washington, DC 20540, and Music Division Recording Laboratory, Washington, D.C. 20540
AMERINDIAN. Examples of the music of many groups are included in various LPs produced by the Library, especially in the *Folk Music in America* series.

Lira Records, *See* Norteño Records

Love Records, Vuorimiehenkatu 29, 00140 Helsinki 14, Finland
1965; catalog available; 250 titles (see below); LP & 45 rpm discs, cassette tapes.
SCANDINAVIAN. "This company has issued 3 LPs of Finnish-American music (from old 78s). Bulk of product is Finnish pop, etc."

Luna Records, 434 Center Street, Healdsburg, CA 95448
Many labels distributed.
1976; catalog available; extensive line with an average of 5 new releases per year; LP & 45 rpm discs, 8-track & cassette tapes.
MEXICAN

Marjon Records, 159 Eastern Road, Sharon, PA 16146
YUGOSLAV (Serbo-Croatian).

Victor 1920 Romanian catalog. Music Division, Library of Congress.

MCA Records (Canada), 2450 Victoria Park Avenue, Willowdale, Ontario, M2J 4A2, Canada
MCA Coral; Carnaval Records
CANADIAN FRENCH

Monitor Records, 156 Fifth Avenue, New York, NY 10010
1956; catalog available; ca. 400 titles, with 15–20 new releases per year (small percentage of relevant material); LP & 45 rpm discs, 8-track & cassette tapes.
ITALIAN; LATVIAN; DUTCH; POLISH; HUNGARIAN; ARMENIAN; GREEK; UKRAINIAN; RUSSIAN; MIDDLE EASTERN; CHINESE; JEWISH.

M.O.R.E. (Minority Owned Record Enterprises), 1205 Lester Drive NE, Albuquerque, NM 87112
MEXICAN

Morningstar Records, 11 River Road, Nutley, NJ 07110
LOUISIANA FRENCH

Walter Naglich, R.D. 1, Box 81, Mount Pleasant, PA 15666
YUGOSLAV

Navajo Sundowners, P.O. Box 15, Farmington, NM 87401
AMERINDIAN

Nichoach Records, c/o Merkos L'inyonei Chinuch, 770 Eastern Parkway, Brooklyn, NY 11213
Catalog available; ca. 15 titles; LP discs.
JEWISH

Nikola Records, 1 Hortus Court, St. Louis, MO 63110
YUGOSLAV

Norteno Record Co., 2606 Ruiz Street, San Antonio, TX 78228
Sombrero Records; Lira Records
1955; catalog available; 4 new LP & tape releases per month, 5 new single releases per month; LP & 45 rpm discs, 8-track tapes.
MEXICAN

Old-Timey Records, *See* Arhoolie Records

Olle i Skratthult Project, P.O. Box 14171, University Station, Minneapolis, MN 55414
1972; catalog available; 6 titles, with 1 new release per year; LP & 45 rpm discs. "A non-profit organization, only a part of whose efforts are devoted to production of recordings."
SCANDINAVIAN

Olympia Records, 230 West 18th Street, New York, NY 10019
POLISH

Philo Records, The Barn, North Ferrisburg, VT 05473
Fretless Records
1973; catalog available; 80 titles, with an average of 25 new releases per year (small percentage of relevant material); LP & a few 45 rpm discs, 8-track & cassette tapes (tapes in Canada only).
IRISH; CANADIAN FRENCH

Popovich Brothers, 11110 Avenue E, Chicago, IL 60617
Ca. 6 titles (privately produced); LP discs.
YUGOSLAV (Serbian)

Ray Records, P.O. Box 128, Columbus, NE 68601
Heritage Records
Catalog available; ca. 60 titles; LP discs, 8-track tapes.
CZECH; POLISH

RBF Records, *See* Folkways Records

Rene Records, Rene Sound Studios, David City, NE 68632
CZECH

Request Records, 3800 South Ocean Drive, Second Floor, Hollywood, FL 33019
1949; catalog available; ca. 300 titles (small percentage of relevant material; most of their product seems to be imported); LP discs, 8-track & cassette tapes.
AMERINDIAN; POLISH

Rex Records, 34 Martin Street, Holyoke, MA 01040
1957; catalog available; ca. 120 titles, with an average of 6 new releases per year; LP discs, 8-track & a few cassette tapes.
IRISH; POLISH

Rodeo Records, P.O. Box 651, Peterborough, Ontario, Canada
Banff Records; Celtic Records
SCOTTISH; CANADIAN FRENCH

Rounder Records, 186 Willow Avenue, Somerville, MA 02144
1970; catalog available; ca. 150 titles, with an average of 30 new releases per year (small percentage of relevant material); LP & a few 45 rpm discs, 8-track tapes.
SCOTTISH; LOUISIANA FRENCH; HAWAIIAN; SCANDINAVIAN

Royal Tamburitzans, J. A. Trosley, 557 George Street, Wood River, IL 62095
Privately produced.
YUGOSLAV

Royden Records, P.O. Box 332, Lemont, PA 16851
POLISH

Saha Records, 409 North Willis, Visalia, CA 93277
Descriptive information available; 4 titles; LP discs.
MIDDLE EASTERN

St. Anthony's Tamburica Orchestra "Croatia," 712 North Grand Avenue, Los Angeles, CA 90012

1959; no catalog available; 3 titles produced, only 1 still available (privately produced); LP discs.

YUGOSLAV (Croatian)

Salt City Records, P.O. Box 162, Provo, UT 84601

AMERINDIAN

Sävel Records, Helsinki, Finland

SCANDINAVIAN (Finnish)

Shanachie Records, Dalebrook Park, Hohokus, NJ 07423

Many other labels distributed.

1975; catalog available; ca. 35 titles, with an average of 10 new releases per year; LP discs.

IRISH. Also distributor of Canadian French and Scottish recordings.

Silwani Records, 6513 Hollywood Boulevard, Hollywood, CA 90028

ARABIC

Sombrero Records, *See* Norteno Records

Standard-Colonial Records, Catalog has been sold and is now handled through: Jo-Ra Enterprises, 3694 Wrightwood Drive, Studio City, CA 91604

Catalog available; ca. 200 titles (small percentage of American material); LP discs, 8-track tapes.

IRISH; SCANDINAVIAN (Finnish, Swedish, Norwegian); GERMAN; ITALIAN; POLISH; GREEK; UKRAINIAN; JEWISH; ARMENIAN.

Swallow Records (Flat Town Music Co.), P.O. Box 10, Ville Platte, LA 70586

Jin Records

1958; catalog available; 40 titles, with an average of 4 new releases per year; LP & 45 rpm discs, 8-track tapes.

LOUISIANA FRENCH

Taos Recordings & Publications, P.O. Box 246, Taos, NM 87571

1961; catalog available; 10 titles, new releases produced when possible; LP discs (12" & 7").

AMERINDIAN; MEXICAN

Tikva Records, c/o International Records, P.O. Box 593, New York, NY 10019

Catalog available; ca. 50 tities; LP discs.

JEWISH

Topsoil Music, 22283 Cass Avenue, Woodland Hills, CA 91364

1974; catalog available; 3 titles, with 1 new release per year; LP & 45 rpm discs.

HAWAIIAN

A 1952 custom recording probably produced by the artist, who appeared on KELO radio, Sioux Falls, South Dakota. Courtesy of Pekka Gronow.

UK Records, 221 Flora Avenue, Winnipeg, Manitoba R2W 2P8, Canada
K Records; V Records
Catalog available; ca. 200 titles; LP discs, 8-track tapes.
UKRAINIAN

University of Washington Press, 4045 Brooklyn NE, Seattle, WA 98105
1950; catalog available; 15 titles, with 1–2 new releases per year (small percentage of relevant material); LP discs.
AMERINDIAN (1 disc of Eskimo music)

V Records, *See* UK Records

Vanguard Recording Society, 71 West Twenty-Second Street, New York, NY 10010
1950; catalog available; ca. 500 titles in catalog (small percentage of relevant material); LP & 45 rpm discs, 8-track cassette tapes.
JEWISH (ca. 10 releases)

Viking Records, P.O. Box 5657, University Station, Seattle, WA 98105
SCANDINAVIAN

Voyager Recordings, 3727 Seattle-First National Bank Building, Seattle, WA 98122
1967; catalog available; 22 titles, with an average of 4 new releases per year (small percentage of relevant material); LP discs.
CANADIAN FRENCH (1 disc); RUSSIAN (1 disc)

Waltiska, P.O. Box 243, Albuquerque, NM 87103
AMERINDIAN

Wam Records, 1214 Ivanhoe, Youngstown, OH 44502
CZECH (Slovakian); HUNGARIAN

Waverly Records, c/o Math Sladky, Waverly, NE 68462
CZECH

Zuni Midnighters, Zuni, NM 87327
AMERINDIAN

Archives

Information for the following list of archives was gathered mainly through direct solicitation. Form letters and questionnaires were sent to more than a hundred institutions and individuals, requesting a description of their holdings of sound recordings of the music of ethnic Americans. For some archives that seemed to have relevant holdings but did not respond to our request, we have taken information from Ann Briegleb, *Directory of Ethnomusicological Sound Recording Collections in the U.S. and Canada,* Society for Ethnomusicology Special Series no. 2 (Ann Arbor, Mich., 1972); such cases are noted in the listings. Information on some Canadian archives was obtained from Renee Landry, "The Need for a Survey of Canadian Archives with Holdings of Ethnomusicological Interest," *Ethnomusicology* 16 (September 1972):504–12; these instances are also noted.

The format for the archives listings is as follows:

Archive Name, Address

Person in charge; hours of operation; availability and nature of playback equipment; duplication procedures.

ETHNIC GROUPS INCLUDED IN ARCHIVE'S HOLDINGS. Remarks.

The completeness of information varies widely from entry to entry, depending on the nature of each archive's response to us. United States archives are listed first, followed by those in Canada, with one Finnish institution also listed.

United States

Arizona **Arizona State Musuem,** University of Arizona, Tucson, AZ 85721

Seth M. Schindler; Monday–Friday, 8:00–5:00; Wollensak F-1700 tape player; recordings duplicated at cost.

AMERINDIAN.

California **Eugene W. Earle,** P.O. Box 2632, Culver City, CA 90230

Private collection; all use by special arrangement.

HAWAIIAN (ca. 1,000 commercial 78s, 30 16" electrical transcriptions); CANADIAN FRENCH (ca. 20 commercial 78s); LOUISIANA FRENCH (ca. 100 commercial 78s).

Ethnomusicology Archive, Music Department, University of California, Los Angeles, CA 90024

Ann Briegleb; Monday–Friday, 9:00–5:00; 4 Tandberg 1541F tape players, 2 Dual 1225 turntables; recordings duplicated "subject to copyright restrictions on commercial recordings and written permission from collector/depositor for field recordings."

AMERINDIAN (67 commercial LPs, 16 field tapes); MEXICAN (8 commercial LPs).

Lowie Museum of Anthropology, Audio Archive, University of California, Berkeley, CA 94720

Geoffrey I. Brown; 8:00–5:00, by appointment; tape and cylinder players available for preview and checking, but not for extended listening; duplication restricted to educational/research use, signed statement of intent required, fee charged.

AMERINDIAN ("approximately 3,000 entires on wax cylinders which are also transcribed on open reel tapes; approximately 650 entries on original open reel tape; approximately 30 noncommercial discs; approximately 10 commercial discs").

Southwest Museum, P.O. Box 42128, Highland Park, CA 90042

Use of sound recordings by appointment only; duplication restricted to noncommercial use and requires museum permission.

AMERINDIAN; MEXICAN. Includes material collected by Charles F. Lummis. Material has been duplicated for the Library of Congress Archive of Folk Song and is available in its "most useable form" there.

Columbia advertisement in the Ukrainian newspaper *Svoboda,* Jersey City, New Jersey, June 20, 1918, Serial Record Division, Library of Congress.

Chris Strachwitz, P.O. Box 9195, Berkeley, CA 94709

Private collection; all use by special arrangement.

LOUISIANA FRENCH (ca. 600 commercial recordings, many field tapes); MEXI-
CAN (ca. 5,000 commercial recordings, many field tapes); MISCELLANEOUS
(ca. 3,000 commercial recordings).

UCLA Folklore Archive, Center for the Study of Comparative Folklore and Mythology, University of California, Los Angeles, CA 90024

D. K. Wilgus; open by appointment; portable tape players and one portable phonograph; recordings duplicated by special arrangement.

IRISH (ca. 10 LPs, a few 78s); CANADIAN FRENCH (ca. 10 LPs); LOUISIANA
FRENCH (ca. 50 LPs); MEXICAN (ca. 5 LPs); PORTUGUESE (ca. 20 field
tapes); LITHUANIAN (ca. 65 field tapes); RUSSIAN (ca. 5 field tapes); JEW-
ISH (ca. 5 LPs). Bulk of collection comprises commercial LPs of Anglo-American and blues traditions.

Colorado **Southwest Folklore Collection,** Tutl Library, Colorado College, Colorado Springs,
CO 80903

Joe Gordan; variable hours of operation; playback and duplication by special permission.

AMERINDIAN; MEXICAN. "Nearly 1,000 tapes on both sides of songs, stories,
music etc. in English, Spanish and various Indian languages. These materials
were collected by J. D. Robb and Rubin Cobas."

State Historical Society of Colorado, Documentary Resources, Colorado Heritage
Center, 1300 Broadway, Denver, CO 80203

Maxine Benson; weekdays; no playback facilities; tape duplication is possible by special arrangement.

AMERINDIAN (ca. 30 discs, representing the music of Acoma Pueblo, Apache,
Hopi, Kiowa, Navajo, Oglala Sioux, Sioux, and Ute tribes).

Connecticut **Laboratory of Ethnomusicology,** Department of Anthropology, Wesleyan University, Middletown, CT 06457

Current information on operation and facilities unavailable. See Briegleb for status
as of 1971.

AMERINDIAN (commercial recordings; field recordings of David P. MacAllester).

District of Columbia **Archive of Folk Song,** American Folklife Center, Library of Congress, Washington,
D.C. 20540

Joseph C. Hickerson; Monday–Friday, 8:30–5:00; disc and tape playback facilities
available; recordings may be duplicated.

AMERINDIAN; IRISH; CANADIAN FRENCH; LOUISIANA FRENCH; MEXI-
CAN; POLISH; JEWISH; and other. "Hundreds of hours of recordings in all
formats relating to ethnic performers in America."

Florida   **Study Center of American Musical Pluralism (SCAMP)**, 214 Banana Street, Tarpon Springs, FL 33589

IRISH; SCOTTISH; WELSH; LOUISIANA FRENCH; SCANDINAVIAN; MEXICAN; PUERTO RICAN; RUSSIAN; UKRAINIAN; YUGOSLAV (including Serbian and Croatian); SLOVENIAN; CZECH; POLISH; LATVIAN; LITHUANIAN; HUNGARIAN; DUTCH; GERMAN; SWISS; BULGARIAN; GREEK; ITALIAN; CHINESE.

Hawaii   **Bernice Pauahi Bishop Museum**, Audio-Visual Department, P.O. Box 6037, Honolulu, HI 96818

Current information on operation and facilities unavailable. See Briegleb for status as of 1971.

HAWAIIAN

Hawaii Archives of Ethnic Musics, Music Department, University of Hawaii, Honolulu, HI 96822

Byong-won Lee; Monday–Friday, 8:00–5:00; playback facilities for reel-to-reel and cassette tapes, open-reel videotape and 8mm and 16mm sound film; recordings duplicated according to restrictions specified by depositor, fee charged.

HAWAIIAN.

Idaho   **Idaho State University Archives**, Idaho State University, Pocatello, ID 83201

Current information on operation and facilities unavailable. See Briegleb for status as of 1971.

AMERINDIAN.

Illinois   **University of Illinois Archives of Ethnomusicology**, School of Music, University of Illinois, Urbana, IL 61801

Bruno Nettl; open during academic year and only by special arrangment to non–University of Illinois personnel; "modest" playback facilities; recordings duplicated only by special arrangement and normally only for trade and with permission of collector.

AMERINDIAN (field recordings from many different tribes, more than 100 tapes); AFRO-AMERICAN (42 field tapes of black Sacred Harp singing); GERMAN (field tapes of Amish hymns).

Northwestern University Music Library, Northwestern University, Evanston, IL 60201

Current information on operation and facilities not available. See Breigleb for status as of 1971.

AMERINDIAN.

Indiana   **Archives of Traditional Music**, 057 Maxwell Hall, Indiana University, Bloomington, IN 47401

Frank J. Gillis; Monday–Friday, 8:00–12:00/1:00–5:00; 10 reel-to-reel tape decks for use with headphones or in private room for group listening; recordings may be duplicated, generally with permission of collector.

Vast holdings, encompassing many types of music. Collection described in *Catalog of Phonorecordings of Music and Oral Data Held by the Archives of Traditional Music* (Boston: G. K. Hall, 1975).

Kansas **Sioux-Dakota Indian Oral Narrative,** English Department, Kansas State University, Manhattan, KS 66501

Current information on operation and facilities not available. See Briegleb for status as of 1971.

AMERINDIAN (ca. 15 field tapes).

Louisiana **George Reinecke,** Department of English, University of New Orleans, New Orleans, LA 70122

Private collection; all use by special arrangement.

LOUISIANA FRENCH (ca. 80 field discs, ca. 40 field tapes). Material includes Corinne Saucier recordings, property of Louisiana Folklore Society. Some commercial 78 and LP recordings also held.

Maryland **Richard K. Spottswood,** 711 Boundary Avenue, Silver Spring, MD 20910

Private collection; all use by special arrangement.

CANADIAN FRENCH; LOUISIANA FRENCH; MEXICAN; POLISH; UKRAINIAN.

Massachusetts **Peabody Museum of Archaeology and Ethnology,** Harvard University, 11 Divinity Avenue, Cambridge, MA 02138

Sally Bond; Monday–Friday, 9:00–5:00; no playback facilities; no facilities for duplication.

AMERINDIAN (field and commercial recordings of the music of a variety of tribes and regions).

Michigan **Ethnomusicological Audio-Visual Lab,** School of Music, University of Michigan, Ann Arbor, MI 48105

Current information on operation and facilities not available. See Briegleb for status as of 1971.

AMERINDIAN (field recordings of Gertrude Kurath, ca. 14 hours).

Wayne State University Folklore Archive, 238 General Library, Wayne State University, Detroit, MI 48202

Current information on operation and facilities not available. See Briegleb for status as of 1971.

Field tapes, ca. 400 hours, of the music of various ethnic groups in Detroit.

Minnesota **Collection of Minnesota Ethnic Music,** Department of Music, University of Minnesota, Minneapolis, MN 55455

Alan Kagan; open by appointment; open-reel and cassette tape decks; "no recordings may be duplicated and dispensed except for depositors."

SCANDINAVIAN (86 7" open-reel field tapes; 60 5" open-reel field tapes; 10 half-hour videotapes). Material includes some Estonian folk music. Music recorded in Minnesota, Iowa, Wisconsin, North and South Dakota, and Montana.

New Mexico **Archive of Southwestern Music,** Fine Arts Library, University of New Mexico, Albuquerque, NM 87131

James B. Wright; 8:00–5:00; complete listening facilities for discs and open-reel and cassette tapes; recordings may be duplicated, with restrictions in some specific cases.

AMERINDIAN; MEXICAN. Total collection consists of ca. 500 10″ open-reel field tapes, ca. 233 long-playing commercial discs and ca. 265 78 rpm commercial discs of Amerindian and Mexican music. Included in this material is the John Donald Robb Collection and a portion of the Ruben Cobos Collection.

Mary Cabot Wheelwright Research Library, Museum of Navaho Ceremonial Art, 704 Camino Lejo, Santa Fe, NM 87501

Current information on operation and facilities not available. See Briegleb for status as of 1971.

AMERINDIAN (large collection of cylinders, discs, and tapes, largely of Navaho music)

New York **Archive of Folklore, Traditional Music and Oral History,** Center for Studies in American Culture, Samuel Clemens Hall, State University of New York at Buffalo, Buffalo, NY 14260

Bruce Jackson; consult archive for current operating hours; "all the necessary equipment for listening to and duplicating half- and quarter-track mono and stereo open reels and cassettes. Video playback and editing decks"; recordings duplicated, but restrictions vary with material.

SCOTTISH; MEXICAN; GERMAN; POLISH; others. Total holdings of archive consist of about 2,200 tapes, and include much "nonethnic" material. Tapes of almost all Newport Folk Festival concerts and workshops are contained in the archive.

OKeh 1926 Italian catalog. Music Division, Library of Congress.

Center for Studies in Ethnomusicology, 417 Dodge Hall, Columbia University, New York, NY 10027

Deiter Christensen; Monday–Friday, 9:00–5:00, 3 Viking tape decks; "field recordings are copied only with the consent of the depositor."

AMERINDIAN ("extensive"); IRISH; SCOTTISH; CANADIAN FRENCH; UKRAINIAN. See Jay Rahn, "Canadian Folk Music Holdings at Columbia University," *Canadian Folk Music Journal* 5 (1977):46–49, for more detailed listing.

Martin Steinberg Center, American Jewish Congress, 15 East 84th Street, New York, NY 10028

Jeff Obeler; 9:00–5:15 (9:00–4:00 on Friday); cassette decks and turntables; recordings duplicated in special cases only.

JEWISH (Yiddish, Hebrew, Judezmo). Holdings not yet completely cataloged.

Rodgers and Hammerstein Archives of Recorded Sound, New York Public Library at Lincoln Center, 111 Amsterdam Avenue, New York, NY 10023

David Hall; Monday–Saturday, 12:00–6:00; disc and tape playback facilities; "in general, staff limitations preclude duplication save under very special circumstances."

JEWISH. "The Benedict Stambler Collection of Jewish Music Recordings is part of the Rodgers and Hammerstein Archives. About two-thirds of its 4,000 items consist of Yiddish-American materials, about equally divided between cantorial repertoire . . . and Yiddish theater 'pop' repertoire." Various other forms of ethnic music on commercial recordings.

Johanna Spector, 400 West 119th Street, New York, NY 10027

Private collection; all use by special arrangement.

CHINESE; KOREAN; JEWISH; MIDDLE EASTERN (Armenian, Egyptian, Persian, Arabic, Iraqi, Yemenite).

YIVO Institute for Jewish Research, 1048 Fifth Avenue, New York, NY 10028

Marek Webb; Monday–Friday, 9:30–5:30; no playback facilities; recordings not duplicated for others.

JEWISH (ca. 60 field tapes, ca. 1,000 78 rpm commercial records, ca. 125 long-playing commercial records). Holdings include the Ruth Rubin Collection of Yiddish Folksong and Folklore and the Ben Stonehill (Steinberg) Collection of Yiddish songs. In addition to Yiddish folksongs, the Institute's holdings contain cantorial music, Hebrew music, religious holiday songs, and theater music.

Pennsylvania   **American Philosophical Society Library,** 105 South Fifth Street, Philadelphia, PA 19106

Whitfield J. Bell, Jr., librarian and executive officer; Murphy D. Smith, associate librarian; Monday–Friday, 9:00–5:00; one open-reel tape machine; no duplication facilities at library, duplication could be done through Language Laboratory at University of Pennsylvania with some time and expense involved.

AMERINDIAN (ca. 45 reels of wire recordings [some redubbed on tape], ca. 150 field tapes, ca. 35 field discs, some commercial discs). The music of many different tribes is included. The library also has many recordings of nonmusical material from various Indian tribes. For more details see John F. Freeman, *A Guide to Manuscripts Relating to the American Indian in the Library of the American Philosophical Society* (Philadelphia: American Philosophical Society, 1966).

Abner and Mary Schreiber Jewish Music Library, Bertha and Monte H. Tyson Music Department, Gratz College, 10th Street and Tabor Road, Philadelphia, PA 19141

Shalom Altman, director; Idelle S. Wood, librarian; Monday–Thursday, 9:30–5:00; playback facilities for discs, cassettes, reel-to-reel, and 8-track, advance reservations required for use of equipment; "all duplication is subject to copyright law."

JEWISH. "The Abner and Mary Schreiber Jewish Music Library maintains collections of the following types of American Jewish Music: music of the immigration period; Yiddish theater in America; popular songs of the Jews in America (all periods); liturgical music of the Jews in America (all periods); serious music by American Jewish composers (secular and Jewish); traditions of various American Jewish communities; humor and literature of the Jews in America."

Utah   **University Archives,** Brigham Young University, Provo, UT 84601

Current information on operation and facilities unavailable. See Briegleb for status as of 1971.

AMERINDIAN; HAWAIIAN (from Briegleb).

Victor 1924 Greek catalog.
Music Division, Library of
Congress.

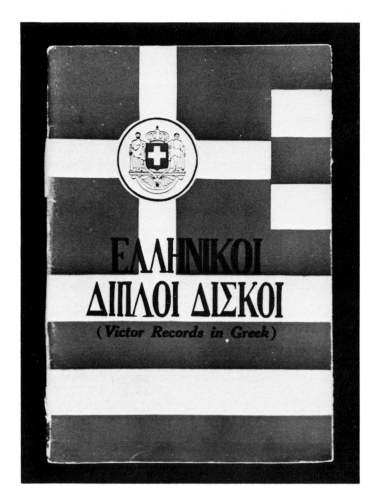

ΕΛΛΗΝΙΚΟΙ
ΔΙΠΛΟΙ ΔΙΣΚΟΙ
(*Victor Records in Greek*)

Washington **Archives of Ethnic Music and Dance,** School of Music, University of Washington,
Seattle, WA 98105

Current information on operation and facilities not available. See Briegleb for status
as of 1971.

AMERINDIAN (from Briegleb).

Wisconsin **Mills Music Library,** Room B162, University of Wisconsin, Madison, WI 53706

Lenore Coral; Monday–Friday, 9:00–5:00; playback facilities for discs and open-reel
and cassette tapes; recordings duplicated if no copyright or other restrictions
apply, if tape is provided, and if staff has time.

"The collection of recordings of the music of American residents in the Mills Music
Library . . . consists of: ca. 200 commercially recorded discs; 15 7" tapes of the
music of Wisconsin residents, both European traditions and Native American
music collected by Helene Stratman-Thomas Blotz."

State Historical Society of Wisconsin, Division of Archives and Manuscripts, 816
State Street, Madison, WI 53706

Current information an operation and facilities not available. See Briegleb for status
as of 1971.

AMERINDIAN (from Briegleb).

Canada

Alberta   **Provincial Museum and Archives of Alberta,** Human History Division, 12845 102nd Avenue, Edmonton, Alberta

Current information on operation and facilities not available. See Landry for status as of 1972.

AMERINDIAN (from Landry).

Provincial Museum and Archives of Alberta, Provincial Archives Division, 12845 102nd Avenue, Edmonton, Alberta

Current information on operation and facilities not available. See Landry for status as of 1972.

CANADIAN FRENCH (7 field tapes); GERMAN (Moravian) (7 field tapes); POLISH (20 field tapes); UKRAINIAN (12 field tapes). Information on holdings from Landry.

Manitoba   **Ukrainian Cultural and Educational Centre,** P.O. Box 722, Winnipeg, Manitoba

Current information on operation and facilities unavailable. See Landry for status as of 1972.

UKRAINIAN ("a limited number of Ukrainian recordings"). Information on holdings from Landry.

Newfoundland   **Memorial University of Newfoundland Folklore and Language Archive,** Department of Folklore, Memorial University of Newfoundland, St. John's, Newfoundland A1C 5S7

Neil V. Rosenberg; Monday–Friday, 9:00–1:00/2:00–5:00; playback facilities for discs and reel-to-reel and cassette tapes; duplication by arrangement, subject to restrictions on specific items.

SCOTTISH (Gaelic); CANADIAN FRENCH. "Holdings include approximately 2,500 tapes. These are field recordings made primarily in Newfoundland along with a few recordings from the Maritimes, Quebec, and Ontario. Material from the dominant English-Irish culture of Newfoundland predominates, with lesser amounts of Highland Scots, Newfoundland French, and Acadian (Maritimes) French resident in Newfoundland. Approximately 500 LP phonograph recordings are owned by the Archive, with about half being representative folk and non-western materials . . . the balance are commercial recordings made by Newfoundlanders. We attempt to purchase all recordings by Newfoundland performers as they come on the market; these recordings include a high percentage of tradition-based materials."

Nova Scotia   **Angus L. MacDonald Memorial Library,** St. Francis Xavier University, Antigonish, Nova Scotia

Current information on operation and facilities not available. See Landry for status as of 1972.

SCOTTISH (Gaelic). Information on holdings from Landry.

Canadian Centre for Folk Culture Studies, National Museum of Man, Ottawa, Ontario K1A OM8

Renee Landry; open 7½ hours daily; playback facilities for use by appointment; duplication possible ("each request is considered on its own merits").

SCOTTISH; CANADIAN FRENCH; SCANDINAVIAN; AUSTRIAN; GERMAN; BULGARIAN; YUGOSLAV; LATVIAN; LITHUANIAN; ITALIAN; HUNGARIAN; POLISH; RUSSIAN (Doukhobor); CZECH; UKRAINIAN; CHINESE; JAPANESE; JEWISH (Yiddish). Information on holdings from Landry.

Edward Johnson Music Library and Recording Archives, Faculty of Music, University of Toronto, Toronto, Ontario

Current information on operation and facilities unavailable. See Landry for status as of 1972.

AMERINDIAN (35 field tapes of Eskimo music). Information on holdings from Landry.

Finland

Suomen Äänitearkisto, (Finnish Institute of Recorded Sound), Pietarinkatu 12A21, 00140 Helsinki 14

Pekka Gronow; open by appointment only; playback facilities for disc and tape, use by appointment; duplication possible depending on time of staff.

SCANDINAVIAN (Finnish) (ca. 500 78 rpm commercial discs); MISCELLANEOUS (ca. 1,000 78 rpm commercial discs of various American ethnic groups). "The main interest of the Archive is in Finnish recordings. Total holdings ca. 12,000 records of all types."

OKeh-Odeon 1928 Russian catalog. Music Division, Library of Congress.

Contributors

Norm Cohen is executive secretary of the John Edwards Memorial Foundation and editor of the *JEMF Quarterly*. He is also head of the Chemical Kinetics Department of the Aerospace Corporation, El Segundo, California. He is the author of a recent book, *Long Steel Rail: The Railroad in American Folksong.*

James S. Griffith is a cultural anthropologist and folklorist living near Tucson, Arizona. He has studied southwestern music, crafts, and architecture, and is currently state folk arts coordinator with the University of Arizona. With his wife, Loma, he puts on "Tucson Meet Yourself," an annual multi-ethnic festival.

Pekka Gronow is employed by the TSL (Workers Educational Association) in Helsinki, Finland. His background includes work as a record and radio producer. For many years he has been interested in the music of industrial societies and the history of the record industry, and he has been active in founding the National Record Archive in Finland.

Joseph C. Hickerson is head of the Archive of Folk Song at the Library of Congress. Among the many bibliographies and research aids he has compiled is "Annotated Bibliography of North American Indian Music North of Mexico." He is co-compiler of "Current Bibliography and Discography" in the journal *Ethnomusicology.*

Alan Jabbour is director of the American Folklife Center at the Library of Congress. While head of the Archive of Folk Song, he edited *American Fiddle Tunes* and the two-LP set *The Hammons Family: A Study of a West Virginia Family's Traditions.* He is also an accomplished fiddler.

Lydia Mendoza made her first records in 1928. In the 1930s she enjoyed an extremely active and successful concert and recording career, which was revived in the late 1940s and continues to the present day. Some of her music has been reissued in the Folklyric series *Una historia de la music de la frontera.* She currently records on the Sombrero label (San Antonio).

Mick Moloney has been conducting research on Irish music in the United States. Presently a graduate student in folklore at the University of Pennsylvania, he is himself a skilled musician.

Richard K. Spottswood has a dual background in public library service and American vernacular music studies. He compiled and edited the fifteen-LP set *Folk Music in America* for the Library of Congress and has contributed to the preparation of many other LPs. A founder and contributing editor of *Bluegrass Unlimited*, he is now at work on a discographics study of ethnic recordings, sponsored jointly by the John Edwards Memorial Foundation, the Library of Congress, the National Endowment for the Humanities, and the National Endowment for the Arts.

Paul F. Wells has a master's degree in folklore and mythology from UCLA and has worked closely with the John Edwards Memorial Foundation for several years. He is currently in the employ of CMH Records. His area of special interest is American traditional fiddling.

Index

This index is divided into two parts, a subject index and an index of people, performers, and performing groups.

People, Performers, Performing Groups